KEY C
POPULAR MUSIC

Key Concepts in Popular Music presents a comprehensive A–Z glossary of the main terms and concepts used in the study of popular music. The book includes definitions of:

- key musical genres, from bhangra to punk rock

- musical subcultures, from hippies to goths

- methodologies, from Marxism to postmodernism

- musicological terms, from harmony to sampling

- musical phenomena, from girl groups to concept albums.

Each entry includes suggestions for further reading and is cross-referenced with related concepts.

Roy Shuker is Associate Professor in the School of English and Media Studies at Massey University. He is the author of *Understanding Popular Music* (1994), also published by Routledge.

KEY CONCEPTS SERIES

Other titles available from Routledge

Key Concepts in Communication and Cultural Studies (second edition)
Tim O'Sullivan, John Hartley, Danny Saunders, Martin Montgomery and John Fiske

Key Concepts in Cinema Studies
Susan Hayward

Key Concepts in Post-Colonial Studies
Bill Ashcroft, Gareth Griffiths and Helen Tiffin

KEY CONCEPTS IN POPULAR MUSIC

Roy Shuker

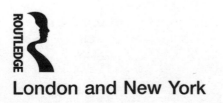

London and New York

First published 1998
by Routledge
11 New Fetter Lane, London EC4P 4EE

Simultaneously published in the USA and Canada
by Routledge
29 West 35th Street, New York, NY 10001

© 1998 Roy Shuker

Typeset in Bembo by Florencetype Ltd,
Stoodleigh, Devon

Printed and bound in Great Britain by Clays Ltd, St Ives PLC

British Library Cataloguing in Publication Data
A catalogue record for this book is available from the British
Library

Library of Congress Cataloging in Publication Data
Shuker, Roy.
  Key concepts in popular music / Roy Shuker.
    p.   cm.
  Includes bibliographical references (p.   ) and index.
  1. Popular music – Encyclopedias. I. Title.
ML102.P66S58   1998
781.64'03–dc21   97–39979
                                                            CIP
                                                            MN

ISBN 0–415–16103–7 (hbk)
ISBN 0–415–16104–5 (pbk)

CONTENTS

Introduction   vii

Acknowledgements   xiv

List of Key Concepts   xv

KEY CONCEPTS   1

Further Resources and Bibliography   318

Name Index   346

Subject Index   356

INTRODUCTION

During 1996 hip-hop performers the Fugees' album *The Score* (Sony) sold more than 8.5 million copies world-wide, 4.2 million of them in their native United States alone; 'Killing Me Softly', a remake of Roberta Flack's 1973 hit and the second international single to be taken from *The Score*, went to number one in twelve countries and sold 2.4 million copies. In the same year, after every major US label had been bidding for the band, REM re-signed to Warner Brothers, securing the biggest record contract in history – an estimated $80 million; UK 'girl group' the Spice Girls' 'Wannabe' (Virgin) became the most successful debut single of all time after selling 4.8 million copies world-wide; and the value of the UK music industry hit a new peak of £1.1 billion, while the value of the total recorded music market in the United States was $12.5 billion. In February 1997, Peter Gabriel's CD-ROM *Eve* won the top prize at the four day Milia conference in Cannes, the computer equivalent of the Cannes film festival, which attracted 1,200 companies from 36 countries. At Milia, in a rare appearance, George Michael declared the Internet to be the future of the music industry; subsequently new media awards for UK music Web sites were launched by *Music Week* and its on-line sister magazine *dotmusic*.

Such events and statistics indicate the international commercial and cultural significance of popular music. Its global and ubiquitous presence is undeniable. We are exposed to its various forms through 'muzak' in shopping malls; on the streets and in the parks with 'ghetto blasters' and Walkmans; on film sound-tracks and in popular musicals; as music video through MTV and television; on the radio at home and work; in club culture; through the music press; and 'live' in a variety of settings, from the stadium concert to dance clubs.

In cultural terms, popular music is clearly of enormous importance in people's daily lives, and for some is central to their social identities. In economic terms, the products of the music industry still outweigh those of any other cultural industry, with income including not just the sales of recorded music, but also copyright revenue, tour profits, sales of the music press, musical instruments, and sound systems. For example, in 1992 Sony's recorded music sales alone, of $3.8 billion, and Polygram/Philips' recorded music sales of $3.7 billion, can be compared favourably with leading video game company Nintendo's total sales of $5.5 billion (Sadler, 1994). The importance of music to the UK economy was revealed by a 1995 report on invisible exports (in this case primarily income from royalties), which showed they grossed $2.25 billion in overseas receipts.

How are we to understand the term 'popular music'?

The term 'popular music' defies precise, straightforward definition. Culturally, all popular music consists of a hybrid of musical traditions, styles, and influences. At the same time, it is an economic product which is invested with ideological significance by many of its consumers. In one sense, popular music encompasses any style of music that has a following, and would accordingly include many genres and styles which are largely excluded from this volume, most notably the various forms of classical music and jazz. Obviously the criteria for what counts as popular, and their application to specific musical styles and genres, are open to considerable debate. Record sales, concert attendance, numbers of performers, radio and television air play, are all quantifiable indicators of popularity, but classical music clearly has sufficient following to be considered popular while, conversely, some forms of popular music are quite exclusive (e.g. thrash metal). Further, many musical forms now cross over in the market place, with distinctions between 'high' and 'low', or popular, culture increasingly blurred. Consider, for example, the highly commercial marketing of The Three Tenors, whose classical music has topped the 'pop' charts.

For the purposes of this study, I have largely followed conventional academic practice, equating 'popular music' with the main commercially produced and marketed musical genres, primarily in a Western context. I am conscious that this emphasis is open to charges of ignoring many significant forms of popular music, located primarily in non-Western settings, but boundaries were necessary to make the project viable. Further, Western styles of popular music continue to dominate the international market place, at the same time appropriating local musics or being absorbed by them. The emphasis is accordingly on traditional 'rock' and 'pop' forms, and their various derivative styles/genres, along with more recently prominent genres such as reggae, rap, 'world music', and the various dance musics. Styles such as jazz, blues, and gospel are only dealt with here in so far as they have fed into contemporary, mainstream popular music.

The state of popular music studies

Popular music studies has become a growth area, and the field is now both extensive and highly active, with new emphases and agenda evident. The international music industry has changed, as have governmental attitudes towards supportive involvement in popular music as a cultural industry. The global music industry is no longer so dominated by the United States and Britain; it is less concerned with the production and management of commodities, and more with the management of rights. The conventional distinction between the major record companies and the independents has become blurred. The significance of the national, and questions of popular music and national cultural identity now tend to be subsumed under broader issues of the globalization of the culture industries and the tensions and communalities between the local and the global. The advent of new technologies of sound recording and reproduction, especially digital sampling, has fundamentally changed the way that popular music is produced and consumed. Associated with this are issues of intellectual property rights, copyright, and the control of sounds. Concern has shifted from a focus on production and textual issues to a concern with consumption. Subcultural theory, once the dominant approach to the study of audiences, has been combined with greater attention to the concepts of scene and locality. The traditional emphasis on rock, pop, and soul as the major constituent genres in popular music, situated around particular notions of musical value, has given way to a proliferation of musical styles, with audiences splintering accordingly. While the historical tension between musicological and sociological approaches to popular music remains, it is being rethought through the reconceptualization of the politics of musical production: 'what's at issue is not which analytical technique better gets at music's "meaning", but how to account for the different musical experiences involved in making and hearing music' (Frith, in Straw *et al.*, 1995: iii). Embracing all of the above is a continued concern with popular music as cultural politics. I have tried to incorporate these new emphases, and capture something of the present diversity and complexity of popular music studies, in this volume.

Why this guide?

The economic and cultural importance of popular music, and the enormous amount of popular and academic discourse surrounding it, suggests that an attempt to provide a guide to the terminology and concepts commonly applied to the field is timely. While there are a number of general studies which introduce students to many of the concepts used in the study of popular music, these 'definitions' are embedded within the general text, and thus are not always easily accessible to students. Further, such studies rarely include both sociological and musicological concepts, along with contextual and textual aspects of the topic. This volume seeks to provide, in accessible form, a comprehensive guide to the key terms and concepts present in the broad body of writing within popular music studies.

This is, obviously, an extremely ambitious undertaking. The study of popular music embraces aesthetics and musicology, economics and sociology, and social psychology. It necessarily includes reference to the music industry, the creators of the music, its textual forms, the means whereby it is disseminated, and its reception and consumption. Further, these are active processes, which articulate and interact with one another. There is an obvious danger that dictionary definitions will be simply encapsulations of particular aspects of this complexity, rather than critical engagement with them. In too neatly labelling and packaging the field of popular music studies, there is the danger that students will treat concepts as tablets written in stone, rather than as a dynamic vocabulary which must be actively located within shifting contexts. Accordingly, the entries here must be regarded as introductions, designed to lead into fuller engagement with the concepts and terms; to this end, I have placed considerable emphasis on the extensive provision of key further reading, listening, and viewing sources.

Concepts and terms

A concept is a general notion, or class of objects. The word is broadly interpreted here to mean general analytical framing labels; for example, genre is a concept, exemplified with various degrees of cohesion by genres such as rap, heavy metal, and grunge. The latter constitute terms. Terms are usually more specific and more descriptive of particular musical practices: locality is a concept, while specific local musical scenes can be considered terms, e.g. the Liverpool sound.

While the format of the book is alphabetical, there are identifiable 'sets' of related concepts. These have been written in a linked fashion, and need at times to be read this way. The broad groupings are:

● theoretical paradigms and the methodological approaches associated with them. Here I have included major social/cultural theories (the various 'isms', e.g. Marxism, feminism), along with aesthetics, cultural studies, ethnomusicology, and musicology. These are provided in very abbreviated fashion, as the main concern is with their application and utilization in popular music studies. An interesting group of concepts, indicative of a relatively new emphasis in popular music studies derived from cultural geography, are locality, sounds, scenes, and identities. The main methodologies considered are semiotics, textual analysis, and ethnography.

- concepts and terminology associated with the study of the music industry. Prominent entries here include the operation of the music industry and its key 'cultural intermediaries' (e.g. A & R), market cycles, and the major and independent record companies. Topics such as the development of recording technology, the shifting status of formats, sampling, and copyright also fall within this group.

- popular music genres. There are approximately sixty of these identified here, with more extensive entries devoted to what can be considered the main popular music genres, including rock/rock'n'roll, pop, reggae, rap, dance-music, and heavy metal. The diversity of genres is indicative of the difficulties of defining popular music in any succinct and broadly acceptable manner. Genres defy static, academic definition independent of those making and listening to the music. Each entry includes reference to the historical development and musical characteristics of the genre, its other stylistic attributes, and some of its main performers. Examples of key or illustrative recordings are provided (usually giving their American pressing). Wherever possible, these are currently available in CD format. There is a marked tendency to situate genres simply by referring to exemplars, both artists and recordings. This device is both necessary and important, and I have used it here. However, a certain amount of caution is necessary given the circularity involved (genre X is illustrated by performer Y, who works within, and thereby defines, genre X). Where appropriate, major subgenres are also mentioned. Obviously, the treatment in this context can only be extremely cursory, serving to introduce each genre.

Excluded here are more traditional forms of popular music which can now be considered largely obsolete, and primarily of historical importance, for example music hall, black face minstrel, and vaudeville (though see Pearsall, 1975, 1976;

Pickering and Green, 1987). There are also a number of genres of 'world music', referred to under that meta genre, which could have been accorded separate treatment had space been available (e.g. rai, bossa nova, juju).

- musicians and the process of creating music. This group includes the range of terms applied to performers, most notably stars and auteurs, and the concepts which underpin the value judgements frequently applied to musicians and their musics (e.g. authenticity).
- modes of delivery and sites of reception (e.g. clubs), including formats, radio, the Internet, and MTV.
- consumption and audience-related terminology, such as taste cultures, fans, subcultures (e.g. punk), cultural capital, and identity.

What is consciously omitted? Specific individuals involved in the music industry, particularly musicians, are only mentioned as exemplars of concepts, for example Madonna is not an entry as such, but is used to illustrate aspects of stardom. More specialized musicological terms are excluded; they can be found in studies emphasizing a musicological approach. As already noted, many styles of 'world music' are excluded; they can be found in *World Music: The Rough Guide* (Broughton *et al.*, 1994).

As well as a table of contents, I have provided an alphabetical listing of the concepts. All cross references are in bold; sometimes the actual concept cross referenced may not be in the precise form in the entry.

ACKNOWLEDGEMENTS

The following people have provided me with feedback and advice on the general project and drafts of entries, lent me books and records, broadening my listening horizons in the process: Henry Barnard, Keith Beattie, Tom Gati, Bryan Gibson, Barry Grant, Colin McLeay, Anne Marie O'Neil, Michael Pickering, Jane Prochnow, Carol Shuker, Mary Jane Shuker, Jeff Sluka, and Lucy Watson. I am also indebted to the students in my Media Literacy and Popular Music class, who have been the generally willing recipients of much of the material included here. Three anonymous readers of an initial draft also provided invaluable suggestions. Finally, thanks to my Routledge editors, Rebecca Barden, Ruth Jeavons, and Kieron Corless – without whom drum'n'bass would have remained a mystery – and to my copy-editor, Tim Weiss.

KEY CONCEPTS

A

a capella
A & R (artists & repertoire)
acid rock *see* psychedelic rock
aesthetics
affect
aficionados
Afro-American *see* black music
albums; concept albums/rock operas; tribute albums;
    benefit albums
alternative rock/alternative music
alternative music scenes
ambient
amplification *see* sound; sound recording
appropriation; syncreticism
art rock
articulation
audiences; consumers
auteur; auteurship
authenticity
avant garde; experimental

B

baby boomers *see* demography
back catalogue; reissues; boxed sets
beat; backbeat; rhythm; riff
beat music; British beat
beatniks *see* counter culture
bebop *see* jazz
behaviourism *see* effects
bhangra
black music; Afro-American
blue notes
bluegrass
blues: country blues; classic blues; jump blues; Chicago (electric) blues; British R & B/blues rock; contemporary blues
boogie-woogie
bootlegs
bricolage
British beat: *see* beat music
British invasion
Britpop
broadcasting *see* MTV; radio; State
bubblegum

C

call and response
cassette audio tape; cassette tape players; cassette culture; home taping
CD (compact disc)
CD-ROMs; multimedia; ROMagazines
Celtic music
censorship; New Right; Parents' Music Resource Center
charts
chords; chord extensions; dominant chords
Christian rock
class

classic rock *see* rock
clubs; club culture; club scene
cock rock *see* hard rock
commodification
communication
concentration
concept albums *see* albums
concerts; mega events
consumer sovereignty
consumption
content quotas *see* State
copyright
counter culture/underground; beats; hippies
country; C & W/country & western; country rock
cover bands *see* musicians
cover versions; song families
crossover
cultural capital
cultural imperialism
culture industries; entertainment industries
cultural intermediaries
cultural policy *see* State cultural policy
cultural studies
culture; mass culture/society; popular culture
curriculum *see* education

D

dance; dancing
dance music; dance-music: jungle; house; trip-hop;
  drum'n'bass
dance pop
deadheads
demography; baby boomers; Generation X
deregulation *see* State cultural policy
disco
discourse analysis
DJ

doo-wop
drum'n'bass *see* dance-music
Dunedin sound

E

education: curriculum; pedagogy; school commitment
effects; 'rock suicides'
enculturation
entertainment industries *see* cultural industries
EPs *see* singles
ethnicity; race
ethnography; participant observation
ethnomusicology
experimental *see* avant garde

F

fans; fandom
fanzines
fashion
feminism
festivals
fiction
film: Hollywood musicals; popular/rock musicals;
  youth movies; rockumentaries; soundtracks
FM radio *see* radio
folk culture; folk music; folk rock
Fordism; post-Fordism
formats *see* radio; record formats
Frankfurt School
functional music *see* muzak
funk

G

garage bands; garage rock
gatekeepers

gender
Generation X *see* demography
genre; meta genres; subgenres
geography
girl groups
glam rock; glitter rock
globalization
gospel
goth/gothic rock; goths
gramophone *see* phonograph
grunge

H

hard rock; cock rock; stadium rock
hardcore
harmony
heavy metal
hegemony
high culture
hip-hop *see* rap
hippies *see* counter culture
history; social history (of popular music)
Hollywood musicals *see* film
home taping *see* cassette audio tape
homology
hook
house music *see* dance-music

I

identity
independents/indies; indie music
Internet; World Wide Web

J

jazz; bebop; jazz rock/fusion; acid jazz
jungle *see* dance-music

L

labelling theory *see* moral panic
lifestyle *see* taste cultures
listening
live performance *see* performance
Liverpool sound/Merseybeat
locality; local scenes; local sounds
lyric analysis

M

majors
making music *see* musicians
managers
Manchester sound
market cycles
marketing; retail
Marxism
mass culture/society *see* culture
mediation
mega events *see* concerts
melody
memorabilia
meta genre *see* genre
mods
moral panic; labelling theory
Motown
MTV *see* music video
multimedia *see* CD-ROMs
music industry; record companies
music press; music journalism; music magazines
music video; MTV
musicals
musicians; making music; cover bands; tribute bands;
  session musicians
musicology
muzak

N

new age
New Right *see* censorship
new romantics
new wave
northern soul *see* soul

O

oi! *see* skinheads

P

Parents' Music Resource Center *see* censorship
participant observation *see* ethnography
payola
performance; live performance
phonograph
piracy
pirate radio *see* radio
political economy
politics; social movements
pop music
popular culture *see* culture
popular music
popular/rock musicals *see* film
postmodernism; postmodern rock
post-structuralism *see* structuralism
power pop
preferred readings *see* textual analysis
producers
progressive rock
psychedelic rock; acid rock
pub rock
punk
punk rock

R

R & B *see* rhythm & blues
race *see* ethnicity
radio; FM radio; radio formats; pirate radio
ragtime
rap; hip-hop
Rastafari *see* reggae
raves; rave culture
realism
record companies *see* music industry
record covers
record formats
recording *see* sound recording
reggae; ska; Rastafari
reissues *see* back catalogue
retail *see* marketing
rhythm & blues (R & B)
rhythm; riff *see* beat
riot grrrls *see* gender
rock *see* rock'n'roll
Rock Against Racism
rock criticism *see* music press
rockabilly
rock'n'roll; teddy boys; rockers; rock; classic rock
rockumentaries *see* film
roots

S

salsa
sampling
San Francisco sound *see* psychedelic rock
scene *see* alternative music scenes; locality
Seattle scene; Seattle sound
semiotics *see* structuralism
session musicians *see* musicians
sexuality

singer songwriters *see* songwriters
singles; **EPs**
ska *see* reggae
skiffle
skinheads; **Oi!**
social history (of popular music) *see* history
social movements *see* politics
song families *see* cover versions
songwriters; **songwriting**; **Brill Building**; **singer song-writers**
soul; **northern soul**
sound; **stereophonic sound**; **amplification**
sound recording; **sound mixers**
sound systems
sounds *see* locality, and entries on various sounds
soundtracks *see* film
stars; **stardom**
State; **State cultural policy**; **regulation/deregulation of broadcasting**; **content quotas**
stereophonic sound *see* sound
structuralism; **semiotics**; **post-structuralism**
style *see* fashion; genre; youth subcultures
subcultures *see* youth subcultures
subjectivity *see* identity
surf music; **surfies**
syncreticism *see* appropriation

T

taste cultures; **lifestyles**
techno
technology
teddy boys *see* rock'n'roll
teenagers; **teenyboppers**; **teen idols**
television
Tex–Mex
text; **textual analysis**; **preferred readings**; **textual poaching**
thrash metal; **speed metal**

timbre
Tin Pan Alley
tours; touring
transculturation *see* globalization
tribute bands *see* musicians
trip-hop *see* dance-music

V

voice

W

women in rock *see* gender
world music; world beat

Y

youth *see* counter culture; demography; youth cultures; youth
movies (in film)
youth cultures; youth subcultures
youth movies *see* film

a capella Group or choral singing without instrumental accompaniment. Religious orders, **blues** field hollers, and some traditional **folk music** all exemplify early forms of a capella. Sometimes regarded as a 'purer' and more **authentic** musical form, since it is not mediated by technology, a view connected to the notion of the human **voice** as the instrument *par excellence*. In addition to a capella groups as such, some contemporary popular songs and **genres** (e.g. **doo-wop**) include close vocal harmony sections without instrumental accompaniment, a form of a capella. Interestingly, given their relative absence from many genres, women dominate membership of a capella groups. For example, Sweet Honey on the Rock are an all-woman, Afro-American a capella group, active since the mid 1970s; heavily gospel-influenced, their work comments on contemporary political, social, and personal concerns.

See: **doo-wop**; **voice**
Listening:
Crosby, Stills, and Nash, *Déjà-vu*, Atlantic, 1970.
'All Around My Hat', on Steeleye Span, *Portfolio*, Chrysalis, 1988.
Sweet Honey on the Rock, *Live at Carnegie Hall*, Flying Fish, 1988.

A & R The artists and repertoire (A & R) department of a recording label is responsible for working with acts who are already under contract, and finding new talent; it is constantly seeking out new material and acts to sign, attempting to develop a roster of artists for the company. A & R staff are frequently involved in all aspects of an artist's relationship with the record company, including the initial negotiations and the signing of the contract, the rehearsal, arrangement, and recording of songs, and liaising with the marketing, video production, and promotion divisions of the recording company. It is a male-dominated sphere, a hierarchy divided according to seniority and experience, with successful A & R people among the highest-paid employees in the music industry. The criteria A & R personnel generally use for judging potential artists are identified by Negus as 'the live, stage performance; the originality and quality of the songs or material; the recorded performance and voice; their appearance and image; their level of personal commitment, enthusiasm and motivation; and the achievements of the act so far' (1992: 53). A & R staff base their acquisition and development of artists on a mix of information about rapidly shifting styles and who are 'hot' new performers, acquired through extensive networks of contacts, and assessed largely through intuition and subjective response ('gut feeling').

See: **music industry**; **record companies**
Further reading: Barrow and Newby, 1996: ch.7; Cusic, 1996; Negus, 1992: ch.3.

acid rock – *see* **psychedelic rock**

aesthetics In a general sense, aesthetics is the philosophical study of art, with particular emphasis on the evaluative criteria applied to particular styles/texts in order to distinguish the identifying characteristics of those of value. In its traditional form, aesthetics concentrates on the study of the work of art in and of itself (cf. an emphasis on the context of artistic production), and developed out of idealist philosophy. This approach included the notion that there existed universal and timeless criteria to determine beauty, 'good taste', and (aesthetic) value in art works: 'transcendent values'. This has been challenged by more recent work, including **Marxist** and **feminist** aesthetics, and '**postmodern**' aesthetics (for an overview, see O'Sullivan *et al.*, 1994).

An aesthetic approach can be seen in several aspects of popular music studies. First, in a negative fashion, it underpins the frequent criticism of popular culture forms, including popular music, as debased, commercialized, devalued, and lacking in artistic value, for example the **high/mass culture** critique, primarily associated with the **Frankfurt School**. Second, and more significantly, although in a rather amorphous and general sense, aesthetic criteria are routinely applied to various forms of popular music. This occurs in everyday discourse around music, amongst fans and musicians, and in the judgements of critics. The evaluative criteria employed are often unacknowledged, but are frequently underpinned by notions of **authenticity**, and perceptions about the relative value of musical **genres** associated with particular gender and ethnic groups (eg. the denigration of **dance pop** and its female audience, compared with the validation of various styles of **black music**). Distinct aesthetic modes may coexist within the same genre, for example, **rap** and **bhangra** (see Manuel, 1995). Third, and more specifically, there is the aesthetic analysis of popular music through the application of **musicology**. This varies in the degree to which such analysis simply takes as a given the concepts/tools of traditional musicology, which is largely oriented towards classical music, or modifies these in relation to popular music. Indeed, there is argument as to whether popular music even merits such a 'serious' analysis.

All this raises the central questions, posed by Frith (1987: 134): 'how do we make musical value judgements? How do such value judgements articulate the listening experiences involved?' The second question raises the significance of differing **listening** competencies. Frith's own response to these questions was to conflate 'the sociological approach to popular music', including a functional dimension drawn from **ethnomusicology**, and the aesthetic, through musicology.

See: **listening**; **musicology**
Further reading: Chester, 1970; Frith, 1987, 1996; Gracyk, 1996; Manuel, 1995; Meyer, 1995; Moore, 1993; Tagg, 1982.

affect A concept developed by the American cultural theorist, Lawrence Grossberg, who argues that the major aspect of popular music is that it brings its audience into an affective space: 'Affect is closely tied to what we often describe as the "feeling" of life. Such "feeling" is a socially constructed domain of cultural effects. The same experience will change drastically as its affective investment or state changes ... different affective contexts inflect meanings and pleasures in very different ways. Affect operates across all our senses and experiences, across all of the domains of effects which construct daily life' (1992: 79–80). Affect is not purely emotional/physical, but also functions in a social sense, as a form of **cultural capital** contributing to the formation of **taste cultures**. Our response to music is one aspect of affect. Although maintaining a distinction between them is central to his thesis, Grossberg arguably tends to conflate affect and pleasure.

Further reading: Grossberg, 1992; Longhurst, 1995.

aficionados Those who see themselves as 'serious' devotees of particular musical styles or performers. Aficionados are **fans** in terms of the word's origins in 'fanatic', but their emotional and physical investments are different from mainstream 'fans', as are the social consumption situations in which they operate. Aficionados' intense interest is usually at more of an intellectual level and focused on the music *per se* rather than the persona of the performer(s). Aficianados prefer to describe themselves as 'into' particular performers and **genres**, and often display impressive knowledge of these. They are characterized by what can be termed 'secondary involvement' in music: the seeking-out of rare releases, such as the picture discs and bootlegs; the reading of **fanzines** in addition to commercial music magazines; regular **concert**-going; and an interest in record labels and producers as well as performers. Aficionados frequently become record-collectors on a large scale, supporting an infrastructure of specialist and second-hand record shops. At times, their record-collecting can become a fixation bordering on addiction. They may also be involved in music-oriented subcultures.

See: **fans**
Further reading: Aizlewood, 1994; Lewis, 1992; Shuker, 1994.

Afro-American – *see* **black music**

albums; **concept albums/rock operas**; **tribute albums**; **benefit albums** An album is usually a collection of recordings originally released on a twelve-inch, 33⅓ revolutions per minute disc, later on **cassette audio tape** and **CD**. The album became prominent as a format in the 1960s, but its vinyl form was largely displaced by CDs in the 1980s (see **record formats**). Part of its appeal was the development of **record covers** as an art form, with some creative packaging and the inclusion of supplementary material (e.g. The Small Faces, *Ogden's Nut Gone Flake*, Sony, 1968; The Who, *Live at Leeds*, MCA, 1970). Several special types of album can be identified: concept albums, including rock operas, and tribute and benefit albums.

Concept albums and **rock operas** are unified by a theme, which can be instrumental, compositional, narrative, or lyrical. In this form, the album changed from a collection of heterogeneous songs into a narrative work with a single theme, in which individual songs segue into one another. Concept albums first emerged in the 1960s as **rock** music aspired to the status of art, and some were accordingly termed 'rock operas'. Pete Townshend of The Who is usually credited as pioneering the concept with the double album *Tommy* (MCA, 1969) although Townshend was partly inspired by the Pretty Things' *P.F. Sorrow* (Edsel, 1968), which had appeared the previous year. Subsequent examples included Frank Zappa and the Mothers of Invention, *We're Only In It For the Money* (Verve, 1967); The Kinks' *Arthur, or Decline of the British Empire* (Reprise, 1969), initially planned as a TV musical and one of several concept albums penned by Ray Davies, the leader of the group; The Who's *Quadrophenia* (MCA, 1973); and the Eagles' *Desperado* (Asylum, 1973), which equated rock'n'roll musicians with Old West outlaws. The Beatles' *Sgt. Pepper's Lonely Hearts Club Band* (Capitol, 1967) is often considered a concept album, for its musical cohesion rather than any thematic unity. These and similar efforts enjoyed various levels of success, and there is debate around the utility of the album format for such conceptual projects.

Tribute albums are compilations of covers of a performer's songs, put together ostensibly in celebration of or homage to the original work. The form has become increasingly popular, though there is some cynicism about the economic motives behind their release. Artistically well-received examples include albums on the music of Neil Young, The Carpenters, Gram Parsons, and Van Morrison. A related form is that of **benefit albums**, collections of songs by artists who have donated their performances/recording to a particular political or humanitarian cause, for example *Red Hot and Blue* (Chrysalis, 1989), supporting Aids awareness and research.

See: **record covers**

alternative rock/alternative music A broad label, and (arguably) a loose **genre**/style, which has been used since the late 1960s for popular music seen as less commercial and mainstream, and more **authentic** and 'uncompromising'. At the historical heart of alternative music was its rejection of the commercial music industry, and the emphasis it placed on **rock** music as art or expression rather than as a product for sale for economic profit. This makes the 'function' or meaning of alternative rock the classic purpose of 'art'. Alternative rock emerged in response to the co-option of rock music by the record industry in the late 1960s and through the 1970s. For instance, in the late 1960s the slogan 'The Revolution is on CBS' was used by the record company to market **psychedelic rock**. The broad genre was closely associated with independent record labels (**independents/ indies**), and was accordingly sometimes referred to as **indie music**.

Like rock, however, alternative soon became a marketing category: in the 1990s, major record retail outlets usually feature an 'alternative' section. The term was originally used in the late 1960s to refer to UK and US underground or **counter culture** performers, while **punk** in the late 1970s was clearly alternative, and the present scene builds on the remains of punk. The alternative label has subsequently been applied to the **grunge** bands of the late 1980s and 1990s and remnants of the underground/counter culture. Such is its considerable commercial success, due in part to its association with the influential US college **radio** scene, that Kirschner refers to it as the new 'hip-mainstream' (1994: 72). Part of this process of mainstreaming has been the move of leading performers, such as REM and Nirvana, from independent labels to **major** companies.

While there is a distinctive musical style here, it is an extremely broad constituency. Kirschner sees alternative as embracing a number of strands, but with **hard rock** at its centre. He approvingly quotes *Spin* writer Jim Greer's 1991 description of alternative:

this music, which encompasses college rock, rap, thrash, metal and industrial, and has as many variants as adherents, has slowly attracted a larger and larger audience, to the point where alternative no longer means anything. Alternative music is purely and simply the music kids are listening to today (1994: 73).

A similar view is evident in an *Entertainment Weekly* (August 21, 1992) cover story on alternative music, 'The New Rock', which includes as constitutive subgenres dream pop, **goth**, grunge, industrial, jangle pop, pranksters, thrashcore, funk and roll, and UK **dance pop**. While observing that such breadth

7

makes alternative 'a ridiculously vague term', the feature notes that the rubric performs a useful function for the music industry, indicating an *attitude*. This is commonly accompanied by an attention to internal, personal demons rather than public sphere political concerns, addressed to youth very much in terms to which they can relate. Another common thread to the patchwork of alternative music is the appearance of many of the performers in the high-profile Lollapalooza tours of 1991 onward, and in feature films such as *Singles* (Cameron Crowe, 1992) and documentaries such as *Hype!* (1996).

Fairchild observes how the evolution of alternative music has been a process of constantly incorporating existing artistic elements into a new ensemble:

> Current alternative bands like Rage Against the Machine, Fishbone, the Disposable Heroes of Hiphoprisy, and [a.k.a. London] Suede (and countless others) have united any number of styles into a broad coalition of unique genres. Funk, '70s dinosaur rock, hip-hop, country, punk, thrash, reggae, and a small number of significant 'worldbeat' elements have slowly been incorporated into the repertoire of numerous bands. It is impossible to adequately chart out the musical evolution of the alternative scene between 1980 and 1994 without tracing the developments and diaspora of a multitude of styles and genres. It is sufficient to note here that the broad contours of the musical development of the alternative music industry throughout the past 15 years have been consistently marked by detournment, negation, confrontation, localism, and a sometimes startling, often extreme stylistic experimentation (1995: 22–3).

Tucker (1992) refers to a variety of American and British performers in his broad discussion of 'Alternative Scenes', including late 1970s **punk/new wave** bands such as Pere Ubu and Devo in Ohio, 1980s LA punk-oriented bands such as X, and the more melodic REM and the B-52s in Athens, Georgia. His UK section includes **pub rockers** such as

Brinsley Schwarz, post-punk/new wave perfomers such as Graham Parker and the Rumour, and Elvis Costello and the Attractions. Such scope clearly demonstrates, yet again, the extreme fluidity of the concept of alternative.

See: **authenticity**; **counter culture**; **grunge**; **indies**; **locality**

Further reading: Fairchild, 1995; Felder, 1993; Heylin, 1993; Kirschner, 1994; Larkin, 1995; Tucker, 1992 (includes useful discographies); Weisband *et al.*, 1995.

Listening:

Pere Ubu, *Terminal Tower: An Archival Collection*, Twin/Tone, 1985.

X, *See How We Are*, Elektra, 1987.

B-52's, *The Best of the B-52's – Dance This Mess Around*, Reprise/WEA, 1990.

Pearl Jam, *Vs*, Epic/Sony, 1993.

Hole, *Live Through This*, Geffen, 1994.

alternative music scenes　**Alternative music** is frequently associated with **local** music scenes. These fall into two basic categories: they are either college/university towns or large cities that are somehow 'alternative', usually to even larger urban centres nearby. Most important American college towns had local music scenes self-consciously perceived as such in the 1980s. The most prominent were Athens, Georgia (source of the B-52s, Love Tractor, Pylon, and REM); Minneapolis (source of the Replacements, Hüsker Dü, Soul Asylum, and Prince), which exemplifies a large 'alternative' city, being alternative to Chicago to the south; and **Seattle**. Often large cities, like Minneapolis, are themselves college towns, while sometimes a small college town and nearby large city have contributed to a shared scene, like Boston and Amherst, Massachussets (sources of Dinosaur Jr, the Pixies, Throwing Muses, and The Lemonheads), with bands moving back and forth between the two centres. Alternative scenes world-wide appear to conform to this basic dichotomy, such as Dunedin, New Zealand, home to the **Dunedin sound**, which is a university city, as is Bristol in the United Kingdom, with a significant **dance–music** scene.

While alternative music is often linked to particular local scenes, the question is why there, and why then? Such scenes have generally developed out of a combination of airplay on the local college radio stations, access to local live venues, advertisements and reviews in local **fanzines** and free papers, and, especially, the existence of local **independent** record companies. Bertsch (1993) argues that there are fundamental links between alternative music scenes and hi-tech areas, with both sharing a decentralized, do-it-yourself approach to production, and with **indie** isolationism not far removed from the entrepreneurial spirit of capitalism, with 'every one out for himself'. Music-making, equipment design, and programming are undertakings one person or a small group can succeed at without much start-up capital. Sub-Pop co-owner Jonathan Poneman goes so far as to envisage that 'Eventually, there are going to be pop stars on every block . . . Recording technology is becoming so accessible, and the networking is becoming so sophisticated, that pretty soon we'll have Nirvana in every precinct' (Kaufman, 1997).

The relationship of the local to the global is a key part of the dynamic of local music scenes, alternative or otherwise. For many participants in alternative local scenes, the perceived dualities associated with indie and **major** record labels are central to their commitment to the local. Here 'the celebration of the local becomes a form of fetishism, which disguises the translocal capital, global management, and the transnational relations of production that enables it' (Fenster, 1995). However, the 'local' is increasingly allied with other localities, for both economic and **affective** reasons. Fenster notes 'the degree to which "independent" non-mainstream musics, while clearly based upon local spaces, performances and experiences, are increasingly tied together by social networks, publications, trade groups and regional and national institutions in . . . locally dispersed formations' (1995: 83). This internationalization of the local is a process encouraged and fostered economically by the major record companies, who place particular local sounds within larger structures, reaching a larger market in the process, such as the marketing of the

Seattle sound. Similarly, local sounds/scenes and their followers are ideologically linked through internationally distributed **fanzines**, **music press** publications and the **Internet**.

See: **locality**; **Dunedin sound**; **Seattle sound**.
Further reading: Fenster, 1995; Bertsch, 1993; Jipson, 1994 (on Athens, Georgia); Straw, 1992.

ambient A broad musical **meta genre**, the term ambient and its variants (ambient dance; ambient house; ambient trance; hardtrance) have been used to refer to **new age** music, and to several subgenres/styles which developed out of, and alongside, **techno**. Broadly, ambient music is designed to lull your mind through more soothing rhythms, with the addition of **samples** in the case of ambient dance. Central figures are Brian Eno, whose records of the early 1970s practically invented the form; Dr Alex Patterson, who formed The Orb; and Richard James, of Aphex Twin. Ambient trance, while similar to ambient and acid house, is softer on the ears and body but still 'keeps you dancing'; hardtrance has a higher number of beats per minute (bpm).

See: **new age; techno**
Listening:
Brian Eno, *Another Green World*, Editions EG Records, 1975.
The Orb, *U.F.Orb*, Big Life, 1992: 'a hypnotic series of trance inducing rhythms and interweaving synths' (Erlewine *et al.*, 1995: 577).
Aphex Twin, *Selected Ambient Recordings 85–92*, R & S, 1993.

amplification – *see* **sound; sound recording**

appropriation; syncreticism Borrowing and reworking from other sources; in relation to popular music, appropriation has been applied to: (i) the creative adaptations of subcultural style – **bricolage**. This can include adoption of particular preferred musical styles, for example white youth's appropriation of black

11

musical styles (see Jones, 1988). This involves considerable contradictions, as with **skinheads**' adoption of **ska**, a musical **genre** popular among the West Indian immigrants targeted by the racist skins; (ii) musical reworkings, ranging from musical borrowings by individual performers of musical sounds, accents, styles (adoptions, copies, reworking), to whole genres/works being based on earlier ones, such as 1990s **Britpop** bands using 1960s British performers as reference points for much of their music (e.g. Oasis: the Beatles, T Rex, etc.).

Syncreticism is a closely-related term for these same processes, indicating a reconciliation, in a blending or fusion of pre-existing elements. In popular music, syncreticism involves the creation of a new style by combining rhythms, timbres, vocal styles, etc. from earlier forms; for instance, rock'n'roll in the 1950s was the result of blending **R & B** (itself derived from **blues**, **boogie-woogie**, and **gospel**), and southern **country** and **bluegrass**. In a sense, all contemporary popular music is the result of syncreticism, with the co-existence of various genres fuelling the emergence of new styles, like the combination of **pop**, **rock**, and **rap** genres with various styles of **world beat/music** in the 1990s (as with **bhangra**).

The concept of appropriation is a contested one, with difficulties associated with determining when musical homage and acknowledged borrowings become musical 'rip-off', for example the debate around Paul Simon's *Graceland* album (Warner Brothers, 1986), and similar excursions into **world music**. Simon won a Grammy Award for album of the year, but his critics accused him of exploiting the South African music and musicians featured on *Graceland* (see the discussion of the album and its reception in Keil and Feld, 1994: ch. 8). Appropriation is often seen as exploitative of weaker social and ethnic groups' music by more dominant cultures; but reverse appropriation also occurs, like the adoption of US country music by Australian aboriginal performers.

See: **bricolage**; **world music**

Further reading: Chester, 1970; Hatch and Millward, 1987; Keil and
    Feld, 1994; Mitchell, 1996.
Listening:
Paul Simon, *Graceland*, Warner Brothers, 1986.
Oasis, *Definitely Maybe*, Epic, 1994.

art rock   A broad musical style/**genre**, linked to **progressive
rock** (Moore (1993) conflates the two terms), art rock was associated with attempts to combine classical, **jazz**, and **rock** forms,
while at the same time importing ideas from other forms in a
variety of ways. It emerged with early 1970s groups such as The
Nice, Yes, and Emerson, Lake, and Palmer; then with Brian
Eno (early Roxy Music etc.), Pink Floyd, and Genesis through
into the 1980s. The genre was prominent primarily in the
United Kingdom, where it had a strong art school connection,
and in Europe (Kraftwerk, Can). Many of the performers were
classically trained musicians. In the United States, bands such as
Kansas, Styx, and Boston fall into the genre. Procol Harum's
single, 'A Whiter Shade of Pale' (1967), whose distinctive organ
sound was based on Bach's Suite No. 3 in D Major, is much
cited as the classic example of art rock.

While there were large differences between the bands which
can be included in the eclectic art rock camp, 'all shared a
commitment to unprepared abrupt transitions from one mood
to another. Sometimes the shifts were between tempos, sometimes between levels of volume, sometimes between whole
styles of music. The effect in any case was violent, disruptive and nervously tense' (Rockwell, 1992: 494). Art rock is
characterized by (i) the use of obscure and changing time
signatures; (ii) not being dance-oriented; and (iii) having a
certain obscurity, especially of **lyrics**. Goertzel (1991) argues
that 'the exact words, good or bad, were never all that important . . . these mystical art rock songs served to help induce
in the listener a state similar to that which had inspired the
composition of the songs. What was essential was the mystical
feel, the cosmic *expression*'. To these characteristics can be
added an emphasis on the electric guitar solo, some use of

13

synthesizers; a preference for extended songs, up to 20 minutes in length; and an emphasis on performance techniques derived from the theatre.

Some art rock performers integrated their work with classical music (e.g. Rick Wakeman, *Journey to the Centre of the Earth*, A&M, 1974); the results were frequently scorned by critics: 'classical pastiche . . . genuinely appalling' (Rockwell, 1992: 493); 'brutally synthesises overkill' (DeCurtis, 1992, on Emerson, Lake, and Palmer). Conversely, some classical composers have adapted art rock (and other styles of popular music) to symphonic conventions. In 1995 Jaz Coleman arranged *Us and Them: Symphonic Pink Floyd*; recorded with the London Philarmonic Orchestra, the album spent 36 weeks at the top of the *Billboard* **crossover** charts in the United States and has sold nearly 750,000 copies.

See: **progressive rock**

Further reading: Frith and Horne, 1987; Goertzel, 1991; Moore, 1993: 79–87; Rockwell, 1992 (includes useful discography); Walker, 1987.

Listening:

Yes, *The Yes Album*, Atlantic, 1971.

Procul Harum, 'A Whiter Shade of Pale' on *The Best of Procul Harum*, A&M, 1972.

Pink Floyd, *Dark Side of the Moon*, Harvest, 1973.

Emerson, Lake, and Palmer, *The Best of ELP*, Atlantic, 1980.

Radiohead, *OK Computer*, Capitol, 1997.

articulation   The connection of two dimensions or elements; linked to the notion of communication as articulation, and to articulated vehicles. Accounts of popular cultural forms, including popular music, often privilege either production or consumption. A middle course has been argued, with an emphasis on the dynamic interrelationship of contexts, creators, texts, and audiences:

> By adopting the concept of articulation, we can start to examine how the meanings of popular music arise

not only out of how artists and audiences articulate, but out of the various audio, visual, and verbal elements that are combined and connected at the same time (Negus, 1996: 135).

See: **mediation**
Further reading: Grossberg, 1992; Middleton, 1990; Negus, 1996.

audiences; **consumers** The study of media audiences is broadly concerned with the who, what, where, how, and why of the consumption of individuals and social groups. Historically we can identify a range of competing media studies approaches to the investigation of audiences. At the heart of theoretical debates has been the relative emphasis placed on the audience as an active determinant of cultural production and social meanings. Music is a form of communication, and popular music, as its very name suggests, always has an audience.

Social theorists critical of the emergence of mass society/culture in the later nineteenth and early twentieth centuries first used the term 'mass audience', alarmed at the attraction of new media for millions of people. Their fears were based on a conception of the audience as a passive, mindless mass, directly influenced by the images, messages, and values of the new media such as film and radio (and later TV). This view emphasized the audience as a manipulated market; in relation to popular music, it is best seen in the work of Adorno (1991). Later analyses placed progressively greater emphasis on the uses **consumers** (the term represents a significant change of focus) made of media: uses and gratifications, which emerged in the 1960s, largely within American media sociology; reception analysis, and subcultural analysis all stressed the active role of the audience. Most recently there has been an emphasis on the domestic sphere of much media consumption, and the interrelationship of the use of various media forms. The opposition between passive and active views of audiences must not be overstated. What need highlighting are the tensions between musical audiences as collective social groups and, at the same time, as individual consumers. (For an overview of the development of audience theory, see Ang, 1991; Morley, 1992.)

Studies of the audience(s) and consumer(s) of popular music reflect these broad shifts in the field of audience studies. Historically, such studies have drawn on the sociology of youth and the sociology of leisure and cultural consumption to explore the role of music in the lives of 'youth' as a general social category, and as a central component of the 'style' of youth subcultures and the social identity of **fans**. The previously neglected adult audience for popular music is also now being examined. The main methodologies used are: (i) empirical surveys of consumption patterns, relating these to sociological variables such as gender and class, and sometimes supplemented by more qualitative data from interviews and participant observation; and (ii) work primarily in a qualitative vein, especially studies of music and **youth subcultures**.

While there is considerable overlap and movement between different audiences/consumers, two factors are seen to underpin the consumption of popular music: the role of popular music as a form of **cultural capital**, records as media products around which cultural capital can be displayed and shaped, and as a source of audience pleasure. To emphasize these is to privilege the personal and social uses of music in people's lives, an emphasis which is within the now dominant paradigm of audience studies. This stresses the *active* nature of media audiences, while also recognizing that such consumption is at the same time shaped by social conditions.

See: **consumption**; **demography**; **Frankfurt School**; **high culture**

Further reading: Adorno, 1991; Ang, 1991.

auteur; **auteurship** Auteur theory attributes meaning in a cultural **text** to the intentions of an individual creative source. The auteur concept is historically linked to writing and literary studies, where it has been applied to 'significant' works deemed to have value, which are accordingly considered part of **high culture**. An ideological construct, it is underpinned by notions of creativity and **aesthetic** value. The concept of auteur has been especially important in relation to film, emerging as a core part of fresh critical studies in the 1950s, with the auteur usually regarded as the director (see Hayward, 1996). The concept has since been applied to other forms of **popular culture** and their texts, partly in an attempt to legitimate their study *vis-à-vis* literature and art.

Applying auteurship to popular music means distinguishing it from **mass** or popular culture, with their connotations of mass taste and escapist entertainment, and instead relating the field to notions of individual sensibility and enrichment. The concept underpins critical analyses of popular music which emphasize the intentions of the creator of the music (usually musicians) and attempts to provide authoritative meanings of texts, and has largely been reserved for figures seen as having outstanding creative talents. It is central to the work of **musicologists**, who identify popular music auteurs as producers of 'art', extending the cultural form and, in the process, challenging their listeners. Auteurship has been attributed primarily to the individual performer(s), particularly **singer songwriters**, but has also been attributed to **producers**, **music video** directors, **songwriters**, and **DJs**.

In the late 1960s, rock criticism began to discuss rock musicians in auteurist terms. John Cawelti, for example, claimed that 'one can see the differences between pop groups which simply perform without creating that personal statement which marks the auteur, and highly creative groups like the Beatles who make of their performance a complex work of art' (Cawelti, 1971: 267). American critic Jon Landau argued that 'the criterion of art in rock is the capacity of the musician to create a personal, almost private, universe and to express it fully' (cited in Frith, 1983: 53). By the early 1970s

> self-consciousness became the measure of a record's artistic status; frankness, musical wit, the use of irony and paradox were musicians' artistic insignia – it was

17

such self-commentary that revealed the auteur within the machine. The skilled listener was the one who could recognise the artist despite the commercial trappings (Frith, 1983: 53).

At a common-sense level, auteurship would appear to be applicable to popular music, since while they are working within an industrial system, individual performer(s) are, at least primarily, responsible for their recorded product. There are 'artists' – the term itself is culturally significant – who, while working within the commercial medium and institutions of popular music, are seen to utilize the medium to express their own unique visions. Such figures are frequently accorded autuer status (and will frequently be **stars** as well). The concept of auteur stands at the pinnacle of a pantheon of performers and their work, an hierarchical approach used by fans, critics, and musicians to organize their view of the historical development of popular music and the contemporary status of its performers. Auteurs enjoy respect for their professional performance, especially their ability to transcend the traditional aesthetic forms in which they work.

Popular musicians accorded the status of auteur include the Beatles, The Rolling Stones, Bob Dylan, Aretha Franklin, James Brown, Jimi Hendrix, David Bowie, Prince, Michael Jackson, and Bruce Springsteen, who have all achieved commercial as well as critical recognition. (The relative absence of women from this list should be noted: see **gender**.) While the status of several may have diminished, with later work largely being found wanting when placed against their earlier output (as with Bob Dylan and The Rolling Stones), such figures retain auteur status on the basis of their historical contribution. So too do auteur figures whose careers were cut short, such as Buddy Holly, Jimi Hendrix, and Janis Joplin. There are also performers whose work has had only limited commercial impact but who are regarded as having a distinctive style and *oeuvre* which has taken popular music in new and innovative directions, for example Frank Zappa, Brian Eno, or Captain Beefheart.

Among **musicians**, in the 1980s and 1990s it is singer song-writers who are most likely to be considered auteurs, such as Sting, Elvis Costello, Tracy Chapman, and Tori Amos. The auteur status of some star performers has been a contested issue, especially with regard to Madonna.

Since all music texts are social products, performers working within popular genres are under constant pressure to provide their audience with more of the music which attracted that same audience in the first place. This explains why shifts in musical direction often lose established audiences while, hopefully for the performer, creating new adherents. This is to emphasize the contradiction between being an 'artist' and responding to the pressures of the market, and to claim particular performers as auteurs despite their location within a profit-driven commercial industry (a similar process to that applied in film studies in the 1950s to Hollywood cinema's studio system). This leads to pantheons of musical value which are problematic, since all musical texts 'arrive on the turntable as the result of the same commercial processes' (Frith, 1983: 54). Furthermore, as in any area of creative endeavour, there is a constant process of reworking the 'common stock' or traditions of generic popular forms, as continuity is self-consciously combined with change (see **appropriation**).

As in literary studies, auteurship in popular music is open to criticism: only some musicians are accorded such status, while achieving auteurship is regarded as possible in some musical **genres** but not others. Further, as with contemporary film-making, the creative process in popular music is a 'team game' with various contributions melding together, even if the particular artist is providing the overall vision (see **cultural intermediaries**). The concept of auteur represents a form of cultural **hegemony**, based on a Romantic conception of art, used to validate certain performers and styles of work.

See: **stars**

Further reading: Cawelti, 1971; Frith, 1983; O'Sullivan *et al.*, 1994; Shuker, 1994. Studies of individual musicians use the concept of auteur, even if only implicitly; see, for example, the following biographies: Marsh, 1983, on The Who; Murray, 1989, on Hendrix; and Norman, 1981, on the Beatles.

authenticity   A central concept in the discourses surrounding popular music, authenticity is imbued with considerable symbolic value. In its common-sense usage, authenticity assumes that the producers of music texts undertook the 'creative' work themselves; that there is an element of originality or creativity present, along with connotations of seriousness, sincerity, and uniqueness; and that while the input of others is recognized, it is the **musicians**' role which is regarded as pivotal. Important in identifying and situating authenticity is the commercial setting in which a recording is produced, with a tendency to dichotomize the music industry into **independent** labels (more authentic, less commercial) and the **majors** (more commercial, less authentic). Perceptions of authenticity (or non-authenticity) are also present in the degree to which performers and records are assimilated and legitimized by particular **subcultures** or communities. Authenticity is traditionally associated with **live performance**, a view undermined by the rise of **disco** and **club cultures**. Thornton (1995) suggests the existence of two distinct kinds of authenticity here, one involving issues of originality and aura, and another, natural to the community and organic to the subculture.

The use of authenticity as a central evaluative criterion is best seen in the discussions of the relative nature and merits of particular performers and genres. For example, commerce and artistic integrity are frequently dichotomized to identify particular artists with either **pop** or **rock**. During the 1960s, leading American critics – Landau, Marsh, and Christgau – elaborated a view of rock music as correlated with authenticity, creativity, and a particular political moment: the 1960s protest movement and the **counter culture**. Closely associated with this leftist political ideology of a rock authenticity was *Rolling Stone* magazine, founded in 1967. This view saw authenticity as underpinned by a series of oppositions: mainstream versus independent; pop versus rock; and commercialism versus creativity, or art versus commerce. Inherent in this polarization is a cyclical theory of musical innovation as a form of street creativity, versus business and market domination and the co-option of rock into the mainstream. It assumes commerce dilutes, frustrates, and negates artistic aspects of the music. This uneasy alliance between art and commerce is frequently placed at the heart of the **history** of popular music, and is widely alluded to by musicians, fans, and critics. Counter to this is the view that **popular culture** is never simply imposed from above, but reflects the complex interrelationship of corporate interests, the intentions of those who create the music, and the **audience** perceptions and use of musical texts (see **articulation**; **mediation**).

Authenticity continues to serve an important ideological function, helping differentiate particular forms of musical **cultural capital**, and is central to debates around the use of studio musicians (see **bubblegum**), **sampling** and other innovative recording techniques (see **rap**), and lip-synching (as in the Milli Vanilli affair: see Martin, 1993).

See: **sampling**
Further reading: Friedman, 1993; Jones, 1995a; Negus, 1996; Pickering, 1986; Thornton, 1995.

avant garde; **experimental** Terms applied to innovative new movements in art; usually associated with breaks with established traditions, styles, and convention. The recordings of a number of performers working within popular music genres have been considered to be avant garde, or experimental; although their commercial success has usually been limited, they often have something of a cult following. Performers working at the interface between various musical **genres** are more likely to be labelled avant garde, with their work claimed as in some sense more **authentic**, for example as John Cale, Laurie Anderson, and classical musicians the Kronos Quartet, with their several reworkings of Jimi Hendrix, most notably 'Purple Haze'.

In the late 1960s, musical experiment was part of the work of The Velvet Underground, associated with Andy Warhol and the New York avant garde art scene, and also that of Frank Zappa and the Mothers of Invention ('Help I'm A Rock' on their first album, *Freak Out*, Rykodisc, 1966). In his ambitious volume *Lipstick Traces* (1989), Greil Marcus argues for a clear connection between the avant garde European 'bauhaus' movement and **punk rock** in the late 1970s. In the 1980s, **alternative** bands such as Sonic Youth and My Bloody Valentine (who 'combine ear-splitting volume with rolling sheets of gorgeous dissonance' (Erlewine *et al.*, 1995: 552) experimented with unusual tuning systems, dissonant sounds, and song structures, and performers such as Mary Margaret O'Hara utilized unique **vocal** styles. Performers working within **art** and **progressive rock** also frequently experiment with sound and song structures.

See: **art rock**; **progressive rock**

Further reading: Erlewine *et al.*, 1995; Bloomfield, 1993; Hesmondhalgh, 1996b.

Listening:

Brian Eno, *Another Green World*, Editions EG Records, 1975.

Laurie Anderson, 'O Superman', on *Big Science*, WB, 1982.

My Bloody Valentine, *Isn't Anything*, Creation/Sire, 1988.

Sonic Youth, *Daydream Nation*, DGC, 1988.

baby boomers – *see* **demography**

back catalogue; **reissues**; **boxed sets** The back catalogue are the recordings available to record companies for reissue, which they still hold **copyright** on. These are often of commercial value given the introduction of new formats, especially the **CD**, and new technology enabling the remastering of originals, combined with the lack of development capital required since the recordings already exist.

The **major** labels realized the sales potential of listeners, especially the affluent **baby boomer** generation, upgrading their vinyl collections by replacing them with CDs. There is also the appeal of adding bonus/rarity/alternative takes to the longer space available on the CD format as, for instance, with the 1996–7 reissue of The Byrds' original 1960s albums. In some cases, the majors have licensed **reissue** rights, or created subsidiary labels for the purpose. The 1970s saw the first companies dedicated to reissues, producing 'thoughtful, intelligent compilations of vintage rock and roll' (Erlewine *et al.*, 1995); Sire in the United States (along with its contemporary artists) and Charlie in the United Kingdom were joined in the 1980s by Ace, Demon/Edsel, and Rhino (US), the leading contemporary reissue company, with 'an extensive catalogue. These companies exploited the market niche created by the

23

major labels' reluctance to release obscure, vintage material for small, specialized audiences.

In its most extreme form, the exploitation of the back catalogue is represented by the **boxed set**: the extensive repackaging of performers' work to present a career overview. Recent commercially and critically successful boxed sets include Eric Clapton, *Crossroads* (Polydor, 1988); The Byrds, *The Byrds* (Columbia, 1994); and The Who, *Thirty Years of Maximum R&B* (MCA, 1994). While sometimes criticized as exploiting consumers, such releases also preserve popular music **history**, making it more accessible, especially to younger listeners. A case in point is the phenomenal success of the Robert Johnson boxed set, *The Complete Recordings* (Columbia, 1990), bringing the **blues** legend to the attention of a new audience. Other types of boxed sets have been multi-album releases by a performer (e.g. George Harrison, *All Things Must Pass*, Capitol, 1970), concert packages (e.g. *Woodstock*, Cotillion, 1970), and, a recent trend, collections of singles (e.g. The Smashing Pumpkins; Alanis Morissette).

Further reading: Erlewine *et al.*, 1995: 950–1; *ICE* magazine.

beat; **backbeat**; **rhythm**; **riff** Rhythm is the beat pattern(s) underlying most forms of communication, pulsations which last various lengths of time. Rhythms are often recurring or repetitive (as in a heartbeat) and follow a consistent pattern. In music, rhythm patterns generally indicate the emotional feel of different types of song, such as slow connoting emotional. A rhythm section is the group of musical instruments which maintain the beat pattern and the harmonic flow of a piece of music; these usually include drums, bass, and guitar/keyboards. Tempo is the pace of the beat. With popular music styles which include percussion, rhythm is best followed by listening to the drums, and counting the beat aloud. The **backbeat** is beats two and four of a four-beat pattern, the accenting of which creates rock's basic rhythm. This beat pattern is usually very simple and easily identified in early **rock'n'roll**. A **riff** is a short melodic or rhythmic pattern repeated over and over while changes take place in the music along with it.

See: **musicology**
Further reading: Brown, 1992; Charlton, 1994.

beat music; British beat A music style, and loose **genre**, characterized by a simple, strong **beat**. The term beat music was applied to the music of the Beatles and other English groups in the early 1960s: Gerry and the Pacemakers, The Dave Clark Five, The Searchers, The Hollies. Accordingly, the form is sometimes referred to as **British beat**. These performers had a repertoire grounded in **rock'n'roll** and **rhythm & blues**. Initially encouraged by the simplicity of **skiffle**, beat groups characteristically had a line up of drums, lead guitar, bass and rhythm guitars, and a lead vocalist (sometimes, as with the Beatles, this would be one of the instrumentalists). Strong regional versions were present, with Liverpool (**Merseybeat**) the major focus. The beat bands were central to the **British invasion** of the American charts in the early 1960s.

See: **British invasion**; **Liverpool sound**
Further reading: Clayson, 1995; Houghton, 1980; McAleer, 1994.
Listening:
The Beatles, *Live at the BBC (1962–1965)*, Apple/Capitol, 1994.
The Searchers, *The Most of The Searchers*, EMI, 1994.

beatniks – *see* **counter culture**

bebop – *see* **jazz**

behaviourism – *see* **effects**

bhangra An Anglo-Indian musical **genre**, based on traditional Punjabi folk dance music played on percussion instruments, bhangra developed in three waves in Britain: as dance pop music played on synthesizers, guitars, and drum kits in migrant Indian communities in the late 1970s; incorporating **house** and **dance-music** and drum machines in the 1980s; and combining with **rap**, **sampling**, and Jamaican ragga or dancehall rhythms in the early 1990s to become 'bhangramuffin' (Mitchell, 1996). The last was commercially successful throughout Asia, and in the United Kingdom with artists such as Sheila Chandra and Apache Indian. For young Asians, bhangra is part of an assertion of cultural **identity** distinct from that of the establishment and their parents.

Further reading: Lipsitz, 1994; Mitchell, 1996; O'Brien, K., 1995 (profile of Sheila Chandra); Oliver, 1990.

Listening:

East 2 West: Bhangra for the Masses, Music Collection International, 1993.

Sheila Chandra, *The Struggle*, Caroline Records/Indipop, 1995.

Apache Indian, *Make Way for the Indian*, Island, 1995.

black music; **Afro-American** The concept of black music is sometimes equated with Afro-American music, or the two terms are used interchangeably. Both concepts are linked to emotive arguments over essentialism, **authenticity**, and the historical incorporation and marginalization of the music of black performers. The existence of black music is predicated on a notion of musical coherence and an identifiable constituency. According to George, 'black music is that which is recognized and accepted as such by its creators, performers and hearers . . . encompassing the music of those who see themselves as black, and whose musics have unifying characteristics which justify their recognition as specific genres' (1989: xii). In such formulations, particular **genres** are considered 'black', most notably **blues**, **soul**, and **rap**. This has led to questions and debate over how this 'blackness' can be musically identified, how 'black' performers can be defined/recognized, and how we situate a song by a white composer being performed by a black artist.

In the development of popular music it has generally been agreed that the interaction between black and white styles, genres, and performers has been crucial. Early Afro-American music had three characteristics: a melodic line; a strong rhythmic accent; and songs which alternate improvised lines, shouts, and cries, with repeated choruses (Gammond, 1991: 61). These were incorporated into **ragtime**, blues, and **R & B**. These general characteristics aside, it has been argued that it is difficult to identify common factors which characterize black music, rejecting the idea that there is an 'essence' to black music (Gilroy, 1993; Tagg, 1989).

Nonetheless, some writers consider black music to be a useful and important term. Brackett uses 'the presence or absence of musical elements that many writers have identified with African-American musical styles, elements derived in particular from gospel music and African-American preaching' (1995: 24) to consider the relative success of a number of songs which crossed over from *Billboard*'s R & B charts to the Hot 100 charts in 1965 (see also Hatch and Millward, 1987).

The concept of diaspora, referring to the scattering or dispersal of a people and historically applied to the Jews, has been applied to the notion of black music to signal a community of musical expression which transcends nationalism, but avoids musical essentialism – see, for example, Gilroy's notion of 'the Black Atlantic'.

See: **crossover**; **history**
Further reading: Gilroy, 1993; Manuel, 1995; Mitchell, 1996.

blue notes Notes that are lowered a half step or less. Early **blues** musicians lowered the third and seventh scale degrees and **bebop** musicians lowered the fifth degree as well.

Further reading: Charlton, 1994.

bluegrass A style of American country music with regional origins in Kentucky in the mid-1940s, though with antecedents in 'hillbilly' music and minstrel styles. The style became recognizably formalized and widely popular through the work of Bill Monroe and his original Bluegrass Boys (who gave the music its name) during the years 1945–8. Prominent features are a melodic, three-finger style of banjo picking, the mandolin as a lead instrument, often soloing against a rhythmic background, and close harmony singing. Bluegrass influenced **rockabilly** such as Elvis Presley's version of Monroe's 'Blue Moon of Kentucky' on his Sun debut.

Further reading: Clarke, 1990; Gammond, 1991; Gillet, 1983; Hardy and Laing, 1990 (the entries on Bill Monroe, Flatt and Scruggs, the Osborne Brothers); Larkin, 1993.

Listening:
Bill Monroe, *Best of Bill Monroe*, MCA, 1975.

blues: **country blues**; **classic blues**; **jump blues**; **Chicago (electric) blues**; **British R & B/blues rock** A major musical **genre**, the blues has been hugely influential on the whole corpus of popular music. Initially a fundamental part of black secular music, which emerged in the early 1900s, the blues includes a number of identifiable subgenres, which can be historically and geographically located. These are dealt with only briefly here, primarily to indicate their influence on other genres of popular music.

1 **Country blues**: a two-bar, three-line format, played on acoustic guitar or piano. The country blues emerged in the still largely rural southern United States during the early 1900s, and became widely recorded during the 1920s. There were strong regional variants, with Texas and the Mississippi Delta (Delta blues) the most prominent. Leading performers included Skip James, Robert Johnson, Leroy Carr, Blind Lemon Jefferson, and Bukka White. Country blues was characterized by its strong social realism, with many songs or recordings which are both beautiful and tortured, with a sense of anguish and desperation in their vocals.

The country blues players developed the bottleneck or slide guitar technique, shaping the instrument's sound into another 'voice'. (A glass or metal tube is fitted over the guitarist's ring or little finger, stopping the strings of the guitar when it is slid up or down the fingerboard; the term comes from the use of the neck of a bottle that had been broken off and sanded down for the purpose.)

Country blues fed into other forms of the blues, and strongly influenced later **R & B**, **rockabilly**, **rock'n'roll**, and **rock** performers (e.g. The Rolling Stone's version of Johnson's 'Love in Vain', on *Let It Bleed*, ABKCO, 1989).

The early 1960s saw the 'discovery' of the blues by white middle-class youth. In the US and the UK (and then internationally), Delta blues legends such as Mississippi John Hurt and Skip James were recorded anew by such small folk-oriented labels as Vanguard, Prestige, and Piedmont. These performers were embraced by folk music, then enjoying a boom period, and appeared at the Newport Folk Festival in Rhode Island and other **festivals**. Interest in the country blues continues: a **boxed set** of Robert Johnson's complete recordings was a somewhat unexpected huge commercial success in the 1990s; other reissues have also done well with the advent of the **CD**.

Further reading: Barlow, 1989; Guralnick, 1989; Ward, 1992a.
Listening:
Blind Lemon Jefferson, *Blind Lemon Jefferson*, Milestone, 1974.
Robert Johnson, *The Complete Recordings*, Columbia, 1990.
Skip James, *Skip James Today!*, Vanguard, 1991.

2 **Classic blues** evolved in the 1920s, usually a woman vocalist, with **jazz** group or piano backing, sometimes as part of a minstrel show. Examples of this are Bessie Smith and Ma Rainey, who gave her music the name 'blues'.

Further reading: Barlow, 1989; Shaw, 1986.
Listening:
Bessie Smith, *The Complete Recordings, vols 1 & 2*, Columbia/ Legacy, 1991 (includes her first major success, 'Downhearted Blues', 1923).

3 **Jump blues**: a hard, swinging transitional style of blues, which anticipated both **R & B** and **rock'n'roll**. For example, Louis Jordan and the Tympany Five, who **crossed over** to enjoy success in both the black and pop charts in the late 1940s with dance-oriented and novelty numbers.

See: **R & B**
Listening:
Louis Jordan, *The Best of Louis Jordan*, MCA, 1975; 1989 (CD).

4 **Chicago (electric) blues** developed when blacks from the south moved to urban centres such as Chicago, Memphis, and New Orleans, looking for work and better lifestyle opportunities. Larger audiences necessitated the use of greater amplification, and saw the popularization of the electric guitar and the use of drums. Major performers included Muddy Waters, B.B. King, John Lee Hooker, and Willie Dixon, also a prolific and successful **songwriter**.

Further reading: Dixon, 1989; Herzhaft, 1992; Santelli, 1993.
Listening:
B.B. King, *Live at the Regal*, MCA, 1971.
John Lee Hooker, *The Healer*, Chameleon, 1989.

5 **British R & B/blues rock**: English musicians popularized the electric blues in the early 1960s, producing a variant that is sometimes referred to as British R & B, which developed into blues rock in the later 1960s. Alexis Korner's Blues Incorporated, The Rolling Stones, The Yardbirds, John Mayall's Bluesbreakers, Cream, Led Zeppelin, and the Pretty Things all mined the blues for inspiration and material, and brought the style to **rock** audiences, and the British and American charts, through the 1960s and early 1970s.

Further reading: Santelli, 1993.
Listening:
The Yardbirds, *Five Live Yardbirds*, 1964; Rhino 1988 (includes Howlin' Wolf's 'Smokestack Lighting').
John Mayall with Eric Clapton, *Bluesbreakers*, London, 1965

(includes Freddie King's 'Hideaway'; Robert Johnson's 'Rambling on My Mind').

Cream, *Fresh Cream*, Polydor, 1966 (includes Skip James' 'I'm So Glad').

Viewing: Dancing in the Street, Episode 5: 'Crossroads'.

6 Contemporary blues: major black bluesmen still performing include John Lee Hooker, B.B. King, and Buddy Guy, while there is a new generation of black blues performers, such as Robert Cray. Prominent blues labels include Alligator. While there is still a debate about the **authenticity** of 'white blues', through the 1980s and 1990s white artists have contributed much to the form, such as Stevie Ray Vaughan, Eric Clapton, John Hammond, and ZZ Top.

See: **black music**; **R & B**; **rock'n'roll**
Further reading: Santelli, 1993; *Living Blues: The Magazine of the Afro-American Blues Tradition.*
Listening:
ZZ Top, *Deguello*, WB, 1979.
Robert Cray, *Strong Persuader*, Mercury, 1986.
The Blues, vols 1–6, MCA, 1986–9 (originally released by Chess in the mid 1960s as a sampler of the label's extensive blues catalogue).
Buddy Guy, *Damn Right I Got The Blues*, Silvertone, 1991.
Eric Clapton, *From the Cradle*, Reprise, 1994.

boogie-woogie A percussive, rhythmic style of black piano-playing, boogie-woogie began in the mid- to late 1920s and flourished during the 1930s. Sometimes referred to as 'the left hand of God' because of the left hand playing repeated bass patterns, while the right hand plays short melodic figures (**riffs**). The style was based on the **blues** progression, but was freely improvised. Boogie is derived from bogey, meaning spirit, while woogie was the name of pieces of wood tying railway tracks together; many of the black piano players associated with the style travelled on the railroad from town to town, playing for 'rent' parties (held by people to raise the rent money). Boogie-woogie strongly influenced the development of **rockabilly** and early **rock'n'roll** in the 1950s.

See: **rock'n'roll**

Listening:

Little Richard, *His Biggest Hits*, 1959; Speciality, 1991.

Blues Piano Orgy, Delmark, 1972.

Jerry Lee Lewis, 'Whole Lotta Shakin' Goin' On' (1957) on *18 Original Sun Greatest Hits*, Rhino, 1984.

Fats Domino, *My Blue Heaven: Best of Fats Domino*, EMI, 1990.

bootlegs Bootlegs are illegally produced and distributed recordings, which enjoy a rather ambivalent status. Frequently associated with a mystique/cultural cachet for avid consumers/completist fans, they are an irritant to record companies, and anathema to many artists. There are several kinds: (i) unauthorized **reissues**, usually of rare or out-of-print material; (ii) counterfeits, which simply duplicate official, authorized releases (see **piracy**); and (iii) unreleased **live performances**. At times these are semi-condoned: *ICE* magazine refers to them as 'gray area, live recordings'. Although containing a regular column on bootleg releases, the magazine notes that while bootlegs are readily available in Europe, they 'cannot definitely advise as to their legality in the United States'.

In some cases, bootlegs attain legendary status, occasionally prompting record companies to release an official/original recording. Three examples are Prince's *Black Album* (Warner Brothers, 1995), originally recorded in 1987 but not commercially released; Bob Dylan, *The Basement Tapes* (Columbia, 1995); and Bruce Springsteen, *Live 1975–1985* (Columbia, 1986), the last two being a reaction against the flood of bootlegs of the artists' concert performances. In some instances, artists have condoned concert recordings – most notably the Grateful Dead (see **deadheads**). Bootleg recordings have been prolific, and have warranted a substantial history (see Heylin, 1995).

See: **copyright**; **piracy**

Further reading: Erlewine *et al.*, 1995; Heylin, 1995; *ICE: The CD News Authority:* 'Going Underground' section.

bricolage The concept of bricolage was initially developed by anthropologist Levi-Strauss, who observed that primitive people's modes of magic – superstition, sorcery, myth – while superficially bewildering, can be regarded as implicitly coherent, connecting things which enable their users to satisfactorily explain and make sense of their own world. Bricolage has been applied in popular music studies primarily in considerations of the nature and cultural significance of cultural style, especially in youth **subcultures**, and in relation to musical **appropriations**.

The Birmingham **cultural studies** writers, most notably Hebdige and the contributors to Hall and Jefferson (1976), applied and developed the structured improvisations of bricolage to explain the spectacular youth subcultures which emerged in the United Kingdom in the 1950s and 1960s. These subcultures appropriated a range of goods from the dominant culture, assigning new meanings to them. Symbolic objects – music, language, dress, appearance – formed a unified signifying system in which borrowed materials reflected and expressed aspects of the subcultural group (see the essays in Hall and Jefferson, 1976). **Punk** best emphasized such stylistic bricolage.

'Normal' youth can also operate as bricoleurs. Clarke suggests that an examination of male working-class youth in the United Kingdom reveals that 'normal' dressing means using elements drawn from government surplus stores, sportswear, subcultural clothing appropriated from different historical eras via the second-hand clothing markets (in Hall and Jefferson, 1976). McRobbie (1988; 1991) demonstrates that this is not a process confined to boys, with **fashion**-conscious young girls also putting together ensembles. Mass market fashion itself contains forms of recontextualized meaning, as with ski jumpers, track suits, and work overalls.

A number of studies have utilized bricolage in a more general sense to examine the social role of particular musical styles. Grossberg argued that **rock'n'roll** is a particular capitalist and postmodernist form of bricolage: 'It functions in a constant play of incorporation and excorporation (both always occurring simultaneously), a contradictory cultural practice' (in Gelder and Thornton, 1997: 481) in which youth celebrates the very conditions of its leisure – boredom, meaninglessness, and dehumanization – through technology, noise, commodity fetishism, repetition, fragmentation, and superficiality. In more precise terms, various musical styles have been credited with bringing a sense of play to the arts of bricolage, utilizing different musical sounds, conventions, and instrumentation. For example, Los Angeles' Chicano rock'n'roll musicians

> draw upon street slang, car customizing, clothing styles, and wall murals for inspiration and ideas, as well as upon more traditional cultural creations such as literature, plays, and poems. Their work is intertextual, constantly in dialogue with other forms of cultural expression, and most fully appreciated when located in context (Lipsitz, in Gelder and Thornton, 1997: 358).

All this is to see a process of semiotic guerrilla warfare at work in and through popular music, operating in sites such as the home, school, and the workplace.

Further reading: Gelder and Thornton, 1997; Hebdige, 1979.

British beat – *see* **beat music**

British invasion A term used by the popular press, and subsequently by historians of popular music, for the impact of British groups on the US popular music scene and their dominance of the American charts from early 1960 to 1964–5. A strong British grassroots popular music scene emerged in the late 1950s, encouraged by **skiffle**, and drawing on American **rock'n'roll** and **R & B** for inspiration. The **beat** boom bands inflected these sounds with their own styles and increasingly produced their own material. The main centres were Liverpool (Merseybeat) and London's R & B-based scene.

The Beatles were the crucial performers of the era, their success opening the way for The Dave Clark Five, Gerry and the Pacemakers, The Rolling Stones, etc. Prior to this, few British recording artists had found sustained popularity in America. Indeed, Capitol Records, the US subsidiary of EMI, initially declined to release Beatles records in the United States, licensing them to smaller labels. For instance, Vee Jay Records released 'Please Please Me' in February 1963, and a modified version of the group's first album (*Please Please Me*) as *Introducing the Beatles* in July 1963. With little accompanying promotion, these releases failed to do well in the **charts**, despite their UK success. This all changed with the band's first US tour in 1964, and the accompanying 'Beatlemania' and chart domination (see Whitburn, 1988). The British invasion withered in the mid-1960s, as the Beatles stopped touring in 1966 and the United States produced a number of successful bands who drew heavily on the British groups and their music (eg. The Byrds).

Lester Bangs is critical of much of the music as 'by and large junk: perfect expressions of the pop aesthetic of a disposable culture' and 'innocuous but raucous' (1992a: 199). The British invasion was nonetheless important in reshaping American popular music in the early 1960s, while validating the emerging youth culture. Although it stifled the emergent black **R & B** and the **girl groups**, it prompted the emergence of **garage bands** and American **power pop**. The success of the Beatles, followed by other British groups, created a standard rock group line-up, usually consisting of four, or possibly five players, with drum kit, lead, rhythm, and bass guitars, plus vocals delivered by one (on lead) and all (chorus). The Beatles also established the importance of the singer **songwriter**, and the cultural significance of groups performing their own material.

See: **garage bands**; **girl groups**; **Liverpool sound**; **power pop**
Further reading: Erlewine *et al.*, 1995; Bangs, 1992a; Clayson, 1995; Ennis, 1992; Friedlander, 1996; Garofalo, 1997.
Viewing: Dancing in the Street, episode 3: 'So You Wanna Be a Rock'n'Roll Star?'.

Britpop   The general label applied to the British guitar-based **pop/rock** bands of the 1990s, initially by the UK music press. Britpop has been a loose movement, whose performers draw musically on 1960s British pop/rock bands such as the Beatles, The Who, and The Kinks; post-punk British rock of the 1980s (The Smiths, The Jam); elements of **glam rock** (T Rex was an acknowledged influence); and British 'new pop' of the 1980s (see **new romantics**). From an American perspective, Britpop has been described, not unfairly, as a 'defiantly nationalistic anti-grunge movement'. Whereas **grunge** had idealized an anti-star approach, Britpop was regarded as 'firmly cemented in snotty arrogance and aspirations to stardom' ('The Empire Gobs Back', *Rolling Stone, Yearbook 1995*: 32–4). The major Britpop bands are Blur, Suede, Pulp, and Oasis, with the label also applied to Ash, Echobelly, Supergrass, and Kula Shaker, among others. Along with **dance-music**, Britpop dominated the British charts through the 1990s, with Oasis' *(What's the Story) Morning Glory?* (Epic, 1995) one of the biggest-selling records in UK history. Oasis also succeeded in the American market, where *Morning Glory* sold 3.26 million copies during 1995–6, supported by extensive touring there, but otherwise Britpop had only limited impact in the United States. There has more recently been talk of the 'death of Britpop', as the music moved away from its original perky, cockney/patriotic style, while several of its performers, previously classed as **indie** bands, joined the commercial mainstream, most notably Oasis.

Listening:

Suede, *Suede*, Columbia, 1993.

Blur, *Parklife*, Capitol, 1994.

Pulp, *Different Class*, Island, 1995 (featuring 'Common People' which is arguably one of the defining songs of Britpop).

Kula Shaker, *K*, Columbia/Sony, 1996.

broadcasting – *see* **MTV**; **radio**; **State**

bubblegum   A derogatory label initially applied to a **genre** of highly commercial and rather cynically manufactured **pop** of the late 1960s, usually aimed at pre-teenage listeners and reflecting their emerging purchasing power. The term came from the **rock**-based jingles that were produced for bubblegum adverts in the United States. It was largely an American phenomenon, associated with the Buddah label and performers like The Lemon Pipers, The Archies (whose 'Sugar Sugar' single was the best selling single of 1969), and the Ohio Express ('Yummy Yummy Yummy'). Bubblegum recordings often made extensive use of **session musicians**. Although frequently critically denigrated, bubblegum was at the core of commercially very successful performers such as The Monkees, Tommy Roe, and Tommy James and the Shondells: 'trash pop made in heaven' (Bangs, 1992b: 360). Subsequently, bubblegum became the general term for popular music regarded as 'lightweight' and chart-oriented. Musically, it is associated with strong melodies and rhythms: insidious, catchy **hooks** that 'get inside your brain and don't leave'.

See: **power pop**
Further reading: Bangs, 1992b (includes discography); Garofalo, 1997.
Listening:
Ohio Express, *The Very Best of the Ohio Express*, Buddah, 1970.
Tommy James and the Shondells, *Anthology*, Rhino, 1980.

call and response The practice of singing in which a solo vocalist, the caller, is answered by a group of singers. The practice is also used with instruments, but its origins are vocal. Call and response was an especially important part of early **country blues**.

Further reading: Hatch and Millward, 1987.

cassette audio tape; **cassette tape players**; **cassette culture**; **home taping** Compact cassette audio tape and cassette tape players, developed in the mid-1960s, appealed because of their small size and associated portability. Initially a low-fidelity medium, steady improvement of the sound, through modifications to magnetic tape and the introduction of the Dolby noise reduction system, enhanced the appeal of cassettes. The transistor radio and the cassette had become associated technologies by the 1970s, with widely popular cheap radio cassette players, and the cassette player incorporated into high-fidelity home stereos. The development of powerful portable stereo players ('boom boxes' or 'ghetto blasters'), associated with inner-city Afro-American youth, created a new form of social identification and a new level of noise nuisance.

An efficient format for the expansion into remote markets, tape cassettes became the main sound carriers in developing countries, and by the end of the 1980s cassettes were outselling other formats there by three to one. As a portable recording technology, the tape cassette has been used in the production, duplication, and dissemination of local musics and the creation of new musical styles, most notably **punk** and **rap**, thus tending to decentralize control over production and consumption. The term **cassette culture** has been applied to the 'do-it-yourself' ethic that underlies such practices, and the network of musicians and listeners it embraces. On the negative side, tape cassettes pose considerable problems of illegal copying and the violation of **copyright**.

Home taping is *individual* copying (to audio or video tape) from existing recordings, or off-air. Making *multiple* copies is considered **piracy**, although both forms breach copyright, and the general practice is frequently criticized by the mainstream music industry, and many artists, because of the perceived loss of revenue involved. Others regard home taping as a legitimate cultural practice, asserting consumer autonomy. Home taping was made possible by the development of cassette audio tape and the cassette tape player.

Making tape compilations is a significant aspect of people's engagement with popular music. Aside from the convenience of ensuring access to preferred **texts**, selected (particularly with **albums**) to avoid any 'dross' or material not liked sufficiently to warrant inclusion, there is an economic aspect to home taping: 'Home taping of music is, in one sense, a strategy directly tailored to recession conditions. The tape cassette has proved to be a practical, flexible and cheap way of consuming and distributing music' (Willis, 1990: 62). Home taping is primarily from the radio, but 'Young people frequently rely on friends, with larger record collections, to make tapes for them. There is something of an informal hierarchy of taste operating here' (ibid.: 63). The tastes reflected in home taping as a consumption practice remain largely outside of the influence of the music industry.

Further reading: Erlewine *et al.*, 1995; Jones, 1992; Millard, 1995: ch. 15; Willis, 1990.

CD (**compact disc**) The compact disc is a 4.5-inch plastic, aluminium-looking disc, similar to the computer disc. In the 1980s the CD became established as the main medium for the recording and marketing of popular music (see **record formats**), fuelled by (often debated) claims of a clearer, sharper sound, and greater durability and permanence compared to vinyl. The shift to CDs was a major factor in the exploitation and availability of the **back catalogue**.

CD-ROMs; **multimedia**; **ROMagazines** CD-ROMs are 4.5-inch plastic, aluminium-looking discs, the same size as the musical **CD**, which can each hold up to 700 megabytes of data, in multimedia form. This is equivalent to approximately one thousand 300 page books. Although they have gone largely untreated in the critical literature on popular music, the music **CD-ROM** represents a new marketing niche and a new advertising avenue for the popular music industry.

CD-ROMs are part of the explosion of **multimedia** in the 1990s. While this term is frequently loosely used, it generally refers to the communication of messages or information through the combined use of text, graphics, animation, audio, and motion video. In the modern sense, it goes with another basic concept of new technology – interactivity. Multimedia has come to imply more than just the convergence of voice, music, alpha-numeric text, and so on, it also implies that the user has some degree of interactive control over these, instead of being a passive viewer, as with broadcast **television**.

In a broader perspective, multimedia is a synonym for convergence: major media companies working together, often under corporate umbrellas. Thus any product system or venture agreement or technology that brings together components of more than one previously distinct sector of the media industry – be it publishing and computers, or TV and computers – can be described as multimedia. Music CD-ROMs are one fruit of the on-going convergence of the electronics and music industries which began in the 1980s. There is an associated drive for control of both the hardware and software dimensions of the market place, along with the cross-fertilization and maximization of texts (one text, many forms). According to Volpe, Welty & Co., a market analysis company in San Francisco, the North American market for 'edutainment' software is expected to grow to $1 billion by 1997. They claim it grew by 47 per cent in 1993, compared to just 14 per cent for all software. This expansion reflects the rapid increase in the titles available, and the lowered cost of multimedia hardware. This market growth is in part the result of education, modified by contemporary electronic media, returning to the home setting.

By the early 1990s, record companies, including EMI and the Warner Music Group, began forming multimedia distribution divisions, which started exploring the possibilities of new technologies, including music CD-ROMs. For example, in 1994 EMI spokesperson Don Harder (senior vice-president of information technology) announced a CD-ROM featuring **heavy metal** band Queensryche, to be released with the band's new album: 'We are looking at creating as much synergy as possible between the CD and the CD-ROM. With both of those titles being carried in many of the same locations, we want to do a lot of cross marketing' (*Billboard*, April 30, 1994; pp. 1, 98). In addition to CD-ROMs, there are now music/artist specific computer screen–savers and video/computer games, complete with sound bites.

CD-ROMs are now an important and influential part of the music industry. There is an increasing number of popular music CD-ROM titles available. These are usually artist-specific, but there are also music CD-ROMs which let users compose, play guitar, and edit music videos, along with music encylopedias (e.g. *Music Central 96,* Microsoft, 1996). Best-selling titles include *XPLORA 1 Peter Gabriel's Secret World* (Interplay, 1993); and releases from The Artist Formerly Known As Prince, Heart, and The Cranberries. Some regular CD releases are now including multimedia material which can be accessed when the recording is played through the appropriate computer (e.g. The Rolling Stones, *Stripped*, Virgin, 1996).

Another avenue for the marketing of popular music is through the exposure of artists and their products in **ROMagazines**, which are published on CD-ROM using multimedia techniques. The pioneer ROMagazine was *NautilusCD*, a monthly consumer/business journal of all things multimedia, which began in 1990 and became the model for others. ROMags, as they are now known, are a mix of text, graphics, sound bites, videos, and music, all organized in roughly the same way as their paper equivalents, in departments and 'articles' – the latter are often a form of advertising. Articles run up to ten pages (screens) with text and pictures. Each screen also has icon buttons; you click on these to bring up additional text, a movie, a blow-up of a picture, or a sound or CD audio file. They are a very compelling publishing medium. For example, the May 1994 edition of *NautilusCD* included a track from a new CD by New Orleans rock group The Subdudes. You can listen to the group in CD audio format – the sound quality is as good as regular audio CDs if you play it through a stereo system – and you can view a postage stamp-sized version of the video of the song. Several regularly produced, current 'lifestyle/entertainment' CD-ROMs include a good deal of coverage of popular music (e.g. *Blender*).

There are some questions to be asked of the new medium. Who is buying music CD-ROMs, and how popular are they? It seems likely that their market is primarily older/affluent consumers. Do they change one's engagement with the music, and, if so, in what ways? Music has always had an element of participation in it, even if this is generally at one remove from the actual performance/recording. CD-ROM arguably extends the possibilities for listeners/viewers to interact with the musical performance. Currently, due to the development costs involved, the format privileges established or commercially successful artists, but as the technology inevitably becomes cheaper and more available, CD-ROM will be utilized by more artists.

Further reading: Hayward and Orrock, 1995.

Celtic music Irish in origin but more widely influential, contemporary Celtic popular music is an example of a hybrid, **meta genre**, variants of which have **crossed over** into the mainstream of popular music. The influence of Celtic music is evident in the 'mainstream', commercially and critically successful music of Van Morrison, Clannad, the Chieftains, Enya (Celtic **new age**), and the Corrs. Celtic music frequently involves a blending of traditional and modern forms, as in the Celtic-**punk** of the Pogues; the **ambient** music of Enya and Canada's Coreena McKennitt; the Celtic-**grunge** of Cape Breton fiddle-player Ashley MacIsaac; the Celtic-**rock** of Rawlins Cross and Horslips. In much of this work, traditional Irish melodies are given a pop/rock dimension, with the lyrics sometimes in Gaelic. The emergence of various hybrids of Celtic and popular music forms is part of a broader awakening of interest in Celtic traditional music and Gaelic culture and language. This appeal, according to the musicians involved, is based on the 'realness' and 'honesty' of the music, in other words, its **authenticity** as a music of the people. To some extent, the perceived authenticity of this music has led to its exploitation as a selling-point, as in the advertising of other Irish products such as beer.

An 'East Coast Sound' in Canadian popular music, centred around Atlantic Canada, has as its principal feature a blending of the conventions of traditional Celtic or Gaelic folk music with those of contemporary rock music; leading performers include Rawlins Cross, Ashley MacIsaac, The Barra MacNeils, and the Rankin Family. As with other such **scenes**, the emergence of the East Coast Sound has been encouraged by the development of institutional support structures, with local record labels and the Annual East Coast Association Conference and Awards, and national and international media coverage (see Baxter-Moore, 1996).

See: **world music**
Further reading: Broughton *et al.*, 1994.
Listening:
Horslips, *Dance Hall Sweethearts*, RCA, 1974.

Enya, *Watermark*, Reprise, 1988.
Sarah McLachlan, *Solace*, Arista, 1991.
The Cranberries, *No Need to Argue*, Island, 1995.
The Pogues, *Rum, Sodomy and the Lash*, MCA, 1995.

censorship; New Right; Parents' Music Resource Center
Censorship occurs whenever particular words, images, sounds, and ideas are suppressed or muted. This usually occurs through legislation at the national or local level, but can also take place through self-regulation and codes of practice within the media and communications industries. In a major study of the operation of popular music censorship in Britain, Cloonan initially defines it as 'an attempt to interfere, either pre- or post-publication, with the artistic expressions of popular music artists with a view to stifling, or significantly altering, that expression. This puts the emphasis on censorship as a *deliberate* act' (1995: 75).

Censorship operates at a number of levels in popular music. There is a long history of **record companies** refusing to distribute potentially controversial records or videos, of recordings subject to bans by **radio**, and recordings being subject to court action. Much of the associated debate is between supporters of the basic right of free speech, and those calling for the regulation of obscenity. A further dimension is a more covert one, where the market effectively acts as a censor. This includes record companies' decisions not to sign artists, or to fully support releases, because of their perceived lack of commercial potential; decisions by large **retail** outlets not to stock less commercial or controversial artists/genres; and decisions by radio stations not to play records which do not fit their general format. While these decisions are based on commercial rather than moral considerations, their net effect may be censorial. The licensing and regulation of **live** venues by local authorities also operates as a form of censorship.

In Britain and the United States, recent calls for stricter censorship of popular media culture have been strongly associated with the political activism and influence of the **New Right**, a loose amalgam of religious and conservative groups (see Grossberg, 1992). Cloonan (1996) details a number of themes in the censorship of popular music in the United Kingdom: the ebb and flow of censorship in relation to contemporary events, with often high-profile crimes linked to violent media texts (e.g. the Jamie Bulger case in 1993); the tendency of proponents of censorship to portray the popular music audience as passive dupes of the industry, accompanied by an aesthetic critique of **pop**; a concern for the welfare of children and adolescents; and xenophobia, as with the early British attacks on **rock'n'roll** which emphasized its American roots. Variants of these are present internationally, particularly in the views of the **Parents' Music Resource Center** (PMRC) in the United States.

A key organization in the debates around popular music and censorship from the mid-1980s, the PMRC was formed in 1985, headed by a group of 'Washington wives' (most were married to Senators or Congressmen, and were also born-again Christians). The PMRC has been described as 'the most effective adversary that rock and roll has ever faced' (Gilmore, 1990: 14). The group dedicated themselves to 'cleaning up' **rock** music, which they saw as potentially harmful to young people, terming it 'secondary child abuse'. The PMRC published a *Rock Music Report*, condemning what they claimed to be the five major themes in the music: rebellion, substance abuse, sexual promiscuity and perversion, violence-nihilism, and the occult, and began a highly-organized letter writing campaign. They argued for the implementation of a ratings system for records, similar to that used in the cinema, suggesting an 'X' rating for those seen as dealing in profanity, suicide, and sexually explicit themes; a 'V' rating for violence; a 'D/A' rating for lyrics that glorified drug or alcohol use; and an 'O' for those referring to the occult, which they regarded as virtually anything dealing with spirituality/religion in a non-Christian manner. In response, some commercial record companies placed warning labels on records containing explicit lyrics. The PMRC also sent copies of lyrics of songs they saw as objectionable to programme directors at radio and television stations, to be screened for 'offensive material', and pressed record companies to reassess the contracts of artists who featured violence, substance abuse, or explicit sexuality in their recorded work or concerts.

All these measures were aimed at encouraging self-censorship in the **music industry**, and the group's tactics met with considerable success. The high point of their efforts was the 1985 US Senate Commerce Committee hearings on pornography in rock music (Denselow, 1990: ch. 10). No legislation came out of the hearings, but the Record Industry Association of America voluntarily responded by introducing a generic 'Parents Advisory – Explicit Lyrics' label to appear on albums deemed to warrant it. (A number of authors have addressed the episode and the cultural politics underpinning it; see, in particular, Denselow, 1990; Pratt, 1990; also Zappa, 1990.) The PMRC remains active.

During the 1990s, **rap** music became the main target of pro-censorship forces internationally. The new **genre** had already been attacked from the political left for its sexism and homophobia, and was now criticized from the right for its profanity and obscenity. A judge in Florida declared the rap group The 2 Live Crew's album *As Nasty as They Wanna Be* (Luke, 1989) to be obscene, the first such ruling for a recorded work in US history. The anti-authority political attitudes and values in some rap music also attracted considerable criticism. The Los Angeles rap group NWA's (Niggers With Attitude) song 'Fuck the Police' (on their debut album, *Straight Outta Compton* (Priority, 1989), which was critically acclaimed for its depiction of black ghetto life) and Ice-T's song 'Cop Killer' both caused considerable controversy and calls to ban their performers' concerts and records.

The Ice-T song is a fantasy narrative about the disempowered going out 'to dust some cops off'. A warning sticker on the **cassette audio tape** version of the album *Body Count* (Warner Brothers, 1992), which includes the track 'Cop Killer', reads 'Warning: This tape contains material that may be offensive to someone out there!' This was hardly enough to appease the critics of the record, who claimed that the song glorified the murder of police, and both President Bush and Vice-President Dan Quayle sided with law-enforcement groups in protesting Time Warner's release of the record. Several US national record store chains stopped selling *Body Count*, and in July 1992, Time Warner pulled the song at Ice-T's request after police groups picketed the media conglomerate's shareholders' meeting in Beverley Hills. In September, Warner Music Group executives met with several of the rappers on the label, including Ice-T, and warned them to change their lyrics on some songs or find another label for their work.

Rap records and performers were also the target of censorship in the United Kingdom, Australia, and New Zealand. In July 1992, New Zealand's Police Commissioner unsuccessfully attempted to prevent an Ice-T concert in Auckland, arguing that 'Anyone who comes to this country preaching in obscene terms . . . the killing of police, should not be welcome here' (Press Association report). Several record shop owners refused to stock the album containing the song. The local music industry, student radio stations, and several leading rock journalists responded by defending the song as a piece of 'role play', linking it with the singer's recent performance in the film *New Jack City* (Mario Van Peebles, 1991) and the right to free speech. Undeterred, the police took *Body Count* and Warners, the song's publishers and distributors, to the Indecent Publications Tribunal, in an effort to get their work banned under New Zealand's Indecent Publications Act (1963). After reviewing the various submissions, and listening carefully to the album, the Tribunal concluded that 'the dominant effect of the album is complex'. While 'its lyrics are repugnant to most New Zealanders . . . It is a much bigger step to link those lyrics to subsequent anti-social behaviour'. It found the song 'Cop Killer' to be 'not exhortatory', saw the album as displaying 'an honest purpose', and found *Body Count* not indecent (Press Association report).

In the United Kingdom in October 1990, gangsta rappers NWA released a single called '100 Miles and Running'. The

B-side of the 12-inch format, 'She Swallowed It', dealt with oral sex, and many of the major department store chains refused to stock the record. The Midlands chain, Music Junction, also refused to stock the single, conscious of the lack of clarity surrounding the UK obscenity legislation (the 1959 Obscene Publications Act), and fearing prosecution. In June 1991, NWA released their second album, *Efil4zaggin* (Niggaz 4 life, backwards) (Priority, 1991) in the United Kingdom, after it had already topped the American *Billboard* chart and sold nearly a million copies in its first week of release. The album contained a number of tracks depicting sexual degradation and extreme violence toward women, along with considerable swearing. The police raided the premises of Polygram, the record's UK distributor, and seized some 12,000 copies of the album, and shops which already had stock withdrew the album from sale. A prosecution followed, using the Obscene Publications Act's definition of an 'obscene article' as one which 'tend(s) to deprave and corrupt'. The high-profile court case revolved around free speech arguments versus claims that the record was obscene, especially in its portrayal of women. The magistrates who judged the case ruled that the album was not obscene under the terms of the Act; the seized stock was returned and the album went back on sale (see Cloonan, 1995, for a detailed treatment of this episode and the associated issues).

See: **State**

Further reading: Cloonan, 1995; Denselow, 1990; Garofalo, 1992b; Kennedy, 1990; Pratt, 1990.

charts   The popular music chart is a numerical ranking of current releases based on sales and airplay, usually over a one-week period of time; the top ranked **album/single** is No. 1 and the rest are ranked correspondingly. The first UK chart appeared in 1928 (*Melody Maker*'s 'Honours List'); in the United States, *Billboard*, the major trade paper, began a 'Network Song Census' in 1934. Such charts quickly became the basis for **radio** 'Hit Parade' programmes.

The precise nature of how contemporary charts are compiled, and their basis, varies between competing trade magazines, and national approaches differ. In the United States, singles charts are based on airplay, while the album charts are based on sales. Current releases are generally defined for the singles charts as twenty-six weeks after the release. In the UK, the charts are produced by market research organizations sponsored by various branches of the media. In both countries, data collection is now substantially computerized and based on comprehensive sample data. Airplay information is compiled from selected radio stations, sales information from wholesalers and retailers, assisted by bar-coding. This represents a form of circular logic, in that the charts are based on a combination of radio play and sales, but airplay influences sales, and retail promotion and sales influence radio exposure.

Changes in the presentation of the charts can have important repercussions for the relative profile of particular **genres/** performers. The charts are broken down into genre categories; these can change over time, acting as a barometer of taste, as with the change of 'race' records to **R & B**. The decline of the single has influenced the way the charts are constructed. In the UK, in 1989 the music industry reduced the number of sales required to qualify for a platinum award (from one million to 600,000) to assist the promotional system, with the charts continuing to fuel excitement and sales.

The popular music charts represent a level of industry and consumer obsession with sales figures almost unique to the record industry. The charts are part of the various trade magazines (e.g. *Billboard*, *Variety*, *Music Week*), providing a key reference point for those working in sales and promotion. The record charts play a major role: 'to the fan of popular music, the charts are not merely quantifications of commodities but rather a major reference point around which their music displays itself in distinction and in relation to other forms' (Parker, 1991: 205).

The charts both reflect and shape popular music, especially through their influence on radio playlists. Historically there

49

has been frequent controversy over attempts to influence the charts (see **payola**), and debate still occurs over perceived attempts to manipulate them. For instance, in the United Kingdom, RCA's *Robson and Jerome* album (1995) rebounded up the chart following a WH Smith promotion which offered the cassette format for £1 (to those spending £20 or more in the store). Angry rival firms saw the promotion as 'like giving away free records for the chart' and 'not good for the business because it devalues the product' (*Music Week*, 18 March 1996). In 1996, the BPI (British Phonographic Industry) brought legal action against Rock Box Promotions, the company it identified as a buying team in a chart-hyping probe, in an attempt 'to protect the integrity of the chart' (ibid.). Also controversial are recent attempts to promote the single as more of a collector's item, by selling two versions of CD singles, with different 'bonus' tracks accompanying the main song.

Charts provide the music industry with valuable feedback and promotion, and help set the agenda for consumer choice. They have been an influential source of data for analyses of trends in the music industry (see **concentration**, **market cycles**), and the historical impact, commercially at least, of genres/performers. In addition to music magazines and the trade press, there is a market for chart listings (eg. Whitburn, 1988). Only rarely, however, has the operation and significance of the charts received sustained academic attention.

See: **payola**
Further reading: Brackett, 1995; Cusic, 1996; Negus, 1992; Parker, 1991.

chords; **chord extensions**; **dominant chords**   Chords are groups of notes sounded together. Chord extensions are notes that lie beyond the normal three or four notes of a chord, and are dissonant to the basic chord. A **dominant chord** is a triad built on the fifth degree of the scale. For example, in the key of C, the dominant chord is G major, made up of the notes G, B, and D.

Christian rock   A rather loose musical style/**genre**, applied
initially to those artists associated with the emergence of a
Christian music industry established by American evangelicals
(in the 1970s) as an alternative to the mainstream 'secular'
entertainment business. *Billboard* magazine has a Top Contemporary Christian Music category. While the **beat** and **melody**
are indistinguishable from other mainstream music forms,
differences are noted in the **lyric** content, where themes
frequently used are personal salvation, the witnessing of one's
faith, living by example, human frailties, rebellion, sin,
forgiveness, God's love and mercy.

There is a debate over whether Christian music is primarily
'ministry' or 'entertainment', or whether particular artists'
work is 'sacred' or 'secular'. The considerable commercial
success of some artists have fuelled this debate (e.g. Amy
Grant). The work of some mainstream performers has, at
times, been influenced by their Christian beliefs, usually in
terms of a more mystic Christian spirituality, such as Bob
Dylan, Van Morrison, or U2.

See: **gospel**
Further reading: Reid, 1993; Romanowski, 1993.
Listening:
Bob Dylan, *Slow Train Coming*, Columbia, 1979.
U2, *The Joshua Tree*, Island, 1987 (particularly 'I Still Haven't Found
   What I'm Looking For').
Van Morrison, 'When Will I Learn to Live in God?' on *Avalon
   Sunset*, Polydor, 1989.
Amy Grant, *Heart in Motion*, A&M, 1991.

class   Class is one of the fundamental types of social classification. The main theoretical tradition within sociology derives
from the work of Marx and Weber, with an emphasis on
defining classes primarily in economic terms. Subsequent
theoretical debates have centred around the primacy of
economic determinations of classes, compared with cultural
indicators. Most contemporary classifications of class rely on
employment categories, with class formation and identity

variously related to educational attainment and life chances, and to patterns of cultural consumption. It is the last that has been a significant part of popular music studies.

The French social theorist Pierre Bourdieu observes that 'nothing more clearly affirms one's class, nothing more infallibly classifies, than tastes in music' (1984: 18). The class nature of popular music preferences is internationally evident, with class-linked taste cultures seemingly fairly fixed over time. It is now clear that music consumption patterns, most notably **genre** preferences, follow discernable trends in terms of gender, age, ethnicity, and, in particular, class. In a pioneering study, Murdoch and Phelps established that English adolescents' popular music preferences were strongly differentiated by social class:

> The tastes of the majority of working class pupils were confined to the routine pop music of the Top Twenty and to the main Negro styles (Tamala Motown and Jamaican Reggae), whereas many middle class pupils largely rejected this 'mainstream' pop and preferred the various minority styles, generally lumped together under the umbrella heading of 'underground-progressive' rock music (Murdoch and Phelps, 1973: 8).

The internationally evident class nature of music preferences was documented consistently in studies through into the 1990s, with class-linked taste cultures seemingly fairly fixed over time. For example, Tanner (1981) found Canadian working-class senior high school students were more likely than their middle-class counterparts to favour the Top 40, while **progressive rock** was more likely to be the choice of middle-class students than working-class students. (The category progressive rock was a broad one here, including groups fusing classical and rock forms – Procul Harum; electronic innovations – Pink Floyd; and 'intellectual' singer songwriters – Bob Dylan.) Similar surveys in New Zealand, ten years later, found working and lower middle-class youth favoured **heavy metal**, **punk**, and **reggae**, while the higher social economic status students favoured **jazz**, **folk**, and **blues**

(Shuker, 1994). The class in music issue revealed itself in the United Kingdom in the late 1990s with the media battle between the groups Oasis and Blur, with the former championing their working-class origins and criticizing the latter as middle-class art students who were mocking the working class in songs like 'Parklife'.

The relative and sometimes greater influence of **gender**, **ethnicity**, age, and **location** as influences shaping musical tastes has also been acknowledged.

See: **consumption**; **cultural capital**; **taste cultures**
Further reading: Hakanen and Wells, 1993; Roe, 1983; Shepherd, 1986; Willis *et al.*, 1990.

classic rock – *see* **rock**

clubs; **club culture**; **club scene**   Clubs emerged historically as venues where people met regularly to pursue shared interests, usually paying a membership fee. During the early 1900s, clubs became major venues for live music on a regular and continuing basis, often associated with particular **genres** (e.g. **jazz** or **blues**). They have continued to serve as training grounds for aspiring performers operating at the local level, and provide a 'bread and butter' living for more established artists, often through being part of an organized circuit of venues.

The equation of live performance with musical **authenticity** and 'paying your dues' as a performer remains a widely-held ideology among fans, musicians, and record company executives. Clubs have historically assumed mythic importance for breaking new acts, as with The Who at the Marquee in London in 1965. They can also establish and popularize trends, as in English **punk** at London's 100 Club and the Roxy in the late 1970s. A community network of clubs or pub venues can help create a local **club scene**, at times based around a particular sound. See, for example, the **Liverpool/Merseybeat sound** associated with the Beatles, Gerry and The Pacemakers, and The Searchers in the early

1960s; and the **Manchester sound** (the Happy Mondays, James, and The Stone Roses) of the early 1990s. While the cohesion of their 'common' musical signatures is frequently exaggerated, such localized developments provide marketing possibilities by providing a 'brand name' with which club-bers can identify.

Despite the importance of **music video** as a marketing tool, club venues remain important for establishing new trends and their associated groups, such as the various forms of **techno**. The UK music press has documented the contemporary resurgence of the club and disco scene, along with the growth of Acid House and rave culture from the late 1980s. The cult of the **DJ** is a central part of the current club scene, a star figure whose skill is to judge the mood on the dance floor, both reflecting and leading it, all the while blending tracks into a seamless whole.

Dance clubs have historically been important to growing up in Britain, where young people have traditionally less mobility than their American counterparts. **Club culture** is

the colloquial expression given to youth cultures for whom dance clubs and their eighties offshoots, raves, are the symbolic axis and working social hub. The sense of place afforded by these events is such that regular attenders take on the name of the spaces they frequent, becoming 'clubbers' and 'ravers'   (Thornton, 1995: 3).

Club cultures are associated with specific locations which continually present and modify sounds and styles,

regularly bearing witness to the apogees and excesses of youth subcultures. Club cultures are **taste cultures**. Club crowds generally congregate on the basis of their shared taste in music, their consumption of common media, and, most importantly, their preference for people with similar tastes to themselves. Crucially, club cultures embrace their own hierarchies of what is authentic and legitimate in popular culture   (ibid., my bold).

See: **DJ**; **dance-music**
Further reading: MUZIK magazine; Thornton, 1995.

cock rock – *see* **hard rock**

commodification   A sociological concept referring to the process whereby a product (including labour, but more usually some form of material good) is created as a commodity for the market place. Applied to the **culture industries** by the **Frankfurt School** theorists, who stressed the commodification of popular cultural forms under the conditions of capitalist production and the constant quest for profit. The concept is related to the classical Marxist view of the economic base essentially determining the nature of cultural products.

Commodification has been used in popular music studies to critically analyse the relationship between the music industry, the market, and music-making. The term is largely used in a negative sense, in critiques of the incorporation of initially rebellious genres, including **rock'n'roll**, **rock**, **reggae**, and **punk**, into the commercial mainstream of the music industry:

> In light of the music industry's profitable involvement in all facets of the commercial mainstream, the story of rock and roll should be used by the Harvard School of Business as one of its case studies. Far from the threat that social and political critics would have it seem, rock and roll has become the corporate spine of American entertainment   (Eliot, 1989: 201).

The ideological side of this view is that **genres** initially couched in the language of rebellion have metamorphosed into the language of the cash register. Commodification is seen in the aggressive and calculated marketing of popular music trends, as with the British 'New Pop' performers of the early 1980s, associated with the rise of **music video** and **MTV**.

Other analyses seek to balance commodification against **consumer sovereignty**:

55

My starting point is what is possible for us as consumers – what is available to us, what we can do with it – is a result of decisions made in production, made by musicians, entrepreneurs and corporate bureaucrats, made according to governments' and lawyers' rulings, in response to technological opportunities. The key to 'creative consumption' remains an understanding of these decisions, the constraints under which they are made, and the ideologies that account for them   (Frith, 1988: 6–7).

Further reading: Eliot, 1989; Frith, 1988b; Harron, 1988; Hill, 1986; Negus, 1996; Rimmer, 1985.

communication Communication is (i) the conveying of information from A to B, with effect (Lasswell's classic flow model); and (ii) the negotiation and exchange of meaning (for a discussion of these, see O'Sullivan *et al.*, 1994). Music is a fundamental form of human **communication**: along with many other animal species, humans use organized sound to communicate. We are musically 'wired' at birth; infants respond to intonation and by six months are able to recognize musical structures and identify wrong notes. There has been a good deal of experimental, laboratory research on the manner in which the brain handles such processes.

'Music is a passionate sequencing of thoughts and feelings that expresses meaning in a manner that has no parallel in human life' (Lull, 1992: 1). That music produces 'sense' and conveys meanings is clear and unquestionable. What needs to be considered are 'the attributes of the processes governing *musical* meaning' (Middleton, 1990: 172), and how these operate in particular contexts. This requires an examination of: (i) the communicative role of musicians, who communicate – 'speak' – directly to individual listeners and to particular **audience** constituencies, often through particular **genres**; (ii) the communicative role of the music; for example, the conveying of implicit political messages ('protest song') and, often at a more implicit level, ideologies of romance, personal and social identity, and so forth; (iii) the communicative role of the means by which the music is transferred to its audiences, and the influence of these 'communicative vehicles' (Negus, 1996: 169), which is far from neutral (see **technology**); and (iv) the ways in which music is received, listened to, interpreted, and used by listeners in a wide variety of contexts.

This last dimension has been the subject of considerable analytical discussion. People and groups interact with popular music in a physical way (e.g. singing along, clapping, foot tapping, dancing, 'air guitar'); emotionally (e.g. romanticizing, letting the music 'wash over you', becoming 'lost in music'); and cognitively (e.g. stimulating thought, framing perceptions, processing information). These different modes of engagement can be in a very personal manner, through individual listening to relax or escape or distance oneself from other commitments and people, but it is the social experience of music which is more frequent. Music provides a soundtrack for daily experiences, such as studying, doing domestic chores, or shopping (see **muzak**); and the stimulus to physical activities, notably **dancing**, but also aerobics, driving, and sex. Music can operate as a companion, something to 'unwind' and relax with; its use contributes to the context and meaning of many other activities, for instance in a **film soundtrack**, weddings, and sporting events.

Music as organized sound is traditionally defined in terms of **beat**, **harmony**, and **melody**, and, in much popular music, song **lyrics**. Particular popular music texts shape audience consciousness through sheer thematic repetition (**hooks**), and by repeated exposure via **radio** and **music video** channel playlists.

See: **musicology**
Further reading: Middleton, 1990: ch. 6; Lull, 1992.

concentration   Concentration refers to 'the decreasing dispersal of ownership in advanced capitalist economies, where the means of production in market sectors become owned by progressively fewer and larger groups' (O'Sullivan *et al.*, 1994: 54). The continued concentration of the **culture industries** as a whole is increasingly obvious, and the music industry has been part of this process of consolidation. A number of internationally based large corporations have spread their interests across a variety of media, resulting in multimedia conglomerates, such as Time Warner (Barnet and Cavanagh term these 'imperial corporations' (1994: 14), and provide several instructive case studies).

At issue is the consequent question of control of the media and in whose interests it operates, and the relationship between diversity and innovation in the market. Free market economists argue that innovation will occur more frequently under conditions of oligopoly (increased concentration), since larger firms are better able to finance innovation and pass the costs and benefits along to consumers. Conversely, other analysts argue that oligopolistic conditions mean a lack of incentive for firms to depart much from the tried and tested, resulting in a high level of product homogeneity. Researchers applying this debate to the culture industries, including the **music industry**, have utilized the concentration ratio, which indicates the proportion of a market sector owned and controlled by the five leading firms; or the similar 'C4 index', which is the sum of the market shares of the four largest firms.

A major part of the music industry is constituted by the activities of a group of major international companies and lower tiers of **independents**. The latter in many cases are dependent on the **majors** for distribution and also act as 'farm teams', finding and developing new talent for them. Each of the majors is part of a larger communications or electronics conglomerate. The crucial issue which has pre-occupied analysts here is how such concentration affects the range of opportunities available to musicians and others involved in the production of popular music, and the nature and range of products available to the consumers of popular music. In other words, what is the cultural significance of this situation, and what role does it play in the creation of meaning in popular music?

Initial analyses of the relationship between concentration, innovation, and diversity in popular music suggested a negative relationship between concentration and diversity in the recording industry, relating this to a cyclical pattern of **market cycles** (Peterson and Berger, 1975). The basis for this analysis was the proportion of top-selling records (as indicated by the American *Billboard* singles **charts**) sold by the leading companies (majors). During the periods of greatest market concentration, there were fewer top-selling records. Conversely, during periods of greater market competition, with noticeable competition from newer/smaller record companies (independents), there were a greater number of top-selling records in the charts. Rothenbuhler and Dimmick (1982) showed that this relationship continued to hold between 1974 and 1980, confirming Peterson and Berger's thesis.

However, this view was challenged by Burnett (1996) and Lopes (1992), who both argued that a very high level of concentration was accompanied by a high level of diversity. Lopes analysed the period 1969–90 and used both albums and singles charts, and the Top 100 rather than simply the Top 10. He concluded that innovation and diversity in popular music in a period of high market concentration depends on the system of development and production used by major record companies. Major record companies establish an open system of development and production, based on 'a multidivisional corporate form linked with a large number of independent producers' (Lopes, 1992: 70). This incorporates innovation and diversity as an effective strategy in maintaining the viability and control of the market: 'major record companies find it advantageous to incorporate new artists, producers and styles of music to constantly reinvigorate the popular music market and to ensure that no large unsated demand among consumers materializes' (ibid.).

More attention is now being paid to the **gatekeeping** process, the filtering processes at work before a particular piece of music reaches the charts. Building on Lopes,

59

Christenson points out the importance of the number of decision-makers within a firm, as a variable in explaining the diversity and innovation generated by a major record company. In a sophisticated analysis of the Dutch music industry, he argues that the pattern between innovation and diversity is more complex than previous analysts had suggested. Christenson

> found a cyclical movement where, at present, we seem to witness an increase in competition together with an increase in diversity and innovation. The independent record companies have in the past few years contributed a lot to diversity and innovation. At the same time, the major record companies, while concentrating on exploiting their back catalogue and squeezing money out of their superstars, have neglected to invest in the talent of the future. As a consequence, independent record companies have gained market share at the expense of the majors. Currently the majors are trying to re-establish their position by large investments in new talent   (Christenson, 1995: 91).

See: **charts**; **culture industries**; **independents**; **majors**; **market cycles**; **music industry**

Further reading: Barnett and Cavanagh, 1994; Burnett, 1996; Christenson, 1995; Lopes, 1992; O'Sullivan *et al.*, 1994; Peterson and Berger, 1975; Rothenbuhler and Dimmick, 1982.

concept albums – *see* **albums**

concerts; **mega events**   Popular music concerts are complex cultural phenomena, involving a mix of music and economics, ritual and pleasure, for both performers and their audience. Concerts are about pleasure, the assertion and celebration of the values of the music, the endorsement of performers, and solidarity in a community of companionship. There is a tension between concerts as exemplifying a sense of community, albeit a transient one, and their economic and promotional importance:

> Backstage is the world of the media, governed by functional specialization, calculations of financial interest, and instrumental rationality. Frontstage is the realm of the audience, ruled by a sense of community, adherence to the codes of a valued subculture, and expressive-emotional experience. The stage itself is the site of the mediation of these two worlds by the performing artist who binds them together with the music (Weinstein, 1991b: 199–200).

The backstage area is a highly complex work site, with a range of specialized workers. The number of personnel reflects the size of the tour and the economic 'importance' of the performers, but can include technicians in charge of the instruments and equipment (amplifiers etc.), stage hands, who often double as roadies, people to work the sound and lighting boards, security guards, and the concert tour manager. The successful operation of the backstage area at concerts involves the integration of these workers into a stable and impersonal time schedule, where each person does their job as and when required.

Concerts are a ritual for both performers and their audience. Classical symphony orchestra concerts celebrate 'the power holding class in our society' (Small, 1987: 7); popular music concerts frequently celebrate youth, not purely as a demographic group, but the *idea* of youth. The behaviour of concert-goers depends on the performer(s) and their associated musical style(s). For example, audiences at **rock** and **heavy metal** concerts are considerably more outgoing and demonstrative, consistent with the essential physicality of the music.

Part of the ritual of attending concerts is getting 'pumped up' for the occasion, a process which can include spending hours in queues to ensure tickets (many concerts by top acts sell out in a matter of hours), listening again to the performer's albums, talking with friends about the coming event (especially where expectations have been generated by previous concerts by the performer), travelling, often over long distances, to the concert venue, possible pre-concert drug use, and 'dressing up' for the concert. These all become part of the celebratory experience.

The performers themselves conform to ritual forms of behaviour in performance, with particular performance styles and images associated with specific **genres**. Take, for example, the model of the rock band, at least at the level of image, as anti-hierarchical: 'on stage the players come close to one another, even lean on one another, and circulate to interact with different members of the band' (Weinstein, 1991b: 99). This public image often hides any personal animosities present within the group, which are frequently concealed or played down in the common interest of maintaining the group's career. The typical rock stage performance is heavily theatrical and physically energetic, especially in the case of the lead singer and lead guitarist.

The term **mega events** has been used by Garofalo and others for the large-scale outdoor concerts and festivals which came to prominence in the 1980s. Some, most notably Live Aid (1985), were to raise funds and publicize causes; these have also been referred to as 'conscience rock' (Shuker, 1994: 274). Most mega events are straight money-making ventures, such as Rock in Rio (1985, 1991), or the Knebworth festivals in the United Kingdom.

See: **tours**

Further reading: Eliot, 1989; Fink, 1989; Garofalo, 1992a; Walser, 1993; Weinstein, 1991b: ch. 6.

consumer sovereignty The view that consumers/audiences exercise of their 'free' choice in the market place is a major determinant of the nature and availability of particular cultural and economic commodities. Consumer sovereignty emphasizes the operation of human agency: 'while the elements of romance and imagination that have informed individual personal histories and the history of popular musical genres are frequently marginalised in the commodification process, they remain essential to the narratives people construct to help create a sense of identity' (Shuker, 1994: 36). In some contemporary forms of cultural studies, consumer sovereignty has been tied to the notion of the active audience, to produce a debated view of semiotic democracy (see Fiske, 1989).

An emphasis on consumer sovereignty as the primary factor whereby social meaning is created in the music is in contra-distinction to the view that the process of **consumption** is constrained by the processes of production: production deter-mines consumption (see **political economy**). Yet production and consumption are not to be regarded as fixed immutable processes, but must be regarded as engaged in a dialectic. Economic power is obviously wielded by institutional struc-tures and practices, in this case, the record companies and their drive for market stability, predictability and profit, but this power is never absolute. Recent writing in popular music studies has emphasized a 'middle way' approach to the issues here, utilizing the concepts of **articulation** and **mediation** (see Negus, 1996).

See: **audiences**; **fans**

consumption The study of the consumption of economic and cultural goods has paid particular attention to the patterns of such consumption and the processes whereby it occurs. Popular music consumption embraces the purchase of recorded music, attending **live** performances, watching **music videos**, listening to the **radio**, and making tape compilations (**home taping**). The discussion here covers patterns and processes evident in the consumption of popular music (for a general discussion of the concept of **consumers**, and its relationship to audience studies, see **audience**).

1 *Patterns of consumption*: Historically, the main consumers of contemporary (post-1950) popular music, especially **rock** music, have been young people, between 12 and 25. At the same time, as the **charts** have frequently indicated, adult tastes are significant; indeed, they have become

increasingly so, with the ageing of rock's original audience (see **demography**).

As a general social category, one factor youth has in common internationally is an interest in popular music, and cultural surveys in North America, the United Kingdom, and New Zealand all indicate youth's high levels of popular music consumption. The profiles of this consumption show a clear pattern of age and **gender**-based **genre** preferences. Younger adolescents, particularly girls, prefer commercial **pop**; older adolescents express greater interest in more **progressive** forms and artists. High school students tend to be more interested in **alternative/ indie** genre tastes, and less interested in the more commercial expressions of popular music. As consumers get older, their tastes in music often become more open to exploring new genres and less commercial forms. This trend is particularly evident amongst tertiary students, reflecting the dominant forms of musical **cultural capital** within their peer groups. There is some evidence of an association between commitment to school, 'anti-social' attitudes and behaviours, and preferences in popular music (see **education: school commitment**). In studies of music consumption in ethnically mixed or diverse populations, black adolescents are demonstrably more likely (than their white or Asian counterparts) to favour black music genres, most notably **soul**, **R & B**, **blues**, **reggae**, and **rap**. Such genres are carriers of ideology, creating symbols for listeners to identify with. Rap has emerged as a major genre preference among black youth internationally.

Adult music tastes generally remain fixed at the commercial level, or they largely abandon more direct interest – through record purchases, **concert**-going, etc. – in popular music. However, there is a substantial older audience for popular music, especially genres/styles such as **country**, easy listening, **jazz**, and blues.

2 *Modes of consumption*: Studies of the process and nature of music consumption have used qualitative methodologies to examine individual record buyers, concert-goers, radio

listeners, and music video viewers. Exposure to the radio, music video programmes and **MTV**, and live performance all influence the construction of individual popular music consumption. Even younger adolescent consumers, who are often seen as relatively undiscriminating and easily swayed by the influence of market forces (see **teeny-boppers**), see their preferences as the product of a more complex set of influences, with the views of their friends paramount. Young people's musical activities, whatever their cultural background or social position, rest on a substantial and sophisticated body of knowledge about popular music. Most young people have a clear under-standing of its different genres, and an ability to hear and place sounds in terms of their histories, influences, and sources. Young musicians and audiences have no hesitation about making and justifying judgements of meaning and value (see Willis *et al.*, 1990). Patterns of consumption are complex, involving record-buying, video-viewing, radio-listening, and home taping; along with the various secondary levels of involvement: the **music press**, **dance**, **clubbing**, and concert-going.

Buying recorded music in its various formats is central, constituting

> an important sphere of activity in itself, one that can range in intensity from casual browsing to earnest search-ing for particular records. It is a process that involves clear symbolic work: complex and careful exercises of choice from the point of view of initial listening to, seeking out, handling and scrutinizing records . . . large numbers of young people now do their own archeologies of popu-lar music history   (Willis *et al.*, 1990: 61).

This involves gathering information from peers, older siblings, and retrospectives in the music press; and systemat-ically searching for items out of the **back catalogue**. This search is primarily through second-hand record shops, which are currently thriving because of the limited purchasing power of unemployed youth and the high prices of new **CDs** and **albums**. It can also be seen in the bargain bins and at record sales.

Radio remains the major source for most people's engagement with popular music, with surveys indicating that young people in particular frequently listen to the radio (and watch less television). Although this is generally listening at an unfocused level, with the radio acting as a companion and as background to other activities, at times listening to the radio is deliberately undertaken in order to hear and tape new music. This is frequently done in relation to particular specialist shows or **DJs**. Preferences for particular radio stations/formats are related to factors such as age and ethnicity.

Further reading: Hakanen and Wells, 1993; Negus, 1996; Roe, 1983; Weinstein, 1991a; Willis *et al.*, 1990.

content quotas – *see* **State**

copyright   Copyright is central to the **music industry**. The basic principle of copyright law is the exclusive right to copy and publish one's own work. That is, the copyright owner has the right to duplicate or authorize the duplication of their property, and to distribute it. The full legal nature of copyright is beyond our scope here (see Fink, 1989: 36–47); its significance lies in its cultural importance. The role of new technologies of **sound recording** and reproduction have been associated with issues of intellectual property rights, copyright, and the control of sounds. For the music industry, the 'bogeyman' of the 1990s is posed by threats to copyright.

In addition to deriving income from unit sales of records, record companies, performers, songwriters, and music publishers derive income from the sale of rights. Ownership of rights is determined by copyright in the master tape, the original tape embodying the recorded performance from which subsequent records are manufactured. The global music industry is now less concerned than previously with the production and management of commodities, with the management of rights providing an increasingly important share of its revenues.

This rights income includes: (i) mechanical income, payable by the record company (to the owner of the copyright) for permission to reproduce a song on record. This is a fixed percentage of the recommended retail price; (ii) performance income, a licence fee paid by venues, TV and **radio** stations for the right to publicly perform or broadcast songs; and (iii) miscellaneous income, payment for the use of songs in films, advertisements, and so on.

The first US copyright statute was enacted in 1909, and protected the owners of musical compositions from unauthorized copying (**piracy**), while making a song into a commodity product that could be bought and sold in the market place. With copyright protection, sheet music writer-publishers could afford to spend a great deal of money promoting a new song because other printers could not pirate the valuable properties thus created. Their activity fostered musical innovation, most notably in **ragtime** and **jazz** (Peterson, 1990: 99). Similar legislation was enacted in Britain in 1911. The development of recording raised the question of whether the publishers of recorded and sheet music could claim the same rights as literary publishers. British and American legislation differed on this, with the former being more restrictive in its approach.

Copyright laws provided no mechanism for collecting the royalties from the public performance of music. In 1914, the American Society of Composers, Authors, and Publishers (ASCAP) was formed, to issue licences and to collect all due royalties from three sources: the performance of songs, with recording artists receiving income based on the revenue made from the sale of their records; the sale of original music to publishers, and subsequent performance royalties; and money paid to the publishers for their share of the sales and performances, usually split 50/50 between composers and publishers. ASCAP's role was confirmed by a Supreme Court decision in 1917 validating the organization's right to issue membership licences and collect performance royalties. However, broadcasters resisted all ASCAP's attempts to collect royalties for music played on the radio, and went so far as to create their own organization to break what they claimed were ASCAP's monopolistic tactics, establishing Broadcast Music Inc. (BMI) in 1939.

Frith (1993) has observed that the advent of new technologies of sound recording and reproduction have coincided with the globalization of culture, and the desire of media/ entertainment conglomerates to maximize their revenues from 'rights' as well as maintaining income from the actual sale of records. What counts as 'music' is changing from a fixed, authored 'thing' which existed as property to something more difficult to identify.

The Rome Convention and the Berne Convention are the major international agreements on copyright. The International Federation of the Phonographic Industries (IFPI) globally regulates the application and enforcement of copyright (not always successfully – see **piracy**). Rights income is collected by various local and regional agencies, such as The Australasian Mechanical Copyright Owners Society (AMCOS); or the Australasian Performing Rights Association (APRA).

Attempts to ensure international uniformity in copyright laws have met with only partial success; even within the European community conventions and practices vary considerably. Attitudes towards copyright diverge, depending whose interests are involved. There is an emerging hostility towards copyright among many music consumers and even some musicians, due to its regulatory use by international corporations to protect their interests. On the other hand, the companies themselves are actively seeking to harmonize arrangements and curb piracy, while the record industry associations (especially the IFPI), which are almost exclusively concerned with copyright issues, largely support the industry line. Ultimately, it is market control which is at stake. There is a basic tension between protecting the rights and income of the original artists, and the restriction of musical output.

Canada, the United States, Australia, Japan, and Ghana all demonstrate different responses to the development of copyright, depending on the nature of interest groups that make up the local performing rights societies, and national concerns about the potential exploitation of local music, the outflow of funds to overseas copyright holders, and the stifling of local performers' ability to utilize international material. (The following studies are to be found in Frith, 1993.) Through a detailed exposition of the regulatory structures and networks in the Australian recorded music industry, and the 1990 Public Inquiry into copyright, Breen (1993) shows how in Australia copyright law has largely helped protect the interests of the major music companies. Théberge traces the situation in Canada, which 'maintains only the most basic levels of copyright protection' (1993: 52). The controversy and legal battles surrounding composer John Oswald's 'Plunderphonics' (the term he has used for his sampling practices) provides a further example of the need for the legal system 'to redefine the legal concept of a musical work, its value and its social uses in light of present technical and creative realities' (ibid.: 62). Jones shows how current copyright controversies in the United States 'must be viewed as part of the recording industry's exploitation of all income-generating means at its disposal' (1993: 82). Théberge and Jones both pay considerable attention to the highly problematic issue of **sampling**. Gaines (1993) provides an extended example of Bette Midler and 'the piracy of identity' case in the United States, stressing the danger of confirming culture as private property over culture as a shared experience.

Mitsui's study of Japan is particularly interesting, showing how copyright laws were originally imported from the West to a situation where social and moral conditions were basically different: 'the Japanese people do not take well to copyright, or more properly, the idea of the individual right' (1993: 141). Historically, Japan tried to avoid paying for translation rights, out of a concern not to impede the influx of Western ideas and information, while the observance of domestic copyright law was also dubious. The case of Ghana also illustrates the problems arising from the attempt to straightforwardly apply a Eurocentric concept in Third World countries, where there is 'a living folk tradition existing along-side private creativity' (ibid. 146). Collins (1993) identifies the difficulties of applying European musical ideology to the African music realm. For example, in the West, song composer royalties are equally divided, with 50 per cent paid for the lyrics and 50 per cent for the music or melody. He suggests that, in African music, rhythm is so important that royalties should be broken down into three components, with a third each (33 per cent) accorded to lyrics, melody, and rhythm.

As case studies of the legal and moral arguments surrounding the sampling used in records by The JAMS, M/A/R/R/S, De La Soul, and others show, there are extremely complex issues involved. These centre around questions of what is actually copyrightable in music; who has the right to control the use of a song, a record, or a sound; and what the nature is of the public domain. As Théberge concludes:

> The introduction of digital technologies in music production during the past decade has resulted in the development of new kinds of creative activity that have, on the one hand, exacerbated already existing problems in the conceptualisation of music as a form of artistic expression and, on the other, demanded that even further distinctions be made in copyright legislation   (in Frith, 1993: 53).

See: **bootlegs**; **home taping**; **piracy**; **sampling**
Further reading: Beadle, 1993; Fink, 1989; Frith, 1993; Harley, 1993; Jones, 1992; Negus, 1992.

counter culture/underground; **beats**; **hippies**   Indicating a loose, expressive social movement, the term counter culture was initially applied to groups such as the beats in the 1950s (see below), and subsequently to the largely middle-class **subcultures** of the mid- to late 1960s. The 1960s counter culture was especially evident in North American communal and anti-conformist lifestyles, but it quickly became an international phenomenon. It was strongly present in the UK, where it was more commonly referred to as the **underground**. The term counter culture continues to be applied to various groups/subcultures outside of, and at times in opposition to, the social and economic mainstream.

The counter culture had its origins in the **beats** (or beat-niks) of the 1950s. The beats developed in post-war Paris in the student area the Left Bank, influenced by the French bohemian artistic intelligentsia. Strongly centred around existentialist values, the futility of action, and a nihilism about social change, the beats also took on board Eastern mysticism, **jazz**, poetry, drugs (primarily marijuana), and literature. Popularized by writers such as Kerouac and Ginsberg, the movement spread across America in the early 1960s, initially centred on Greenwich Village in New York. The beats had a romantic, anarchic vision, with individualism a major theme, and were highly antagonistic to middle-class lifestyles and careers. They were influential on the values of the later counter culture and **Generation X**, and helped bring jazz, especially its more modern forms such as **bebop**, to wider attention.

In the 1960s, the term counter culture was used by social theorists, such as Roszak and Marcuse, as an integrative label for the various groups and ideologies present in the American movement. The counter culture was seen as a generational unit, the 'youth culture' challenging traditional concepts of career, education, and morality, and seeking an **identity** outside an occupational role or family. The 1960s counter culture/underground embraced a range of groups and life-styles, who broadly shared values of drug use, freedom, and a broadly anti-middle-class stance. In the United States elements of the counter culture were sympathetic to New Left politics (Students for a Democratic Society), and embraced some political concerns, especially community activism in relation to health, education, and the environment. While this led some observers to see youth as a generationally political progressive group, at heart the movement represented a form of symbolic, cultural politics (exemplified by the hippies). The counter culture embodied a series of contradictions. For instance, it developed at a time of relative economic prosperity, enabling the economy to carry substantial numbers of voluntarily unemployed people living on subsistence incomes, who were antagonistic to the mainstream economy and society.

A significant part of the counter culture were the **hippies**. Initially centred on San Francisco's Haight Ashbury district, they came into international focus during 1966–7. 'Soft' drug use (cannabis, LSD), long hair, communes, peace, love-ins/free love, flowers, and **psychedelic/acid rock** were all aspects picked up on by the press. Hippies represented a style of cultural politics, ostensibly rejecting mainstream society and values, but with clear contradictions present. They generally came from comfortable middle-class backgrounds, but the material affluence of the Western economies during the 1960s made their opting-out possible; they were anti-technology but often possessed impressive sound systems; and their espoused 'freedom' at times sat uneasily alongside sexism and **gender** stereotyping.

Musically, the counter culture was linked to the **genres** of **progressive** and psychedelic **rock**. The hippies' preference for psychedelic rock was consistent with the other values of the subculture, especially its 'laid back' orientation and drug use (see Pichaske, 1989; Willis, 1978). Counter culture 'radical' youth, mainly students, were part of the US Civil Rights movement, with its use of political **folk** songs and negro spirituals, and supported the Campaign for Nuclear Disarmament in the United Kingdom, which drew on similar sources, along with trad. **jazz** during its marches in the late 1950s. All of these musics were soon subject to **commodification**, with sincerity becoming highly marketable during the mid-1960s.

The counter culture persisted into the 1980s and beyond, though arguably more in terms of the encapsulation of its values in the private lives of the **baby boomer** generation.

See: **jazz**; **progressive rock**; **psychedelic music**
Further reading: Brake, 1985; Garofalo, 1997: ch. 6; Nuttal, 1968; Reich, 1972.

country; **C & W/country & western**; **country rock**
Country music is an American **genre** now internationally
popular; it has been variously known in the past as **folk
music**, old-time music, hillbilly, and C & W/country &
western. According to Bill Malone (1985: 1) 'it defies precise
definition, and no term (not even 'country') has ever successfully encapsulated its essence'. As an identifiable genre, C &
W can be traced back to the American rural south in the
1920s; Okey issued the first country catalogue in 1924. It
has evolved into primarily an American form with two general
strands: traditional country, and a more commercial mainstream of **pop** country. Within these are various identifiable
subgenres and related styles: progressive country, **country
rock**, **bluegrass**, **rockabilly**, Western Swing, new country,
Tex Mex, Cajun, Zydeco, and Conjunto. Leading traditional
country performers included Johnny Cash, the Carter Family,
Hank Williams, Willie Nelson, and Dolly Parton.

Country emerged in the United States as a major market
force in popular music in the 1990s, and classic stereotypes
associated with the genre (especially its maudlin themes and
limited appeal) no longer hold up. *Billboard* placed Garth
Brooks as Top Country Album Artist *and* Top Pop Album
Artist for the years 1990, 1991, and 1993. In 1993, all six of
his albums were included among the 100 most popular albums
of the year, with two – *No Fences* and *Ropin' the Wind*
(Capitol, 1991) – having sold about ten million copies each.
In performance, Brooks adopted an arena **rock** aesthetic,
using theatre smoke, fireworks, and sophisticated lighting
shows (Garofalo, 1997: 457). His **crossover** success opened
the way on the pop **charts** for other country artists, with
Billy Ray Cyrus, Dwight Yoakum, Mary Chapin Carpenter,
and Reba McIntyre among the best-selling artists of the early
to mid-1990s. Along with Brooks and others, these artists are
often referred to as 'new country'. At the same time, country
radio became the second most listened to music format in
the United States, second only to adult contemporary.

Further reading: Endres, 1993; Ennis, 1992; Lewis, 1993; Malone, 1985.

Listening:

Hank Williams, *Hank Williams*, Polydor, 1986 (series covering his 1946–52 releases).

Garth Brooks, *No Fences*, Capitol/EMI, 1989.

Rosanna Cash, *Retrospective 1979–1989*, CBS, 1989.

Representing an amalgam of country and rock styles, the term **country rock** was first applied in the mid-1960s to American rock performers who looked to country music for inspiration, including The Byrds, The Flying Burrito Brothers, and Gram Parsons (a short, but influential career). Country rock was carried into the 1970s with the Eagles, Poco, Ozark Mountain Daredevils, and the Amazing Rhythm Aces, all of whom mixed country with other rock genres and enjoyed commercial success. In the 1980s and 1990s country has been drawn on by various artists as part of a hybridization of musical styles, like Jason and the Scorchers or The Blasters. While primarily a male-dominated genre, some female performers enjoyed critical and commercial success with soft country rock (e.g. Emmylou Harris). In the 1990s, country rock became indistinguishable from much contemporary country music. The audience for country rock is under-researched, but appears to be a mix of those favouring either, or both, of the parent genres.

Further reading: Garofalo, 1997; Fong-Torres, 1991; Scoppa, 1992.
Listening:

Bob Dylan, *Nashville Skyline*, Columbia, 1969.

Emmylou Harris, *Luxury Liner*, Warner Brothers, 1977.

Gram Parsons, *GP/Grievous Angel*, Reprise, 1990 (rerelease, both albums on single CD).

The Byrds, *Sweetheart of the Rodeo*, Edsel, 1997.

cover bands – *see* **musicians**

cover versions; **song families** Cover versions are performances/recordings by musicians not responsible for the original recording. Historically, these were often 'standards' which were the staples of singers for most of the 1940s and 1950s. More recently, with the 1960s emphasis on a rock **aesthetic** valuing individual creativity and the use of one's own compositions, covers have become regarded as not as creative, or authentic, as the originals. At times, however, they have been perceived as creative in their own right. Take, for example, Elvis Presley's cover of 'That's Alright Mama' (Sun, 1955), originally recorded by **R & B** singer Arthur 'Big Boy' Crudup; or The Chimes' 'I Still Haven't Found What I'm Looking For' (CBS, 1990), first recorded by U2. Some covers have replicated the popularity of the original, like Joan Jett's version of 'Crimson and Clover', originally a No. 1 hit for Tommy James and the Shondells in 1967; others have been successful renditions of relatively ignored originals, like Tommy James and the Shondells' 'Hanky Panky' (1966, a US No. 1). Cover songs are a proven product with which an audience can often identify. While some reinterpret the original song in a fresh and distinctive way, the majority are regarded as simply 'retreads'. Covers have featured strongly in the **charts** throughout the late 1980s and into the 1990s. There is a fresh generation of listeners and a new market for the recycled song, as reissue/compilation albums and film soundtracks also demonstrate.

Song families are particular songs which are revived and reworked; the term has been developed primarily by Hatch and Millward (1987). Constructed out of existing lyrical, melodic, and rhythmic structures, they are adapted to new musical developments by successive generations of musicians, reshaping generic conventions in the process. Willie Dixon's 'Spoonful', which has been recorded by a number of artists, illustrates this process, both musically and in terms of the social meanings ascribed to various renditions of the song. Elvis Presley's reinterpretations of 'That's Alright Mama', a **blues** song, and the **bluegrass** classic 'Blue Moon of Kentucky' (originally sung by Bill Monroe), contributed to the formation of **rockabilly** and **rock'n'roll** in the 1950s.

75

See: **authenticity**

Further reading: Hatch and Millward, 1987; Moore, 1993.

Listening:

Joan Jett, 'Crimson and Clover' (1981) on *The Hit List*, Epic, 1990.

Howlin' Wolf, 'Spoonful', several renditions, on various compilations.

Cream, 'Spoonful', *Fresh Cream*, Polydor, 1966; and extended live
version on *Wheels of Fire*, Polydor, 1968.

crossover   The move of a record or performer from success
in one **genre** or **chart** area to another, usually with a more
mainstream audience. The term is usually associated with
black music achieving more mainstream chart success. Less
commonly, crossover has also been applied to the early 1990s
success of 'new **country**', and to gay musicians 'coming out'.
With the exception of a brief period (November 1963 to
January 1965), *Billboard* had a separate **R & B** chart, with
some R & B records 'crossing over' to the **pop** chart, such
as The Four Tops, with 'I Can't Help Myself' (Motown,
1965). Music classified as R & B was neither promoted as
heavily as pop, nor did R & B recordings have access to the
extensive distribution network of pop records, though Gordy
at **Motown** in the 1960s successfully pursued a policy of
making black music attractive to a white audience (e.g. The
Supremes, The Four Tops). In the 1980s, with the success
of performers such as Michael Jackson and Prince, *Billboard*
inaugurated a Hot Crossover 30 chart (1987–), codifying the
pace-setting nature of black music.

Crossover is predicated on the existence of discreet boundaries, and a hierarchy of racially distinct genres and audiences.
At times it sits awkwardly with the bi-racial composition of those
working within particular genres (e.g. 1950s **rock'n'roll**).
Brackett (1995) provides an interesting case study of five R & B
songs that achieved varying degrees of crossover success in 1965,
demonstrating clear connections between their musical style
and the degree to which they crossed over. He argues that the
country and R & B charts served as 'testing grounds' to identify
potential crossover records to the mainstream pop chart.

Crossover music has been criticized by some (notably Nelson George) as a sell-out of the tougher styles of black music, and as a threat to the livelihoods of independent black entrepreneurs. There are black nationalist underpinnings to such views, linked to the notion of compromising the **authenticity** of black music. Other commentators (notably Perry, 1988) view crossover as a metaphor for integration and the upward social mobility of the black community. Crossover is not such an issue in music markets outside the United States. In the United Kingdom the term is rarely used, and then usually to refer to successful **dance** and **indie music** doing well in the main pop charts (see *Music Week, NME*, and *Melody Maker*).

See: **R & B**; **soul**

Further reading: Brackett, 1995; Garofalo, in Bennett, 1993; George, 1989; Perry, 1988.

Listening:

Marvin Gaye, 'I Heard it Through the Grapevine', *Anthology*, Motown, 1974.

Michael Jackson, *Thriller*, Epic, 1982.

James Brown, 'Papa's Got a Brand New Bag', *20 All Time Greatest Hits*, Polydor, 1991.

cultural capital   Originating in the work of Pierre Bourdieu, cultural capital 'describes the unequal distribution of cultural practices, values and competencies characteristic of capitalist societies', with classes defined not only by their economic capital, but also by their differential access to cultural capital and symbolic power (O'Sullivan *et al.*, 1994: 73). In simple concrete **consumption** terms, in relation to the media, this means the preference of individuals and social groups for particular **texts** – for example, European movies or Hollywood action movies – and the role such tastes play as both means of self-identification and as social indicators to others.

The designation of popular music is as much sociological as musical, a view reinforced by the varied reception of specific music texts. Bourdieu (1984) showed how 'taste' is both conceived and maintained in social groups' efforts to differentiate and distance themselves from others, and underpinning varying social status positions. Music has traditionally been a crucial dimension of this process. The musical tastes and styles followed or adopted by particular groups of consumers are affected by a number of social factors, including **class**, **gender**, **ethnicity**, and age. Consumption is not simply a matter of 'personal' preference, but is, in part, socially constructed. Linked to this process is the manner in which musical tastes serve as a form of symbolic or cultural capital.

Musical cultural capital is demonstrated through a process whereby the individual, in acquiring a taste for particular artists, both discovers the broader history of popular music and assimilates a selective tradition. He or she is then able to knowledgeably discuss artists, records, styles, trends, recording companies, literature, etc. This process occurs with music which is popular among the individual's peer group or subculture. In both cases, it serves a similar function, distancing its adherents from other musical styles. In the case of allegiance to non-mainstream **genres**/performers, cultural capital serves to assert an oppositional stance; this is the pattern with many **youth subcultures**, which appropriate and innovate musical styles and forms as a basis (subcultural capital) for their identity.

There is a tendency to dichotomize cultural capital in popular music by distinguishing between listeners oriented toward a commercial mainstream and a marginalized minority preferring more **independent** or **alternative music**. For example, in 1950, Reisman distinguished between two teenage audiences for popular music in the United States. First, a majority group with 'an undiscriminating taste in popular music, (who) seldom express articulate preferences', and for whom the functions of music were predominantly social. This group consumed 'mainstream', commercial music, following the **stars** and the hit parade. Second, Reisman identified a minority group of 'the more active listeners', who had a more rebellious attitude toward popular music, indicated by 'an insistence on rigorous standards of judgement and taste in a relativist culture; a preference for the uncommercialized, unadvertised small bands rather than name bands;

the development of a private language ... (and) a profound resentment of the commercialization of radio and musicians' (Reisman, 1950: 412; also in Frith and Goodwin, 1990).

More recently, Trondman (1990) saw contemporary Swedish youth **rock** as split between two major genres: a mature 'artistic' rock, and a commercial 'idol rock'. The mature was identified with what Bourdieu refers to as legitimate culture, while the other expresses distance from legitimate culture. The adherents of artistic rock are found primarily among university students and graduates, people who have good prospects of becoming part of the legitimate culture. For them, there is an emphasis on music that satisfies demands of 'intellectuality', 'aesthetic appeal', and 'association with tradition'. Those who have an avid interest in the 'right' kind of rock can develop their taste into a 'learned discourse' or 'scholastic jargon' in the periphery of legitimate culture. For some, this form of assimilation can offer a port of entry into legitimate culture and preparatory schooling in the tradition of assimilation.

See: **class**; **youth subcultures**
Further reading: Reisman, 1950; Trondman, 1990; Willis *et al.*, 1990.

cultural imperialism   Cultural imperialism developed as a concept analogous to the historical, political, and economic subjugation of the Third World by the colonizing powers in the nineteenth century, with consequent deleterious effects for the societies of the colonized. This gave rise to global relations of dominance, subordination, and dependency between the affluence and power of the advanced capitalist nations, most notably the United States and Western Europe, and the relatively powerless underdeveloped countries. This economic and political imperialism was seen to have a cultural aspect:

> namely the ways in which the transmission of certain products, fashions and styles *from* the dominant nations *to* the dependent markets leads to the creation of particular patterns of demand and consumption which are

underpinned by and endorse the cultural values, ideals and practices of their dominant origin. In this manner the local cultures of developing nations become dominated and in varying degrees invaded, displaced and challenged by foreign, often western, cultures (O'Sullivan *et al.*, 1994: 74).

Evidence of cultural imperialism was provided by the predominantly one-way international media flow from a few internationally dominant sources of media production, notably the United States, to media systems in other national cultural contexts. This involved the market penetration and dominance of Anglo-American popular culture, and, more importantly, established certain forms as the accepted ones, scarcely recognizing that there are alternatives. The international dominance of the media conglomerates and the associated major record companies suggested that cultural imperialism was applicable to popular music. The extent to which this situation should be seen in terms of cultural invasion and the subjugation of local cultural identity has been debated.

The cultural imperialism thesis gained general currency in debates in the 1960s and 1970s about the significance of imported popular culture. Such debates were evident not only in the Third World, but in 'developed' countries such as France, Canada, Australia, and New Zealand, which were also subject to high market penetration by American popular culture. Adherents of the thesis tended to dichotomize local culture and its imported counterpart, regarding local culture as somehow more **authentic**, traditional, and supportive of a conception of a distinctive national cultural **identity**. Set against this identity, and threatening its continual existence and vitality, was the influx of large quantities of commercial media products, mainly from the United States. Upholders of the cultural imperialism view generally saw the solution to this situation as some combination of restrictions upon media imports and the deliberate fostering of the local cultural industries, including music.

Although the existence of cultural imperialism became widely accepted at both a common-sense level and in left-wing academia, its validity at both a descriptive level and as an explanatory analytical concept came under increasing critical scrutiny into the 1980s. In a sustained critique of the concept, Tomlinson (1991) argued that it concealed a number of conceptual weaknesses and problematic assumptions about 'national' culture and the nature of cultural homogenization and consumerism. In the 1980s, the 'active audience' paradigm in media and **cultural studies**, with its emphases on resistance and polysemy, challenged the value of cultural imperialism.

The cultural imperialism thesis is predicated on accepting the 'national' as a given, with distinctive national musical identities its logical corollary. However, the validity of a local/authentic versus imported/commercial dichotomy is difficult to sustain with reference to specific examples, while media effects are assumed in a too one-dimensional fashion, conflating economic power and cultural effects. This is to underestimate the mediated nature of audience reception and use of media products. Since the 1950s Anglo-American popular culture has become established as the international preferred culture of the young. Locally produced texts cannot be straightforwardly equated with local national cultural identity, and imported product is not to be necessarily equated with the alien. Indeed, local music is frequently qualitatively indistinct from its overseas counterpart, though this in itself is often a target for criticism. While specific national case studies demonstrate the immense influence of the transnational music industry on musical production and distribution everywhere, they 'just as clearly indicate that world musical homogenization is not occurring' (Robinson *et al.*, 1991: 4). A complex relationship, often more symbiotic than exploitative, exists between the **majors** and local record companies in marginalized national contexts such as Canada and New Zealand. Local musicians are immersed in overlapping and frequently reciprocal contexts of production, with a cross-fertilization of local and international sounds. Attempts at the national level to foster local popular music production are primarily interventions at the level of the distribution and

81

reception of the music. They attempt to secure greater access to the market, particularly for local products in the face of overseas music, notably from England and the United States.

The **globalization** of Western capitalism, particularly evident in its media conglomerates, and the increasingly *international* nature of Western popular music undermined the applicability of cultural imperialism, at least in any straightforward fashion. However, it remains a useful concept in popular music studies, providing that it refers to the manner through which dominant power is exerted (see Negus, 1996: ch. 6), rather than simply its effects or impact on the culture.

See: **content quotas**; **globalization**; **identity**; **majors**; **mediation**
Further reading: Laing, 1986; Lealand, 1988; Negus, 1996; Roach, 1997; Robinson *et al.*, 1991; Rutten, 1991; Tomlinson, 1991; Wallis and Malm, 1984

culture industries; **entertainment industries**   A term first coined and developed by Adorno (1991), the cultural industries are those economic institutions 'which employ the characteristic modes of production and organization of industrial corporations to produce and disseminate symbols in the form of cultural goods and services, generally, though not exclusively, as commodities' (Garnham, 1987: 25; see also Adorno, 1991). In analyses situated in business economics, they are referred to as the **entertainment industries**. Such industries are characterized by a constant drive to expand their market share and to create new products, so that the cultural commodity resists homogenization. In the case of the record industry, while creating and promoting new product is usually expensive, actually reproducing it is not. Once the master copy is pressed, further copies are relatively cheap as economies of scale come into operation; similarly, a **music video** can be enormously expensive to make, but its capacity to be reproduced and played is then virtually limitless.

The cultural industries are engaged in competition for limited pools of disposable income, which will fluctuate according to the economic times. With its historical association with youthful purchasers – though their value as a **consumer** group is not as significant as it once was – the music industry is particularly vulnerable to shifts in the relative size of the younger age cohort and their loss of spending power in the recent period of high youth unemployment world-wide (see **demography**). The cultural industries are also engaged in competition for advertising revenue, consumption time, and skilled labour. **Radio** especially is heavily dependent on advertising revenue. Not only are consumers allocating their expenditure, they are also dividing their time amongst the varying cultural consumption opportunities available to them. With the expanded range of leisure opportunities in recent years, at least to those able to afford them, the competition amongst the cultural, recreational, and entertainment industries for consumer attention has increased.

The music industry demonstrates most of the features identified by Vogel (1994) as characteristic of the entertainment industries: (i) profits from a very few highly popular products are generally required to offset losses from many mediocrities; overproduction is a feature of recorded music, with only a small proportion of releases achieving **chart** listings and commercial success, and a few mega-sellers propping up the music industry in otherwise lean periods (e.g. Michael Jackson's *Thriller* (Epic, 1982), with sales of some 20 million copies through the 1980s); (ii) marketing expenditures per unit are proportionally large; this applies in the music industry to those artists and their releases with a proven track record; (iii) ancillary or secondary markets provide disproportionately large returns; in popular music through licensing and revenue from copyright (e.g. for film soundtracks); (iv) capital costs are relatively high, and oligopolistic tendencies are prevalent; in the music industry this is evident in the dominance of the **majors**, in part due to the greater development and promotional capital they have available; (v) on-going technological development makes it ever easier and less expensive to manufacture, distribute, and receive entertainment products and services. This is evident in the development of recording technology; and (vi) entertainment products and services have universal appeal; this is evident in the international appeal of many popular music **genres** and performers, enhanced by the general accessibility of music as a medium, no matter what language a song may be sung in.

In addition to these characteristics, it is noteworthy that the music majors and their associated media conglomerates reveal different patterns of ownership in relation to the levels of production, distribution, and retail (see the case studies in Barnett and Cavanagh, 1994).

See: **concentration**; **music industry**
Further reading: Adorno, 1991; Garnham, 1987; Vogel, 1994.

cultural intermediaries   Bourdieu's notion of cultural inter-mediaries has been used to examine the role of personnel in the music industry in terms of their active role in the production of particular artists and styles of music, and the promotion of these: 'Although often invisible behind star names and audience styles, recording industry personnel work at a point where the tensions between artists, consumers and enter-tainment corporations meet and result in a range of working practices, ideological divisions and conflicts' (Negus, 1992). These personnel include **A & R** (artists and repertoire), responsible for finding new artists and maintaining the company's rosta of performers; the record **producers** and **sound mixers**, who play a key role in the recording studio; **music video** directors; **marketing** directors and the associ-ated record pluggers; press officers; record retailers; **radio** programmers and **DJs**; and concert and club promoters.

While there is an anarchic aspect of many of these industry practices, resulting from the essential uncertainty endemic to the music business, the industry has come to privilege partic-ular styles of music and working practices, and quite specific ways of acquiring, marketing, and promoting performers. Such established modes of operating work against new artists, styles outside of the historically legitimated white **rock** main-stream, and the employment of women. The concept of cultural intermediaries is more useful than the related concept of **gatekeepers**, primarily because of its greater flexibility.

See: **A & R**; **marketing**; **producers**; **retail**; **sound mixers**
Further reading: Bourdieu, 1984; Negus, 1992.

cultural policy – *see* **State cultural policy**

cultural studies The term cultural studies became current in the late 1960s and early 1970s, and was initially associated with its institutional base at England's Birmingham University: the Centre for Contemporary Cultural Studies (BCCCS). Cultural studies was a reaction against the **high culture** tradition's strongly negative view of popular culture. Stuart Hall initially mapped the field according to a distinction between the paradigms of culturalism and **structuralism**, a neo-Gramscian synthesis of 'hegemony theory' and a series of post-structural variants. Cultural studies expanded and became more diverse, with developing international interest, especially in North America, and the establishment of further institutional bases. There in no sense exists a cultural studies orthodoxy, although there is a general recognition that cultural studies focuses on the relations between social being and cultural meanings. This embraces the analysis of institutions, texts, discourses, readings, and audiences, with these understood in their social, economic, and political context. (For an overview of the development and scope of cultural studies, see Brantlinger, 1990; Grossberg *et al.*, 1992, and Turner, 1994; for a helpful summary, see O'Sullivan *et al.*, 1994.)

Several key figures working within British cultural studies have been primarily concerned with the question of how the media actually undertake the production of 'consent' for social, economic, and political structures which favour the maintenance of dominant interests. Their approach was markedly influenced by Gramsci's concept of ideological or cultural **hegemony**. This vein of cultural studies has exerted the greatest influence on popular music studies, primarily through the 1970s work on music and **youth subcultures** associated with the BCCCS (Hall and Jefferson, 1976; Hebdige, 1979; Willis, 1978), and critics who attempted to place popular music, especially **rock**, at the centre of oppositional ideology (Chambers, 1985; Grossberg, 1992; Middleton, 1990). These writers emphasize the place of the individual in the determination of cultural meaning; for example Chambers' theme is the constant interplay between commercial factors and lived experience:

> For after the commercial power of the record companies has been recognised, after the persuasive sirens of the radio acknowledged, after the recommendations of the music press noted, it is finally those who buy the records, dance to the rhythm and live to the beat who demonstrate, despite the determined conditions of its production, the wider potential of pop (1985: xii).

Middleton similarly places popular music in the space of contradiction and contestation lying between 'imposed' and 'authentic', and also emphasizes the relative autonomy of cultural practices.

See: **youth subcultures**
Further reading: Agger, 1992; Chambers, 1985; Grossberg, 1992; Middleton, 1990.

culture; **mass culture/society**; **popular culture** The meaning and utility of 'culture', and the words used to qualify culture, namely 'popular' and 'mass', have been the subject of considerable discussion and debate. The difficulties surrounding these linked concepts is evident in their application to popular music.

1 **Culture** is one of the most difficult words in the English language. It is used in a variety of discourses, including **fashion**, the arts, nationalism, and **cultural studies**, with each discursive context signalling a particular usage.

Cultural and media studies, which have underpinned this volume, maintain a sociological rather than an **aesthetic** sense of culture, with a focus on popular culture rather than artistic pursuits associated with particular values and standards: elite or mass culture. In this approach, evident throughout popular music studies, culture is a sphere in which social inequalities are reproduced; a site of struggle over meanings. An aspect of this is the way in which music studies in **education** have historically largely stressed the classical musical tradition, seeing popular music as inferior and paying it little attention.

2 **Mass culture/society** refers to the manufacture of culture as a commodity on a massive scale to mass markets, composed of undiscriminating consumers, for large-scale profit; as such, it clearly includes popular music. The notion of mass culture/society is closely allied to two broad sociological traditions: (i) the **high culture** tradition of a narrowly defined high or elite culture; and (ii) the **Frankfurt School**. Both critique popular music for its commodification and negative social influence (see their respective entries).

3 **Popular culture** was historically a term applied during the nineteenth century to the separate culture of the subordinate classes of the urban and industrial centres (see Storey, 1993). This culture had two main sources: a commercially oriented culture, and a culture of, and for, the people (often associated with political agitation). While some subsequent usages of popular culture reserve it for the second of these, the term became more generally associated with the commercial mass media: print, aural, and visual communication on a large scale, including the press, publishing, **radio** and **television**, **film** and video, telecommunications, and the recording industry.

Used as an adjective here, 'popular' indicated that something – a person, a product, a practice, or a belief – was commonly liked or approved by a large audience or the general public, with this popularity indicated by ratings, sales, and so on. To a degree, this definition of popularity reifies popular cultural texts, reducing them to the status of objects to be bought and sold in the market place, and the social nature of their consumption must always be kept in mind. In considerations of popular music as a form of popular culture, the emphasis has been on **texts** and **audiences**, and the relationship between them – the way individuals and social groups use popular music within their lives.

Further reading: O'Sullivan *et al.*, 1994; Swingewood, 1977; Williams, 1983.

curriculum – *see* **education**

D

dance; **dancing** As a social practice dance has a long history, closely associated with music, ritual, courtship, and everyday pleasure. Historically, social dancing dates back at least to the sixteenth century and the private balls of the aristocracy, with ballroom dancing popularized in the early nineteenth century (especially the waltz). 'The demands of the dancer tended to shape the course of ragtime and jazz rather than the obverse . . . and this status has continued into the rock age' (Gammond, 1991: 144). Dance is associated with the pleasures of physical, rather than intellectual, expression, the body rather than the mind. At times, the closeness and implied sexual display of dance has aroused anxiety and led to attempts to regulate dance, or at least to control who is dancing with whom.

Forms of dance subject to considerable social criticism included the Charleston, jitterbugging, **rock'n'roll** in the 1950s, the twist in the 1960s, and **disco** dancing in the 1970s. Adorno saw jitterbugging, a popular and flamboyant form of dance in the 1940s, as a 'stylized' dance style whose performers had 'convulsive aspects reminiscent of St. Vitus's dance or the reflexes of mutilated animals' (1991: 46). As Negus (1996) observes, such responses reflected a distaste for overt expressions of sexuality, a racist fear of 'civilized' behaviour being undermined by 'primitive rhythms', and a concern that young people are being manipulated and effected by forms of mass-crowd psychology (see **effects**).

Dance is central to the general experience and leisure lives of young people and many adults, through their attendance at, and participation in, school dances, parties, discos, dance classes, and **raves**. The participants in the dance break free of their bodies in a combination of 'socialised pleasures and individualised desires', with dancing operating 'as a metaphor for an external reality which is unconstrained by the limits and expectations of gender identity and which successfully and relatively painlessly transports its subjects from a passive to a more active psychic position' (McRobbie, 1991: 194, 192, 201). Dance also acts as a marker of significant points in the daily routine, punctuating it with the freedom of Saturday night. These various facets of dance are well represented in films such as *Flashdance* (Adrian Lyne, 1983), *Dirty Dancing* (Emile Ardolino, 1987), and *Strictly Ballroom* (Baz Luhrman, 1995), with the attraction of these dance narratives lying in 'the fantasies of achievement they afford their subjects' (McRobbie, 1991: 201). The film and music industries now work together to maximize the potential of both mediums, with carefully chosen music for the associated soundtrack album (see **film**).

Dance is associated with some popular musical **genres** to a greater extent than others, most prominently disco, **rap**, and rock'n'roll. Chambers (1985) documented the clubs and dance halls of English post-war urban youth culture, referring to 'the rich tension of dance' in its various forms, including the shake, the jerk, the **northern soul** style of athletic, acrobatic dance, and the breakdancing and body-popping of black youth. There are forms of dance which are genre and **subculture** specific, such as 'line-dancing' in **country**, 'slam-dancing' and the pogo in **punk**, 'break-dancing' in some forms of rap, and 'headbanging' and 'moshing' at concerts by **heavy metal**, **grunge**, and **alternative** performers.

These represent new forms of dance, less formally constrained than traditional dance forms. For example, while the audience does not 'dance' at heavy metal concerts, as the subculture stresses male bonding rather then male–female pairing, it is 'nonetheless engaged in continuous kinesthetic activity' (Weinstein, 1991a: 216), moving the body in time with the beat. This includes headbanging, which involves keeping the beat by making up-and-down motions of the head, and moshing, a form of circle dance: 'a hard skipping, more or less in time to the music, in a circular, counter-clockwise pattern. Elbows are often extended and used as bumpers, along with the shoulders' (Weinstein, 1990a: 228). There is a moshing circle, the 'pit', located close to centre stage, and visible to both performers and the audience.

The close link between dance and contemporary popular music is indicated in the title of a recent major documentary series on popular music, *Dancing in the Street*, which throughout shows changing dance styles and their associated musical genres.

Further reading: Chambers, 1985; Gammond, 1991; McRobbie, 1991; Mungham, 1976; Thomas, 1995.
Viewing: Dancing in the Street, 1995.

dance music; dance–music: jungle; house; trip–hop; drum 'n'bass Dance bands and dance music came into general use as phrases from around 1910 onwards, with **radio** playing a major role in the popularization of dance. Dance bands, notably 'Big Bands', were a feature of many hotels and clubs during the inter-war period and into the early 1950s. Dance music came to be used in a general sense, for those popular music **genres** capable of being danced to. Accordingly, it can be regarded as a **meta genre**, including music from a range of styles and genres, most prominently **disco**, **funk**, **soul**, **Motown**, **ska**, **hard rock**, and **techno**. In most cases, certain styles of dance and venues or locations are associated with particular styles of dance music (e.g. **northern soul**).

More specifically, in the 1990s 'dance' has become associated with dance club scenes, and various styles of **dance–music**. This meta genre has become a prominent part of the UK music scene, with substantial sales and its own **charts**. It is also evident internationally: in the United States, 'electronica' is currently the vogue dance-music, with commercial success for the Prodigy and the Chemical Brothers. In Britain and Europe, dance has become part of mainstream popular music, embraced by the music industry as a possible antidote to the declining sales in the highly fragmented rock/pop market. While the contemporary music market is volatile and unclear, in the United States dance is arguably overtaking **grunge** as the major commercial force, while it has become hugely popular in Asia and is making inroads in Australia and New Zealand.

In the 1980s techno, which had become practically synonomous with contemporary dance-music, mutated into a number of different musical styles (and associated **scenes** and loose **subcultures**), most notably **jungle**, **house**, **trip-hop**, and **drum'n'bass**. These were broadly characterized by their use of state-of-the-art technology, extensive use of samples, musical eclecticism, and links to dance or club scenes. As music press reviews and articles and marketing hype indicate, there is considerable overlap between the various forms, with shifting and unclear boundaries present, and **subgenres** splintering off:

1 **jungle**: frenetic, speeded-up **hip-hop** breaks, with 'bad boy' lyrics, and extremely heavy sub-bass.

   Listening: Goldie, *Timeless*, FFR, 1995.

2 **house** was a direct descendant of disco and an important element of the **dance** club scene in the mid-1980s. House music got its name from the late-night parties held in warehouses, originally in New York but then more prominently in Chicago, where '**DJs** mixed the music in elaborate and lengthy sets in which segments of many songs were interspersed with one another. House music was propelled by the throbbing rhythms of disco, but with the emphasis less on lyrics and more on atmosphere and beat' (*Music Central 96*). House music used synthesizers, remixing, sampling, multi-layered computerized tracks, and drum machines to produce repetitive and hypnotic dance music. Several identifiable variants of house developed: (i) Chicago House, with DJs combining German techno pioneers

Kraftwerk with soul and drum machines; (ii) Acid House, in which musicians used Roland 303 and similar drum machines/synthesizers; and (iii) Deep House, a 'combination of gospel and old Chicago house beats; wailing divas, spooky organs, and chord progressions' (ibid.). Acid House attained cult status in Britain in the late 1980s (see **raves**);

3 **trip-hop** began to circulate as a term in the British music press during 1995, referring to a 'movement' led by the Bristol-based artists Massive Attack, Portishead, and Tricky, dance-music which was 'a dark, seductive combination of hip-hop beats, atmospheric reverb-laden guitars and samples, soul hooks, deep bass grooves and ethereal melodies' (Erlewine *et al.*, 1995: 506). The style had actually been around for several years, in several mutating guises, all forms of slowed-down **hip-hop**.

Further reading: Steve Daly, 'Tricky', in *Rolling Stone*, February 1997, pp. 47–8;
Listening:
Massive Attack, *Blue Lines*, Virgin, 1991.
Portishead, *Dummy*, Polygram, 1994.
Tricky, *Maxinquaye*, 4th & Broadway, 1995.

4 **drum'n'bass** is the latest variant of dance-music to achieve a high profile in the UK music press. An eclectic style, its practitioners (e.g. Goldie, Roni Size) draw variously on funk, techno, jazz fusion, house, and hip-hop. Associated labels include Moving Shadow, Prototype, and, especially significant, Metalheadz.

Listening:
Breakbeat Science vol. 1, Volume/Vital, 1996.

See: **techno**
Further reading: Mitchell, 1996: ch. 4; Thornton, 1995; Weisband, 1995; the contemporary British music press (*NME*'s 'Vibes' section, or 'Orbit' in *Melody Maker*).
Listening:
Ragga Groove: 20 Ragga, Jungle & Dance Hits, Cookie Jar, 1994.
Nathan Haines, *Soundkilla Sessions Volume 1*, Huh!/Polygram, 1996.

dance pop A broadly constituted musical **genre**, dance pop is often maligned, in part because of its perceived commercial orientation and its main audience of adolescent girls (**teeny-boppers**). Commercially highly successful exponents include Kylie Minogue (in the late 1980s), Paula Abdul, Bananarama, Milli Vanilli, and the Spice Girls. The success of these performers was frequently attributed to the svengali-like influence of **producers** (e.g. Stock, Aitken, and Waterman for Kylie Minogue in the late 1980s), and exposure through **MTV** and high-energy **music videos** (e.g. Paula Abdul), as much as or more than talent. In 1989, after Milli Vanilli had won the Grammy Award for Best New Group, there was an uproar when it emerged that the duo did not sing on their records (see Martin, 1993). Nonetheless, dance pop is a continuing staple of contemporary popular music, and is undergoing a critical reappraisal as part of audience-oriented **cultural studies** analysis.

See: **authenticity**; **dance**; **pop**; **producers**
Listening:
Paula Abdul, *Forever Your Girl*, Virgin, 1988.
Bananarama, *Greatest Hits Collection*, London, 1988.
Milli Vanilli, *Girl You Know It's True*, Arista, 1989.

deadheads An affectionate slang term for **fans** of the American band the Grateful Dead. Leading figures in San Francisco's **psychedelic** scene since the early 1960s, the Grateful Dead continued to tour and record extensively until the death of band leader Jerry Garcia in 1996. Deadheads attended large numbers of the band's **concerts**, often making extensive tape compilations of the various performances, or purchasing **bootlegs** of such performances, with the band unofficially condoning such practices. The Grateful Dead's concerts functioned as secular rituals for hardcore followers of the band, who also frequently identified with the broadly **counter culture** values and style of the band. This last point led some municipalities to ban Grateful Dead concerts, because of the 'undesirable elements' attending.

See: **concerts**; **counter culture**; **psychedelic rock**
Further reading: Sardiello, 1994.

demography; **baby boomers**; **Generation X** Demography
is the study of human populations, primarily with respect to
their size, their structure, and their development. It includes
aspects of the age structure and its relationship to social,
economic, and cultural structures. In popular music studies,
research drawing on demography has been primarily
concerned with examining the relationship between age structure and consumption, and the relevance of this to explaining
the historical advent of particular **genres** and **radio** formats,
and their shifting popularity/market share.

A major example of such an approach is the explanation
for the emergence of **rock'n'roll** in the mid-1950s in terms
of a combination of age-group demographics and individual
musical creativity. The post-war baby boom was 'a crucial
condition of the rearticulation of the formations of popular
culture after the Second World War and the Korean War';
there were 77 million babies born between 1946 and 1964,
and by 1964, 40 per cent of the population of the United
States was under twenty (Grossberg, 1992: 172). The baby
boom and the emergence of a youth market made the young
a desirable target audience for the cultural industries: 'post-
1945 American teenagers enjoyed an unprecedented level of
affluence. Their taste in film, music, literature and entertainment was backed up by enormous purchasing power which
record producers and film-makers were quick to satisfy'
(Welsh, 1990: 3). One aspect of this search was the development of a youthful white audience for **rhythm & blues**.

American suburbia, where the **baby boomers** were
concentrated, neither represented nor catered for the desires
of American youth. As Grossberg (1992: 179) puts it: 'Rock
emerged as a way of mapping the specific structures of youth's
affective alienation on the geographies of everyday life.' This
is to emphasize the point that the social category of youth
'is an affective identity stitched onto a generational history'

(ibid.: 183); the particular configuration of circumstances in the 1950s forged an alliance of 'youth' and **rock music** as synonomous with that particular age cohort of young people. For Grossberg, 'Rock's special place (with and for youth) was enabled by its articulation to an ideology of authenticity', an ideology which involved providing youth with cultural spaces 'where they could find some sense of identification and belonging, where they could invest and empower themselves in specific ways' (Grossberg, 1992: 204–5). **Authenticity**, in Grossberg's sense of the term, is here equated with the ability of rock to resonate with youth's common desires, feelings, and experiences in a shared public language.

The baby boom elevated youth to a new social, political, and economic visibility, and clearly the emergence and vitality of any cultural form is dependent on the existence of an **audience** for it. However, we must not overprivilege this 'audience explanation' for the emergence of rock in the 1950s. Audiences are selecting their cultural/leisure **texts** from what is available to them, and the nature of the market is determined by much more than the constitutive qualities of its potential audience (see **history**).

More recently, demographical analysis has revealed the changing audience for popular music. As Goodwin observed at the end of the 1980s: ' "older" music has become contemporary for audiences of *all* ages' (Frith and Goodwin, 1990: 259). Throughout 1994 and 1995 'nostalgia rock' has continued to be prominent in popular music, with the release of 'new' Beatles material (*Live at the BBC*, *Anthology* 1–3, the video *Anthology* documentary); the launch of *MOJO* magazine, placing rock history firmly at its core and with 35 per cent of its readers aged 35-plus; and successful **tours** by The Rolling Stones, Pink Floyd and the reformed Eagles, among other ageing performers. British journalists have termed some 'retro' **Britpop** bands such as Ocean Colour Scene 'dadrock', while several 1980s **stars** such as Paul Weller (ex-The Jam) have enjoyed renewed success. This continued high level of interest in popular music's past was evident amongst both greying consumers and younger people, with the latter being constructed by the popular and academic media and the advertising industry as **Generation X**: a very media self-conscious group of youth, primarily associated with **grunge** as a style.

This repackaging and marketing of our collective musical memories is hardly new, but the scale is different, and it raises questions about the vitality of popular music in the 1990s. As an age cohort, seen usually as around 13–24 years of age, youth has historically been among popular music's major consumers, and young people continue to have considerable discretionary income for the leisure industries to tap. The straightforward association of popular music with youth, however, now needs qualifying. The absolute numbers of young people entering the labour market in the United Kingdom and Europe declined for the first time during the 1980s, and have continued to fall toward the end of the century. By the late 1980s, Frith could accurately observe that 'In material terms, the traditional rock consumer – the "rebellious" teenager – is no longer the central market figure' (Frith, 1988c: 127). Similar demographic trends have been observed in most other Western countries. The market for popular music has extended to those who grew up with the music in the 1950s and 1960s and who have continued to follow it. Ageing along with their favoured surviving performers of the 1960s, these older listeners largely account for the present predominance of 'golden oldies' radio formats and occupy an increasing market share of record sales, especially **back catalogue** releases. These trends illustrate how demography continues to play a significant role in reshaping the cultural market place.

See: **audience**
Further reading: Dychtwald, 1989; Grossberg, 1992; Welsh, 1990.

deregulation – *see* **State cultural policy**

disco A term derived from the French *discothèque* – record library – referring to a club where you dance to records. In the United States the **genre** had a strong initial association with gay bars, and remained a cult there until the huge hit of the film and soundtrack *Saturday Night Fever* (RSO, 1977). Internationally, disco was a pervasive and commercially highly successful genre in the late 1970s and early 1980s.

As a musical form, disco is frequently denigrated. Clarke describes it as a 'Dance fad of the '70s, with profound and unfortunate influence on popular music . . . because the main thing was the thump-thump beat, other values could be ignored; producers used drum machines, synthesisers and other gimmicks at the expense of musical values' (1990: 344). Other commentators celebrated the form's vitality and emphasis on dance: 'Superficial, liberating, innovative, reactionary, sensuous, disco emerged out of a subculture at the beginning of the '70s, dominated pop music for a few years at the end, and then shrank back. But during its brief dominance, it restored the dance groove as pop imperative' (Smucker, 1992: 562).

While most disco hit-makers were virtually anonymous, with **producers** to the fore (e.g. Giorgio Moroder), there were a few **stars**: Labelle, Hot Chocolate, Donna Summer, KC and the Sunshine Band, and the Bee Gees. Although disco had faded by the mid-1980s, it has enjoyed something of a mid-1990s revival, helped by a renewed interest in Abba, whose music featured on several hit film soundtracks, such as *Muriel's Wedding* (P.J. Hogan, 1994). In the United Kingdom, impetus for the Abba revival also came from various covers and tributes to their songs, such as Erasure's version of 'Take a Chance on Me' (on *Pop!: The First 20 Hits*, Sire/Reprise, 1992) and the success of the **covers** band Björn Again. Disco has also been an element in the eclectic make-up of the hybrid **meta genre** of contemporary **dance–music**.

See: **dance–music**
Further reading: Charlton, 1994; Dyer, 1990; Smucker, 1992.
Listening:
KC and the Sunshine Band, *Greatest Hits*, Rhino, 1990.
Abba, *Abba Gold: Greatest Hits*, Polydor, 1992.

Donna Summer, *Endless Summer: Donna Summer's Greatest Hits*, Polygram, 1994.

discourse analysis   At a popular level, discourse refers to a body of meaning associated with a particular topic or field, regardless of the form of its transmission, such as medical discourse. Discourse is the domain of language use, especially the common ways of talking and thinking about social issues. Discourse analysis is a method of analysing such patterns of language use, and their social function. While discourse is often manifest in language, it is embedded in organizational and institutional practices. Accordingly, discursive practices are real or material, as well as being embodied in language, and function as a form of ideology. They help constitute our personal, individual identity, our subjectivity.

In social science, discourse analysis seeks to tease out the underlying assumptions and belief systems, and their associated meanings, embedded within a particular discourse. This is undertaken through an analysis of various forms of **text**, including documents such as policy statements, novels, and interview transcripts. In post-structuralist social theory, discourse refers to a historically, socially, and institutionally specific structure of meaning(s); statements, terms, categories, and concepts about the nature of individuals and the world they inhabit. While there are dominant discourses – what Foucault terms 'truth generating discourses' – discourses are multiple; they offer competing and frequently contradictory ways whereby we give meaning to the world and our social existence within it.

As with other forms of discourse, popular music contains meanings that both reflect and help constitute wider social systems and structures of meaning. There are discourses around many of the terms used to describe the field and its constituent **genres** (see the discussion under **popular music**). More specifically, discourse analysis has been utilized to examine **DJ** talk (see Brand and Scannell, 1991, on the Tony Blackburn Show in the United Kingdom; also Gill,

99

1996; Montgomery, 1986), and **music videos** (Goodwin, 1993).

To take one example of the value of such an approach, Gill used discourse analysis to provide 'a thorough and principled approach to analysing *talk*' (1996: 210); in this case, five male DJs and programme controllers from two commercial radio stations in the United Kingdom, and their responses to a question about the lack of female DJs, a pertinent issue given male DJs' domination of the airwaves. She observes that a traditional approach to this issue would use attitude surveys, questionnaires, or structured interviews with those responsible for appointment decisions, trying to pinpoint a single answer as to why there are so few female DJs. 'Discourse analysis, in contrast, takes variability seriously, as something interesting in its own right' (1996: 213). This is facilitated by the use of informal interviews, and an analytical approach which sought to tease out the practical ideologies through which the employment of women DJs are understood and legitimated. The interviewees used a range of reasons to account for the lack of women DJs, including women not applying to become DJs; listeners' preference for male presenters; women's lack of the necessary skills; and the unsuitability of women's voices. 'It is important to note that these were not alternative accounts . . . each was drawn on by all or most of the broadcasters at different points in the interviews' (1996: 213). Utilizing discourse analysis, Gill sought not simply to identify the different accounts selectively drawn upon, but 'to examine how they were constructed and made persuasive' (ibid.). Her analysis shows how the broadcasters constructed the problem as lying in women themselves or in the particular wants of the audience. Both of these discursive practices – the way the broadcaster's accounts were organized – enabled the broadcasters to present themselves as non-sexist: 'The role of the radio station was made invisible, and discussions of employment practices and institutionalized sexism were conspicuous by their absence' (1996: 217).

Further reading: Potter and Wetherell, 1987.

DJ   The disc jockey (DJ) is the person responsible for presenting and playing the music which is a part of **radio** and **music video** programming, and central to many **clubs**, **dances**, **discos**, and other occasions. Popular music studies have concentrated on (i) the role of the DJ in the history of radio, especially the emergence of personality radio and the elevation of DJs to **star** status, initially in the 1950s; and (ii) DJs as central figures in contemporary **club culture**. In each case, the notions of **gatekeeper** and **cultural intermediary** have been used to examine the influence of DJs.

1   *DJs and the history of radio:* Initially, music radio announcers were primarily responsible for cueing records and ensuring smooth continuity, and had little input into the determination of radio playlists. The reshaping of radio in the 1950s was a key influence in the advent of **rock'n'roll**, while radio airplay became central to a performer's commercial success. As Barnes observes, hit radio was 'one of America's great cultural inventions', revitalizing a medium threatened by **television** (Barnes, 1988: 9). The DJ emerged as a star figure, led by figures such as Bob 'Wolfman Jack' Smith , Dick Clark, and Alan Freed. Freed's *Morning Show* on WJW radio in Cleveland in the early 1950s, and his subsequent New York radio programmes and associated live shows, popularized the very term rock'n'roll and helped introduce black **R & B** music to a white audience. The considerable influence wielded by DJs on music radio playlists, and the associated 'pay-to-play' practices, led to official investigations of **payola**. Personality radio and the cult of the DJ was very much part of **pirate radio** in the 1960s. The role and status of contemporary radio DJs depends very much on the type and format of the radio station.

2   *DJs and club culture:* When DJs became mixers, they entered the world of musicianship. For example, DJs played a major role in the emergence of the twelve-inch single as a standard industry product amongst US, then British, record companies in the 1970s. American DJs began mixing

seven-inch copies of the same record for prolonged play, then recording their own mixes, firstly on tape then on vinyl, to play in clubs. The practice became sufficiently widespread to make it worthwhile for record companies to cater for this new market. Initially produced for public performance only, twelve-inch singles became retail products from 1978 on, and by the early 1990s represented roughly 45 per cent of the singles sold (Thornton, 1995). In the process of mixing, DJs created new music, becoming 'turntable musicians'.

The role of the DJ is vital to dance club culture. The club atmosphere, mood, or 'vibe' is created in the interaction between the DJ, the crowd, and the physical space which they share. The DJ's choice and sequencing of records, in a dialectic with the mood of the clubbers, is central to this interaction.

See: **payola**; **radio**
Further reading: Barnes, 1988; Brand and Scannell, 1991; Brennan, 1996; Thornton, 1995.

doo-wop   Doo-wop is derived from two of the many nonsense syllables sung by back-up vocalists. As a **genre**, doo-wop is primarily equated with the mainly black vocal-harmony music of the 1950s, although its origins were in the late 1930s and the ballad style of the Ink Spots. Doo-wop evolved out of the **gospel** tradition, and was characterized by close (four-part ballad) harmonies. As an essentially **a capella** style, doo-wop was developed by New York groups, often originally singing on street corners, in the period 1945–55. The songs were relatively simple and extremely formulaic, with a sentimentalized romance as the dominant theme. Pioneer performers included the Ravens, and the Orieles. The Orieles' single 'Crying in the Chapel' (The Bear Family, 1953) was the first doo-wop release to gain acceptance with white listeners. Doo-wop spread to other US cities, reaching its zenith in the late 1950s, with The Platters, The Clovers, The Coasters, Dion, and the Belmonts.

Gribin and Schiff (1992) argue that doo-wop deserves greater recognition for its contribution to **rock** music's development during the 1950s. Groups such as The Drifters and The Coasters added a stronger beat and more pronounced gospel elements, providing a bridge to what became known as **soul** music. The genre did not survive the **British invasion** of the early to mid-1960s, although it remained evident in the work of artists such as The Four Seasons, who enjoyed considerable chart success between 1962 and 1967. The genre enjoyed a brief, nostalgic revival in the 1970s, with the popularity of groups such as Manhatten Transfer and Sha-Na-Na, whose name is taken from the background harmony of The Silhouettes' earlier doo-wop classic 'Get a Job' (Ember, 1958). In the 1990s, the influence of doo-wop is evident in the work of performers such as Boys II Men (sometimes referred to as 'hip-hop doo-wop').

Further reading: Gillet, 1983; Gribin and Schiff, 1992; Hansen, 1992a (includes a useful discography).

Listening:

The Four Seasons, *Anthology*, Rhino, 1988.

The Best of Doo Wop Up Tempo, Rhino, 1989.

Boys II Men, *Cooleyhighharmony*, Motown, 1991.

drum'n'bass – *see* **dance-music**

dub – *see* **reggae**

Dunedin sound　New Zealand South Island city Dunedin was home to an arguably distinctive **alternative** music sound which developed during the 1980s, associated with the **independent** label Flying Nun, founded in 1981, and later Xpressway (founded in 1988). Leading bands included The Chills, The Verlaines, The Clean, and Toy Love.

The Dunedin sound was generated through a cultural geography of living on the margin, producing a 'mythology of a group of musicians working in cold isolation, playing music purely for the pleasure of it' (McLeay, 1994: 39). As with similar **local** sounds, there has been debate over the constituent elements, distinctiveness, and coherence of the Dunedin sound. 'Pure pop melody' and 'guitar jangle' were frequently used descriptors, although in themselves these are hardly geographically distinctive. There was also a tendency, initially at least, towards low-tech production values, and a shared aesthetic which emphasized the primary importance of the song, and valorized the 'roughness' of the music.

For many, especially overseas followers of alternative music, Dunedin and Flying Nun became a metonym for New Zealand music as a whole, although the Flying Nun label embraced a range of performers and styles (see Mitchell, 1996). Flying Nun rarely achieved local commercial success, but built up a considerable reputation in the international indie/alternative scene. In the 1990s, the notion of the Dunedin sound continues to be present in discussions of New Zealand music, although the Flying Nun label has relocated (to Auckland and London), and many of the bands associated with it are not based on 'guitar jangle'.

See: **locality**
Further reading: Erlewine *et al.*, 1995; McLeay, 1994; Mitchell, 1996.
Listening:
Tuatara: A Flying Nun Compilation, Flying Nun, 1985.
The Clean, *Compilation*, Flying Nun/Homestead, 1986.
The Chills, *Solid Cold Hits*, Flying Nun, 1995.

education: **curriculum**; **pedagogy**; **school commitment**
There has been a good deal of discussion of the validity and place of popular music within the school and post-school curriculum, and how the study of popular music can best be approached.

Popular music can be taught as a subject in its own right, but is more commonly found as a component of other courses. For example, in the school systems of Canada, the United Kingdom, the United States, and Australia, popular music may be studied within music, social studies, and media studies. In the tertiary sector, it is usually found within departments of music, media/communication studies, and cultural studies. Such courses usually emphasize Anglo-American pop/rock music and its associated **genres**, representing a form of musical **hegemony**. There are two major areas of discussion and debate: the status of the field, primarily in terms of its inclusion in the school curriculum, and pedagogy – how it should be taught. Another topic of interest has been the relationship between attitudes towards school and pupils' tastes in popular music.

1 *The **curriculum** status of popular music studies:* At all levels, the subject has usually had to struggle to be accepted as a legitimate educational study. Writing in 1982, Vulliamy and Lee argued that the majority of young people faced a clear opposition between music which is acceptable to

the school, usually based in the classical tradition, and their own (usually popular) musical preferences, which by inference they were led to see as of little value or significance. This situation exacerbated the conflict between the cultural values transmitted through schools and the cultural values of young people. Vulliamy and Lee argued that forms of musical analysis through notation are inappropriate to popular music, which can be legitimated in school by establishing different evaluative criteria (from traditional **musicology**). This is in line with the view that all music is bounded by particular styles and traditions and occurs within a sociocultural context (e.g. Shepherd *et al.*, 1977). These views have continued to be debated into the mid-1990s (see, for example, the journal *Music Education*, published by Cambridge University Press).

At tertiary level, popular music has only recently been accorded much recognition within cultural and media studies. 'Popular music scholars draw the fire of rock journalists (and musicians and music fans) who resent their wordy intrusions and see their theorising as desiccating rock's supposed spontaneity' (John Street, *The Times*, 31 July 1993). However, the attainment of a certain level of academic respectability for the field is indicated by senior academic appointments, most notably Peter Wicke as the world's first professor of popular music studies (at Humboldt University of Berlin); the creation and growth of specialist research centres and research archives (e.g. the Institute of Popular Music at Liverpool University; the John Logie Baird Centre in Glasgow); the proliferating tertiary level courses, both industry-oriented and of a more general media and **cultural studies** nature; the existence of a number of academic journals on popular music, considerable cultural journalism in the commercial **music press** and in **fanzines**, and an explosion of the critical literature; and the existence, since 1981, of the International Association for the Study of Popular Music, with over 600 members in 36 countries.

2 *Pedagogy:* Attempts to teach popular music programmes are seen to confront a number of difficulties, both theoretical

and practical in nature. There is a tendency to either over-theorize, or not to theorize. 'Theoretical abstractions and rote memorization tend to take students further away from the music itself, while musical transcriptions and technical analyses are scarcely more effective at getting the energy that made the music so exciting to begin with' (Gass, 1991: 731). Accordingly, many commentators consider it neces-sary to begin with students' own consumption, the context which it occurs in, and the meanings they attach to it. However, to neglect theoretical concerns and terminology is to risk the danger of turning popular music studies into a nostalgic form of populism, largely focused on the prod-ucts of the record industry and viewing their **history** as one of shifts in genre popularity and the relative status of musicians. While it is necessary to engage with theory, constantly seeking to demonstrate its links with students' own lives and experiences, this creates its own problems. First, there is the difficulty of problematizing the popular, and opening popular music up for critical discussion. This is particularly difficult in the school situation, where for many students popular music is associated with the out-of-school self, and its inclusion in the curriculum represents a form of incorporation: 'Not only is the critic's discourse distinctly other than the students' discourse, but it wounds the students' narcissism because it claims to be a superior discourse and seeks therefore to deprive the students of their previous claim on the music' (Shumway, 1989: 229). Further, whatever the teaching context, the study of popular music can place the teacher in an awkward bind, as Grossberg found:

> If I positioned myself as a scholar and cultural critic, I lost my credibility as a 'fan' and the students in my class became suspicious and skeptical. But to speak with the voice of a fan was to relinquish my position as a critic and professor   (Grossberg, 1986: 178–9).

It has been suggested that these problems can be avoided by recognizing the value of Barthes' dictum that to be a critic you first have to be a **fan**, and combine with this a willingness on the part of the teacher to make available for student analysis his or her own readings of texts (Shumway, 1989). This serves to open up the complex issue of the polysemic and open-ended nature of popular music narratives, and the nature of pleasures in popular music.

Current 'textbooks' offer various approaches to the study of popular music, emphasizing **musicology**, usually in a modified form (Brown, 1992; Charlton, 1994); cultural studies/sociology (Longhurst, 1995; Negus, 1996; Shuker, 1994); and an historical/sociological approach (Ennis, 1992; Friedlander, 1996; Garofalo, 1997).

Further reading: Gass, 1991; Grossberg, 1986; Richards, 1995; Shumway, 1989; Tagg, 1990; Vulliamy and Lee, 1982.

3 *School commitment and music preferences:* During the 1980s, a number of studies established an association between commitment to school and preferences in popular music. Tanner (1981), for example, found that students with a low commitment to school (an attitudinal scale of six items was used to judge this) were more likely to favour 'heavy' rock than those with a high school commitment, were correspondingly less committed to 'Top 40' rock, and were, as a group, predominantly working class; they also were more likely to be associated with delinquent activity. This relationship between delinquent activities, social class, and school commitment, on the one hand, and the predilection for heavy rock, on the other, was the clearest association uncovered by Tanner's study. He plausibly suggested that **heavy metal** provided 'a symbolic rejection of the prevailing values and assumptions of the schooling process', and indicated 'a correspondence between "heavy metal" and a **subcultural** solution rooted in action physicality and collective solidarity' (Tanner, 1981: 10; for a recent corroboration of this view, see Arnett, 1996). In his study of Scandinavian adolescents, Roe similarly concluded that music functions to symbolically express 'alienation from

school', and that low school achievement and a greater preference for 'socially disapproved music' (1983: 196ff.) were strongly linked. Weinstein confirmed the findings of these earlier studies, citing peer descriptions of school adherents to the heavy metal subculture to support her view that it is 'distinctive and marginalised from the mainstream' (Weinstein, 1991a: 139).

Further reading: Arnett, 1996; Roe, 1983, 1990.

effects; **'rock suicides'** A major tradition in American media research seeks to identify the specific effects of the media on behaviour, attitudes, and values. This approach is most evident in studies of **television**, but is also seen in many of the claims made for the negative influence of popular music. Groups such as the Parents' Music Resource Center in the United States (see **censorship**) have used 'effects' research to support their arguments.

The effects tradition is based on behaviourism. A major school of psychology, based on stimulus–response theory and the work of B.F. Skinner, behaviourism was developed in the 1920s in the United States. Although remaining influential, it has been strongly criticized for its lack of attention to the importance of the complex social situation in which media consumption occurs, the absence of any satisfactory theory of personality, and the neglect of the particular self of the individual consumer. The behaviourist approach reduces the interaction between medium and recipient to a simple communication-flow model, and accordingly fails to offer a satisfactory explanation for the operation of the popular media (see O'Sullivan *et al.*, 1994).

An example of the use of effects research, and the assumptions underpinning it, is the debate surrounding the relationship between popular music and adolescent suicide. During the 1980s, there were several celebrated court cases in the United States, in which unsuccessful attempts were made to hold popular music responsible for teenage 'rock suicides'. More recently, similar arguments resurfaced following a spate of teenage suicides in the New York/New Jersey areas, and 'copy-cat' suicides after Kurt Cobain's suicide in 1994. These featured prominently in the popular press, where objective reasons for such tragedies were ignored in favour of more sensational accounts. **Heavy metal** and **gothic rock** were the main **genres** held accountable by critics. While they did not always reach the courts, similar claims and arguments about a connection between adolescent suicide and genres such as heavy metal have been evident in other countries.

The relationship between popular music and behaviour in such cases, and the public and press response to them, have been the subject of a number of academic studies (on the US cases, see Gaines, 1991; Walser, 1993; and Weinstein, 1991a; Shuker (1994) gives an account of the New Zealand experience). These consider how the press coverage of rock suicides has treated them as a form of **moral panic**, and critically examine the claims of causality, perceived subliminal messages in the music, and the **preferred readings** of songs such as Ozzy Osbourne's 'Suicide Solution' (1981) present in such cases. These studies largely conclude, along with more balanced press accounts, that popular music could hardly be held accountable (at least solely) for such suicides, observing that teenagers attempt suicide for complex, and frequently interrelated reasons: growing unemployment, family breakdown, lack of communication in families, peer pressure, sexuality, and low self-esteem. In the case of the suicides picked up on by the press, it is possible that the music may have acted as a final catalyst, contributing to depression. More likely, however, is that the youths involved were already depressed or unstable.

See: **audiences**; **gothic rock**; **heavy metal**
Listening:
Judas Priest, *Stained Glass*, Columbia, 1978.
Ozzy Osbourne, 'Suicide Solution', on *Blizzard of Ozz*, Jet, 1981.

enculturation An anthrological concept, enculturation is something of a blanket term for the complex process of assimilation or integration of new cultural forms and practices. Enculturation is relatively new to media/popular music studies, where it has been used for (i) the integration of a technology or social practice: for example, Thornton (1995) discusses the enculturation of records in terms of the changing sites at which people danced to discs, most recently the enculturation of records into the public sphere of **dancing**; (ii) the dynamic process of engagement between various forms of **world music** and Western popular music.

See: **appropriation**; **world music**
Further reading: Guilbault, 1993; Mitchell, 1996; Thornton, 1995.

entertainment industries – *see* **cultural industries**

EPs – *see* **singles**

ethnicity; **race**   While the term race is still widely used in popular discourse and in some academic work, it has been superseded by the more correct term, ethnicity. Race is a biological concept, whereby humans can be classified according to a number of physical criteria. Ethnicity is defined on the basis of shared cultural characteristics for a group of people, based in part on cultural self-identification, but is often an overlay of cultural criteria on to perceived racial characteristics. (There is considerable debate around both concepts: see O'Sullivan *et al.*, 1994: 'race'.)

Ethnicity has been an important consideration in virtually all aspects of popular music studies, particularly in regard to **black music** in the United States, but also in relation to the music of ethnic minorities and **world musics**. (With the exception of ethnicity and consumption, the following topics are covered separately and only summary reference is made to them here – see the related entries in each case.)

1   The lack of black ownership of record companies (with a few exceptions, notably Berry Gordy and **Motown**), or representation in management, has been critiqued and

debated, along with the **marketing** of black music, and the use of racist practices, such as the term 'race music' to describe **R & B** (see Garofalo, 1994; George, 1989).

2 The **appropriation** of black music is a contentious issue, as is the status of **crossover**.

3 The use of the term black music, and the associated notion of an identifiable 'black voice' in vocal **timbres**, is debated.

4 Ethnicity as a factor in consumption patterns. Studies of the **consumption** of popular music in ethnically mixed or diverse populations, show that blacks are more likely (than their white or Asian counterparts) to favour black music **genres**, most notably **soul**, R & B, **blues**, **reggae**, and **rap**. These genres have become virtually synonymous with 'black music' and black culture, especially among black adolescents and young adults, although their following is hardly confined to black populations alone.

To take reggae as an example, black youth internationally identify with the genre, with Bob Marley continuing to enjoy God-like status. For instance, in New Zealand, a multicultural society with some 15 per cent of the population being either descendants of the indigenous Maori people or Pacific (Polynesian) Islanders, and the majority population descendants of the British and European immigrants ('Pakeha'), Maori and Polynesian youth prefer reggae performers and records because these reinforce Maori self-esteem. Reggae does not simply describe an experience, but it politicizes it through creating symbols for listeners to identify with. Many Maori and Polynesian youths are knowledgeable about rasta, and familiar with some of the metaphors in the music ('Babylon', 'Jah', etc.). They regard reggae as relevant to the structural location of the Maori-Polynesian as a major part of New Zealand's socially dispossessed working class. Such views are also expressed by black youth in England and North America (Brake, 1985; Jones, 1988). More recently, rap has emerged as a major genre preference among black youth internationally (Spencer, 1991).

ethnography; **participant observation** A research method initially developed in social anthropology, ethnography has been utilized in a variety of disciplines. In the anthropological sense, ethnography refers to the description and analysis of a way of life, or culture, and is based on direct observation of behaviour in particular social settings. In contemporary usage, ethnography has become a broad term, associated with a range of methods, including case study, participant observation, life history, and symbolic interactionism. There is considerable debate over the status of ethnography as a form of knowledge, and the various approaches to 'field work'. In the traditional, anthropological sense, ethnography involves extensive and intimate involvement in the community studies, but much contemporary ethnography is limited to forms of participant observation (e.g. Willis, 1978).

Cohen (1993) has argued that popular music studies (at least in Western contexts) lack ethnographic data and micro-sociological detail, especially in relation to the grassroots of the industry – 'the countless, as yet unknown bands struggling for success at a local level' (1993: 6) – and the actual process of music-making. Recent studies along such lines, drawing on various forms of ethnography, include community studies (e.g. Cohen's work in Liverpool, 1991; Finnegan's examination of music-making in Milton Keynes, 1989); studies of the geographic popularization of specific **genres**, along with local music scenes (e.g. Guilbault on zouk, 1993; Kruse on the American **alternative** scene, 1993; Bjornberg and Stockfelt on Danish **pub rock**, 1996); and work on popular music and youth cultures and **subcultures** (e.g. Fornas *et al.* on rock music and Swedish youth, 1994); and studies of the process of music-making and becoming a musician (e.g. Becker on **jazz** musicians, 1997; Bennett on **rock** musicians, 1990).

Cohen argues that

An ethnographic approach to the study of popular music, involving direct observation of people, their social networks, interactions and discourses, and participation in their day-to-day activities, rituals, rehearsals and

113

performances, would encourage researchers to experience different relationships, views, values and aesthetics, or to view familiar contexts from an alternative perspective (1993: 135).

Her own study of the music scene in Liverpool in the mid-1980s illustrates the value of such an approach, examining

the process of music-making and the complexity of social relationships involved, analysing the way in which music not only reflects but affects the social environment, and highlighting the underlining conceptions of music which determine the musical terminology and categories used and the evaluation of music, musicians, musical knowledge and skills (1991: 7).

Accounts of music-making in non-Western settings are more numerous, and there is a rich tradition of ethnography within **ethnomusicology**. Recent interest in ethnographic approaches reflects a shift within cultural and media studies, from the global to the **local**, and an emphasis on the study of **consumption** and **audiences**.

See: **ethnomusicology**; **youth subcultures**
Further reading: Bennett, 1990; Bjornberg and Stockfelt, 1996; Cohen, 1991, 1993; Finnegan, 1989; Fornas *et al.*, 1994; Guilbault, 1993; Keil and Feld, 1994; Kruse, 1993.

ethnomusicology A division of **musicology**, emphasizing the study of music in its cultural context – the anthropology of music. The term ethnomusicology gained currency in the mid-1950s, replacing 'comparative musicology'.

Ethnomusicology includes the study of **folk music**, Eastern art music and contemporary music in oral tradition as well as conceptual issues such as the origins of music, musical change, music as symbol, universals in music, the function of music in society, the comparison of musical systems and the biological basis of music and dance (Myers, 1992).

This broad compass aside, the main areas of study in ethno-musicology have been music in the oral tradition and living musical systems, usually in non-Western settings or in relation to indigenous people in Western societies (e.g. the American Indians, Australian Aboriginals, New Zealand Maori), with particular reference to the relation of cultural context and musical style. Fieldwork has been the main research method, using various forms of **ethnography**, and with considerable use of recordings and written notation. While historically the field was split between musicology and anthropology, the two strands fused in the 1980s, as 'interest shifted from pieces of music to processes of musical creation and performance – composition and improvisation – and the focus shifted from collection of repertory to examination of these processes' (Myers, 1992: 8). A fascinating example of ethnomusicology is Neuenfeldt's edited collection (1997), tracing the changing place of the didgeridu in Australian Aboriginal culture, from a range of musical, cultural, and sociological standpoints.

See: **ethnography**; **folk music**
Further reading: Myers, 1992; Neuenfeldt, 1997.

experimental – *see* **avant garde**

F

fans; fandom Fans are people who avidly follow the music, and lives, of particular performers, and the histories of musical **genres**, with various degrees of enthusiasm and commitment. Fandom is the collective term for the phenomenon of fans and their behaviour: concert-going, record-collecting, putting together scrapbooks, filling bedroom walls with posters, and discussing the **star** with other fans.

Lewis correctly observes that while fans are 'the most visible and identifiable of audiences', they 'have been overlooked or not taken seriously as research subjects by critics and scholars' and 'maligned and sensationalized by the popular press, mistrusted by the public' (Lewis, 1992: 1). This situation reflects the traditional view of fandom, which situates it in terms of pathology and deviance, and reserves the label 'fans' for teenagers who are generally presented as avidly and uncritically following the latest pop sensation. These fans are often denigrated in popular music literature and, indeed, by many followers of popular music. Their behaviour is often described as a form of pathology, and the terms applied to it have clear connotations of condemnation and undesirability: 'Beatlemania', '**teenyboppers**', and 'groupies'. The last can be considered an extreme form of such fan, moving beyond vicarious identification and using their sexuality to get close to the stars – even if the encounter is usually a fleeting one.

Fandom is a complex phenomenon, related to the forma-
tion of social **identities**, especially sexuality. An active process,
fandom offers its participants membership of a community
not defined in traditional terms of status. Fiske (1989) sees it
as the register of a subordinate system of cultural **taste**, typically associated with cultural forms that the dominant value
system denigrates, including popular music. Grossberg defines
fandom as a distinct 'sensibility', in which the pleasure of
consumption is superseded by an investment in difference:
'A sensibility is a particular form of engagement or mode of
operation. It identifies the specific sorts of effects that the
elements within a context can produce; it defines the possible
relations betwen texts and audiences located within the spaces'
(1992: 54). Fandom is located within a sensibility in which
the fan's relation to cultural texts 'operates in the domain of
affect or mood' (ibid.: 56; and see **affect**). Pleasure and difference are central to fandom.

A distinction can be made between fans and **aficionados**,
with the latter more focused on the music, and with whom
different affective investments are present (see the entry on
aficionados). Fans, in the more widely accepted perjorative
sense of the term, will collect the records put out by their
favoured stars, but this is only one aspect of an interest which
focuses rather on the image and persona of the star. For
example, studies of the post-**punk** British 'New Pop'
performers of the 1980s (Culture Club, Duran Duran,
Wham!, Spandau Ballet, Nik Kershaw, and Howard Jones),
showed how they drew upon a fanatical female following.
Such fans represent a merchandising dream, buying up practically anything associated with the group, with their support
in extreme cases bordering on the pathological. At the
same time, it was clearly shown that such 'Pop fans aren't
stupid. They know what they want. And ultimately, all the
media manipulation in the world isn't going to sell them
something they haven't got any use for' (Rimmer, 1985: 108).
This is to argue that whatever the constraints of 'context' –
the intentions of the industry, the pop press, and musicians
themselves – meaning in the music is ultimately created by

the consumers. For many fans, their idols function almost as religious touchstones, helping them to get through their lives and providing emotional and even physical comfort. Such strong identification with the star becomes a source of pleasure and empowerment. The discomfort or even pain involved is an important part of this, since it is its resolution – or, at least, the possibility of resolution – which provides the pleasure.

In fandom,

> moods and feelings become organized and particular objects or personas take on significance. By participating in fandom, fans construct coherent identities for themselves. In the process, they enter a domain of cultural activity of their own making which is, potentially, a source of empowerment in struggles against oppressive ideologies and the unsatisfactory circumstance of everyday life (Lewis, 1992: 3).

Examples of such empowerment are as diverse as **heavy metallers** and Bay City Rollers fans. There is an assertion of female solidarity evident in the activities of girl fans. Similar cultural self-assertion is present in many adherents of **youth subcultures**' knowledge of the associated music.

Beyond possible empowerment, popular music fandom as a form of cultural activity has a number of pleasurable dimensions common to both fans and aficionados: **dance** and its associated rituals of display and restraint; the anticipatory pleasure of attending a **concert** or playing a new purchase; the sheer physical pleasure of handling records, tapes, or **CDs**; the pleasure of finding that rare item in a second-hand store bin; and the intellectual and emotional pleasures associated with 'knowing' about particular artists and genres valued by one's peers and associates.

See: **affect**; **aficionados**; **consumption**; **cultural capital**
Further reading: Lewis, 1992; arguably the best accounts of fandom are those which document the perspective of the fans themselves: e.g. Aizlewood, 1994; Cline, 1992; Smith, 1995; Vermorel and

Vermorel, 1985. Fandom is a central theme in some popular music **fictional** narratives, and in many **popular/rock musicals**.

fanzines Fanzines are a form of publication, but they are considered separately from the bulk of the **music press** because of their largely non-commercial nature. Produced by one person, or a group of friends, working from their homes, fanzines are usually totally concentrated on a particular artist or group, and are characterized by a fervour bordering on the religious: 'Fanzines accumulate rock facts and gossip not for a mass readership but for a small coterie of cultists, and they are belligerent about their music' (Frith, 1983: 177). This stance can be a reactionary one, preserving the memory of particular artists or styles, but is more usually progressive. As Savage (1991) acutely observes, fanzines were historically tied to the English radical tradition of pamphleteering. Many of the original **punk** fanzines were characterized by broadly leftish cultural politics, challenging their readers to take issue with the views presented by bastions of the status quo and reasserting the revolutionary potential of rock. Fanzines like *Crawdaddy* in the 1960s and *Sniffin' Glue* in the 1970s had tremendous energy, reflecting the vitality of live performances and emergent **scenes**.

The initial impact of **punk rock** was aided by a network of fanzines and their enthusiastic supporters. Savage argues that in the early days of punk in the United Kingdom, nobody was defining 'punk' from within: 'the established writers were inevitably compromised by age and the minimal demands of objectivity required by their papers. The established media could propagandize and comment, but they could not dramatize the new movement in a way that fired people's imagination' (Savage, 1991: 200). With photocopying cheap and accessible for the first time, the fanzines were a new medium tailor-made for the values of punk, with its do-it-yourself ethic and associations of street credibility, and there was an explosion of the new form. These fanzines provided a training ground for a number of music journalists, and in some cases useful media expertise for those who, taking to heart their own rhetoric of 'here's three chords, now form a band', subsequently did just that. Fanzine producers and writers did not have to worry about deadlines, censorship, or subediting, and 'even the idea of authorship was at issue, as fanzines were produced anonymously or pseudonymously by people trying to avoid discovery by the dole or employers' (Savage, 1991: 279).

The growth of the audience for **heavy metal** in the 1980s was accompanied by a proliferation of (heavy) metal fanzines, which played an important commercial role in the absence of **radio** airplay for metal and the hostility of the mainstream press toward it. The metal fanzines create an information network connecting fans and bands globally. As with fanzines in other **youth subcultures**, 'metal fanzines are characterized by a passionate, almost proselytizing, tone. Fanzine editors adhere *fanatically* to the metal conventions, standards, and practices' (Weinstein, 1991a: 178). Weinstein identifies three basic forms of metal fanzine: those based on a band, such as *Killing Yourself to Die*, an international Black Sabbath fanzine; area-based fanzines, such as *Metal Caos* from Italy, and British regional 'zines; and fanzines that specialize in a specific metal subgenre, such as California's *White Throne*, focused on Christian metal, or *Metallic Beast* from Denmark, concerned with **thrash metal**.

Despite their essentially non-commercial and often ephemeral nature, fanzines remain a significant part of the popular music scene. Fanzines are integral to the development and popularization of **alternative music scenes**. There was a mushrooming of UK **club** fanzines in the early 1990s, linking a network stretching from Manchester to London. The **Internet** has provided a new medium for the international dissemination of fanzines.

See: **music press**; **punk rock**
Further reading: Cohen, 1994b; Savage, 1991; Thornton, 1995; Weinstein, 1991a. The RoJaRo Index of the music press includes many fanzines, and the list is constantly updated (see Bibliography: Web sites).

fashion Fashion is central to popular music. Music preferences and the status of **genres** are subject to fluctuation in critical and commercial popularity, with such 'changing fashions' related to shifts in the constitution of the genre, its audience, the music industry, and social trends. The music aside, genres can be in part based around fashions and style. Their performers and their **fans** present, adopt, and popularize particular clothing and hair fashions, for instance the British **new romantics** of the 1980s. This process is clearly evident in the styles of **youth subcultures**. While fashion and style are indicative of individual and group subjectivities, and serve to demarcate them from other styles and the 'mainstream', they are subject to commodification, as was the case with the **'grunge** look', which was the subject of major spreads in the fashion press in 1992.

Further reading: Ash and Wilson, 1992; McRobbie, 1988; the contemporary music press and lifestyle magazines (e.g. *Sky*, *The Face*, *Pavement*).

feminism Feminism can best be considered as a body of social theory, with a number of distinct strands, or 'schools', each associated with different theoretical assumptions and political agendas: Liberal; **Marxist**; Radical; Psychoanalytic; Socialist; Existentialist; **Postmodern** (for a useful overview, see Tong, 1989). Feminism has most notably informed media and cultural studies through considerations of representation (see, for example, Gamman and Marshment, 1988), the proportion and role of women in the media industries, and gender as a crucial aspect of audience subjectivities.

The following focii are evident in popular music studies (these are only alluded to here; see the entries mentioned):

1 the analysis of **stars**. Madonna, for example, has been the focus of a range of feminist readings;
2 the relationship of girls (and women) to **fandom**, **teeny-bopper** culture, and **music video** and **MTV**;
3 the representation of women in music video, and the

nature of the gaze (usually constructed as male) of the viewer of such texts;

4 general studies of women in the **music industry**, especially the experiences of female **musicians**, who have frequently struggled against the patriarchal and masculinist structures and assumptions which feminist writers see as dominating much popular music;

5 the treatment of women within the **history** of popular music, especially the marginalization of female performers, and their stereotypical representation;

6 the relationship between gender, sexuality, and particular **genres**, most notably **rock**, **country**, and **disco**. One aspect of this is the emergence of a queer musicology.

See: **gender**

Further reading: O'Brien, K., 1995; Reynolds and Press, 1995; Schwichtenberg, 1993; Tong, 1989.

festivals A festival is a concert, usually outdoor, often held over several days. There is an established historical tradition of popular music festivals, with regular events such as the Newport Folk and Jazz Festival and the New Orleans Mardi Gras in the United States, and the United Kingdom's Cambridge Folk Festival, and festivals play a central role in popular music mythology. They keep traditions alive, maintaining and expanding their audience base, legitimating particular forms of that tradition, and giving its performers and **fans** a sense of shared, communal identity.

A number of festivals at the end of the 1960s and in the early 1970s helped create the notion of a youth-oriented **rock** while confirming its commercial potential: Monterey in 1967; Woodstock in 1969; the Isle of Wight in 1970; and the Concert for Bangladesh in 1971, a relief effort organized by George Harrison for victims of Pakistan's civil war. The other side of the 1960s rock ideology was revealed in the violence at The Rolling Stones' free concert at Altamont, near San Francisco, at the end of their 1969 tour of the United States. The 1980s saw the reassertion of the music festival, with the success – both financially and as ideological touchstones – of the politically motivated 'conscience concerts': Live Aid, 1985, and the various Amnesty International concerts. In recent years, the Knebworth and WOMAD (the World of Music, Arts and Dance, began in 1982) concerts have become an established feature of the UK popular music scene, with WOMAD being exported to Australia, New Zealand, Denmark, Spain, and Italy. Also significant, reflecting the rise of **indie** music in general, is the popularity and scale of the previously alternative summer festivals, especially Glastonbury, along with Reading, 'T in the Park' (Glasgow), and the Virgin festivals in Chelmsford and Leeds started in 1996.

The theoretical question is how such festivals create their sometimes considerable symbolic and economic significance. Music festivals, as do **concerts**, reinforce popular music personas, creating icons and myths in the process. The performers are made 'accessible' to those attending the concert and, increasingly with large-scale festivals (e.g. Woodstock in 1994) via satellite television, to a world-wide audience. At the same time as it is forming a temporary community, joined in celebration and homage to the performers and/or the **genre**, the festival audience is being created as a **commodity**. If it attracts the projected audience, the festival is a major commercial enterprise, with on-site sales of food and souvenirs, the income from the associated television broadcasts via satellite to a global audience/market, and the subsequent 'live' recordings (e.g. Knebworth and Rock in Rio).

See: **concerts**

Further reading: Surprisingly, given their scale and significance, festivals have received only limited attention within popular music studies: see Morthland, 1992c; Shuker, 1994; Taylor, 1985.

fiction   Popular music offers to musicians and listeners a form of fictional narratives, presented through songs. This tradition is most fully present in the **folk**, **country**, **pop**, and **blues** genres. In pop, for example, a major form of song narrative is love – celebrated, thwarted, unrequited, lost and found, or found, lost, and found again. Working within generic forms, the work of **singer songwriters** is located primarily as a form of story-telling. Part of the appeal of such song narratives is the sense of identification and associated pleasure they create for listeners.

Popular music has also provided a source of inspiration and theme for prose fiction; sometimes based (loosely) on the author's own experience in music, the **music press**, or associated lifestyles. A major theme is the role of popular music in adolescent rites of passage and **subcultures**. Examples of this are Colin McInnes, *Absolute Beginners*, 1959 (**jazz** and **rock'n'roll**); Irvine Welsh, *Trainspotting*, 1993, and Jim Carroll, *The Basketball Diaries* (**punk/alternative**); Jack Kerouac, *On the Road*, 1957 (the **beats** and **jazz**). The '**rock** lifestyle' and the pressures of **touring** and fame are the focus in Bruce Thomas, *The Big Wheel*, Nik Cohn, *I am Still the Greatest says Johnny Angelo*, 1967, and Ray Connolly, *Stardust*, 1974; **fandom** is central to Nick Hornby, *High Fidelity*, 1996, Linda Jarvin, *Rock n Roll Babes from Outer Space*, 1996, and Jenny Fabian and Johnny Byrne, *Groupie*, 1969. Most recently, the 'ecstasy novel', linked to the **dance–music** scene, has become fashionable (e.g. *Disco Biscuits*, a collection of short stories edited by Sarah Campion, 1987; Alan Warner, *Morvern Callar*, 1987).

Such work has in turn frequently been the basis for feature **films**, such as *Absolute Beginners* (Julien Temple, 1986). This media cross-fertilization has been significant in exposing particular texts to a wider audience, albeit in different forms and contexts. Despite their arguable status as a literary subgenre, these and similar novels have been largely neglected in popular music studies.

See: **film**
Further reading: Taylor, 1985: ch. 7.

film: **Hollywood musicals**; **popular/rock musicals**; **youth movies**; **rockumentaries**; **soundtracks** Film has had an important relationship to popular music. Early silent films often had a live musical accompaniment (usually piano); and with the 'talkies', musicals became a major **genre** in the 1930s, and continued to be important through into the 1960s. Composers and musicians, primarily **stars**, provided a source of material for these films, as did Broadway musicals. The various genres of popular music, its **fans**, and its performers have acted as a rich vein of colourful, tragic, and salutary stories for film-makers. A new form of musical, the 'rock musical', played an important part in establishing **rock'n'roll** in the mid-1950s. Allied to such musicals were youth movies, with a range of subgenres, and 'rockumentaries'. Over the past thirty years or so, considerable synergy has been created between the music and film industries, with film soundtracks representing another avenue of revenue for recordings, including the **back catalogue**, and helping to promote contemporary releases.

The discussion here deals with these various aspects of film and popular music, in each case overviewing the historical development of the form or genre, then attempting to establish its central themes and conventions, and how these create meaning for the viewing and listening audience. Given the vast scope of the topic, the exploration can be only preliminary.

1   *The classic **Hollywood musical*** (for an excellent overview, see Hayward, 1996): The musical is a hybrid film genre, descended from European operetta and American vaudeville and the music hall. While *The Jazz Singer* (Alan Crosland, 1927) was the first feature film with sound, the first 'all-talking, all-singing, all-dancing' musical was *The Broadway Melody* (Harry Beaumont, 1929), which was important also for establishing the tradition of the backstage musical. The musical soon became regarded as a quintessentially American or Hollywood genre, associated primarily with the Warner and MGM studios, and RKO's pairing of Fred Astaire and Ginger Rogers. A major source of Hollywood's musicals was New York's Broadway (see **musicals**).

Early 'classic' musicals had simple, even naïve plots, promoting 'a gospel of happiness' (Hayward, 1996: 235), and were mainly perceived as vehicles for song and **dance**. The routines and performance of these became increasingly complex, culminating in the highly stylized films of Busby Berkeley. *The Wizard of Oz* (Victor Fleming, 1939) introduced a new musical formula, combining youth and music, with the children putting on a show format. Other new forms of the musical were introduced during the 1940s, including composer biographies, and biographical musicals of 'showbiz' stars. The vitality and audience appeal of the musical continued into the 1950s, with contemporary urban musicals such as *An American in Paris* (Vincent Minnelli, 1951), which portrayed the vitality of the Paris music **scene**, including **jazz**; Astaire joined by Gene Kelly; and the involvement of musical stars such as Frank Sinatra and Bing Crosby.

'The period 1930–1960, despite some severe dips, marked the great era of the Hollywood musical' (Hayward, 1996: 239). Although the 1960s did see several blockbuster musicals, notably *The Sound of Music* (Robert Wise, 1965), the heyday of the classic musical had passed, with fewer Broadway hits now making it to the screen. The 1960s saw a move towards greater realism in the musical, exemplified by *West Side Story* (Robert Wise/Jerome Robbins, 1961), an updated version of *Romeo and Juliet*. In the late 1960s and through the 1970s, the classic Hollywood musical was primarily kept alive by the films of Barbra Streisand (e.g. *Funny Girl*, William Wyler, 1968). Subgenres such as the performer biography still appeared (e.g. *Lady Sings the Blues*, Sydney Furie, 1972), along with the occasional backstage musical (e.g. *Fame*, Alan Parker, 1980). The classical musical's place was taken by a plethora of new forms associated with the popular musical genres spawned by the advent of rock'n'roll.

The classic musicals were a narcissistic and exhibitionist genre, extremely self-referential: 'the general strategy of the genre is to provide the spectator with a utopia through the form of entertainment. The entertainment *is* the utopia' (Hayward, 1996: 241), which is constituted and characterized by energy, abundance, intensity, community, and transparency. Pleasure, especially the visual enjoyment of the dance, is derived from both female and male forms. Ideologically, the genre is selling marriage, gender fixity, communal stability, and the merits of capitalism. Classic musicals are situated around a series of binary oppositions, most notably the duality of male and female, which it ultimately resolves; and work versus entertainment. These codes and conventions were questioned by the popular musicals of the 1950s and beyond.

2 *Popular/rock musicals*: Films dealing in some way with popular music, or drawing on it for their soundtrack, are frequently treated as a generic group. They are sometimes termed 'popular musicals', although this term could apply equally to their historical predecessors, and they are also accorded the more appropriate label 'rock film'. There is now a substantial body of such films, including a number of identifiable subgenres, with a considerable literature on them (see the extensive bibliography in Cooper, 1992) and the discussion here is highly selective.

During the 1950s, the decline of the Hollywood studio system and dwindling cinema audiences led to the need to target more systematically particular audience **demographics**. Hollywood linked up with the record industry to target youth, with a spate of teenage musicals. Many of these starred Elvis Presley, who sold sex through his song and dance routines, such as in *Jailhouse Rock* (Richard Thorpe, 1957). *The Blackboard Jungle* (Richard Brooks, 1954) used the new genre of rock'n'roll to symbolize adolescent rebellion against the authority of the school. Most early popular musicals centred around basic plots involving the career of a young rock performer: *Rock Around the Clock* (Fred Sears, 1955), *Don't Knock the Rock* (Fred Sears, 1956), and *The Girl Can't Help It* (Frank Tashlin, 1957). These were frequently combined with the other stock form, films serving purely as contrived vehicles for their real life stars. Most of Elvis Presley's movies, from *Love Me Tender* (Robert Webb, 1956) onward, were of this order, while British examples include Cliff Richard in *The Young Ones* (Sydney Furie, 1961), and Tommy Steele in *The Tommy Steele Story* (Gerard Bryant, 1957).

Any interest such films retain is largely due to their participant's music rather than their acting talents, though they did function as star vehicles for figures like Presley. In helping establish an identity for rock'n'roll, the teenage musicals placed youth in opposition to adult authority, and for conservatives confirmed the 'folk devil' image of fans of the new genre, associating them with juvenile delinquency, a major concern internationally through the 1950s. Thematically, however, the popular musicals actually stressed reconciliation between generations and classes, with this acting as a point of narrative closure at the film's ending. Such musicals also helped create an audience and a market for the new musical form, particularly in countries distant from the initial developments. These related roles continued to be in evidence in the subsequent development of the popular/rock musical.

British beat and the **British invasion** of the early 1960s were served up in a number of films in the early 1960s. Gerry and the Pacemakers brought a taste of the moment to a broader audience with their 1964 film *Ferry Across the Mersey* (J. Summers). This stuck to what had already become a standard formula – struggling young band makes good after initial setbacks – which was only shaken when the Beatles enlisted director Richard Lester to produce the innovative and pseudo-biographical *A Hard Day's Night* (1964). Along with Lester's *Help!* (1965), this consolidated the group's market dominance, and extended the rock film genre into new and more interesting anarchic forms. In the mid- to late 1960s, with the emergence of the **counter culture**, popular music was a necessary backdrop and a cachet of cultural authenticity for films such as *Easy Rider* (Dennis Hopper, 1969) and *The Graduate* (Mike Nichols, 1967). .Both fused effective **rock** soundtracks with thematic youth preoccupations of the day: the search for a personal and cultural **identity** in contemporary America.

During the 1970s and 1980s there was a profusion of popular musicals: the realist Jamaican film *The Harder They Come* (Perry Henzel, 1972); the flower power and religious fantasy of *Godspell* (David Greene, 1973); *Jesus Christ Superstar* (Norman Jewison, 1973) and *Hair* (Milos Forman, 1979); the disco-dance musicals of *Saturday Night Fever* (John Badham, 1977), *Grease* (Randal Kleiser, 1978), and *Staying Alive* (Sylvester Stallone, 1983); and the dance fantasies of *Flashdance* (Adrian Lyne, 1983), and *Dirty Dancing* (Emile Ardolino, 1987). The 'rock lifestyle' was the focus of *That'll Be The Day* (Claude Watham, 1973) and Ken Russell's version of *Tommy* (1975). Nostalgia was at the core of *American Graffiti* (George Lucas, 1973), *The Blues Brothers* (John Landis, 1978), *Quadrophenia* (Franc Roddam, 1979), and *The Buddy Holly Story* (Steve Rash, 1978). Grossberg (1993) claims that the success of these popular musicals prepared the ground for the success of **MTV**, launched in 1981, by redefining the political economy of rock, moving the emphasis from sound to images.

Since the 1980s, popular musical films have continued to mine these themes of youth subcultures (e.g. *Rivers Edge*, Tim Hunter, 1987); adolescent and young adult sexuality and gender relations (e.g. *Singles*, Cameron Crowe, 1992); class and generational conflict; nostalgia; stardom and the rock lifestyle (e.g. *The Doors* (Oliver Stone, 1990); *Sid and Nancy* (Alex Cox, 1986); *Pink Floyd: The Wall* (Alan Parker, 1982); and *Purple Rain* (Albert Magnoli, 1984)); and dance fantasies such as *Strictly Ballroom* (Baz Luhrman, 1992). The attraction of these dance narratives lies in 'the fantasies of achievement they afford their subjects' (McRobbie, 1988: 201). Film dance narratives exemplify Grant's observation that, more generally, for a theme 'musicals have been concerned with articulating a sense of community and defining the parameters of sexual desire, the two themes of course being intimately related' (Grant, 1986: 196). In the highly successful and realistic *The Commitments* (Alan Parker, 1991), the lead character, Jimmy Rabitte, attempts to bring soul to the Irish by forming an R & B band in Dublin. His unlikely collection of individuals, The Commitments, argue constantly, have problems acquiring gear and gigs, and, after one great pub performance, the band disintegrates.

The storylines of these musicals involve popular music to varying extents, ranging from its centrality to the narrative theme, to its use as a contextualizing soundtrack. These films resonate with the hopes and dreams and fantasy lives which popular music brings to young people everywhere. Where an actual artist is drawn on, or featured, such films help the process of mythologizing them, as with Elvis Presley, or the Janis Joplin character in *The Rose* (Mark Rydell, 1979). Dominant themes include youth/adolescence as a rite of passage, frequently characterized by storm and stress, and using subcultural versus 'mainstream' affiliations to explore this; reconciliation, between generations, competing sub-cultures, and genders, frequently expressed through the emergence of couples; and the search for independence and an established sense of identity. Given such themes are ones identified in the academic literature on human development as central adolescent 'tasks' and preoccupations, they clearly appeal to youthful cinema audiences, and to film-makers looking for box office appeal.

The Rocky Horror Picture Show (Jim Sharman, 1975) created a new subgenre: the cult musical. Following its first New York midnight screening in 1976, over the next six years the film played to over 5,000 people each week, only at midnight, in over 200 cinemas throughout the United States. Ironically, the film was only placed in the midnight slot after poor initial box office response to its first American screenings in late 1975 and its withdrawal from general release. Following its New York opening, however, the numbers at screenings gradually increased. People started coming dressed in some of the costumes shown in the film, and began singing and talking back to the screen. This was a new form of film–going, with the audience becoming an integral part of the cinematic experience, an indulgence in fantasy and catharsis. The film went on to become the king of the 'midnight movies' – cult films shown at midnight week after week, usually on Friday and Saturday nights (see Samuels, 1983).

3 **Rockumentaries**: The festival/concert/tour/scene film. Films of music **festivals** have consolidated the mythic status of events like Woodstock; and the 1970 film was a major box office success. A number of other **concert** and concert tour films have had a similar but more limited commercial and ideological impact. See, for example, *The Last Waltz* (Martin Scorsese, 1978), a record of The Band's final concert; *Hail! Hail! Rock'n'Roll* (Taylor Hackford, 1987), featuring Chuck Berry and other seminal rock'n'roll performers; *Stop Making Sense* (Jonathan Demme, 1984), featuring Talking Heads; and Prince's *Sign O' The Times* (Prince, 1987). Such films capture particular moments in 'rock history', while simultaneously validating particular musical styles and performers.

Stop Making Sense won the 1984 Best Documentary Award from the US National Society of Film Critics. A record of **new wave** band Talking Heads in concert, the film used material from three Hollywood shows in December 1983. The documentary is shot in a cool, almost classical style, with the unobtrusive camera subservient to the performances. Instead of stage histrionics and overpowering light shows, Demme used minimalist staging, lighting, and presentation. The film helped bring a moderately successful 'cult' band to a broader audience. The problem for filmmakers with such projects is that there are only so many things you can do with concert performances, given their restricted ambit, and many of the conventions they rely on have become cinematic cliché; e.g. *Rattle and Hum* (Phil Joanou, 1988), the film of U2's 1987 Joshua Tree tour.

Documentaries have also been important in exposing particular scenes and sounds to a wider audience. Prominent examples are *The Decline of Western Civilization, Part One* (Penelope Spheeris, 1981) on the Los Angeles **punk/ hardcore** scene circa 1981, featuring Black Flag, the Circle Jerks, X, and the Germs; its 'sequel', *The Decline of Western Civilization, Part Two: the Metal Years* (Spheeris, 1988), featuring Aerosmith, Alice Cooper, Ozzy Osbourne, Kiss, Metallica, and Motörhead; and *Hype* (Doug Pray, 1996) on the Seattle **grunge** scene. Other popular music documentaries have celebrated major performers, like The Who in *The Kids Are Alright* (Jeff Stein, 1978). As with any genre, the ultimate accolade is parody, represented by *This is Spinal Tap* (Rob Reiner, 1984).

The various rockumentary forms of popular musical have served a number of economic and ideological functions. While celebrating the youth audience and the mythic status of stars, for critics of popular music such films also confirm musicians and their fans as contemporary 'folk devils'. They validate and confirm particular musical styles and moments in the **history** of popular music as somehow worthy of more 'serious' attention.

4 *Soundtracks*: Mainstream narrative cinema has used two types of musical soundtrack to compliment the filmic text: (i) theme music, usually composed specifically for the film (e.g. *Star Wars*, George Lucas, 1977; *Jaws*, Steven Spielberg, 1975); (ii) a soundtrack consisting of selected popular music, usually contemporary with the temporal and physical setting of the film, or representative of the period evoked (e.g. *The Big Chill* (Lawrence Kasdan, 1983), *Singles*, *American Graffiti*). Occasionally, there may be two soundtracks released, and the two approaches are sometimes combined (e.g. *Dead Man Walking*, Tim Robbins, 1996). The emphasis here is on the second of these forms.

Rock Around the Clock (Fred Sears, 1956) and many of the films featuring Elvis Presley demonstrated the market appeal of popular music soundtracks, as indeed had many Hollywood musicals before them. Mainstream narrative cinema has increasingly used popular music soundtracks to great effect, with accompanying commercial success for both film and record, such as the soundtrack to *The Commitments*, featuring some impressive covers of soul classics and the powerful voice of Andrew Strong (who plays the part of the lead singer Deco), which charted internationally, reaching No. 1 in several countries, and spawned a further album of covers from the film.

Such soundtracks feature popular music composed specifically for the film, or previously recorded work which is thematically or temporally related to the film: eg. *The Big Chill*; *Boyz N The Hood* (John Singleton, 1991). This enables multimedia marketing, with accompanying commercial success for both film and record. Prince's soundtrack for the film *Batman* (Tim Burton, 1989) was part of a carefully orchestrated marketing campaign, which successfully created interest in the film and helped break Prince to a wider audience, primarily through exposure (of the promotional video clip) on MTV.

Further reading: Grant, 1986; Romanowski and Denisoff, 1987; Romney and Wootton, 1995; Shuker, 1994; Taylor, 1985.

FM radio – *see* **radio**

folk culture; **folk music**; **folk rock**   The term folk culture is applied to forms of culture which are tightly linked to particular social groups and which are not subject to mass distribution, even if electronically produced (Longhurst, 1995: 145). The concept is sometimes conflated with the notion of **roots** music. Often rooted in specific **localities**, early forms of many popular music **genres** can be regarded as folk culture, for example the pre-**ska** forms of Jamaican **reggae**, and the hillbilly styles which contributed to **country & western** and **rockabilly**. In particular, folk culture has been used in considerations of the musical characteristics and social dynamics of folk music.

While in a sense it can be argued that all popular music is a form of **folk music**, more specifically, and historically, the term is reserved for music passed from person to person or generation to generation without being written down. 'In general, folk is simple, direct, acoustic-based music that draws upon the experiences, concerns, and lore of the common people' (*Music Central 96*).

Folk music includes **ethnic** music, such as the social and religious ceremonial music of Africans or American Indians; negro spirituals and **blues**; work songs (e.g. sea shanties); political and protest songs ('broadsides'); and love songs. Its form and variants exist in every country and are often regionally based (e.g. the Appalachians). Considerable mixing and mingling of different traditions, song structures, and instrumentation is evident. There are important folk music archival collections, associated magazines, and record companies (e.g. Folkways). **Festivals** have been central to the maintenance of folk music in the United Kingdom and the United States, helping to maintain what counts as 'folk music' (e.g. Newport, in America; Cambridge, in England).

Folk music has taken differing paths in the United Kingdom and the United States, and in other national contexts: 'folk is a shifting signifier which continuously mutates in meaning' (Smith, 1997: 130). The genre's history is one of debates around folk's **authenticity**, and its role in **enculturation** of folk culture. The genre experienced a strong revival in the two countries in the late 1950s through to the early 1960s. In the United States, leading performers included Bob Dylan, Joan Baez, and Phil Ochs, who built on the radical activist, popular traditions developed by Woody Guthrie and Pete Seeger in the 1930s. There were influential local scenes in Greenwich Village in New York, and Cambridge, Massachussetts. The British folk scene of the 1960s was oriented more towards a folk club circuit, and regular major festivals. Leading performers included John Renbourne, Davy Graham, and Bert Jansch. Many of these performers went on to be influential in the development of British folk rock styles.

Folk music continues to be an active genre in its own right, while many 'mainstream' musicians have come out of folk, particularly **singer songwriters**. The study of folk music has long been academically regarded as a more valid, or 'respectable' form of popular music studies, reflecting its *perceived* roots in people's common experience, its general lack of mass commercialization and **commodification**, and the associated connotations of authenticity.

Further reading: Ennis, 1992; Gammond, 1991; Hardy and Laing, 1990 (especially entries on Woodie Guthrie, Pete Seeger); Laing, D., 'Folk and Blues', in Collis, 1980. For an essay review of recent folk music scholarship, see Smith, 1997.

Listening:

Joan Baez, *Joan Baez*, Vanguard, 1960.

Bob Dylan, *Bob Dylan*, Columbia, 1962.

Woody Guthrie, *The Legendary Performer*, RCA, 1977.

Tanita Tikaram, *Ancient Heart*, Reprise, 1988.

Folk music provided the basis for **folk rock** in the mid-1960s: a genre built around folk song structures and topical themes, adapting instruments and techniques associated with folk styles while using amplified instrumentation and **rock** conventions. Folk rock also had links with **country rock**, and **psychedelic rock** (the early Grateful Dead, Jefferson Airplane, and Country Joe and the Fish). The new genre arguably first came to wider attention with Bob Dylan's famous double set (half acoustic, half electric) at the Newport Festival in 1965, and subsequent 'electric' tour. As Dylan's hostile reception indicated, such innovations were not always welcomed by folk purists. Leading exponents of folk rock included The Byrds, The Flying Burrito Brothers, and The Loving Spoonful in the United States; and Lindisfarne, Steeleye Span, Pentangle, Donovan, and Fairport Convention in the United Kingdom. The Byrds' 'Mr Tambourine Man' (1966) is regarded as the archetypal folk rock record. The genre has lived on in the guitar-based sound of much mainstream rock music through the 1980s, often blended with **country rock** (e.g. the Long Ryders), and in **alternative** bands such as REM.

Further reading: Garofalo, 1997; Nelson, 1992; Scoppa, 1992; Vassal, 1976.

Viewing: *Dancing in the Street*, episode 3, 'So You Wanna Be A Rock'n'Roll Star?'.

Listening:

Bob Dylan, 'Like A Rolling Stone', on *Highway 61 Revisited*, Columbia, 1965.

The Loving Spoonful, 'Do You Believe in Magic?', on *Do You Believe In Magic?*, Kama Sutra, 1965.

The Byrds, 'Turn! Turn! Turn!', 1965, on *Turn! Turn! Turn!*, CBS, 1966.

REM, *Murmur*, IRS, 1983.

Steeleye Span, *Portfolio – Steeleye Span*, Chrysalis, 1988.

Fordism; post-Fordism A key term in recent writing on the **culture industries**, post-Fordism sees a move away from traditional forms of industrial organization (Fordism), toward flexibility and 'flexible specialization', associated with niche marketing. The term has been applied to new relationships between the **majors** and **independent** record companies, and shifts in the vertical and horizontal integration of the **music industry**.

See: **retail**

Further reading: Garnham, 1990; Hesmondhalgh, 1996a; Negus, 1992.

formats – *see* **radio**; **record formats**

Frankfurt School A group of German intellectuals, the Frankfurt School developed a revolutionary philosophical variant of Western **Marxism**, which became known as 'critical theory'. Initially based at the Institute of Social Research in Frankfurt, the school moved to the United States during the 1930s. Its principal figures included Adorno, Marcuse, Horkheimer, Fromm, and Benjamin.

The Frankfurt theorists criticized mass culture in general, arguing that under the capitalist system of production, culture had become simply another object, the 'culture industry', devoid of critical thought and any oppositional political possibilities. This general view was applied more specifically to popular music by Adorno, especially in his attacks on **Tin Pan Alley** and **jazz**. When Adorno published his initial critique 'On Popular Music' in 1941, the music of the big bands filled the airwaves and **charts**, operating within the Tin Pan Alley system of songwriting that had been dominant since the early 1900s, with the majority of songs composed in the 32-bar 'AABA' format.

Adorno's writings on popular music were only a minor part of his attempt to develop a general **aesthetics** of music (see Paddison, 1993, for a systematic outline and discussion of this intellectual project). Adorno was not opposed to popular music as such, but rather to its ruthless exploitation by the **culture/music industries**. His examination of the development of music utilized the concepts of diachronic, the analysis of change, and synchronic, the analysis of static states. At the heart of his critique of popular music was the standardization associated with the capitalist system of commodity production:

> A clear judgement concerning the relation of serious to popular music can be arrived at only by strict attention to the fundamental characteristic of popular music: standardization. The whole structure of popular music is standardized even where the attempt is made to circumvent standardization   (Adorno, 1941: 17).

In this essay and his subsequent writings on popular music, Adorno continued to equate the form with Tin Pan Alley and jazz-oriented variations of it, ignoring the rise of **rock'n'roll** in the early 1950s. This undermined his critique and resulted in his views generally being strongly rejected by more contemporary **rock** analysts (see, for example, Frith, 1983: 43–8). Gendron forcefully recapitulates 'the failings' of Adorno's theory, particularly his exaggeration of the presence of industrial standardization in popular music, but also suggests that 'Adorno's analysis of popular music is not altogether implausible', and merits reconsideration (Gendron, 1986: 25). To support this argument, Gendron examines the standardization of the vocal group style **doo–wop**, rooted in the black **gospel** quartet tradition, which had a major chart impact between 1955 and 1959.

Adorno's views on popular music remain widely utilized and debated. Paddison, for instance, argues that Adorno's defence of the musical **avant garde** can be applied to the work of composers and performers of popular music such as Frank Zappa and Henry Cow.

See: **culture industries**
Further reading: Adorno, 1941, 1991; Gendron, 1986; Paddison, 1993.

functional music – *see* **muzak**

funk The term funk was originally used in the 1950s to describe a form of modern **jazz** which concentrated on 'swing' and '**soul**' – the latter synonomous with **authenticity** and sincerity. Funk was also used in a more negative sense to refer to music considered low-down, earthy, or crude. Subsequently, funk was applied to the 'anarchic and polyrhythmic' late 1960s and 1970s derivatives of soul: 'High energy, mind-expanding black rock'n'roll, a soulful psychedelic reaction' (DeCurtis and Henke, 1992b: 268). Major performers included James Brown, George Clinton (Parliament, Funkadelic), Kool & the Gang, and Earth, Wind and Fire. Funk was an element in subsequent black-oriented **genres**, such as **hip-hop** and **techno**-funk, and the eclectic work of artists like The Artist Formerly Known As Prince and Living Colour. It also made a major contribution to **disco** (the Ohio Players), and **rap**. Indeed, funk encompasses a variety of associated musical styles and can be considered a **meta genre** (see Vincent, who comprehensively identifies a succession of 'Funk Dynasties' (1996: x–xi), extending from the late 1960s to the 1990s).

Musically, funk tends to have little melodic variation, and **rhythm** is everything (the 'groove'). 'The funk style requires a particular rhythmic ensemble – percussion and bass line – and either sustained chords or rhythmic interpolations by other instruments. Funk is an attitude, which when expressed musically transforms the listener into a particular mood, usually described as laid-back or mellow' (Brown, 1992: 211).

Further reading: McEwen, 1992 (includes discography); Vincent, 1996.

Listening:

James Brown, *Cold Sweat*, King, 1967.

Parliament, *Mothership Connection*, Casablanca, 1976.

Funkadelic, *One Nation Under a Groove*, Warner Brothers, 1978.

Michael Jackson, 'Billy Jean', on *Thriller*, Epic, 1983.

Prince, *1999*, Warner Brothers, 1984.

G

garage bands; **garage rock**   The garage bands of the late 1960s, so called as exponents made the music in the garage or basement, were especially prominent in the United States, where they responded to the **British invasion** of the American market. Playing basic rock music with lots of enthusiasm, these performers produced some classic 'one-hit wonders'. Some bands were more enduring, including The Standells, The Electric Prunes, and The Count Five. Frequently covered standards were 'Gloria' (originally a single B-side for Them in the United Kingdom in 1966), 'Hey Joe' (The Leaves), and 'Louie, Louie' (Kingsmen). In the United Kingdom, garage was best represented by the proto-**punk** of the commercially successful Troggs ('Wild Thing', 1966).

In 1972 a compilation of garage band releases, *Nuggets*, by Lenny Kaye, created new interest in their work, spawning a whole series of reissues (*Nuggets*, vols 1–12, Rhino; and *Pebbles*, vols 1–10, AIP). In his liner notes, Kaye termed the **genre** 'punk rock', a prescient acknowledgement of garage rock's subsequent influence on post-1977 **punk rock**. The advent of punk in the late 1970s and 1980s saw a revival of interest in the garage bands, whose sound is not dissimilar. The term 'garage dance' has recently been applied to a form of New Jersey (the Paradise Garage club) and New York **dance-music**, which has also developed a UK following.

Garage rock's musical characteristics were 'a premium on sheer outrageousness, over-the-top vocal screams and sneers, loud guitars that almost always had a fuzztone' (Erlewine *et al.*, 1995). The genre was the province largely of white, teenage suburbanites. It first emerged around 1965, predominantly on tiny, local record labels, linked to strong regional **scenes** (especially Texas and California), each with a distinctive style. The genre declined in 1967–8 with the impact of the Vietnam War draft and college attendance on band members, and the performers' general lack of commercial success. The surviving garage bands moved towards more **progressive**, **psychedelic** sounds (e.g. The Electric Prunes, The Blues Magoos, and The Chocolate Watchband).

The genre and its performers are strangely neglected in otherwise comprehensive American **rock** histories (Friedlander, 1996; Garofalo, 1997), but have retained a cult following, including **fanzines** and Web sites on the **Internet**.

Further reading: Bangs, 1992d (includes discography); Erlewine *et al.*, 1995; Heylin, 1992.

Listening:

The Chocolate Watch Band, *The Best of The Chocolate Watch Band*, Rhino, 1983.

Nuggets Volume One: The Hits, Rhino, 1984.

The Troggs, *The Best of the Troggs*, Polygram, 1988.

gatekeepers A media studies term initially applied to describe how telegraph wire editors selected items for inclusion in local papers, gatekeepers became an established approach to analysing the way in which media workers select, reject, and reformulate material for broadcast or publication. Based on a filter-flow model of information flow, gatekeepers 'open the gate' for some texts and information, and close it for others.

The music industry has a number of gatekeepers, making the initial decision about who to record and promote, and filtering material at each step of the process involving the recording and marketing of a song. Studies of **radio** have been the main users of the concept. For example, Rothenbuhler (1985) examined one US radio station in depth to determine how, within a given airplay format, the programmer decides which songs to play. The main gatekeepers were the station's programme director and music director, or outside consultant. Subsequent studies of radio have confirmed this finding in various national settings (e.g. Brennan, 1996). Decisions on which releases, artists, and **genres** to accord airplay or screen-time help shape consumption preferences, and can consolidate new genres, such as US college radio and **alternative** rock, and **MTV** and **heavy metal**, in the late 1980s.

Organizations involved in industry regulation (e.g. The International Federation of the Phonographic Industry – IFPI), and government regulatory agencies act as gatekeepers. The editors of music trade publications, and the popular music press, must also be considered a form of gatekeeper, since reviews, artist profiles, chart lists, and publicity information help shape radio programmers' choices.

The concept became critiqued for being too mechanistic, and it has been claimed that 'the gatekeeper concept is now generally regarded as oversimplified and of little utility' (O'Sullivan *et al.*, 1994: 126-7; see also Negus, 1992). Nevertheless it remains useful if used in conjunction with considerations of how musical forms 'arrive' at a 'gate', and how they are subsequently modified.

See: **A & R**; **censorship**; **music industry**; **music press; radio**
Further reading: Barrow and Newby, 1996; Brennan, 1996; Burnett, 1996; Cusic, 1996; Negus, 1992.

gender Gender is the cultural differentiation of females from males, a signifying distinction, compared to sexual differentiation, which is a biological/physical difference. There is considerable debate over the extent to which particular gender differences can be attributed to culture and socialization.

In popular music, the significance of gender is evident in considerations of the following points:

1 the **history** of popular music, where while there is a recognition of women's contributions to **gospel**, the **blues**, and **soul**, there is a tendency to marginalize their place in the development of **rock** and **pop** styles, and to see their contribution in stereotypical terms: divas, rock chicks (Suzi Quatro, Janis Joplin), men-pleasing angels (Doris Day), victims (Billie Holiday), or problem personalities (Judy Garland, PJ Harvey);

2 **musicology's** presentation of a male-dominated musical canon, and a **feminist** challenge to this;

3 the perceived masculine or feminine nature of particular **genres**/styles. To take some examples, **dance pop** is generally seen as 'a girls' genre', while **hard rock** and **heavy metal** are regarded as primarily male-oriented genres. Women performers predominate in **a capella** and gospel music, and are prominent in **folk** and **country**, and among **singer songwriters**;

4 in relation to **audiences**, girl fans and their musical tastes are often denigrated – see **teenyboppers**;

5 the lack of women in the male-dominated music industry. When present, they are largely in stereotypically 'female' roles, like press, or office personnel: there are few women working in **A & R**, or as **producers**, **managers**, and **sound mixers**;

6 youth **subcultures** as largely a male preserve, with girls generally absent, 'invisible', or socially insignificant;

7 the treatment of gender and **sexuality** in song lyrics, with some genres having a clear misogynist strain (e.g. hard rock, light metal);

8 stereotyped gender representations in **music video**. See Lewis, 1990b.

Further reading: Bayton, 1990; Cohen, 1991; Evans, 1994; Frith and McRobbie, 1990; Gaar, 1992; McClary, 1991; O'Brien, 1995 (includes discography); Reynolds and Press, 1995; Steward and Garratt, 1984.

As even this cursory list indicates, much of the work around gender issues in popular music has focused on girls and women. Two further aspects of this are noteworthy. First, the term **women in rock** emerged as a media concept in the early 1970s, and has persisted despite being criticized as a 'generic mushy lump' (O'Brien, L., 1995: 3), unrelated to the wide variety among female performers, even those within the rock genre. There are two dimensions: women as performers, and women in the music industry, with women being marginalized and stereotyped in both. For instance, Cohen found that, in the Liverpool rock music **scene** she studied, women were not simply absent, but were actively excluded. All-male bands tended to preserve the music as their domain, keeping the involvement of wives and girlfriends at a distance. This situation reflects the more restricted social position of women, with greater domestic commitments and less physical freedom; the lack of encouragement given to girls to learn rock instruments; and rock sexuality as predominantly masculine. Consequently, there are few women bands in rock, or women instrumentalists, and most women rock performers are 'packaged as traditional, stereotyped, male images of women' (Cohen, 1991: 203).

In the early 1990s this soundscape changed with the '**Riot Grrrl**' movement. Initially based in Washington DC, and Olympia, Washington, Riot Grrrl quickly became the focus of considerable media attention. Through **fanzines** and sympathetic role models among female musicians, riot grrrls asserted the need to break down the masculine cameraderie of the **alternative** and **hardcore** music scenes, which marginalized girls and young women. They drew on feminism and **punk** 'do-it-yourself' ideology to question conventional ideas of femininity; and rejected rockist ideas of cool and mystique, challenging the view that enhanced technical virtuosity is necessary to create music. Some writers referred to them as 'punk feminists' (see Weisband *et al.*, 1995). Riot grrrls aimed to create a cultural space for young women in which they could express themselves without being subject to male scrutiny and domination. They played with conflicting images and stereotyped conventions, such as their appropriation of 'girl' and their assertive use of the term 'slut'. Musically, the performers linked to the riot grrrl movement sounded very like traditional hardcore and late 1970s punk bands, but their emphasis was on the process rather than the product. Performers and supporters included L7, Bikini Kill, and Kim Gordon of Sonic Youth. Inspired in part by the Riot Grrrls, a number of prominent women-led bands have emerged during the 1990s, for example Hole, Veruca Salt, Echobelly, and Skunk Anansie.

Further reading: Reynolds and Press, 1995; Weisband *et al.*, 1995.
Listening:
L7, *Bricks Are Heavy*, Slash/Warner Brothers, 1992.
Bikini Kill, *Pussywhipped*, Kill Rock Stars (the group's own label, which also puts out material from like-minded bands), originally an EP, 1992, reissued on CD, 1993.

Generation X – *see* **demography**

genre; **meta genres**; **subgenres**   Genre can be basically defined as a category or type. A key component of **textual analysis**, genre is widely used to analyse popular culture texts, most notably in their filmic and popular literary forms (e.g. thrillers, science fiction, and horror). The various encyclopedias, the standard histories, and critical analyses of popular music (see below) all use genre as a central organizing element. Some accounts tend to use style and genre as overlapping terms, or prefer style to genre (e.g. Moore, 1993). The arrangement in retail outlets also suggests that there are clearly identifiable genres of popular music, which are understood as such by consumers. Indeed, **fans** will frequently identify themselves with particular genres, often demonstrating considerable knowledge of the complexities of their preferences (subgenres). Similarly, musicians will frequently situate their work by reference to genres and musical styles.

The usual approach to defining musical genres is 'to follow the distinctions made by the music industry which, in turn, reflect both musical history and marketing categories' (Frith,

1987: 147). Another approach, suggested by Frith, is to 'classify them according to their ideological effects, the way they sell themselves as art, community or emotion' (ibid.). He gives the example of a form of **rock** termed '**authentic**', exemplified by Bruce Springsteen:

> The whole point of this genre is to develop musical conventions which are, in themselves, measures of 'truth'. As listeners we are drawn into a certain form of reality: this is what it is like to live in America, this is what it is like to love or hurt. The resulting work is the pop equivalent of film theorists' 'classic realist text' (ibid.).

Against and in interplay with authentic genres can be placed a tradition of artifice (e.g. **glam rock**).

Critical analysis of popular music genres has concentrated on the question of their fluidity. Chambers (1985) correctly observed that by the mid-1980s there were quite rigid boundaries between genres, as exemplified by **art rock**. Currently, while musical genres continue to function as marketing categories and reference points for musicians, critics, and fans, particular examples clearly demonstrate that genre divisions must be regarded as highly fluid. No style is totally independent of those that have preceded it, and musicians borrow elements from existing styles and incorporate them into new forms. 'Performers have absorbed influences across genre (and colour) lines. In the 1920s, **country** pioneer Jimmie Rogers drew extensively from the **blues** and popular music traditions just as, in the 1980s, Prince reworked the imagery and sounds of white 1960s rock' (Hardy and Laing, 1990: v). Further, many performers can fit under more than one classification, or shift between and across genres during their careers. There is also considerable genre-bending: subverting or playing with the conventions of existing musical genres, or adopting an ironic distance from those same conventions. This process is strongly present in hybrid genres, where different styles inform and engage with each other (e.g. **jazz rock**). Moreover, 'while the surface styles and fashions of popular music change rapidly, the underlying structures move far more slowly' (ibid.).

It is useful to distinguish between **meta genres**, which are rather loose amalgams of various styles (e.g. **alternative rock**, **world music**), and genres, which arguably exist in a purer, more easily understood and specified form (e.g. **disco**). It is also important to acknowledge the significance of **subgenres**, which are particularly evident in well-established and developed styles/genres, and qualify any simplistic depiction of a genre; the blues, **heavy metal**, and **techno** provide good examples of strongly differentiated genres.

'Mainstream' musical genres are operating within a commercial system of record companies, contracts, marketing, publicity, management, support staff, and so on; within this context performers tour and perform, make recordings, and create an image. As Breen has observed, moving into the 1990s 'every genre and sub-genre of popular music shares a location on the totalized map of popular music culture, where the bridges that form the industrial crossovers from one domain of the popular music industry to the next are increasingly interconnected' (1991: 193).

In the light of the above, several general distinguishing characteristics of popular music genres can be identified. First, there are the stylistic traits present in the music: their musical characteristics, 'a code of sonic requirements . . . a certain sound, which is produced according to conventions of composition, instrumentation and performance' (Weinstein, 1991a: 6). These may vary in terms of their coherence and sustainability (as examples such as **Christian rock** and glam rock clearly demonstrate), particularly in meta genres. Along with other aspects of genre, particular musical characteristics can be situated within the general historical evolution of popular music. Of particular significance here is the role of **technology**, which establishes both constraints and possibilities in relation to the nature of performance, and the recording, distribution, and reception of the music. Second, there are other, essentially non-musical, stylistic attributes, most notably image and its associated visual style. This includes standard iconography and record cover format; the locale and structure of performances, especially in concert, and the dress, make-up,

147

and hair styles adopted by both the performers and their listeners and fans. Musical and visual stylistic aspects combine in terms of how they operate to produce particular ideological effects, a set of associations which situate the genre within the broader musical constituency. Third, there is the primary **audience** for particular styles. The relationship between fans and their genre preferences is a form of transaction, mediated by the forms of delivery, creating specific cultural forms with sets of expectations (see Weinstein, 1991a). Genres are accorded specific places in a musical hierarchy by both critics and fans, and by many performers. This hierarchy is loosely based around the notions of authenticity, sincerity, and commercialism. The denigration of certain genres (e.g. disco, **dance pop**) and the elevation of others (e.g. **progressive rock**) reflect this, a situation mirroring the broader, still widely accepted, high/low culture split. We must acknowledge the ultimately subjective nature of these concepts, and the shifting status and constituency of genres. This point becomes clear when we check which genres listed here are also included in the major encyclopedias, compendiums, and histories of popular music. Furthermore, genres are historically located; some endure, others spring briefly to prominence then fade.

In terms of the identification and delineation of various genres, it is instructive to see which have, or have not, been accorded separate treatment in some of the major overviews of popular music. For example, Gammond (1991) excludes, among others, art rock, Christian rock, **folk rock**, and glam rock; Clarke (1990) concentrates on performers, and 'major' genres: blues, country, **folk**, heavy metal, **jazz**, **reggae**, rock, and **soul**, with considerably briefer entries on several other genres (e.g. **doo-wop**; **bubblegum**); DeCurtis and Henke (1992a) have no separate contributions for country, blues, and jazz, though these are necessarily alluded to where they have influenced or fused with **rock'n'roll**. Further, this major history relies on the concept of scenes and sounds, and the role of key performers, as much as genre. Hardy and Laing (1990) include a fairly inclusive glossary of styles and genres, with the brief entries supplemented by the discussions of associated artists. This device works quite well, and is illustrative of how genres defy static or academic definition independent of those actually making the music. (Of course, all this raises the whole thorny question of the definition of **popular music**, an issue considered in the entry for that concept.)

See: genre entries
Further reading: Charlton, 1994.

geography   Cultural geographers have been doing research on music since the late 1960s, seeking to establish 'the nexus between the social, cultural, economic and political in musical analysis' (Kong, 1995: 273). The geographical analysis of popular music has emphasized the dynamics and consequences of the geographical distribution of recorded popular music around the world; and how particular musical sounds have become associated with particular places. Four main areas of research within musical geography have been identified (Carney, 1990; Kong, 1995): (i) a concern with the spatial distribution of musical forms, activities, and performers; (ii) exploration of musical home locales and their extension, using concepts such as contagion, relocation, and hierarchical diffusion; and the examination of the agents of and barriers to diffusion; (iii) the delimitation of areas that share certain musical traits, or, relatedly, on the identification of the character and personality of places as gleaned from lyrics, melody, instrumentation, and the general 'feel' or sensory impact of the music; and (iv) pertinent themes in music, such as the image of the city.

A necessary addition to these emphases is that of the global processes of cultural homogenization and commodification, and the intersection of these with the local. The study of the global geographical distribution of recorded popular music is concerned with the nature, status, and operation of **cultural imperialism**, and the relationship between local musics and the international **music industry**.

Interest in particular sounds has focused on the significance of **locality**, and how music may serve as a marker of **identity**.

Many histories of popular music will refer to particular geographic locales, usually cities or regions, as being identified at a specific historical juncture with a sound, for example the San Francisco Sound, Chicago Blues, and the **Seattle sound**. Somewhat contiguous with this usage, is the application of **scene**, such as that in Athens, Georgia in the late 1980s. This implies a range of activities, loosely centred around and aligned to a particular style of music and its associated performers.

See: **cultural imperialism**; **locality**
Further reading: Kong, 1995; McLeay, 1994.

girl groups   While often the studio creations of **producers** such as Phil Spector, girl groups were on the cutting edge of early 1960s pop music. Leading performers included Darlene Love, who sang lead vocals on a number of groups' records, the Ronnettes, The Supremes, and The Crystals. The girl groups had a clearly identifiable sound: 'girlish vocals fraught with adolescent idealism and pain, plus quirky arrangements embellished by strings and a dramatic drumbeat' (O'Brien, 1995: 68). The vocals were a combination of qualities: nasal, high-pitched, humming, and husky, they owed much to **soul** and **gospel**, yet were at the same time unique. Their song narratives were morality tales about the attractions and perils of 'first love', especially of the forbidden variety, primarily written by several youthful **songwriting** teams (e.g. Gerry Goffin and Carol King). Many girl-group releases were on **independent** labels, including Red Bird, Phillies, Scepter, and an ascendant **Motown**. The girl groups had considerable impact, articulating the optimism present in the United States under the Kennedy administration, and providing the basis for the success of the 1960s **British beat** groups, including the Beatles. By the mid-1960s the girl-group sound had been assimilated into mainstream pop, but they have continued to exercise a fascination, linked to a mythic status associated with innocence and optimism. The 1980s and 1990s equivalents of the 1960s girl groups are performers such as Bananarama, TLC, and the Spice Girls, although they sometimes exercise greater control over their music than did their predecessors.

See: **gender**
Further reading: Gaar, 1992; O'Brien, 1995: ch. 3.
Listening:
The Supremes, *Anthology*, Motown, 1974.
The Best of the Ronnettes, ABKCO, 1992.
The Best of the Crystals, ABKCO, 1992.
There are a number of good compilations of the girl groups; see those issued by Rhino.
Viewing: Dancing in the Street, episode 2, 'Be My Baby'.

glam rock; **glitter rock**   Also referred to as glitter rock, glam rock was a musical style/**genre**, and an associated **subculture**, which flourished in the early 1970s, especially in the United Kingdom. Glam was both a reaction against the seriousness of late 1960s **progressive rock** and the **counter culture**, and also an extension of it. It strongly emphasized the visual presentation of performers and their concerts, with vividly coloured hair, outrageous costumes, heavy make-up, and fire breathing (in the case of Kiss). In glam the music was almost secondary to the act, as the image of the **star** became part of the musician's creative presentation.

British glam pioneers were early-period David Bowie and Gary Glitter, who had three British No. 1 **chart** singles in the mid-1970s: 'With its mammoth drum beat, growling guitar, dumb instrumental hook, and incessant chorus of "hey", his debut single "Rock and Roll, Part Two" was a huge hit' (Erlewine *et al.*, 1995: 342). In the United States, glam was represented by performers such as Kiss, with a huge following of **fans** ('the Kiss Army') for their highly theatrical concerts, the **punk**ish New York Dolls, and, in the 1980s, light **heavy metal** bands such as Bon Jovi. Other glam rockers included the more prosaic pop-oriented styles of Sweet and Slade, and the more **art rock**-oriented Roxy Music and Queen ('Bohemian Rhapsody', 1975).

151

Elements of androgyny and bisexuality were a part of glam's image and appeal. The style of glam performers and their fans combined **hippy** sartorial elegance and **skinhead** hardness: 'Reminiscent of mods in their extravagant clothes, high heels and make up (often offset with tattoos), hard-working lads masculinised their decadent image composed of a collage of Berlin thirties and New York gay' (Brake, 1985: 76). Glam was part of the 1970s embourgeoisement of leisure in the United Kingdom, with new city-centre leisure centres, and influenced and merged into the **new romantics** (eg. Adam and the Ants).

See: **heavy metal (lite metal); new romantics**
Further reading: Charlton, 1994; Garofalo, 1997; Moore, 1993.
Listening:
David Bowie, *The Rise and Fall of Ziggy Stardust*, Rykodisc, 1972.
T Rex, *Electric Warrior*, Reprise, 1972.
Kiss, *Double Platinum (Greatest Hits)*, Casablanca, 1978.
Gary Glitter, *Rock'n'Roll: The Best of Gary Glitter*, Rhino, 1990.
Sweet, *The Best of Sweet*, Capitol, 1993.
New York Dolls, *Rock & Roll*, Mercury, 1994 (contains their 1973 and 1974 albums).

globalization   The result of the world being shrunk into one communications system, dominated by international media conglomerates, globalization emerged as a critical concept in the late 1980s. It was often used to argue that regional and local cultures are squeezed out, overwhelmed, or colonized and 'watered down' and commercialized for mainstream global consumption. Although globalization was frequently used in association with **cultural imperialism**, it is distinguished from it as 'more complex and total, and less organized or predictable in its outcomes' (O'Sullivan *et al.*, 1994: 130).

In relation to popular music, globalization has an economic and a cultural dimension, with the two closely linked. The dominance of the **popular music** industry by the **majors**, and the internationalization of music styles, can be viewed as examples of globalization. Various authorities place the majors' market share of the global production, manufacture, and distribution of recorded popular music at between 80 and 90 per cent. In Europe, the dominance of the multinationals is clear and increasing. International Federation of the Phonographic Industry figures for 1990 placed it around 90 per cent in most countries, ranging from Austria (94 per cent), to Portugal (89 per cent), France (83 per cent), and The Netherlands (75 per cent). Since 1988, several of the majors have embarked on a concerted effort to absorb locally owned record companies and further increase their market share. For example, EMI absorbed Chrysalis in the United Kingdom (in 1991), Medley in Denmark (1991), Minos Matsas in Greece (1991), and Hispavox in Spain (1988). The major companies also take major shareholdings in independent labels with promising artists, an investment which can pay off: Oasis' label Creation is 49 per cent owned by Sony Music.

An important aspect of the role of the majors in national popular music markets is the question of the possible conflict between the **local** and the global, in relation to national musical vitality. The basic concern is that the transnationals will promote their international artists at the expense of local artists, and international preferences and **genres** at the expense of more '**authentic**' local popular music, and only develop those local talents and genres with global sales potential. At a more general level, it is noteworthy that English is the language of popular music, arguably a form of linguistic globalization. Do the policies and activities of the multinationals inhibit the development of indigenous music in local markets? The response is complex, and varies from country to country.

Further reading: Burnett, 1996; Negus, 1992; Robinson *et al.*, 1991; Wallis and Malm, 1992.

gospel   While its religious content has generally kept gospel from enjoying significant commercial success in the mainstream of popular music, it has been hugely influential, especially on **soul** and **R & B**. Garofalo (1997) refers to the

genre as 'sanctified R & B'. Gospel is a *Billboard* chart category, and features among the Grammy awards.

Black slaves in the United States adapted the spiritual as part of the Protestant revival at the beginning of the nineteenth century, and gospel arose from the upsurge in fundamentalist church-going in black urban communities in the 1920s. Thomas Dorsey (b. 1899), a major composer and choir leader, is credited with inventing the term 'gospel'. Vocal **call and response**, and an intense spiritual 'feeling' were central to early gospel music, while the moaning, pleading, and supplicating vocals became part of the repertoire of jump **blues** and early soul singers. Gospel was an important part of the upbringing of many early **rockabilly** singers, and is evident in their vocal style (e.g. Elvis Presley). During the late 1950s, Sam Cooke and Ray Charles performed gospel tunes with secular lyrics, or adapted gospel tunes, anticipating soul music. Other leading gospel performers were Mahalia Jackson, America's most popular gospel artist in the 1950s, and Aretha Franklin, who was a gospel star before singing more secular material. Gospel is clearly influential on the smooth harmonies and lead vocals of contemporary R & B.

See: **doo-wop**; **R & B**; **soul**

Further reading: Cusic, 1990; Ennis, 1992; Gammond, 1991; Hansen, 1992b.

Listening:

Aretha Franklin, *Amazing Grace*, Atlantic, 1972.

Ray Charles, *The Right Time*, Atlantic, 1987 (especially 'I Got A Woman').

Sam Cooke, *Sam Cooke with the Soul Stirrers*, Speciality, rereleased 1991.

Mahalia Jackson, *Gospels, Spirituals, Hymns*, CBS, 1991.

goth/gothic rock; **goths**   A musical **genre**, and associated **subcultural** style, goth was influenced by the proto-**punk** music of American band The Velvet Underground and the sound experiments of the rock **avant garde**. The label goth, or gothic rock, was first applied in the 1970s to bands like

Joy Division, Bauhaus, Siouxie and the Banshees, and the Southern Death Cult. Siouxie Sioux used the term 'gothic' to describe the orientation of her band, and may be the originator of the term. 'The music was generally a dark, angst-ridden and introspective alternative to the light-hearted **disco** sounds that were dominating that era' (*Music Central 96*), and combined gothic images (gloomy medieval castles, vampires, etc.) with a negative view of contemporary society. Goth was primarily a British phenomenon, though it developed internationally and remains evident in the 1990s.

Bauhaus' debut EP, *Bela Lugosi's Dead* (Small Wonder Records, 1979) is credited with introducing the genre in the United Kingdom; the nine-and-a-half minute title track, with its lengthy, haunting, electronically produced sound effects, became a gothic rock anthem. (The thematic gothic connection lay in the fact that Lugosi played the lead part in the original *Dracula* film (Tod Browning, 1931).) While there was a variety of gothic bands and instrumental line-ups, the basic characteristics of the music remained fairly constant: a low bass pulse, pounding drumbeats, electronic sound effects, low-pitched vocals, often spoken rather than sung, and with deep, dramatic vocal **timbre**. Performers such as the Sisters of Mercy used drum machines, low drones (long held notes), and made 'an almost minimalist use of short repeated melodic fragments' (Charlton, 1994: 280). Elements of an austere **psychedelia** were part of the music of Joy Division ('Love Will Tear Us Apart', on *Closer*, Qwest, 1980) and the Jesus and Mary Chain. Through the 1980s and beyond, goth has covered a broader spectrum of music, for example that of Robert Smith and the Cure.

Goth was also a cultural style, with **goths** characterized by their black clothes and the heavy use of dark eye and face make-up. The genre and its **fans** were associated with several **moral panics** around youth suicides in the late 1980s. In New Zealand, for example, press comment and headlines initially fastened on a possible association, quoting song **lyrics** to demonstrate how 'Gothic music preaches a message of despondency wrapped in the mysticism of death'; headlines referred to 'Gothic Cult suicides', the 'Music of mysticism and despair', and how 'Gothic lifestyle puts young at risk – doctor' (Shuker, 1994: 260–2). The episode was an example of the use of an '**effects**' argument to attack popular music.

Further reading: Charlton, 1994.
Listening:
Siouxie and the Banshees, *Once Upon a Time: The Singles*, Geffen, 1984.
The Jesus and Mary Chain, *Psychocandy*, Reprise, 1985.
The Cure, *Staring at the Sea: the Singles*, Elektra, 1986.
The Sisters of Mercy, *God's Own Medicine*, 1986.

gramophone – *see* **phonograph**

grunge   As much a marketing device as an identifiable 'sound' (cf. **alternative music**, into which it is often conflated), grunge initially developed in the **Seattle** area of the United States in the late 1980s, associated with the influential **indie** label, Sub Pop. It went on to become part of a commercially successful alternative mainstream world-wide by the mid-1990s.

Grunge 'de-emphasized appearance and polished technique in favour of raw, angry, passionate songs that articulated the pessimism and anxiety of young people' (*Music Central 96*), fuelled by a broadly anti-establishment attitude. The speciality grunge/alternative albums, *The Trip, vols 1–8* (Warner Brothers), show grunge to be a musically disparate **genre**, with noticeable differences in tempo, **rhythm**, and **melody** within a core structure of dominant guitar sounds and pessimistic lyrics. Many grunge performers straddle genres, such as Green Day, who are on the border between grunge and **punk**. Interestingly, there is usually no 'grunge' category at the various music awards (although there is often an **alternative** section, like that won by Pearl Jam at the 1995 **MTV** Awards).

Grunge embraces clothing and attitude as well as music.

The 'grunge look' includes flannel shirts, big baggy shorts, and opportunity-shop clothing. But in reacting against commercialism and capitalism, grunge arguably established a new conformity, as both the music and clothing styles were soon **commodified**. Pearl Jam and Nirvana have been the two most influential bands, credited as leading the commercial breakthrough of grunge/alternative rock into a relatively moribund music scene in the early 1990s. International versions of grunge are Britain's Bush, and Australia's Silverchair. The enormous world-wide response to the 1994 suicide of Kurt Cobain, Nirvana's lead singer, indicated the impact of grunge.

See: **alternative rock/alternative music**; **Seattle sound**
Further reading: Shevory, 1995; Stanford, 1996; Tucker, 1992 (includes discographies).
Listening:
Nirvana, *Nevermind*, Geffen, 1991.
Pearl Jam, *Ten*, Epic, 1991.
The Trip, vols 1–8, Warner Brothers.

hard rock; **cock rock**; **stadium rock**   A loose, amorphous **genre**/style; hard rock is also referred to as heavy rock, cock rock, or stadium rock. The term has been applied since the late 1960s (the Small Faces, The Who) and early 1970s (Bad Company) to a variety of performers whose music was characterized by hard, driving **rhythms**, strong bass drum, use of **backbeat** (on snare), and short **melodies**, limited in pitch range. The formal structure of hard rock songs is largely verse–chorus–verse–chorus–solo (usually played by the lead guitar) –verse–chorus.

Hard rock is also characterized by loud volume and assertive masculinity, evident in the persona of performers, especially vocalists (e.g. Roger Daltrey, Robert Plant, Axl Rose) and lead guitarists, and the genre's predominantly male following. **Cock rock** emerged as an alternative term for hard rock, highlighting the genre's often explicit and aggressive expression of male sexuality, its sometimes misogynist lyrics, and its phallic imagery. Cock rock performers were regarded as aggressive, dominating, and boastful, a stance, it was argued, evident in their live shows (see Frith and McRobbie, 1990; Reynolds and Press, 1995).

Early hard rock styles drew on **R & B** (eg. The Who), and overlapped with forms of **heavy metal** (eg. Deep Purple). The Who fused melody and raw percussive power, extending the structural limitations of early **rock'n'roll**. In the United

States in the 1980s, hard rock became associated with **stadium rock**, so called because of large-scale concerts held in sports stadiums by bands such as Journey, Loverboy, and Foreigner. Other leading hard rock performers in the 1980s and 1990s included Australia's Cold Chisel (and a solo Jimmy Barnes), Van Halen, The Cult, Bon Jovi, and Aerosmith.

See: **gender**
Further reading: Dunbar-Hall and Hodge, 1993; Marsh, 1992.
Listening:
The Who, *Live at Leeds*, MCA, 1970.
Bad Company, *10 From 6*, Atlantic, 1986.
Guns N'Roses, *Appetite for Destruction*, Geffen, 1987.
Deep Purple, *Smoke on the Water: The Best of Deep Purple*, EMI, 1994.
Viewing: *The Song Remains the Same* (Peter Clifton and Joe Massot, 1976, on Led Zeppelin); *The Kids Are Alright* (Polygram, 1984, on The Who).

hardcore   Part of the US underground in the late 1970s, hardcore developed out of **punk** and was linked with **grunge** and **alternative rock**. By the late 1990s the label had become a cliché. 'Uncompromising' is the word often used to characterize the **genre**. Originally harder and faster than its direct ancestor, **punk rock**, hardcore took punk music and 'sped up the tempos as fast as humanely possible, sticking largely to monochrome guitars, bass and drums, and favoring half-shouted lyrics venting the most inflammatory sentiments the singers and songwriters could devise' (Erlewine *et al.*, 1995: 917).

While internationally in evidence, hardcore's chief breeding ground was the United States. The genre was strongest in the San Francisco Bay area (the Dead Kennedys, Black Flag, the Circle Jerks), and Washington DC (Minor Threat, the Bad Brains). British hardcore and post-punk bands were noted for their melodically minimal, percussive structures (Wire, The Fall). Politics were left of centre, but enmeshed in a mass of contradictions, for instance that hardcore was against sexism and racism, but its performers were generally white and male. Nearly all (early) hardcore bands were on small, **independent** labels. A number of alternative bands had their roots in hardcore, before broadening the scope of their music and signing with **major** labels (e.g. Hüsker Dü, X, the Replacements).

See: **alternative**; **thrash**

Further reading: Erlewine *et al.*, 1995; Tucker, 1992 (includes discography).

Listening:

Wire, *Pink Flag*, Restless, 1977.

The Dead Kennedys, *Fresh Fruit for Rotting Vegetables*, Alternative Tentacles, 1980.

Black Flag, *Damaged I*, SST, 1981.

Viewing: The Decline of Western Civilization, Part One (Penelope Spheeris, 1981): the Los Angeles punk/hardcore scene circa 1981, featuring Black Flag, the Circle Jerks, X, and the Germs.

harmony   The simultaneous sounding of two or more different notes at the same time, such as in guitar chords, blocks of notes on the piano, and the sounds of a chorus. The easiest place to hear harmonies is in the background melodies. Harmony varies from simple to complex, and often distinguishes one style from another. It is important in popular music because it provides the texture of the total sound.

See: **a capella**; **doo-wop**; **melody**
Further reading: Brown, 1992.

heavy metal   The musical parameters of heavy metal (HM) as a **genre** cannot be comfortably reduced to formulaic terms. It is usually louder, 'harder', and faster-paced than conventional **rock** music, and remains predominantly guitar-oriented. The main instruments are electric guitars (lead and bass), drums, and electronic keyboards, but there are numerous variants within this basic framework. Some forms of the genre have enjoyed enormous commercial success, and have a large **fan** base; other, 'harder' **subgenres** have a cult following.

Heavy metal is frequently criticized as incorporating the worst excesses of **popular music**, notably its perceived narcissism and sexism, and it is also often musically dismissed. Even Lester Bangs, one of the few rock critics to view the emergence of heavy metal favourably, wrote of the genre:

As its detractors have always claimed, heavy-metal rock is nothing more than a bunch of noise; it is not music, it's distortion – and that is precisely why its adherents find it appealing. Of all contemporary rock, it is the genre most closely identified with violence and aggression, rapine and carnage. Heavy metal orchestrates technological nihilism (Bangs, 1992c: 459).

Heavy metal was one of the main targets of moves to censor popular music in the 1980s.

Until the publication of Weinstein's comprehensive sociological study (1991a), and Walser's more musically grounded treatment (1993), there were few attempts to discuss the genre seriously. Yet heavy metal displays a musical cogency and enjoys a mass appeal, existing within a set of social relations. There is a well-developed heavy metal **subculture**, predominantly working class, white, young, and male, identifying with the phallic imagery of guitars and the general muscularity and oppositional orientation of the form (there is some debate here: see Walser, 1993). The symbols associated with heavy metal, which include Nazi insignia and Egyptian and Biblical symbols, provide a signature of identification with the genre, being widely adopted by metal's youth cult following (see Arnett, 1996). The genre has maintained its high market profile into the 1990s, despite critical derision and a negative public image.

There are a number of identifiable heavy metal subgenres, or closely related styles, including:

1 heavy/**hard rock**: uses a classic guitar, drums, vocalist line-up. Examples: Deep Purple; Def Leppard; Aerosmith;
2 classic metal: emerged in the 1970s, partly as a 'return to basics' in the face of the excesses of progressive and art

161

rock; it features high-pitched, often wailing vocals, and extended guitar solos. Examples: Black Sabbath; AC/DC;

3 soft/lite metal: a more accessible, commercial style, strong on visual impact, which draws on and intersects with **glam rock**. The subgenre enjoyed huge commercial success in the late 1980s, and was largely responsible for breaking heavy metal with **MTV** and **radio**. Examples: Poison; Kiss; Van Halen; Bon Jovi;

4 funk metal: a more contemporary form, less structured than earlier forms of metal, with the bass guitar relied on more than the lead. Examples: Suicidal Tendencies; Red Hot Chili Peppers;

5 death metal: characterized by a grating vocal, though the music itself ranges from the intensely **hardcore** to 'mellow' with samples. Examples: Death; Pestilence;

6 **thrash metal/speed metal**: typified by clean, clear guitar riffs, and a focused sound overall; generally quite fast, though bands often include slower songs. Examples: Anthrax; Metallica;

7 Christian metal: lyrics drawing on the Bible and Christian values, but within a metal music framework. Example: Mortification;

8 industrial metal: greater use of sampling and computer technology. Example: Ministry.

A much-debated question is why a genre generally panned by the critics (and many other music fans) as formulaic noise, associated with a negative social stance and consequent public controversy, is so popular. Breen argues that the rise of heavy metal is linked to 'firstly, a search for substance and **authenticity** in rock music and, secondly, to advanced methods of marketing music for mass **consumption**' (Breen, 1991: 194; see also Weinstein, 1991a: ch. 4).

See: **glam rock**; **hard rock**; **thrash metal/speed metal**
Further reading: Arnett, 1996; Bangs, 1992c; Cooper, 1993; Eddy, 1992; Kotarba, 1994; Walser, 1993; Weinstein, 1991a; Weisband *et al.*, 1995.
Listening: AC/DC, *Back in Black*, Atco, 1980.

Van Halen, *1984*, Warner Brothers, 1984.

Metallica, *And Justice For All*, Elektra, 1988.

Ministry, *The Mind Is a Terrible Thing to Taste*, Sire, 1989.

Red Hot Chili Peppers, *Blood Sugar Sex Magik*, Warner Brothers, 1991.

Viewing: *Dancing in the Street*, episode 7, 'Hang On To Yourself'; *The Decline of Western Civilization, Part Two: The Heavy Metal Years* (Penelope Spheeris, 1988).

hegemony   Italian **Marxist** theoretician Antonio Gramsci's concept of ideological (or cultural) hegemony was advanced to explain how a ruling class maintains its dominance by achieving a popular consensus mediated through the various institutions of society, including the mass media. Hegemony mystifies and conceals existing power relations and social arrangements. Particular ideas and rules are constructed as natural and universal 'common-sense' and the popular media play a leading role in this process. Hegemony operates in the realms of consciousness and representations, making popular cultural forms important contributors to its formation and maintainence (see O'Sullivan *et al.*, 1994, for a succinct elaboration).

In relation to popular music, hegemony has been utilized to examine the manner in which song **lyrics** and **music videos** underpin dominant conceptions of **gender**, **sexuality**, and **ethnicity**; to investigate the cultural symbolic challenge offered by **youth subcultures** to mainstream, dominant society (e.g. Abrams, 1995); and, perhaps most significantly, to analyse the Anglo-American international dominance of the music industry and its styles. This dominance has waned in recent years, with the reassertion of the European market and the emergence of Japanese media conglomerates as major players in the music industry, but the Anglo-American market remains of major importance, not least for its commercial legitimation of emergent trends. Aside from its market share, the Anglo-American music industries established and continue to privilege particular formats and working practices as 'natural' and accepted, especially those associated with 'international repertoire' (Negus, 1996: 174).

See: **cultural imperialism**; **globalization**; **lyric analysis**; **sub-cultures**

high culture   The high culture tradition emerged during the nineteenth century; it was essentially a conservative defence of a narrowly defined high or elite 'culture', in the classic sense of 'the best that has been thought and said' (Arnold, 1869). This asserted an artistic conception of culture: the only real and **authentic** culture is art, against which everything else is set. It views the valued civilized culture of an elite minority as constantly under attack from a majority or **mass culture** which is unauthentic and a denial of 'the good life'. Its analytic emphasis is on evaluation and discrimination; a search for the true values of civilization, commonly to be found in Renaissance art, the great nineteenth-century novels, and so on. The high culture tradition includes the work of various cultural commentators, including F.R. Leavis, T.S. Eliot, Abbs, Bloom, and most recently Roger Scruton. Elements of it are evident in **Marxist**-oriented critiques of mass culture: the **Frankfurt School**, Raymond Williams *et al.* ('left culturalism').

The high cultural critique of **popular culture** has frequently vehemently attacked **popular music**. While such a view can be traced back to Plato, it emerged more forcefully with the massive social changes of the nineteenth century. For example, writing in 1839, Sir John Herschel claimed: 'Music and dancing (the more's the pity) have become so closely associated with ideas of riot and debauchery among the less cultivated classes, that a taste for them, for their own sakes, can hardly be said to exist, and before they can be recommended as innocent or safe amusements, a very great change of ideas must take place' (cited in Frith, 1983: 39). A succession of commentators have regarded much popular music as mindless fodder, cynically manufactured for mindless youthful consumers. Bloom, for instance, claims that **rock**

presents life as 'a nonstop commercial prepackaged mastur-
bational fantasy' (1987), which he charges as responsible for
the atrophy of the minds and bodies of youth.

Underpinning such views are assumptions about the potentially disruptive nature of 'the popular', and the need for
social control and the regulation of popular pleasures. The
high culture view of popular culture has been criticized for
failing to recognize the active nature of popular culture
consumption; failing to treat the cultural forms seriously on
their own terms; biased by **aesthetic** prejudices, which are
rarely explicated; and resting on outmoded class-based notions
of a high–low culture split. The traditionally claimed distinctions between high and low culture have become blurred.
High art has been increasingly commodified and commercialized, while some forms of popular culture have become
more 'respectable', receiving **State** funding and broader
critical acceptance.

The high culture perspective remains evident in the application of aesthetics to popular music, and the tendency of
musicology to ignore or dismiss popular music **genres**. It
also underpins some State attitudes towards the funding and
regulation of cultural forms. At an everyday level, it is implicit
in the manner in which musicians, fans, and critics make
distinctions of value both between and within particular
genres.

See: **audiences**; **culture**; **Frankfurt School**
Further reading: Abbs, 1975; Bloom, 1987; Hall and Whannel, 1964;
Swingewood, 1977.

hip-hop – *see* **rap**

hippies – *see* **counter culture**

history; **social history (of popular music)**   As a field of
study, the history of popular music has been subject to internal
critiques and debates in a similar manner to other forms of

historical writing. At issue are the boundaries of the field, including its tendency to privilege Western developments; the treatment of various **genres** within it; and the emphasis which should be accorded to the context within which popular music is produced: the producers of music, the music, and its fans and the processes of consumption.

The history of popular music, especially in relation to the emergence of **rock'n'roll** and its subsequent generic development and mutation, has usually been presented in a fairly standard form, based around a chronological sequence of genres (see Bradley, 1992; Friedlander, 1996; Garofalo, 1997; Mitchell, 1996). This sees it as essentially a Western tradition, and privileges rock'n'roll and the genres it mutated into. This tradition has been critiqued as 'rockist' (e.g. by Negus, 1996; on this point, see **popular music**).

The various histories display a tendency to emphasize performers, genres, and texts, with rather less attention to the role of technology and economics. An example of this approach is the weight usually attached to the role of creative individuals in establishing rock'n'roll in the 1950s: Elvis Presley, Little Richard, Bill Haley, Buddy Holly, and Chuck Berry are seen to have virtually created the genre and revitalized popular music in the process. At one level, the impact of these performers is undisputed – even though they were adapting existing styles and forms, they were clearly innovative (see Gillet, 1983). But as Curtis observes, '*all* popular performers come along at the right time' and 'to explain the success of a given act, you need to make the social and cultural context of that success as specific as possible' (1987: 5). Accordingly, other writers have paid greater attention to the social, economic, and demographic situation in the United States and the United Kingdom in the early 1950s, producing rather different accounts (e.g. Peterson, 1990).

It has been asserted that the **social history** (of popular music) is a field of study in itself:

> Although a genealogy of sorts could be constructed from the eighteenth century, the social history of music is

best viewed as a broad tendency within music scholarship, a loose body of writing seeking, with various degrees of thoroughness and with varying emphases, to consider the social and economic roots and consequences of musical production and consumption (Russell, 1993: 139).

Russell notes that until recently only folk song attracted anything resembling sustained critical attention of this type. This locates the 'tendency' within popular music studies as a form of **ethnomusicology**, ignoring the point that much sociological work takes just such an approach to popular music.

Further reading: Bradley, 1992; DeCurtis and Henke, 1992b; Ennis, 1992; Garofalo, 1997; Negus, 1996; Shuker, 1994.
Viewing: Dancing in the Street.

Hollywood musicals – *see* **film**

home taping – *see* **cassette audio tape**

homology In general terms, a reproduction or repetition of structure (O'Sullivan *et al.*, 1994), applied to popular music homology refers to the 'fit' between lifestyle/values and music preferences. The concept was central to the consideration of the place of music in **youth subcultures** by the subcultural analysts of the 1970s. Their answer to the question 'what specifically does a subcultural style signify to the members of the subculture themselves?', was to identify an homology between the 'focal concerns, activities, group structure and collective self-image' of the subculture, and the cultural artifacts and practices adopted by the members of the subculture. The latter were seen as 'objects in which they could see their central values held and reflected' (Hall and Jefferson, 1976: 56). The case of **skinhead** subculture was often used to demonstrate such an homology. The skins' style of heavy 'bovver' boots, braces, and drastically cropped hair communicated and asserted their values of 'hardness, masculinity and working-classness. The symbolic objects – dress, appearance, language, ritual occasions, styles of interaction, music – were made to form a unity with the group's relations, situation, experience' (ibid.).

The most extensive and theoretically sophisticated applications of the concept of homology to the preferred music of specific subcultures are Willis' study of 'bike boys' (rockers) and **hippies**, *Profane Culture* (1978), and Hebdige's various case studies in his hugely influential study *Subculture: The Meaning of Style* (1979). Willis argued that there existed a 'fit' between certain styles and fashions, cultural values, and group identity; for example, between the intense activism, physical prowess, love of machines, and taboo on introspection of motor-bike boys, and their preference for 1950s **rock'n'roll**. For Hebdige, the **punks** best illustrated the principle:

> The subculture was nothing if not consistent. There was a homological relation between the trashy cut-up clothes and spiky hair, the pogo and the amphetamines, the spitting, the vomiting, the format of the fanzines, the insurrectionary poses and the 'soulless', frantically driven music. The punks wore clothes which were the sartorial equivalent of swear words, and they swore as they dressed – with calculated effect, lacing obscenities into record notes and publicity releases, interviews and love songs (Hebdige, 1979: 114).

See: **punks**; **punk rockers**; **skinheads**; **youth subcultures**
Further reading: Gelder and Thornton, 1997; Hebdige, 1979; Middleton, 1990; Willis, 1978.

hook The melodic or rhythmic pattern that is catchy and 'hooks' or attracts the listener to want to listen to the rest of the song, and, more importantly, want to hear repeated playings.

house music – *see* **dance-music**

I

identity Popular music is an aspect of attempts to define identity at the levels of the self, community, and national. It expresses self-identity through the use of music **consumption** to indicate **cultural capital**, especially in **subcultures**; community identity through notions of **local sounds** and **scenes**; and national identity through cultural policies (e.g. quotas) aimed at promoting locally produced music, and the association of particular **genres** and national settings (e.g. **salsa** and the Caribbean).

Popular music is a component in the processes of the construction of individual identity, or subjectivity. Adherence to a musical genre can be used to distance oneself from the parent culture/community/social authority. For example, in the 1950s, 'while **rock'n'roll** was undoubtedly a moment in the expansion and technological development of the entertainment industry, it was also an instance of the use of foreign music by a generation as a means to distance themselves from a parental "national" culture' (Laing, 1986: 338).

National identity can be regarded as a social construct as much as a quality associated with a physical space. While such identities may be constructed or imagined (see Anderson, 1983), they are mobilized for particular interests, and emerge partly in relation to different 'others'. Popular music can be part of this, as evident in Nazi Germany in the 1930s (see Negus, 1996) and in various national cultural movements (see Garofalo, 1992b).

independents/indies; **indie music**   Indies are small record labels which are independent from the **majors** (at least in terms of the productive and creative process of artist acquisition and promotion), though still reliant on a major for distribution. These labels are frequently considered to be more flexible and innovative in their roster of artists. They have also been associated with the emergence of new **genres**: 'It is an attitude with a sound' (Larkin, 1995: 3). The heart and soul of it resides in record labels such as Creation, 4AD, Sub Pop, Demon, Stiff, and such like.

It has been argued that independent record companies in the 1950s did not have the corporate hierarchy of the majors, and so had greater flexibility in picking up on and promoting new trends and talent, and a greater ability to adjust record production. In companies such as Sun, the owner, record **producer**, sound technician, and promoter were often the same person – Sam Philips in this case (see Millard, 1995: 291–2).

Using a case study of Wax Trax! Records, a Chicago-based industrial dance label, Lee argues that market expansion and the necessary links with majors for distribution force such indies increasingly to adopt the business practices of the majors, in the process moving away from their traditional cultural goals of artistry and creativity. The result is a 'hybrid label – a privately-held company that deals with a major for important production elements or that receives some of its operating funds from a major' (Lee, 1995: 196). The interaction between the majors and independents in such situations, however, remains a dynamic process.

The term **indie music** is used for a broad musical style, primarily equated with **alternative music**. This can be problematic: for instance, in the case of the *Guinness Who's Who of Indie New Wave*, indie music is defined as 'music after the Sex Pistols played by creative on the edge musicians with lots of nice guitars that sound a bit like the Byrds, Velvet Underground and MC5' (Larkin, 1995: 3). Not only does this cover a considerable range of musical styles, but the volume includes 'electro synth' bands like Depeche Mode, basic **rock** bands like the Del Lords ('spirited, emotive rock songs delivered with unreconstructed passion' (ibid.: 113)), and the Dead Kennedys, along with a large number of other **punk** performers.

Both senses of indie are linked to a set of dominant musical values, with **authenticity** at their core. These are cast as diametrically opposed to a stereotyped mainstream. For example, indie music is considered to be raw and immediate, while mainstream music is processed and mediated by 'over-production'; indie bands can reproduce their music in concert and even improve upon it, while mainstream bands use too many electronic effects to reproduce their music live.

See: **alternative**; **authenticity**
Further reading: Lee, 1995

Internet; **World Wide Web**   The Internet (or Net) is a computer-linked global communications technology, with dramatically increasing numbers of people accessing it in the 1990s. The World Wide Web (WWW), a major part of the Internet, is the graphical network that contains Web sites dedicated to one topic, person, or company. These locations are known as 'homepages' and allow seamless jumping to other locations on the Internet. The Net has added a major new dimension to the marketing and reception of popular music, while creating new problems for the enforcement of **copyright**. It includes on-line music shops; Web sites for record companies and performers; on-line music journals; on-line concerts and interviews; Web radio, and bulletin boards. In sum, they represent new ways of interlinking the **audience/consumers** of popular music, the performers, and the **music industry**. Most discussions of the significance of such electronic commerce emphasize the business or economic aspects: the benefits to firms and consumers; the barriers and difficulties associated with doing business via the Net; the demographics of Net users; and the opportunities for companies on the Net.

There are also significant cultural issues associated with popular music on the Net, which link up on-going debates in the study of popular music, such as the relative importance of the music industry and the audience for popular music. The Net may create greater consumer sovereignty and choice by bypassing the traditional intermediaries operating in the music industry (primarily the record companies), but the **majors**, initially slow to recognize its potential, are now developing major sites (see Sony's Michael Jackson site – currently at the address *http://www.music.sony.com/Music/ArtistInfo/MichaelJackson/main.html*). Any new medium or technological form changes the way in which we experience music, and this has implications for how we relate to and consume music. In the case of the Net, the question is what happens to traditional notions of the 'distance' between consumer and product, and its technological mediation. Finally, the nature of intellectual property rights, and the regulation of these, has been brought into even sharper focus with the electronic retrieval possibilities implicit in the Net, and the on-going debates over sampling in popular music texts.

See: **retail**

Further reading: Gurley and Pfefferle, 1996; Hayward, 1995; Mitchell, 1997.

J

jazz; **bebop**; **jazz rock/fusion**; **acid jazz**   As a musical style/
genre, jazz is only briefly considered here, primarily in terms
of its links to and influence on more mainstream popular
music genres, fusing with these to create new forms: jazz
rock/fusion, jazz funk, and acid jazz. Jazz was also the first
home for many musicians who moved over into other genres,
notably **skiffle**.

Established at the beginning of the twentieth century, jazz
was an American idiom developed from **ragtime**, **blues**, and
popular music of its day. The key component of jazz was
improvization, in which each performance represents an original and spontaneous creation. Its subsequent genesis spawned
increasingly varied and disparate **subgenres**, spreading regionally from Southern centres to generate distinct styles in St
Louis, Kansas City, Chicago, New York, and beyond.

> Key styles include, but are not limited to, traditional (or
> Dixieland) jazz, swing, bebop, cool jazz, free jazz and
> fusion; recent years have seen renaissances for older styles
> and new fusions alike, from the 'New Traditionalists' of
> the '80s to the acid jazz and hip-bop of the '90s, stirring
> frequent debate even as they reinvent and extend the jazz
> influence across new generations   (*Music Central 96*).

Major jazz artists, who at times shifted between these styles,
include Benny Goodman, Duke Ellington, Dave Brubeck,

Ella Fitzgerald, Count Basie, Sarah Vaughan, Billie Holliday, Louis Armstrong, Miles Davis, John Coltrane, Thelonious Monk, Charlie Parker, and Wynton Marsalis.

Further reading: Carr *et al.*, 1988; Fordham, 1991.

Chronologically these styles are termed premodern (pre-1940), and the more diverse modern (post-1940). It is the latter styles which I am concerned with here, concentrating on two which exerted considerable influence on mainstream popular music: bebop, and jazz rock/fusion.

Bebop is an alliterative word possibly derived from the cry of 'arriba' heard in the Latin American bands of the period. Developed initially in New York, bebop was the popular name given to early modern jazz developments of the 1940s: 'a deliberate attempt by serious jazz musicians to move jazz away from the simple harmonies and basic rhythms of the earlier styles . . . Employing extended chordal harmonies and broken rhythms, bop changed the face of jazz' (Hardy and Laing, 1991). Leading exponents included Dizzy Gillespie, Charlie Parker, and Thelonious Monk. The name fell out of use as the style became more broadly incorporated into modern jazz. Bebop's link with mainstream popular music was via the **beats** in the 1950s; its adoption as part of the musical palette utilized by some **progressive** and **art rock** performers in the 1960s and 1970s; and, more recently, as an element in some styles of **drum'n'bass**.

Further reading: Owens, 1995.
Listening:
Thelonious Monk, *Something in Blue*, Black Lion, 1972.

The term **fusion** is variously used to designate the amalgamation of two styles of music, as in the fusion of folk and rock to form **folk rock**, a mix of electric and acoustic instrumentation and sounds. The term is most commonly applied to the music produced by the fusion of jazz and rock, **jazz rock**. Jazz rock combines jazz improvization with the instrumentation and rhythm of **R & B**, employing technology to a greater extent, such as replacing the piano with the electric piano and the synthesizer. The more 'jazz-oriented' versions are usually refered to as fusion, while some commentators prefer the term **jazz rock fusion** (Gammond, 1991). The most critical and commercially successful rock-oriented exponents include Return to Forever, Blood, Sweat and Tears, and Weather Report who had creative peaks in the early 1970s. Other musicians to work in a jazz rock vein include Stanley Clarke, Chick Corea, Miles Davis, Larry Coryell, and John McLaughlin.

Acid jazz is a popular **dance** genre of the late 1980s and 1990s, which combines elements of jazz, **hip-hop**, **funk**, and **R & B**. It has been primarily a singles medium (for representative compilations, see *Acid Jazz: Collection* 1, Scotti Brothers).

Listening:

Blood, Sweat and Tears, 'Spinning Wheel', on *Greatest Hits*, CBS, 1972.

Weather Report, *Mysterious Traveller*, Columbia, 1974.

Jeff Beck, *Blow By Blow*, Epic, 1975.

jungle – *see* **dance-music**

labelling theory – *see* **moral panic**

lifestyle – *see* **taste cultures**

listening   Listening is a physical process which is situated in social contexts and mediated by technology. Considerations of these aspects of listening have been a small but significant part of popular music studies. Listening to music is an activity which takes place with varying levels of intensity, influenced by the **consumption** context and the style of the performer: 'the "distracted" environment of many club settings and the hushed concentration typical of singer-songwriter concerts might represent two extremes' (Middleton, 1990: 95). More melodious and 'non-abrasive' styles of music form the staple of **radio** 'easy listening', and the loose **genre** of 'lounge music', while louder genres (e.g. **heavy metal; hard rock**) have been seen as dangerous to the listener's hearing. The development of headphones and the Walkman enabled different styles of listening, while reconfiguring the social locations and contexts within which it occurred (see Millard, 1995).

   Negus identifies two groups of listeners focused on by Adorno and later theorists: those lost in the crowd, and easily manipulated into the collectivity, and obsessive individuals, alienated and not fully integrated into social life, with both types part of the anxieties of moral guardians (Negus, 1996: ch. 1). Adorno saw the mass culture products of the music industry as requiring very little effort on the part of listeners. He argued that it led to 'de-concentrated listening in which listeners rejected anything which was unfamiliar, regressing to "child-like" behaviour' (1991: 44–5). One facet of this was what Adorno termed 'quotation listening', where instead of listening to a piece of music and trying to grasp it as a whole, the regressive listener dwelt only on the most obvious aspects of melody. In the process listeners adopted a 'musical child's language' and responded to different works 'as if the symphony were structurally the same as a ballad' (cited in Negus, 1996: 9). Adorno referred disparagingly to the category of 'easy listening', which he regarded as an example of the music industry deliberately encouraging distracted audience activity, with an emphasis on the most familiar harmonies, rhythms, and melodies, with a 'soporific' effect on social consciousness. Adorno saw this as fulfilling an ideological function in pacifying the listening audience and making them unable to reflect critically on their world.

This view of passive listening has been challenged, especially by the active **audience** paradigm which has been prominent in much recent media/**cultural studies**.

Further reading: Middleton, 1990; Negus, 1996.

live performance – *see* performance

Liverpool sound/Merseybeat   Historically, the Liverpool sound emerged with the Beatles *et al.* in the early 1960s. While it was marketed as such, its musical characteristics and coherence are debatable, although the performers were mainly part of **British beat**. Cohen has conceptualized the (contemporary as well as historical) Liverpool sound as a complex amalgam of factors, incorporating a variety of regional, national, and international influences, but all particular to Liverpool, and reflecting 'a range of social, economic and political factors peculiar to the city' (1994a: 117). She relies on the way in which Liverpool musicians situate themselves and their music, especially in relation to other sounds/**scenes**. As Negus observes, however, this is to 'impose a meaning on the music that is grounded more in inter-city rivalries than actual sounds' (1996: 185).

See: **British beat**; **geography**; **locality**
Further reading: Cohen, 1994a; Negus, 1996.

locality; **local scenes**; **local sounds**   Locality is emerging as a key concept in contemporary popular music studies, picking up on trends in cultural **geography**. The basic emphasis is on exploring the role and effectiveness of music as a means of defining locality. The rhetoric of the music press commonly makes reference to where, in the geographic sense, bands have come from. Similarly, **fans** and academic studies both uphold the notion of local sounds/**scenes**. As Street observes, the questions to be asked here are 'whether local factors shape the production and consumption of the music; and whether the locality effects the meaning of the music' (1995: 255).

Locality has been used in a number of overlapping ways in popular music studies:

1 to explore the relationship between dominant centres/the major companies and the periphery, with particular emphasis on the operation/validity of **cultural imperialism**. Here locality becomes a marker of political experience, juxtaposed against the other to ideologically valorize and support local musics;
2 the way in which music has frequently been used to express conceptions of homeland or national, regional, or community **identity**. This can take the form of sexual identity, such as the production of spaces of musical reception for the 'queer' community (Valentine, 1995);
3 locality as a social experience, linked to songwriters as a theme and as a means to authenticate their music (e.g. Bruce Springsteen, John Lee Hooker);

4 the notion of localized scenes/sounds. Particular geographic locales, usually cities or regions, are identified with
a **sound**, like the **Liverpool sound**, **San Francisco
sound**, **Seattle sound**, and Chicago **blues**. Somewhat
contiguous with this usage is the notion of scene: for
example, Athens, Georgia, since the late 1980s; Seattle in
the 1990s. This implies a range of activities, loosely centred
around and aligned to a particular style of music and its
associated performers. Aside from exploring the characteristics of such scenes, a central interest in popular music
studies has been the question of *why* they develop at a
specific location at a particular time (see **alternative
scenes**). Also 'we must question the underpinning assumption that sound and location are in some way connected'
(Street, 1995: 256). In several instances, local music production has revitalized industry following a decline that resulted
from global restructuring (Hudson, 1995).

Cohen suggests locality could be most usefully used in
popular music studies in an anthropological sense:

> to discuss networks of social relationships, practices, and
> processes extending across particular places; to imply a
> methodological orientation concerned with the partic-
> ular rather than the general, the concrete rather then
> the abstract. It could also emphasise interconnections
> and interdependencies between, for example, space and
> time, the contextual and the conceptual, the individual
> and the collective, the self and other   (1995: 65).

See: **alternative music scenes**; **cultural imperialism**; **Dunedin
sound**; **geography**; **identity**; **Liverpool sound**; **San
Francisco sound**
Further reading: Cohen, 1995; De Curtis and Henke, 1992a; Fenster,
1995; Negus, 1996: ch. 6; Street, 1995.

lyric analysis Much textual analysis of popular music has
largely concentrated on the lyrical component of songs. In a
significant historical discussion, 'Why Do Songs Have

Words?', Frith shows how through the 1950s and 1960s the sociology of popular music was dominated by the analysis of the words of songs. This was largely because such an approach was grounded in a familiar research methodology – content analysis – and assumed 'that it was possible to read back from lyrics to the social forces that produced them' (Frith, 1988b: 106). This approach has continued to be important, although its application has been tempered.

There are numerous examples of attempts to analyse song lyrics as examples of shifts in popular ideologies of sex, romance, and relationships. These frequently emphasize lyrics as mirrors of social, political, and personal issues:

> The attitudes and values portrayed in modern tunes demand the reflective consideration of students because they strike at the heart of the major social and political issues of our time: ecology, women's liberation, political cynicism, militarism, drug abuse, and others. Likewise, the literary images and linguistic configurations presented in popular lyrics are as fascinating as communication vehicles, particularly when they reveal rich patterns of attitudes, values, and beliefs. In short, contemporary songs are invaluable tools for pursuing the twin educational goals of self-knowledge and social analysis   (Cooper, 1981: 8; see also Cooper, 1992).

Given that songwriters are social beings, the words of the songs do express general social attitudes, and are worth study. But

> they treat lyrics too simply. The words of all songs are of equal value; their meaning is taken to be transparent; no account is given of their actual performance or their musical setting. Even more problematically, these analysts tend to equate a song's popularity to public agreement with the message   (Frith, 1988b: 107).

Songs create identification through their emotional appeal, but this does not necessarily mean that they can be reduced to a simple slogan or message.

Lyric analysis also tends to valorize certain forms of popular music, most notably **blues**, **soul**, and **country**, and some varieties of **rock** – especially that of the **singer songwriter** (Bob Dylan, Randy Newman, etc.). These are seen as 'the authentic expression of popular experiences and needs', whereas mainstream popular music song lyrics are largely seen in terms of **mass culture** arguments, and criticized for their banality and lack of depth (Adorno, 1941; Hoggart, 1957). In a left-wing version of this critique, Harker (1980) reads off **Tin Pan Alley** lyrics as straightforward statements of bourgeois **hegemony**, equating pop's central themes of love and romance with the 'sentimental ideology' of capitalist society. Conversely, Harker argues for '**authentic**' lyrics as the expression of 'authentic' relationships, with both reflecting direct experience, unmediated by ideology.

Part of the argument for rock music's superiority over **pop** and earlier forms of popular music rested on the claim that its major songwriters were poets. Richard Goldstein's *The Poetry of Rock* (New York: Bantam, 1969) and similar anthologies helped popularize this view. Frith (1988b: 117) points out that this work has emphasized a particular form of rock lyrics – those akin to romantic poetry with lots of covert and obscure allusions. This approach attempts to validate rock in terms of established 'art' forms, elevating the role of the lyrical **auteur** figure and the ability to work in a recognizably high cultural mode. An extension of this position is the relegation of mainstream commercial rock/pop lyrics to banality and worthlessness. Yet clearly such lyrics do in some sense matter to their listeners: *Smash Hits*, focusing on the words of the latest chart entries, remains Britain's biggest selling pop magazine. Frith suggests that the more critical question is 'how do words and voices work differently for different types of pop and audience?' (Frith 1988b: 121). This necessitates addressing how song lyrics work as ordinary language.

Further reading: Cooper, 1992; Frith, 1988b; Garon, 1975; Harker, 1980; Negus, 1996.

M

majors The international record industry is dominated by the six large international companies commonly referred to as the majors. They are: Thorn/EMI (UK-based); Bertelsmann (Germany); Sony (Japan); Time/Warner (USA); MCA (formerly Japan; recently purchased by Canadian-owned company Seagram); and Philips (Holland). 'Middle range' companies (Virgin, Motown, Island) have been absorbed by the majors, while the smaller **independents** are often closely linked to the majors through distribution deals. The music majors are part of a battle for global dominance of media markets, reflecting companies' attempts to control both hardware and software markets, and distribute their efforts across a range of media products – a process labelled 'synergy' – which enables maximization of product tie-ins and marketing campaigns and, consequently, profits.

Each major is part of a larger communications or electronics conglomerate. Some recent corporate reshuffles have produced this configuration, most prominently Sony's purchase of CBS for some $2 billion in 1988. Each major has branches throughout the Americas and Europe, and, in most cases, in parts of Asia, Africa, and Australasia. Each embraces a number of record labels: the Philips labels include Polydor, Deutsche Gramophon, Phonogram, and Decca; the Sony labels include CBS, Epic, and Def Jam. (For an outline of the organization and activities of each of the majors, and their Web sites, see Burnett, 1996; also Barnet and Cavanagh, 1994.)

The market share exercised by the majors varies from country to country, but in some cases is over 90 per cent. There is considerable debate over the economic and cultural implications of such market dominance, especially the strength of local music industries in relation to marked trends toward the **globalization** of the culture industries. Some commentators see the natural corollary of such concentrations of ownership as an ability to essentially determine, or at the very least strongly influence, the nature of the demand for particular forms of popular culture. On the other hand, more optimistic media analysts, with a preference for human agency, emphasize the individual consumer's freedom to choose, their ability to decide how and where cultural **texts** are to be used, and the meanings and messages to be associated with them. The debate in this area is one of emphasis, since clearly both sets of influences/determinations are in operation.

See: **globalization**
Further reading: Burnett, 1996; Cusic, 1996; Negus, 1992; Wallis and Malm, 1992.

managers In industrial organizations which are part of the **culture industries**, those working in management act as important cultural intermediaries. Although not directly integrated into the music industry, managers operating within it play an active role in the production of particular artists and styles of music. Indeed, such managers often have the reputation of being 'starmakers and svengalis', manipulating their artists' music and image. In the 1950s and 1960s, several UK managers (e.g. Larry Parnes) were dominating father-figures for their artists, but managers more usually operate as representatives and advisers, handling the myriad details of daily business decisions, including arranging media interviews and promotional appearances, dealing with correspondence, maintaining record company relations, and organizing **tours** and

concerts. Ideally, managers contribute to the formation of career strategies, resolve conflict and ambiguity, communicate effectively with the different parties involved, control the allocation of resources wisely, shield artists from criticism, and generally provide knowledgable leadership and advice to artists. In the process, they can be influential in determining the prevailing climate of the music industry within which they function.

See: **cultural intermediaries**
Further reading: Cusic, 1996; Negus, 1992; Rogan, 1988.

Manchester sound   A loose **genre** label, popularized by the British music press in the early 1990s, though more of a **scene** than a distinct sound. Manchester is an example of the role of **geography** in forging a distinctive orientation to localized **alternative music**. Since the late 1970s, Manchester has been associated with several styles of **indie**/alternative music:

> in the late 1970s and early 80s, the post-punk sound of Joy Division, which mutated into New Order; 'bedsit blues' in the mid 1980s with the Smiths and James; and the tempo and mood was revived around 1988, in the wake of 'Acid House', with the arrival of the club-and-Ecstasy sounds of 'Madchester', led by the Happy Mondays, the Stone Roses and Oldham's Inspiral Carpets   (Halfacree and Kitchin, 1996).

All three periods and styles fed off the association with Manchester: the songs often included clear geographical references and reflected localized feelings and experiences; **record covers** and other promotional imagery incorporated place-related references; and a network of alternative record labels (especially Factory Records), venues, and an active local press created a supportive network for the bands and their followers. The initial success of the Manchester scene opened the way for many of the **Britpop** bands of the 1990s.

See: **geography**; **locality**

Further reading: Halfacree and Kitchen, 1996; Rogan, 1992.
Listening:
The Smiths, *Strangeways Here We Come*, Rough Trade Records, 1987.
The Stone Roses, *The Stone Roses*, Silvertone, 1989.
James, *Laid*, Polygram, 1993.

market cycles An influential attempt to explain both the emergence of **rock'n'roll** in the 1950s, and subsequent shifts in popular music, is the market cycles explanation developed initially by Peterson and Berger (1975). This suggests that original musical ideas and styles, generated more or less spontaneously, are taken up by the record industry, which then popularizes them and adheres to them as the standard form. Meanwhile new creative trends emerge which have to break through the new orthodoxy.

Thus develops a cycle of innovation and consolidation, a cycle reflected in the shifting pattern of economic **concentration** and market control in the **music industry**. Monopolistic conglomerates are formed during periods of market stability, and inhibit the growth of **independents**, which are usually the source of new ideas. Yet under conditions of oligopoly there is also a growing unsated demand, from those who are not satisfied with the prevailing product available. Bursts of musical innovation – rock'n'roll, the **San Francisco sound**, **punk** – are often associated with **youth subcultures**, who help draw attention to them. Small record labels emerge to pioneer the new sound and style, followed by reconcentration and market stagnation once more as the **majors** regain control. The main evidence used by Peterson and Berger is the relative **chart** shares (in the Top 20) of the competing labels and the relative chart performance of established artists, and new and emerging artists. Subsequent research used a similar approach, but with conflicting conclusions (see **concentration**).

While the market cycles thesis offers an economic rationale for the bewildering historical shifts in popular music tastes, there have been a number of criticisms of it. There are methodological difficulties posed by its (initial) reliance on commercially successful singles, with the underlying assumption that the diversity of rock music is to be found in the hit parade. This overlooks the predominance of **album** sales over **singles** since the early 1970s, and the generally accepted tendency to accord greater **aesthetic** weight to the longer format. Further, it sees market diversity as a direct function of the number of individual hit records in any one year. To confirm this argument it would be necessary to undertake a critical stylistic analysis of the actual recordings that were hits, on the basis of their musical features rather than the companies that released them. It could also be argued that the products of the independents are by no means always characterized by innovation. Indeed, frequently they themselves copied styles already popularized by their major competitors. Finally, as Peterson and Berger themselves acknowledge, the distinction between majors and independents has not been clear-cut since about 1970, while the two tiers of the industry have historically been linked through the majors' control of distribution.

See: **concentration**; **independents**; **majors**
Further reading: Christenson, 1995; Lopes, 1992; Peterson and Berger, 1975; Rothenbuhler and Dimmick, 1982.

marketing; **retail**   Marketing has come to play a crucial role in the circulation of cultural commodities. It is a complex practice, involving several related activities: research, product planning and design, packaging, publicity and promotion, pricing policy, and sales and distribution, and is closely tied to merchandising and retailing. Central to the process is product positioning and imbuing cultural products with social significance to make them attractive to consumers. (For insightful discussions of this, see Ewen, 1988; Ryan, 1992.) In popular music this has centred on the marketing of **genre** styles and **stars**, these having come to function in a similar manner to brand names, 'serving to order demand and stabilize sales patterns' (Ryan, 1992: 185). **Fashion** is a crucial dimension: the commodity is designed to attract the attention and interest of shoppers: 'commodity **aesthetics**' necessitate the construction of a desirable appearance around the commodity, to stimulate the desire to purchase and possess. In the marketing process, cultural products become a contested terrain of signification.

It is noteworthy that by the 1990s the cant term for music within the industry was 'product'. This relates to popular music being an increasingly **commodified** product: merchandise to be packaged and sold. The music can be reproduced in various formats – vinyl, **cassette audio tape**, **CD**, DAT, and **music video** – and variations within these: the dance mix, the cassette single, the limited collector's edition, and so on. These can then be disseminated in a variety of ways – through **radio** airplay, **discos** and dance **clubs**, **television** music video shows and **MTV**-style channels, and live **concert** performances. Accompanying these can be advertising, reviews of the record or performance, and interviews with the performer(s) in the various publications of the **music press**. In addition there is the assorted paraphernalia available to the **fan**, especially the posters and the t-shirts. Further, there is the use of popular music within **film soundtracks** and television advertising. The range of these products enables a multimedia approach to the marketing of the music, and a maximization of sales potential, as exposure in each of the various forms strengthens the appeal of the others.

The marketing of popular music includes the use of genre labels as signifiers, radio formatting practices, and standardized production processes (e.g. Stock, Aitken, and Waterman and **dance pop** in the 1980s). Above all, it involves utilizing star images, linking stars and their music with the needs/demands/emotions/desires of **audiences**.

In terms of the everyday operation of the **music industry**, marketing has been examined in several studies, with particular attention paid to industry personnel responsible for advertising and sales, and the promotional role of radio, music video, and the music press. There is less critical examination of aspects such as packaging (e.g. **record covers**, performers' dress codes), and the retailing of popular music. On this last point, as Du Gay and Negus observe, the record shop has been strangely absent from most popular music histories, and neglected or merely mentioned in passing in accounts of its production and consumption. They demonstrate that recent and 'profound transformations in the distribution system have led to retailers exercising an increased influence within the music industry' (1994: 396). The deployment of new technologies in Electronic Data Processing, combined with greater **concentration** of music retailing, have permitted retail, distribution, and production 'to be arranged as an interconnected logistic package', allowing 'music retailers to delineate, construct and monitor the "consumer" of recorded music more intricately than ever before' (ibid.). This is a trend, exemplified by the rise of 'megastores', that would bear further investigation.

See: **commodification**; **memorabilia**; **stars**
Further reading: Chapple and Garofalo, 1977; Featherstone, 1987; Negus, 1992.

Marxism A social theory based on the nineteenth-century views of Karl Marx and Friedrich Engels, who saw human history as a process rooted in people's material needs and changing modes of production (historical materialism), which 'in the last analysis' determine the nature of class structure. Class struggle and the emergence of socialism were central to this classic Marxist analysis. A very influential critique of capitalism, and imperialism as its highest form, Marxism has informed the subsequent development of social theory, mutating into a range of Marxist perspectives on society. The major variants of Marxism differ in terms of their relative emphasis on base (the classical Marxist term for economic structures – the forces of production, relations of production, and mode of production), and superstructure (the family, schools, the church, etc.), the role of social class as a determinant, and the nature and operation of ideology. Marxism has been a major theory informing media and cultural studies, especially through **political economy**. (*Further reading:* Boyd-Barrett and Newbold, 1995; Curran, Morley and Walkerdine, 1996; Milner, 1991; Storey, 1993.)

The validity of Marxist approaches, especially in their classical variants (see Adorno's views), have been the subject of extended debate within popular music studies. While few writers on popular music would consider themselves 'Marxist', Marxian perspectives and concepts have informed (i) discussions of the music industry and its international operation (see **cultural imperialism, globalization**); (ii) the examination of the constitution of popular music **audiences** and **subcultures**; and (iii) studies of the constitution of individual subjectivities and social structures, through the intersection of popular music with **class**, **ethnicity**, and **gender**.

See: **cultural studies**; **Frankfurt School**; **political economy**
Further reading: Chapple and Garofalo, 1977; Harker, 1980; Rosselson, 1979.

mass culture/society – *see* **culture**

mediation

> The act of interpreting between two parties in order to effect/affect a relationship between them; the act of channelling social knowledge and cultural values through an institutional agency to an audience. Mediation is taken to be one of the primary purposes of the mass media: they are the corporate mediators between the various fragmented groups, classes, and hierarchies of a modern society (O'Sullivan *et al.*, 1994).

Applied to popular music, mediation refers to how media forms (**radio**, **music video**, etc.) re-present music to the listener. Negus has been prominent in developing the concept of mediation as a crucial dimension in the analysis of popular music.

See: **cultural intermediaries**
Further reading: Negus, 1996.

mega events – *see* **concerts**

melody   An organized set of notes consisting of different pitches (high or low sounds). The melody of a song is what we would be singing if we substituted the syllable 'la' for all the regular syllables. Melody is the variation in the lead singer's voice, without accompaniment. Various melodies are present in popular music forms: the main melody (sung by the lead singer), background melodies (sung by other group members, or back-up singers), and bass melodies.

memorabilia   Generally, memorable things not to be forgotten, regarded as worthy of preservation and collection. 'Rock and pop memorabilia has become the fastest growing field of collecting', claimed Phillips auction house writer Fox in 1988 (1988: 5). The first such auction, in London in 1981, included John Lennon's upright Steinway piano. As major auction houses included such items, this field of collecting gained credibility and respectability, and prices began to rise. In 1988 a John Entwistle (The Who's bass player) guitar, used on the group's BBC *Top of the Pops* appearances in the early 1970s, fetched £15,000. More recently, tapes of very early Rolling Stones and Beatles 'performances' have realised high prices. The majority of early interest was in items related to the Beatles and Elvis Presley, but other artists soon attracted interest, especially those from the 1950s and the 1960s. The death of a prominent artist lends great appeal to collectability. Leading auction houses in London and New York (Phillips, Sothebys) now conduct regular sales.

There are a large range of collectable items: various records, including promotional copies and gold discs; musical instruments; autographs; **tour** programmes; posters; tour jackets and **concert** tickets and t-shirts, plus novelty toys and a whole range of ephemera marketed around major artists like the Beatles. Record-collecting is a major aspect of memorabilia, supported by a network of collector magazines (e.g. *Goldmine*, *Record Collector*), discographies and price guides, record fairs, and second-hand shops. Record-collecting can border on the obsessional (Eisenberg (1988: 2) describes the case of 'Clarence', crippled with arthritis and on welfare, living in an unlit, unheated house so crammed with trash that the door wouldn't open – and with three-quarters of a million records; see also Nick Hornby's novel *High Fidelity*, 1995).

See: **fans**; **nostalgia**
Further reading: Fox, 1988; *Goldmine*; *Record Collector*.

meta genre – *see* **genre**

mods   A **youth subculture**, which began in London around 1963. Mod was basically a working-class movement with a highly stylized form of dress, the fashions of which changed frequently, and an interest in **R & B** music. Originally called 'modernists' (a **bebop** jazz phrase), mods were influenced by the urban fashions of young American blacks. Mods wore their hair short and well-cut in a series of changing styles. Mod transport was on highly decorated motor scooters, and their clothes were casual with a parka when out riding, or expensive suits with a specific length of sidevent and the latest Italian shoes. Living for weekend partying, mods took pep pills, particularly 'purple hearts' (amphetamines). Several **class**-based strains of mod appeared, each with distinctive styles: an art school, high camp version; mainstream mods; scooter boys; and the hard mods, who developed into **skinheads**. The mod lifestyle parodied and subverted the respectable conventions of their class backgrounds and the relatively unskilled office jobs many of them held.

The Who and The Small Faces were favourite mod groups, along with Tamla **Motown** artists, and **ska** and blue beat in the late 1970s. The Who's **rock opera** *Quadrophenia* (MCA, 1973;

film: Franc Roddam, 1979) celebrates mod, as does the stutter
vocal of the group's classic **single**, 'My Generation' (1965).
Mods clashed with the **rockers** in a series of holiday weekends
in the mid-1960s, giving rise to a media-fuelled **moral panic**.

There was a revival of the subcultural style in the late 1970s
and the **two-tone** groups used a combination of mod dress
with ska and blue beat rhythms.

Further reading: Barnes, 1979; Brake, 1985; Hebdige, 1979.

moral panic; labelling theory Moral panic is a sociological
concept applied to community over-reaction to new media
forms and (often associated) deviant **subcultural** groups. The
popular media are seen to amplify and exaggerate episodes
or phenomena out of proportion to their actual scale and
significance, thereby contributing to the construction of a
moral panic. Historically, concern over the impact of popular
culture has emerged periodically with the advent of each new
mass medium: silent cinema and the talkies, dime novels and
comics, **television**, and video. The moral panics around these
were episodes in cultural politics, in part representing struggles to maintain dominant norms and values. **Popular culture**
was seen by its critics as diametrically opposed to **high
culture** and something to be regulated, particularly in the
interests of the susceptible young.

The concept of moral panic was utilized in the British sociology of deviance and new criminology studies of the 1970s,
most notably in Stanley Cohen's classic study (1980) of the
clashes between **mods** and **rockers** at several seaside resorts in
the mid-1960s. The writing on deviance and moral panic drew
on **labelling theory**: 'A perspective which considers that
deviance is not an intrinsic quality of specific social acts, but
rather the consequence of social definition, whereby deviant
'labels' are applied to those activities' (O'Sullivan *et al.*, 1994:
160). The approach was initially associated with the work of the
American sociologist Howard Becker, who argued that societies and social groups 'create deviance by making those rules
whose infraction comprises deviance, and by applying them to

particular people, and labelling them as outsiders' (Becker, 1963: 9), that is deviance is a social construct. The mass media are a major source for the labelling process, as they transmit and legitimate such labels (e.g. Cohen's 'folk devils') and contribute to the operation of social control. Labelling theory is evident in popular music studies of various **audiences** and their perceived 'anti-social' behaviour.

Following Becker's study, moral panic was subsequently used in relation to various **youth subcultures** (e.g. **punk**), their associated musical preferences (e.g. **heavy metal**), and to some consumption practices (e.g. **raves**). The concept has also been applied to earlier panics around **genres**; indeed, popular music was seen to have had its own series of moral panics, with particular genres and youth subcultures attracting controversy and opposition, both upon their emergence and sporadically since: for example, **jazz** in the 1920s, the teds and **rock'n'roll** in the 1950s, the mods and rockers of the 1960s, punk in the 1970s, **goths**, heavy metal, and **rap** in the 1980s, and British **rave** culture in the 1990s. In such moral panics, criticism has centred variously on the influence of such genres on youthful values, attitudes, and behaviour through the music's (perceived) sexuality and sexism, nihilism and violence, obscenity, black magic, or anti-Christian nature. The political edge of popular music has been partly the result of this hostile reaction often accorded to the music and its associated causes and followers, helping to politicize the **musicians** and their **fans**.

Further reading: Cohen, 1980; Goode and Ben-Yehuda, 1994; O'Sullivan *et al.,* 1994; Thornton, 1994.

Motown Motown was the **black music** company founded by Berry Gordy in Detroit in 1959. The 'Motown sound' had a pounding beat, strong bass lines, hooks from keyboards and guitars, and 'vocals stripped of ghetto inflections' (McEwen, 1992), as Gordy deliberately targeted the white **crossover** market. In what is regarded as the best of several studies of the company, George (1985) views it as a team effort of performers, **songwriters**, **producers**, and **session**

players, with Gordy overseeing and coordinating. Leading Motown artists included the Miracles, the Four Tops, the Temptations, Marvin Gaye, and Stevie Wonder. Motown represented a blander, more commercial version of the **soul** associated with artists at Atlantic and Stax. Motown was sold to MCA in 1988 (for $61 million), although Gordy retained the lucrative publishing rights to Motown's **back catalogue**.

See: **soul**
Further reading: George, 1985; Hirshey, 1985; McEwen, 1992 (includes discography).
Listening:
The Four Tops, 'I Can't Help Myself (Sugar Pie, Honey Bunch)', 1965, on *The Greatest Hits*, Motown, 1967.
The Temptations, *Anthology*, Motown, 1973.
Marvin Gaye, *Super Hits*, Motown, 1973.
Stevie Wonder, *Looking Back*, Motown, 1977.
Viewing: Dancing in the Street, episode 4, 'R-E-S-P-E-C-T'.

MTV – *see* **music video**

multimedia – *see* **CD-ROMs**

music industry; **record companies**   There is a tendency, especially in general discourse, to equate the 'music industry' with record companies, when the latter are only a part of it. The music industry embraces a range of institutions and associated markets: the recording companies (see **majors**; **independents**) and the **retail** sector, producing and selling recordings in their various formats; the **music press**; music hardware, including musical instruments and sound recording and reproduction technology; merchandising (posters, t-shirts, etc.); and royalties and rights and their collection/licensing agencies. These facets are increasingly under the ownership/control of the same parent company (see **concentration**), enabling the maximum exploitation of a particular product or performer.

The recording industry is a major **cultural industry**, and exhibits their common characteristics. **Record companies** are hierarchically organized business structures, with clearly demarcated roles. In a larger enterprise these would include management, **producers**, **marketing** and public relations, publicity, promotion, business affairs, finance and legal, manufacture and distribution, administrative and secretarial (see Negus, 1992: ch. 3). The major problem faced by record companies is the uncertainty of the music market: only one in eight of the artists **A & R** staff sign and record will achieve sufficient sales to recoup the original investment and start to earn money for the artists and generate a profit for the company. This situation has led to major record companies looking for acts already partially developed and indicating commercial potential.

See: **A & R**; **cultural industries**
Further reading: Barrow and Newby, 1996; Burnett, 1996; Cusic, 1996; Dannen, 1991; Negus, 1992.

music press; **music journalism**; **music magazines** The music press includes a wide range of publications. Many general magazines and newspapers cover popular music, with regular review columns. There has been little critical analysis of how these publications construct popular music and influence the reception of **genres** and performers. Exceptions include Stratton's analysis of the premises 'which writers in the music press take for granted but which inform their understanding of, and attitudes to, the music about which they write' (1982: 267); and Jones' review of media coverage of Kurt Cobain's suicide in 1994 (Jones, 1995b).

More specifically, the music press refers to specialized publications: lifestyle magazines with major music coverage, music trade papers, and weekly and monthly consumer magazines devoted to popular music, or particular genres within it. In addition to these are privately published **fanzines** (as these are usually peripheral to the market economy of commercial publishing they are considered separately). There is also a variety of book-length writing on popular music, which I shall turn to first.

An extensive, annotated bibliography published in 1985, covering the writing on popular music since 1955, revealed a considerable body of literature, which had increased dramatically during the early 1980s. Recently published bibliographic guides show rapid growth has continued during the following decade (see Gatten, 1995; Leyser, 1994; Taylor, 1985). Although categories frequently overlap, we can distinguish between (i) popular (auto)biographies, histories, and genre studies; (ii) various forms of consumer guides, including encyclopedias and dictionaries, discographies, and **chart** listings and compilations; and (iii) bibliographies of records or other musical texts, usually organized by artist, genre, or historical period (e.g. Whitburn, 1988). The last represent an important aspect of popular music history, which they constitute as well as record, and are important texts for **fans** and **aficionados**. There are also more esoteric publications, such as **rock** quiz books, genealogical tables plotting the origin and shifting membership of groups, and 'almanacs' dealing with the trivia and microscopic detail of **stars**' private lives. Taylor's summary of all this is apposite: 'The variety of these publications is matched by the variation in the quality of their writing, accuracy and scholarship, which means one must approach them with a degree of discrimination and care' (Taylor, 1985: 1). This judgement still stands.

Popular **music journalism** includes the proliferation of 'quickie' publications aiming to cash in on the latest **pop** sensation. Reading like press releases and emphasizing the pictorial aspect rather than any extended critical commentary, these are often little more than pseudo-publicity. They reinforce the public preoccupation with stars, feeding fans' desire for consumable images and information about their preferred performers. In these respects, they complement those popular music magazines aimed at the **teenage** market (see below). In work of a more serious vein and intent, 'Two kinds of writing now feed into the study of youth and popular culture. These are the more conventional academic mode, and what might be called a new form of cultural journalism. Each is marked by its own history, its debates and disputes' (McRobbie, 1988: xi). McRobbie's edited collection, *Zoot Suits and Second-Hand Dresses*, showed serious popular music journalism had changed dramatically during the 1980s, 'with interest shifting from the music itself to a more general concern with the cultural phenomena which accompany it'. This new focus was strongly evident in the new 'style bibles' of the 1980s, especially *The Face*. Some of this journalism also colonized the 'mainstream' press and the more 'serious' weekly and monthly magazines.

Alongside this is a similar, though more historically situated, identifiable body of journalistic work on popular music which is not only aimed at a broader readership, but is also thoughtful and critically analytical of its subjects: the work of critics like Greil Marcus, Lester Bangs, Robert Cristgau, and Dave Marsh in the United States, and Jon Savage, Dave Rimmer, Nik Cohen, and Charles Shaar Murray in the United Kingdom. Indicative of the commercial and ideological significance of this work is its appearance in book form, as sustained, in-depth studies of genres and performers (e.g. Savage (1991) on the Sex Pistols and **punk rock**); collected reviews and essays (e.g. Christgau, 1990; Murray, 1991); the publication of several encyclopedias of popular music (e.g. Clarke, 1990; Gammond, 1991); and anthologies (e.g. Heylin, 1992). McRobbie has noted the overlap between this work and academia, and the closing together of the two forms: 'while pop journalism has moved towards a more serious mode, academic writing has, to some extent, shifted towards a lighter, more essayistic style' (McRobbie, 1988: xvii). This in part reflects the proliferation of journals which have grown up around **cultural studies**, which have frequently provided a forum for shorter pieces and work-in-progress statements, and been more receptive to a more 'journalistic' essay-form style. This is work in a more exploratory mode, 'where theoretical questions inform a piece of work without necessarily overwhelming it' (McRobbie, 1988: xix).

Popular **music magazines** have received surprisingly little attention in popular music studies. The major exception to this generalization is the inclusion of advice to performers on how to deal with the music press to best advantage, in guidebooks to successful careers (e.g. Riordan, 1991; York, 1991). General accounts of the development of popular music (e.g. Chambers, 1985; Garofalo, 1997; Szatmary, 1991) make considerable use of the music press as a source, while largely ignoring its role in the process of **marketing** and cultural legitimation. The music press is absent from otherwise far-ranging anthologies (e.g. Frith and Goodwin, 1990), studies of the music business (e.g. Chapple and Garofolo, 1977; Sanjek, 1988), and even encyclopedias of popular music (e.g. Clarke, 1990; Gammond, 1991). The only book-length study of the music press, of its most influential publication, *Rolling Stone* magazine (Draper, 1990), emphasizes biographical exposé rather than extended cultural analysis.

While there is obvious overlap – and market competition – amongst the various types of music magazine, they do have distinctive qualities. The music trade papers keep industry personnel informed about mergers, takeovers, and staff changes in the record and media industries, and changes in **copyright** and regulatory legislation and policies; advise retailers about marketing campaigns, complementing and reinforcing their sales promotions; and provide regular **chart** lists based on extensive sales and radio play data (the main publications are *Billboard*, *Music Business International*, and *Music Week*). Musicians' magazines (e.g. *Guitar Player*) inform their readers about new music technologies and techniques, thereby making an important contribution towards musicianship and musical **appropriation** (see Théberge, 1991).

The various consumer or fan-oriented music magazines play a major part in the process of selling music as an economic commodity, while at the same time investing it with cultural significance. In the United Kingdom, a 1995 survey of the readers of 27 music magazines showed *Smash Hits* to be the most-read title (3.3 million readers across an entire year, reaching 7.1 per cent of the group surveyed), followed by *NME* with 2.4 million readers (5.3 per cent) and *Q* with 2.3 million (5.1 per cent). The survey showed that 57 per cent of those who read music magazines buy an album every month and a further 30 per cent do so every two to three months (*Music Week*, March 1996).

Popular music and culture magazines don't simply deal with music, through both their features and advertising they are also purveyors of style. At the same time, these magazines continue to fulfil their more traditional function of contributing to the construction of **audiences** as **consumers**.

The majority of popular music magazines focus on performers and their music, and the relationship of consumers and **fans** to these. These magazines fall into a number of fairly clearly identifiable categories, based on their differing musical **aesthetics** or emphases, their sociocultural functions, and their target audiences. For example, 'teen glossies' emphasize vicarious identification with performers whose music and image is aimed at the youth market (e.g. *Smash Hits*); *Melody Maker* and *New Musical Express* (the 'inkies') have historically emphasized a tradition of critical rock journalism, with their reviewers acting as the **gatekeepers** for that tradition; and the 'style bibles' (*The Face*) emphasize popular music as part of visual pop culture, especially fashion. Several relatively new magazines offer a combination of the inkies' focus on an extensive and critical coverage of the music scene and related popular culture, packaged in a glossier product with obvious debts to the style bibles (*MOJO*, *VOX*). This is a volatile and highly competitive market: *RAW*, the 'Britpop fortnightly' launched in 1995 to fill the gap between *Smash Hits* and the monthly *Select*, ceased publication after five months, despite selling around 40,000 copies per issue.

Music press reviews form an important adjunct to the record company's marketing of their products, providing the record companies (and artists) with critical feedback on their releases. In the process, they also become promotional devices, providing supportive quotes for advertising and forming part of press kits sent to radio stations and other press outlets. Both the press and critics also play an important ideological function, distancing consumers from the fact that they are essentially purchasing an economic commodity, by stressing the product's

199

cultural significance. This is reinforced by the important point that the music press and critics are not, at least directly, vertically integrated into the music industry (i.e. not owned by the record companies). A sense of distance is thereby maintained, while at the same time the need of the industry to constantly sell new images, styles, and product is met.

See: **fanzines**

Further reading: Barrow and Newby, 1996; Shuker, 1994.

music video; **MTV**   Music video (MV) is a hybrid cultural form, encompassing elements of both television and radio. There are several distinct yet overlapping meanings of the term: individual MV programmes within general broadcast **television** channel schedules (dealt with separately); the long-form music video cassette, available for hire or purchase; and **MTV** and similar cable/satellite music channels. Each of these uses individual music video clips as its central components.

The long-form music video cassette, available for hire or purchase: The value of the video retail market continues to grow, with a 13 per cent increase in 1995 to £789 million in the United Kingdom alone. Boosted by the success of *Riverdance* and *Robson and Jerome*, the two biggest selling music videos of the year, the music genre in 1995 had a 10.6 per cent share of this market. The rental market also grew, reaching its highest level for six years (*Music Week*, March 18, 1996). There appears to be a dearth of research on these products, their production and **marketing**, their purchasers, and the uses they make of such videos.

MTV and similar cable/satellite music channels: MTV: the American cable television channel, 'MTV: Music Television', founded in 1981, has become almost synonomous with music video as a cultural form. Originally owned by the Warner Amex Satellite Company, but subsequently sold to Viacom International, the channel became enormously popular during the later 1980s, and has been credited with boosting a flagging music industry. MTV captured a considerable share of the advertising directed at the youth and young adult 'yuppie'

market, and solved the perennial problem of cable television
– how to generate enough revenue for new programming –
by having the record companies largely pay for the
'programmes' by financing the video clips. In the late 1980s
it was reaching nearly twenty million American homes, and
was regularly watched by 85 per cent of 18–34 year olds.

By 1991 MTV had 28 million subscribers, and was adding
between one and three million new subscribers every year.
MTV's success spawned a host of imitators in the United States,
and a number of national franchises and imitations around the
globe. In 1988 MTV crossed the Atlantic, with the creation of
MTV Europe. After an initial struggle to untangle cable and
satellite regulations in dozens of countries, MTV Europe broke
even for the first time in February 1993, and became the
continent's fastest growing satellite channel, with its 24-hours-
a-day MV programming available in more than 44 million
homes. Thirty per cent of its airtime is reserved for European
performers, and while the programme format is similar to that
of its parent station, a genuine effort appears to have been made
to play a substantial number of European music videos (Burnett,
1990). MTV Asia began broadcasting in late 1991, with a satellite signal covering more than thirty countries from Japan to the
Middle East. The channel's English-language broadcasts reach
more than three million households with a programme dominated by MVs by Western **stars**, but with an approximately
20 per cent quota of Asian performers.

By the late 1980s, the influence of MTV on the United
States' music industry – and, therefore, by association, globally
– was enormous. Getting their music video on regular MTV
play became necessary to ensure chart success, while MTV
has become the most effective way to 'break' a new artist,
and to take an emerging artist into star status. During the
1980s, performers who received considerable exposure on
MTV before they were picked up by radio included Madonna,
Duran Duran, the Thompson Twins, and Paula Abdul. The
'invasion' of the American charts by style-conscious and
photogenic British groups in the mid- to late 1980s was
directly attributed by some analysts to MTV. Innovative videos

and MTV helped American performers such as Paula Abdul and Talking Heads consolidate themselves, and pushed sales of Michael Jackson's albums to dizzy heights – over 40 million copies of *Thriller* (Epic, 1983).

The MTV channels' format is typified by MTV Europe, which uses a weekly playlist of current hits, divided into four categories of song rotation: power plugs, played every 4 hours; high, every 4–6 hours; medium, every 8–9.5 hours; and light, every 13 hours. Classic, older clips are also played at regular intervals. Each week sees a playlist of some eighty MVs, and there is a very high turnover. In terms of their country of origin, 52 per cent of the video clips were British, 31 per cent American, with the rest of the world accounting for the remainder (Burnett, 1990). While MVs are the staple of such channels' programming, they also screen concerts, interviews, and rock-oriented news/gossip items, acting as a visual radio channel. Banks' more recent study (1996) shows that this pattern remains typical of MTV programming.

Given their crucial role in determining commercial success, a key question is how particular MVs are chosen for the playlist. Evidence on this point is sparse, and it is clearly an area for further inquiry. Surprisingly, Kaplan's (1987) study of the channel ignores the selection issue, as do most commentators preoccupied with the videos as **texts**. Rubey (1991) noted that MTV's Top 20 lists are compiled from national album sales, video airplay, and the channel's own research and requests, building circularity and subjectivity into the process.

In easily the most thorough study of the operation of MTV, Banks (1996: ch. 9) looks at the **gatekeeper** role of the American MTV channel, the operation of its Acquisitions Committee and the standards, both stated and unstated, which they apply. He concludes that **major** companies willingly edit videos on a regular basis to conform to MTV's standards, even coercing artists into making changes to song lyrics, while smaller, **independent** companies cannot usually get their videos on MTV.

Despite the heady growth of the 1980s, the American MTV channel began the 1990s by retrenching. MTV executives claimed that the format had lost its freshness and was becoming clichéd. The channel initiated a programme overhaul designed to lessen its reliance on videos; new shows included *Unplugged*, a 30-minute Sunday programme featuring live acoustic performances, which became established as a vehicle for marketing associated recordings, including chart-topping album releases by Eric Clapton and Mariah Carey. These programme changes were a direct response to research on viewership patterns, which indicated, not surprisingly, that people tuned in to MTV for only as long as they enjoy the clips. With MVs making up some 90 per cent of the channel's broadcast day, negative reaction to a few clips can spell problems for audience retention and the sale of advertising time. This is a situation MTV shares with 'mainstream' television and radio, which have always been in the business of delivering audiences to advertisers in a highly competitive market.

The music video clip: Individual music video clips follow the conventions of the traditional 45 single: they are approximately 2–3 minutes long, and function, in the industry's own terms, as 'promotional devices', encouraging record sales and chart action. These clips are the staple component in MTV style television, individual music programmes on television, and the long form music videos. However, their place in each case is different, as are their associated patterns of consumption.

The analysis of MV clips has been one of the major growth areas in both television studies and the study of popular music. The associated literature emphasizes their visual aspect, their perceived violence and sexuality/sexism, and their significance as a central postmodern cultural artifact. Situating themselves in film studies rather than music studies, these analyses accordingly focus on MVs as discrete, self-contained, essentially visual texts. They frequently largely ignore considerations such as MVs' industrial and commercial dimensions, their placement in the flow of television programming, and the links between MVs and rock stardom.

For a fuller understanding of MVs it is necessary to consider their production process and their commercial function for the music industry, the institutional practices of channels such as MTV, and their reception as polysemic texts, open to varying audience interpretations. Music video is both an industrial/commercial product and a cultural form.

See: **television**

Further reading: (a) music video: Goodwin, 1987, 1993; Kaplan, 1987; Mercer, 1988; Shore, 1985

(b) MTV: Banks, 1996; Goodwin, 1993; Kaplan, 1987; Lewis, 1990a, 1990b; Sturmer, 1993.

musicals   Stage musicals are an historically well-established and popular cultural form. While they are part of popular music in a general sense, only a small proportion of such musicals are thematically based on those popular musical **genres** considered here. There have been successful shows based on the lives and careers of Elvis Presley, Buddy Holly, and the Beatles; 'rock operas' such as The Who's *Tommy*, which has periodically been resurrected; and nostalgia-oriented musicals drawing on particular historically situated genres. These productions are often termed 'rock musicals', to distinguish them from the classic musicals which dominate the Broadway and West End theatres. Those musicals featuring popular music and **star** performers serve similar purposes to popular music **films**: they help create and popularize ideologies (e.g. *Hair* and the counter culture of the 1960s) and mythologize their real life stars or those they historically portray.

The Rocky Horror Picture Show, and its subsequent film version (Jim Sharman, 1975), exemplify the cult status rock musicals can attain. Written by Richard O'Brien, *Rocky Horror* was first produced as an experimental work for the Theatre Upstairs, upstairs at the Royal Court Theatre, London, on 16 June 1973. Tim Curry, who had starred in *Hair*, played the part of Frank'n'Furter, 'a sweet transvestite from Transsexual in Transylvania', a modern-day rock-oriented Frankenstein, hard at work on his creation, a boy called Rocky. O'Brien himself played Riff Raff, the devoted servant. The London critics enthused and the fans queued. After a short initial run the show continued in larger theatres. Opening at the King's Road Theatre in Chelsea on 31 October 1973, *The Rocky Horror Show* ran for seven years. The show won critical praise, awards, and a cult audience, many of whom went again and again. The long-running show also proved highly successful when staged in Los Angeles and other centres. *Rocky Horror* was about the fantasy-fun side of popular music, demanding that its audience let go the restraints of everyday reality and have a good time. O'Brien had blended aspects of late-night science fiction and horror movies on **television**, Dr Strange comics, and **rock** history for inspiration. He had spent a year playing in *Hair* and wanted his own **rock opera** to reflect not spirituality, but the sexuality of rock, and developed the songs and dialogue accordingly.

Despite the commercial and critical success of a number of 'rock musicals', they remain an oddly neglected topic within popular music studies.

See: **film**

musicians; **making music**; **cover bands**; **tribute bands**; **session musicians** The bulk of the popular writing on musicians is on those musicians considered **stars/auteurs**; academic study has focused on identifying those who are considered 'musicians', especially within particular social/community settings; the processes whereby musicians 'make music'; and the hierarchies of musician (and associated forms of musician*ship*) which are held among critics, fans, and musicians themselves.

1 *Musicians*: The term musician covers a range of people creating music, from the purely recreational player of a musical instrument through to those who make a specialized contribution to the recording process. With the advent of new technologies, and the importance of **sound mixers** and **producers** as creators of recordings, the term has taken on a more flexible and diffuse meaning. Playing music is for the majority of those who do so an essentially 'amateur' activity, which may become a career option.

However, while the term musician is usually equated with a full-time professional, various studies have found it difficult to distinguish 'amateur' from 'professional' musicians:

> local bands sometimes contained many players in full-time (non-musical) jobs and others whose only regular occupation was their music; yet in giving performances, practising, sharing out the fees and identification with the group, the members were treated exactly alike (except for the inconvenience of those in jobs that had to plead illness or take time off work if they travelled to distant bookings) (Finnegan, 1989: 13).

Finnegan's local musicians tended to use the term professional in an evaluative rather than an economic sense, to refer to a player's standard of performance, musical knowledge and qualifications, and regular appearances with musicians themselves regarded as professional.

2 *Making music*: accounts of how musicians create their music demonstrate a complex process of musical composition, rehearsal, and performance. The musical world of the two bands that Cohen studied was based around a series of polarities: creativity/commerce; musical content and quality/image and superficiality; honest and natural/false and deceitful; artistic integrity/selling out; **independent** record companies/**major** record companies; live music for community, experimentation, and indulgence/recorded music for profit and for a mass market. The bands situated themselves into a combination of these various factors, with tension, constant debate, and shifting allegiances evident among their members. Their creative process was typically incremental and participatory (Cohen, 1991: 134).

3 **Hierarchies of musician(ship)**: value distinctions are evident in the terms used by critics and **fans** to label various performers: **stars**, **auteurs**, **session musicians**, and cover and tribute bands. Beginning bands, with relatively inexperienced musicians, out of necessity rely on cover versions for a large part of their repertoire.

Learning such songs is part of the apprenticeship process in acquiring **rock** musicianship: 'song copying allows the novice to become a competent member of a musical tradition. This applies to both musicians and audiences' (Hatch and Millward, 1987: 3–4).

Cover bands are generally accorded little creative weight and critical artistic merit. The extreme example of cover bands are those performers who not only directly model themselves on established bands, but actually copy them, presenting themselves as simulacra of the originals – and in the process demonstrating a high level of musical competence. Often referred to as **tribute bands**, these have become big business, for example Björn Again, the Australian Abba tribute band, who take their name from a member of the original band. Supporters of these performers argue that the imitators are bringing the music to a new audience of under twenty-fives, opening it up to a generation who never saw the originals, and thereby encouraging them to seek out their material. Detractors point to the difficulties in policing copyright and regard it as at best unfortunate that the original artists are frequently having to share audiences with their imitators.

Session musicians are performers who are contracted, sometimes to studios but usually to particular recording projects, to contribute as directed by the main performers and the producer. Generally anonymous, they function as the pieceworkers of the music industry. Some attain critical recognition for their contributions (e.g. reggae performers Sly and Robbie Dunbar), while the efforts of a few session musicians attain near legendary status – such as Jeff Beck and Jimmy Page's guitar solos on a variety of records in the 1960s – but usually only when they later become successful in their 'own right', creating interest in this aspect of their back catalogue.

See: **cover versions**
Further reading: Bennett, 1990; Cohen, 1991; Finnegan, 1989; Hatch and Millward, 1987.

musicology   In broad terms, musicology is

> the whole body of systematized knowledge about music
> which results from the application of a scientific method
> of investigation or research, or of philosophical specu-
> lation and rational systematization to the facts, the
> processes and development of musical art, and to the
> relation of man in general   (Harvard Dictionary of
> Music, cited in Middleton, 1990: 103).

A major debate in popular music studies has been
constructed around the value of a musicological approach to
music texts. Indeed, there is an argument as to whether
popular music even merits such a 'serious' analysis, a question
related to the **high culture** and mass society critiques of
popular music. Until recently, academic musicologists have
generally neglected **rock/pop music** (notable exceptions
include Mellers, 1974, 1986; Shepherd, 1991), in part out of
an unwillingness to engage with a form of music which is
accorded low cultural value in comparison with 'serious'
music. At the same time, many sociologists writing on popular
music were wary of musicology. For example, the application of traditional musicology to rock music has frequently
provided a rich source for ridicule, due to its tendency to be
distant from the mechanics of much actual composition of
rock, its 'vague pretentiousness' and 'chronic failure to address
what is really at stake in the tunes' (McClary and Walser,
1990: 277). As Frith observed, both rock musicians and rock
commentators generally lack formal musical training: 'They
lack the vocabulary and techniques of musical analysis, and
even the descriptive words that critics and fans do use –
harmony, melody, riff, beat – are only loosely understood
and applied' (Frith, 1983: 13; also Frith and Goodwin, 1990,
part 5).
    Frith saw rock critics as essentially preoccupied with soci-
ology rather than sound, and there has been too ready a
willingness to dismiss musicology as having little relevance to
the study of rock. The arguments here were well rehearsed
through the 1980s: traditional musicology neglects the social

context, emphasizes the transcription of music (the score), and elevates harmonic and rhythmic structure to pride of place as an evaluative criterion. Popular music, on the other hand, emphasizes interpretation through performance, and is received primarily in terms of the body and emotions rather than as pure text. Many rock musicians observed that classical music operated according to a different set of musical criteria, which has little validity for their own efforts (e.g. Pete Townshend, in Palmer, 1970: 131).

More recently, there are signs that the largely negative attitude toward musicology (in relation to popular music) is changing. Several musicologists have engaged with popular music, while popular music scholars have accorded musicology more weight (e.g. McClary, 1991; Middleton, 1990; Walser, 1993). This work varies in the degree to which such analysis simply takes as a given the concepts/tools of traditional (ie. more classical music-oriented) musicology (e.g. Mellers, 1974, 1986), or modifies these in relation to popular music (e.g. Moore, 1993).

A number of authors have argued, with reference to detailed examples, that musical analysis of selected compositions is a workable approach to studying the nature and evolution of popular music, with such analysis presupposing a basic knowledge of the elements of music: **melody**, **rhythm**, **harmony**, **lyrics**, and performance (e.g. Brown, 1992; Hatch and Millward, 1987; Moore, 1993; Vulliamy and Lee, 1982). However, it can be argued that much of this work demonstrates that the traditional conception of musicology remains inadequate when applied to popular music in any straightforward manner (equating the two forms). For example, a concentration on technical textual aspects alone – the score – is inadequate, since it fails to deal with how the effects listeners celebrate are constructed, what McClary and Walser term 'the dimensions of music that are most compelling and yet most threatening to rationality' (1990: 287). This takes into consideration the role of pleasure, the relationship of the body, feelings and emotions, and **sexuality** in constructing responses to rock music. It needs extension into the more affective domains of the relationship between the text and its listeners, and into the generic and historical locations of the text and its performer(s). **Genre** study usefully moves us beyond the music as pure text, alerting us once again to the value of context and consumption. So too does the study of narrative structures and representations in popular music, particularly the ideological and contextual aspects of these.

Ideally, what is needed is an approach which embraces both traditional musicology and these **affective** aspects of music. It is worth remembering that people are more 'musical' than is usually credited. **Radio** listening – switching stations in search of something recognizable or engaging – and selecting which music to play on one's stereo involves an ability to distinguish between different types of music. This is to utilize a more extended definition of 'musical' (Tagg, 1990: 104), where what is crucial is the link between musical structures and people's use of them.

See: **harmony; lyrics; melody; rhythm**

Further reading: Brown, 1992; Chester, 1990; Frith, 1987; Hatch and Millward, 1987; Manuel, 1995; Meyer, 1995; Moore, 1993; Tagg, 1982.

muzak   Muzak is the term applied, rather negatively, to 'functional' or 'background' music. Muzak accounts for the greatest proportion of the music we are exposed to in our daily lives, though we are rarely consciously aware of it. It is used in a deliberate attempt to influence, or manipulate, the buying patterns of supermarket shoppers, the eating habits of restaurant patrons, and so on. Muzak is also used as background music in places such as airport lounges, doctors' waiting rooms, and lifts (elevator music), to 'soothe' the mood of people in such public spaces, and similarly in workplaces to enhance worker satisfaction and output.

Functional music is now economically very significant: Muzak Corporation, the largest of the programmed music companies, grossed over $50 million in 1990, when it had ninety-six franchises supplying 'programmed music' to 135,000 businesses in sixteen countries. Such companies have been paying enormous sums to acquire **copyrights** to songs, rearrange them, and profile and track the behaviour of various **consumer** groups.

Muzak has been critiqued on **aesthetic** or musical grounds, as a form of banal, 'wallpaper' music; or as an example of bureaucratic rationalism, linked to post-Fordist industrial practices perpetuating the alienation of workers. Jones and Schumacher 'examine the practices and discourses of functional music, how they have evolved historically, their role in the regulation of work and consumption, and their reproduction of particular kinds of economic, spatial, and symbolic power relations' (1992: 157).

See: **listening**

Further reading: Jones and Schumacher, 1992; Negus, 1996.

new age A marketing label as much as a truly distinguishable musical **genre**. 'More of a mood than a style, new age was soothing instrumental music of the 1980s, based on the softer kinds of classical, jazz and folk' (Hardy and Laing, 1990). New age is characterized by having precious little vocal accompaniment and making considerable use of **ambient** (natural) sounds, synthesizers, and **samplers**. 'New Age music is commonly marked by minute variations and an abundance of repeats. This music is all middle; it starts and stops, it is turned on and off, but one does not get a distinct sense of beginnings and endings' (Hall, 1994: 14). It is almost exclusively recorded music, produced and consumed via **cassette audio tape** and **CD**. The Wyndham Hill label was prominent in popularizing the genre, which has its own specialist radio programmes, and is a genre sales category in many **retail** outlets.

New age is sometimes scorned as 'yuppie muzak' (Gammond, 1991), in part because of its appeal amongst relatively well-off and liberally educated listeners. Hall claims new age to be a postmodernist musical style, 'due to its eclectic, constantly shifting character and confusion of boundaries; its spirit of playfulness, taste for irony, and textual looting; its aggressive multiculturalism; and its anti–intellectualism yet devotion to learning' (see Hall, 1994: 17–18, for an elaboration of these claims). Other observers regard the genre as musically a heavily conservative one, leaning towards the formulaic, and oriented toward private introspection.

Further reading: Hall, 1994; Hardy and Laing, 1990: entries on John Fahey, Ian Mathews; Schaefer, 1987.

Listening:

Mike Oldfield, *Tubular Bells,* Virgin, 1973 ('a harbinger of the wallpaper music that is now called New Age' – Sinclair, 1992: 230).

New Right – *see* **censorship**

new romantics   A rather general label or movement, applied to British synthesizer-based bands of the mid-1980s, who did well in the US market partly because of extensive exposure on **MTV**. The term is often used interchangeably with (British) New Pop. The new romantics often adopted extravagant dress, make-up, and period clothes (e.g. Adam and the Ants). Other leading performers were Soft Cell, Duran Duran, Culture Club, Howard Jones, and the Human League.

See: **MTV**; **glam rock**

Further reading: Hill, 1986; Rimmer, 1985.

Listening:

Duran Duran, *Notorious*, Capitol, 1986.

At Worst . . . The Best of Boy George and Culture Club, Virgin, 1993.

new wave   The origins of the term lie with its application to **avant garde** French film-makers of the 1950s to signal a radical break with dominant conventions. Musically new wave performers were innovative and progressive, but not necessarily threatening (cf. **punk**). New wave was usually more melodic and more accessible, in some cases with a greater emphasis on song **lyrics**. In part, new wave provided a convenient **marketing** label for record label **A & R** people, journalists, and **DJs** to distinguish music they did not want identified as punk, owing to punk's negative marketing connotations, especially in the United States.

213

New wave embraced a wide range of styles. In the United Kingdom, The Police (with **reggae** associations), XTC, Elvis Costello and the Attractions, and Graham Parker and the Rumour. In the United States, Devo, the Cars, the B–52s, Talking Heads, Blondie (overlayed with **disco**), Tom Petty and the Heartbreakers (with **rock'n'roll** antecedents), and Jonathan Richman and the Modern Lovers. The term is also sometimes used to refer to new strains of British **heavy metal** in the 1980s.

See: **punk**

Further reading: Erlewine *et al.*, 1995; Heylin, 1993; Larkin, 1995.

Listening:

Talking Heads, *More Songs about Buildings and Food*, Sire, 1978.

Blondie, *The Best Of Blondie*, Chrysalis, 1981.

Elvis Costello and the Attractions, *The Best of Elvis Costello and the Attractions*, CBS, 1985.

northern soul – *see* **soul**

Oi! – *see* **skinheads**

P

Parents' Music Resource Center – *see* **censorship**

participant observation – *see* **ethnography**

payola A term used for the offering of financial, sexual, or other inducements in return for promotion. In 1955 the US House of Representatives Legislative Oversight Committee, which had been investigating the rigging of quiz shows, began looking at pay-to-play practices in rock music **radio**. Payola, as the practice was then known, had long been common-place, but was not illegal. 'Song plugging', as the practice was originally termed, had been central to music industry **marketing** since the heyday of **Tin Pan Alley** in the 1920s. By the 1950s, **DJs** and radio station programmers frequently supplemented their incomes with 'consultant fees' and musical credits on records, enabling them to receive a share of song-writing royalties.

During the committee hearings, Dick Clark admitted to having a personal interest in around a quarter of the records he promoted on his influential show. He divested himself of his music business holdings and was eventually cleared by the committee. A clean-cut figure, Clark survived the scandal because he represented the acceptable face of **rock'n'roll**. Pioneer DJ Alan Freed was not so fortunate; persecuted and eventually charged with commercial bribery in 1960, his health and career were ruined.

Payola did not target all music radio, but was rather 'the operative strategy for neutralizing rock'n'roll' (Garofalo, 1997: 170), and part of a conservative battle to return to 'good music'. The campaign against payola was underpinned by economic self-interest. The American Society of Composers, Authors and Publishers (ASCAP) supported it by attacking rivals BMI (Broadcast Music, Inc.), whose writers were responsible for most rock'n'roll. The **majors** supported it as part of a belated attempt to halt the expansion of the **independents**. Hill goes so far as to conclude that one way to see the payola hearings was as an attempt – ultimately successful – 'to force a greater degree of organization and hierarchical responsibility onto the record industry so that the flow of music product could be more easily regulated' (1991: 667). The involvement of conservative government officials, and a number of established music figures (including Frank Sinatra), was largely based on an often intense dislike of rock'n'roll, a prejudice with only loosely concealed racist overtones, given the prominence of black musicians in the **genre**.

See: **censorship**; **charts**; **DJ**; **radio**
Further reading: Friedlander, 1996; Hill, 1991; Morthland, 1992b.

performance; **live performance**   Musical performance occurs in a wide variety of contexts. It can be impromptu and domestic, the classic singing in the shower, but the focus here is on public performance. This is either 'live' or a mediated form of the live (pseudo-live): the **club scene**; **concerts** and concert **tours**; **music festivals**; on **film**; **musicals**; **radio**; and **music video**. All of these forms mediate the music, creating a link between performer, **text**, and **consumer**. Their significance in determining cultural meaning lies in the interrelationship of ritual, pleasure, and economics. Popular music performance shapes audiences, fuels individual fantasy and pleasure, and creates icons and cultural myths. At times, performance events have had the capacity to encapsulate and represent key periods and turning points in rock. Their significance is indicated by their use in a cultural shorthand fashion among **fans**, musicians, and writers (for example, 'Woodstock', with an assumed set of connotations: the **counter culture**, music festivals, the 1960s, etc.). Investigating the processes involved in how performance communicates musical meaning to its constituent audiences in such different contexts has been a major preoccupation of popular music scholarship.

Historically, prior to the advent of recorded **sound**, all music was live, and was experienced as such. The term 'live' performance is now usually reserved for those situations where the audience is in physical proximity to the performance, and the experience of the music is contiguous with its actual performance. Live music in this sense can be experienced in a variety of settings: by buskers in the streets or subways, in clubs and concert halls, and in the 'open air', most notably at outdoor concert venues and festivals. However, much live performance is experienced at a distance from its actual physical and temporal location, being captured and re-presented via music video, film, radio, and recordings (see **mediation**). The status of live recordings is regarded as rather ambivalent, given that many are technologically sonically upgraded prior to their release.

Historically, for both fans and musicians there was a perceived hierarchy of **live performances**, with a marked tendency to equate an audience's physical proximity to the actual 'performance' and intimacy with the performer(s) with a more **authentic** and satisfying musical experience. While this view was central to the ideology of **rock** created during the 1960s, it has since been undermined by performers who work primarily, and at times exclusively, in the studio setting, such as Steely Dan in the 1970s. Some **genres** are now largely studio creations (e.g. recent styles of **dance–music**).

See: **authenticity**; **concerts**; **mediation**
Further reading: Gracyk, 1996.

phonograph Edison invented the phonograph, a 'talking machine', in November 1877. This followed his work, along with researchers such as Bell and Watson, on the electrical transfer of speech, which led to the development of the telephone. The phonograph represented the true beginning of recorded sound technology, replacing 'the shared Victorian pleasures of bandstand and music hall with the solitary delight of a private world of sound' (Millard, 1995: 1). Edison's phonograph used cylinders and was able to record and reproduce **sound**. Other researchers developed the new technology further: Berliner developed the gramophone (1888), using a disc instead of a cylinder, while Edison considerably improved on his original in 1887. The phonograph and the gramophone are the forerunners of contemporary home stereo systems.

The phonograph was originally intended primarily as a business tool, but moved into entertainment initially through coin-operated phonographs (from 1889). With the development of pre-recorded cylinders in the early 1900s, the phonographic industry took off: while in 1897 only about 500,000 records had been sold in the United States, by 1899 this number had reached 2.8 million, and continued to rise.

Various commentators have identified a succession of phases in the technological history of the phonograph: an acoustic one, from 1877 to the 1920s; the use of electrical/magnetic tape, from the 1920s; and the digital age, with the **CD**, from 1982: 'the industry built on the phonograph was driven forward by the constant disruption of innovation: new systems of recording, new kinds of machine, and newer types of recorded music' (Millard, 1995: 5–6; see also Jones, 1992; Read and Welch, 1977). By the 1970s, most homes in developed countries had a home stereo, the modern phonograph, consisting of an amplifier, a record player, tape recorder, and radio in one or more units.

See: **sound recording**
Further reading: Eisenberg, 1988, especially ch. 8; Jones, 1992; Millard, 1995.

piracy The same **technologies** that have made commercially recorded popular music a global commodity have also made it one of the world's most stealable. The International Federation of Phonogram and Videogram Producers (IFPI), the 'watchdog' of the global **music industry**, noted that world-wide **CD** piracy had doubled during 1993 to about 75 million units with a corresponding value of almost $700 million (IFPI, *For the Record*, April 1994, 'CD Piracy'). Subsequently, the IFPI put the retail value of pirate sales in 1994 at some 6 per cent of legitimate sales (January 1996 press release; cf. Burnett (1996: 88), who shows that in 1990 the IFPI estimated that 25 per cent of the 'music phonographs' sold throughout the world were pirate copies). In some countries in Asia, Africa, the Middle East, and Latin America, the proportion of pirate copies is considerably higher, with China a major offender. The IFPI has had only limited success in curbing these activities, since many governments are reluctant to act against their own **bootleggers**, who are part of an important 'informal economy', and provide a major source of income and jobs. Concern about piracy extends to **home taping**, with the IFPI and the music industry lobbying for a levy on blank tapes.

See: **bootlegs**; **copyright**; **home taping**; **pirate radio**
Further reading: Burnett, 1996.

pirate radio – *see* **radio**

political economy While mainstream economics views the 'economy' as a separate domain, 'critical political economy is interested in the interplay between economic organization and political, social and cultural life' (Golding and Murdoch, 1991: 18). Political economy has as its starting point the fact that the producers of mass media are industrial institutions preoccupied with profit-making, and the broadcast media are engaged in selling audiences to advertisers (see **culture industries**). That these institutions are owned and controlled by a relatively small number of people, and their marked tendency towards increased **concentration**, is a situation involving considerable ideological power.

Classical political economy analysis tended to devalue the significance of culture, seeing it primarily as the reflection of the economic base. The influence of classical political economy is evident in the arguments of contemporary **Marxists** who emphasize the power of the corporate capitalist music industry to manipulate and even construct markets and audiences:

> More than any of the other performing arts, the world of song is dominated by the money men on the one hand and the moral censors of the media on the other. The reality is that song is the private property of business organisations   (Rosselson, 1979: 40).

This position can all too easily slip into a form of economic determinism, married to a form of capitalist conspiracy theory; seeing **culture** as produced by the economic base, and omitting any sense of the relative autonomy of the superstructure. It ignores the point that the consumption of popular music is not (necessarily) a passive activity, and tends to overlook or negate the many instances of oppositional politics in popular music.

In contrast, critical political economy has appreciated the reciprocal relationships between base and superstructure: 'the interplay between the symbolic and economic dimensions of public communications' (Golding and Murdoch, 1991: 15). This involves examining media institutions by asking of media **texts**: Who produces the text? For what audience? In whose interests? What is excluded? Such an interrogation necessitates examining particular media in terms of their production practices, financial bases, technology, legislative frameworks, and their construction of audiences.

Recent popular music studies have revisited, reworked, and revitalized the political economy tradition. To a degree, their collective emphasis on issues of cultural production and cultural policy have displaced earlier preoccupations of popular music analysis, particularly the concern with **subcultures** and the **textual**. In this respect, they reflect shifts in the theoretical orientation of **cultural studies** and the relative privileging of particular 'ways into' the analysis of culture. Collectively these authors demonstrate that the practice of music takes place within a nexus of government policies, broadcasting regimes, technology, media corporations, and cultural politics. Both macro and micro studies are present here: the broad brushstrokes of the national and the international are placed alongside the analysis of local music scenes and historical moments such as **pirate radio**.

For example, in his detailed account of the music industry, Negus' central concern is the process of discovery and development of recording artists, which he uses 'as an organising principle to provide a more general account of the recording industry and the production of pop music' (1992: vi). In so doing, he consciously avoids what he sees as the two dominant approaches to the analysis of popular music: political economy analysts in the tradition of the **Frankfurt School**, who reduce the music industry to the organizational conventions and commercial logic of capitalism; and, secondly, subcultural and postmodernist accounts which stress the activities of **audiences** in their **consumption** of popular music. Negus is at pains to emphasize 'the cultural worlds being lived and constantly remade, highlighting the webs of relationships and multiple dialogues along and around which the musical and visual identities of pop artists are composed and communicated' (1992: vii). (Other recent studies which draw on political economy are Burnett, 1996, on the international **music industry**; and Banks, 1996, on **MTV**.)

See: **majors**; **Marxism**
Further reading: Bennett *et al.*, 1993; Frith, 1993; Negus, 1992.

politics; **social movements**   In the general sense of the word, politics permeates popular music studies. Practically every aspect of the production and **consumption** of popular music involves theoretical debates about the dynamics of economic,

cultural, and political power and influence, and the reproduction of social structures and individual subjectivities (see
**Frankfurt School; political economy; cultural studies;
feminism; structuralism**). In a more specific sense, politics
is reflected in direct **State** intervention in the cultural sphere,
such as through forms of **censorship** and the regulation of
broadcasting. Here the discussion focuses rather on the question of the role of popular music in creating social change,
and its mobilization within **social movements**.

A central problem in social theory has been to explain how
cultures change, and to identify the forms of social activity
at work in processes of social transformation. A key part of
social change are changes in the cognitive identity of the
individuals involved. Popular music has played a prominent
role in articulating this process, at both the individual and
collective group level. At various historical points, popular
music has translated political radicalism into a more accessible idiom, identifying social problems, alienation and
oppression, and facilitating the sharing of a collective vision.
Performers and songs contribute to forging a relationship
between politics, cultural change, and popular music. Popular
music has frequently acted as a powerful means of raising
both consciousness about and funds for political causes. At
the same time, however, there is a tendency for such popular
music forms to be co-opted, **commodified**, and watered
down or neutralized by the **music industry**.

Examples of popular music playing an overt political role
include the Campaign for Nuclear Disarmament (CND)
movement in the United Kingdom in the late 1950s; Civil
Rights in the United States in the 1960s; **Rock Against
Racism** (RAR) in the United Kingdom in the late 1970s
and early 1980s; and the global phenomenon of Live Aid in
1985 (as RAR is one of the most fully documented of these,
it has been considered separately). Further, there is a strong
historical tradition of protest song, particularly in **folk music**,
which has been carried on in **genres** such as **reggae**, **punk**,
and **alternative** music. Within these, and other genres, many
artists have individually used their music to make political

223

statements on a variety of issues, including racism, class, gender politics, **sexuality**, and the environment.

There is disagreement as to the cultural significance and force of such statements. For Grossberg, 'on the one hand, so much activity is attempting to explicitly articulate rock to political activism; on the other hand, this activity seems to have little impact on the rock formation, its various audiences or its relations to larger social struggles' (1992: 168). This argument rests on a perceived 'radical disassociation' of the political content of the music of bands such as U2, REM, and Midnight Oil 'from their emotionally and affectively powerful appeals' (ibid.). It is clear that many listeners derive pleasure from such performers without either subscribing to their politics, or, indeed, even being aware of them. On the other hand, a variety of examples can be adduced to illustrate that many listeners do indeed have their ideological horizons both confirmed and extended by association with political rock, which can also have practical benefits – the Amnesty International tours of 1988 are estimated to have added some 200,000 new members to the organization in the United States alone (see Denselow, 1990; Garofalo, 1992b; Herman and Hoare, 1979; Street, 1986).

As Street concludes, referring to RAR in the United Kingdom, such episodes showed how political strategies were 'played out and resolved in terms of musical choices', a process which indicated 'the limitations of a politics organized around music' (1986: 78). Similar difficulties were evident in attempts to harness rock to the cause of the striking British miners in 1984–5, and with Red Wedge, Labour's attempt to use rock to win the youth vote in the 1987 UK general election. In both cases, strongly held views about the correct relationship of political principle and musical style arguably seriously limited the impact of the efforts (see Denselow, 1990: ch. 8; Frith and Street, 1992).

It has been argued that the history of such attempts to use popular music to forge mass movements will always face two problems. First, the power of popular music is transitory by nature: novelty and shock value have a short life span, and routinization and disempowering follows. Second, there is the confused nature of musical power's 'collectivity': 'The power of mass music certainly comes from its mobilization of an audience; a series of individual choices (to buy this record, this concert ticket) becomes the means to a shared experience and **identity**. The question, though, is whether this identity has any political substance' (Frith and Street, 1992: 80).

A further dimension of this question is the tendency of many commentators to assume incorrectly that 'youth' represents some sort of 'natural left' political constituency. Yet popular music is hardly the preserve of the political left and broadly progressive politics. It can, and has been, used to support a broad range of political positions. President Bush's inaugural performances included an impressive line-up of **blues** and **soul** artists; white supremacist organizations like the National Front in the United Kingdom and neo-Nazi groups in Germany have used the appeal of **punk rock** and **Oi!** to attract new recruits; and US anti-abortion activists have co-opted 'We Shall Overcome' to maintain solidarity at sit-ins outside abortion clinics.

See: **censorship**; **concerts**; **Rock Against Racism**
Further reading: Eyerman and Jamison, 1995; Garofalo, 1992b; McDonnell, 1992; Pratt, 1990.

pop music   It has been observed that

> While the use of the word 'popular' in relation to the lighter forms of music goes back to the mid-19th century, the abbreviation 'pop' was not in use as a generic term until the 1950s when it was adopted as the umbrella name for a special kind of musical product aimed at a teenage market   (Gammond, 1991: 457).

The term pop is often used in an oppositional, even antagonistic sense, to **rock** music, a dichotomy linked to notions of art and commerce in popular music. For example, Hill claims:

225

Pop implies a very different set of values to rock. Pop makes no bones about being mainstream. It accepts and embraces the requirement to ˙be˙ instantly pleasing and to make a pretty picture of itself. Rock on the other hand, has liked to think it was somehow more profound, non-conformist, self-directed and intelligent (Hill, 1986: 8).

Rock'n'roll was created by the grafting together of the emotive and rhythmic elements of the **blues**, the folk elements of **country & western** music, and **jazz** forms such as **boogie-woogie**. Pop is seen to have emerged as a somewhat watered-down, blander version of this, associated with a more rhythmic style and smoother vocal harmony – the period of **teen idols** in the late 1950s and early 1960s (e.g. Bobby Vee). Subsequently the term was used to characterize **chart** and **teenage** audience-oriented music, particularly the **genres** of **dance pop**, **bubblegum**, **power pop**, and the **new romantics**, and performers such as the **girl groups** of the 1960s. Along with **songwriters**, **producers** are often regarded as the main creative force behind pop artists (e.g. Stock, Aitken, and Waterman; Chinn and Chapman; Phil Spector).

Much of pop is regarded as disposable; the best of it survives as 'golden oldies'. Musically it is defined by its general accessibility, an emphasis on memorable **hooks**, and a preoccupation with romantic love as a theme.

Further reading: Friedlander, 1996; Garofalo, 1997; Hill, 1986.

popular culture – *see* **culture**

popular music   Historically, the term popular has meant 'of the ordinary people'. It was first linked in a published title to a certain kind of music that conformed to that criterion in William Chapple's *Popular Music of the Olden Times*, published in installments from 1855. Not until the 1930s and 1940s did the term start to gain wider currency (Gammond, 1991; see also Williams, 1983).

Popular music defies precise, straightforward definition. As Negus observes, unlike film studies,

> popular music is broader and vaguer in scope and intentions. The moving media image can be traced to particular social and technological developments within a particular period of history, and this provides a boundary for study in a way that has no parallel in popular music studies (1996: 5; and see Hayward, 1996).

Such difficulties lead some writers on popular music to slide over the question of definition, and take a common-sense understanding of the term for granted.

This aside, various attempts to provide a definition can be identified:

1 *Definitions placing an emphasis on 'popular'*: Middleton observes that the question of 'what is popular music' is 'so riddled with complexities . . . that one is tempted to follow the example of the legendary definition of folk song – all songs are folk songs, I never heard horses sing 'em – and suggest that all music is popular music: popular with someone' (1990: 3). However, the criteria for what counts as popular, and their application to specific musical styles and **genres**, are open to considerable debate. Classical music clearly has sufficient following to be considered popular, while, conversely, some forms of popular music are quite exclusive (e.g. **thrash metal**).

2 *Definitions based on the commercial nature of popular music, and embracing genres perceived as commercially oriented*: Many commentators argue that it is commercialization that is the key to understanding popular music: 'When we speak of popular music we speak of music that is commercially oriented' (Burnett, 1996: 35). This approach is related to the emphasis on the popular, arguing that such appeal can be quantified through **charts**, **radio** airplay, and so forth. In such definitions, certain genres are identified as 'popular music', while others are excluded (e.g. Clarke, 1990; Garofalo, 1997; and of course the same process of

227

selection is at work in this volume). However, this approach can suffer from the same problems as those stressing popularity, since many genres, especially **meta genres** such as **world music**, have only limited appeal and/or have had limited commercial exposure. Moreover, popularity varies from country to country, and even from region to region within national markets. It also needs to be noted that this approach is largely concerned with *recorded* popular music.

3 *Identification by general musical and non-musical characteristics:* Tagg (1982), in an influential and much-cited discussion, characterizes popular music according to the nature of its distribution (usually mass); how it is stored and distributed (primarily recorded sound rather than oral transmission or musical notation); the existence of its own musical theory and **aesthetics**; and the relative anonymity of its composers. The last of these is debatable, and I would want to extend the notion of composers and its associated view of the nature of musical creativity (see **auteurs**; **producers**; **songwriters**). However, **musicologists** have usefully extended the third aspect of this definition, while sociologists have concentrated on the first two dimensions.

In sum, it seems that a satisfactory definition of popular music must encompass both musical and socioeconomic characteristics. Essentially, all popular music consists of a hybrid of musical traditions, styles, and influences, and is also an economic product which is invested with ideological significance by many of its consumers. At the heart of the majority of various forms of popular music is a fundamental tension between the essential creativity of the act of 'making music' and the commercial nature of the bulk of its production and dissemination (see Frith, 1983: ch. 1).

Further reading: Burnett, 1996; Longhurst, 1995; Middleton, 1990; Negus, 1996; Stratton, 1983; Tagg, 1982.

popular/rock musicals – *see* **film**

postmodernism; **postmodern rock** Postmodernism is a 'portmanteau term encompassing a variety of developments in intellectual culture, the arts and the fashion industry in the 1970s and 1980s' (O'Sullivan *et al.*, 1994: 234). Postmodernism seeks to blur, if not totally dissolve, the traditional oppositions and boundaries between the **aesthetic** and the commercial, between art and the market, and between high and low **culture**. The precise nature of postmodernism, however, proves hard to pin down, and there is a marked lack of clarity and consistency in all the varying usages of the term.

In a key contribution, 'Postmodernism, or the Cultural Logic of Late Capitalism', Jameson overviews postmodernism as the cultural expression of a new phase of capitalism, characterized by communications technologies facilitating the virtually instantaneous shifting of international capital, the emergence of new centres of capital (e.g. Japan) in a global economy, new **class** formations breaking with the traditional labour/capital division, and a consumer capitalism which markets style, images, and tastes as much as actual products. The **commodification** of culture has resulted in a new populism of the mass media, a culture centred around the marketing and **consumption** of surfaces and appearances, epitomized by the ubiquity of commercial **television** (Jameson, 1984). Despite its obvious plausibility as a general explanation of developments in popular culture, postmodernism suffers from a number of difficulties, including its frequent lack of specificity; its over-preoccupation with **texts** and **audiences** at the expense of locating these within their economic and productive context, within which cultural products reside; its reduction of history and politics and ignoral of 'traditional' sociological notions of production, class, and **ideology**.

The postmodernist view of popular music generally regards it as exemplifying the collapse of traditional distinctions between art and the commercial, the aesthetic and unaesthetic, and the **authentic** and unauthentic. This view has been most prominent in discussions of **music video**, with its affinities to advertising (Kaplan, 1987); and, during the 1980s, with commentators on popular music, especially **rock**, who saw the music, once associated with youthful rebellion and political activism, as now thoroughly commercialized and incorporated into the postmodernist capitalist order. Frith (1988a, 1988b) suggested the arrival of a curious entity, post-modernist pop, a value-free zone where aesthetic judgments are outweighed by whether a band can get its video on **MTV** and its picture in *Smash Hits*. In an analysis of a number of major 1980s pop **stars**, Hill echoed Adorno's critique of popular music as manufactured mass culture. Appropriately subtitled 'Manufacturing the 80's Pop Dream', Hill's study of performers such as Michael Jackson, Duran Duran, Wham!, and Madonna, demonstrated that 'this fresh species of genuinely talented practitioners are *ready and willing* to manu-facture themselves' (his emphasis), and that 'never before have commerce and creativity so happily held hands' (Hill, 1986: 9; and see **commodification**). While both Frith and Hill conceded that popular music had always been about style as well as music, they argued that it was now increasingly subverted to the services of commercialism.

Aside from general commodification and **marketing** tendencies in popular music being drawn on to elaborate a postmodern view of the cultural form, postmodernism has also been applied to particular styles of music, treating them almost as a form of **genre** category. Goodwin (1991) offers three definitions for **postmodern rock**: (i) music that is outside the mainstream of popular music and is to be taken seriously; (ii) music that is created by musicians who come chronolog-ically after 'modern rock'; and (iii) music that has evolved from **punk rock**. He observed that because popular music is con-ceptually used to define theory, culture, and practice, 'further analysis of its relation to music will have to take account of this epistemological feedback loop' (1991: 188). A number of contemporary genres demonstrate such characteristics (see **rap**; **dance-music**) although these could no longer be regarded as outside of the mainstream; indeed, they have to a considerable extent actually become the mainstream.

Further reading: Gracyk, 1996; Kotarba, 1994; Longhurst, 1995.

power pop   The term power pop is often seen as a post-**punk**, **major** record label **marketing** device, but it actually has a longer history, being applied to various performers since the 1960s.

The musical source point for nearly all power pop is the Beatles, who established its style. Other major performers credited with developing the **genre** in the 1960s included The Who, The Kinks, and the Move, who all featured aggressive melodies and loud, distorted guitars (the 'power'). Leading American power pop bands during the same period were The Byrds, who originally consciously modelled themselves on the Beatles; Tommy James and the Shondells, and Paul Revere and the Raiders (the last two have also been considered as **bubblegum**).

Subsequent British exponents of power pop included Badfinger, Nick Lowe, Slade, and Sweet (the last two with strong **glam/glitter** associations), along with US bands the Raspberries and Big Star in the early 1970s, and Cheap Trick and the Knack in the 1980s. All were strongly influenced by their 1960s antecedents, and produced 'smart, punchy hook-filled pop' (Erlewine *et al.*, 1995). During the 1980s, many of the **new wave** and **alternative** British and American bands incorporated elements of power pop (e.g. the Replacements, The Stone Roses), as did the bands identified with the **Dunedin sound** (especially The Chills), while contemporary **Britpop** owes major musical debts to it.

See: **British beat**; **Britpop**; **bubblegum**; **glam rock**
Further reading: Erlewine *et al.*, 1995; Garofalo, 1997.
Listening:
The Raspberries, *Raspberries' Best*, Capitol, 1975.
The Knack, 'My Sharonna', on *Get the Knack*, Capitol, 1979.
The Move, *Great Move! The Best of the Move*, EMI, 1994.

preferred readings – *see* **textual analysis**

producers   The occupation of producer emerged as a distinct job category and career path in the popular **music industry**

during the 1950s, initially as someone who directed and supervised recording sessions. Successful producers (e.g. **songwriters** Leiber and Stoller at Atlantic; George Martin at EMI) began exerting pressure on their recording companies to receive credits (on recordings) and royalties. By the mid-1960s, the studio producer had become an **auteur** figure, an artist employing multi-track technology and stereo sound to make recording 'a form of composition in itself, rather than simply as a means of documenting a performance' (Negus, 1992: 87). The main example of this new status was Phil Spector. In the 1970s and 1980s, the producer's important role as a **cultural intermediary** was consolidated with the development of new **technology**: synthesizers, samplers, and computer-based sequencing systems. Producers became central figures in **genres** such as **dub** and **dance-music**.

Currently, the way producers operate, their contribution to the session, and the level of reward they are accorded vary widely, depending on the stature of the musicians they are working with and the type of music being recorded. Producers' approaches to recording vary from the naturalistic, 'try it and see what happens', to a more calculated, entrepreneurial attitude. Production practices represent an amalgam of established techniques and the possibilities offered by the new technologies.

See: **auteurs**; **cultural intermediaries**; **reggae**
Further reading: Blake, 1992; Cohn, 1992; Millard, 1995; Negus, 1992.

progressive rock Progressive rock is a loose musical **meta genre**, closely related to, and often conflated with, **alternative**, **independent**, and **art rock**. Its broad constituency leads Moore (1993, ch. 3) to observe that it is best to always consider the word as qualified by quotation marks. Progressive rock was initially associated with the **counter culture**/underground movement of the mid- to late 1960s, especially in the United Kingdom. It soon became a **marketing** category, with a number of commercially successful performers.

Progressive rock 'is marked, above all, by its diversity, a diversity suggestive of a constellatory, rather than a linear, account' (Moore, 1993: 101–2). In common with art rock, Moore sees it as embracing the use of fantastic and obscure imagery, mixing conventions from disparate styles. This is evident in the names of several of the key albums (e.g. King Crimson's *Lark's Tongues in Aspic*, EG, 1973). The music is primarily not intended for **dancing**, so largely avoids the standard rock **beat**, with **timbre** and texture more important. In performance, progressive rock has made considerable use of theatrical conventions.

Downing describes Pink Floyd's 'Set the Controls for the Heart of the Sun' (from *Saucerful of Secrets,* Capitol, 1978) as:

melodically and rhythmically simple in the extreme. The bass lays down a monotonous riff which is picked up first by the drums and then the organ, creating an irresistible sense of motion. This is amplified by the whispered lyrics, frequently indecipherable but for the oft-repeated hook line. Around this structure are added occasional wailing runs on the organ, rises and falls in volume, and fairly minimal use of electronic atmosphere. All in all a seemingly skeletal piece of music. Yet it is riveting, somehow perfectly conjuring the images pouring from the title line; a journey through space in all its futuristic grandeur, a sense of mystery both enticing and vaguely frightening   (Downing 1976: 99).

Progressive rock enjoyed considerable chart success through the 1970s with bands like Pink Floyd, Tangerine Dream, and Hawkwind. **Punk rock** was in part a reaction against the perceived excesses of what punks derogatorily called 'prog rock'.

See: **alternative rock**; **art rock**
Further reading: Erlewine *et al.*, 1995; Moore, 1993; Thompson, 1994.
Listening:
King Crimson, *In the Court of the Crimson King*, EG, 1969 (rereleased 1989).

Hawkwind, *In Search of Space*, One Way, 1971.
Kansas, *The Best of Kansas*, CBS, 1984.

psychedelic rock; **acid rock**   A musical style usually regarded as a **genre**, which emerged in the mid-1960s, psychedelic rock describes **rock** music inspired by or related to drug-induced experience, with the term used more or less interchangeably with **acid rock** (e.g. Whiteley, 1992; the label 'acid' was the common name for the mind-expanding drug LSD). Various artists recorded songs assumed to refer to drugs. Whiteley provides extensive discussions of several key releases, including the Beatles' 'Tomorrow Never Knows' and 'Strawberry Fields Forever' singles, referring to 'the LSD coding' in these (1992: 66).

Brown claims 'The emphasis is on loud sounds from the lead guitar and the singer, although the words themselves are not very significant' (1992: 145). However, this is debatable with songs like Jefferson Airplane's 'White Rabbit' (1967). Musicians used fuzztone, feedback, synthesizers, and sheer volume, mimicking the supposedly mind-expanding properties of marijuana and LSD. Much of the music was characterized by experimentation and indulgence, with an emphasis on **albums** rather than **singles** (though there were some chart successes, such as Jefferson Airplane's 'Somebody to Love' in 1967). Psychedelic/acid rock was related to fashion, poster and record design, and concert visual effects as well as the music, and was broadly linked with the youth **counter culture** and, more specifically, with the hippy **subculture**.

Psychedelic rock had two main focii in the mid- to late 1960s: the West Coast of the United States, and London. In San Francisco around 1967–9, a psychedelic scene emerged, based around the Haight-Ashbury area, and free, open-air gatherings and commercial Fillmore **concerts**. With the success of the Monterey Pop Festival, US record companies realized the commercial potential of the genre. The main performers included Jefferson Airplane, The Grateful Dead,

Moby Grape, and Quicksilver Messenger Service (see **counter culture**).

In the United Kingdom, psychedelic rock was linked to the 'swinging '60s' London-based **scene**, tending to be conflated with **progressive rock**, and featuring prominently in the **charts** in the late 1960s. Major artists included Cream, Arthur Brown, and Jimi Hendrix; and psychedelia also influenced the leading groups of the period: the Beatles (with *Sgt. Pepper's Lonely Hearts Club Band*, Capitol, 1967) and The Rolling Stones (*Satanic Majesties*, ABKO, 1967).

Psychedelic rock strongly influenced the subsequent development of other genres, especially **alternative**, **art rock**, **heavy metal**, and **progressive rock**; its contemporary influence is clear in some exponents of **Britpop** and some styles of **dance-music**.

See: **counter culture**

Further reading: DeRogatis, 1996; Perry, 1992; Puterbaugh, 1992; Selvin, 1994; Whiteley, 1992.

Listening:

Cream, *Disraeli Gears*, Polydor, 1967.

Jefferson Airplane, *Surrealistic Pillow*, RCA, 1967.

The Grateful Dead, *Anthem of the Sun*, Warner Brothers, 1968.

Quicksilver Messenger Service, *Happy Trails*, Capitol, 1969.

pub rock Initially a musical style/**genre**, pub rock is now identified more in terms of the pub as a context for the **performance** and **consumption** of popular music.

The term originated in England during the early 1970s, when some musicians reacted to the excesses of **glam/glitter rock** by forming energetic bands that derived their sound from early **rock'n'roll** and **R & B**; they played primarily in public houses, hence the label. Pub rock was important because it brought music back into small venues. The style tended to be a very muscular, male-dominated musical form. Pub rock had little commercial impact (until the advent of **punk**, which it influenced, and provided many of the musicians for) although a number of bands recorded and/or charted. The term also gained some currency in Australia and New Zealand, due to the significance of the pub (and the pub circuit) as a venue for live music (see Turner, 1992). Major UK performers included Brinsley Schwarz; Ducks Deluxe; Dr. Feelgood; Eddie and the Hot Rods; and the Motors. Contemporary band Oasis have been ironically referred to as 'pub rock', with their songs being easily sung along to and played a lot in British pubs.

Further reading: Bennett, 1997; Bjornberg and Stockfelt, 1996; Tucker, 1992; Turner, 1992.

Listening:

Brinsley Schwarz, *Brinsley Schwarz*, Capitol, 1970.

Dr. Feelgood, *Malpractice*, United Artists, 1975.

punk A **youth subculture**, closely associated with **punk rock,** during 1977–80 punk became the most visible youth subculture in the United Kingdom and in most Western metropolitan centres (notably London, Los Angeles, and Melbourne). In part punk was a reaction to **hippy** romanticism, and a lack of social status – some commentators saw punks as unemployed youth, celebrating their unemployability. There were several strata: middle-class, art school-influenced punks, influenced by bohemianism; and working-class, 'hard' punks. Punk style was very 'DIY' (do-it-yourself): old school uniforms, plastic garbage bags, and safety-pins combined to present a shocking, self-mocking image. Punks adopted the swastika as an element of their style, though removed from its Nazi setting and adopted as shock-provoking jewellery. Hairstyles were either close-shaved and dyed in bright colours, or (later) Mohican haircuts: spiked up into cockatoo plumes. Punk dances were the robot, the pogo, and the pose: 'collages of frozen automata' (Brake, 1985: 78). Hebdige (1979) stresses the **homology** of these elements in the subculture. Punks tended to align themselves with **Rock Against Racism**, but theirs was a cultural rather than a political phenomenon.

While punk has been regarded by some commentators as originating in England, and then being taken up internationally, there is a strong case for its origins being rather in New York's **alternative music scene** in the 1970s. Punk has maintained itself as a subcultural style through into the 1990s, while being subjected to considerable **commodification**.

Further reading: Brake, 1985; Hebdige, 1979.
Viewing: Sid and Nancy, Alex Cox, 1986; *The Decline of Western Civilization, Part One*, Penelope Spheeris, 1981.

punk rock A musical style/**genre** which, while usually associated with the UK 'punk explosion' of c.1977–80, clearly had its antecedents in the **garage rock** bands of the late 1960s, such as the Troggs, and early 1970s American bands, most notably The Velvet Underground, Iggy and the Stooges, and the New York Dolls. Punk has continued to be a major influence on popular music, with elements of punk style present in a variety of genres into the 1990s (see **alternative rock**; **grunge**; **hardcore**).

Stylistically, much punk music was loud, fast, and abrasive. The myth endures that it was all three chords and an attitude, but the performers actually included some very capable and experienced musicians (in the case of Britain, many were from the **pub rock** scene of the mid-1970s), although 'the issue of skill and competence in punk rock remains ideologically charged' (Laing, 1988: 83). Punk bands relied on **live** shows to establish an **identity** and build a reputation, and 'techniques of recording and of arrangement were adopted which were intended to signify the "live" commitment of the disc' (ibid.: 74). In short, punk records generally sound 'live', as if the studio had not come between the intentions of the musicians and their listening **audience**. While popular music typically foregrounds the voice, 'punk voices . . . seem to want to refuse the perfection of the "amplified" voice' (ibid.: 75). With often shouted, snarled vocals, punk emphasizes the sound (voice plus instruments), rather than lyrical meaning. The ideology of sincerity was central to punk; in interviews, 'the stated beliefs of musicians, and their congruence with the perceived messages of their lyrics,

237

became routine topics' (ibid.: 90). But, as Laing demonstrates, in many cases punk **lyrics** are like collages, a series of often fractured images, with no necessarily correct reading.

Punk's mode of address was 'confidential and declamatory', but with only rare use of the confidential stance; there is also an emphasis on addressing individuals other than 'lovers', and a 'plural specific' address (ibid.: 79). The tempo of punk is usually described using terms such as 'basic' and 'primitive'. As a more minimalist genre, punk rock eschewed the growing use of electronic instruments associated with **progressive rock**, and featured a strict guitar and drums instrumental line-up: 'this was a sound best suited to expressing anger and frustration, focusing chaos, dramatizing the last days as daily life and ramming all emotions into the narrow gap between a blank stare and a sardonic grin' (Marcus, 1992: 595). The lack of importance of virtuosity in instrumental solos reflected punk's frequent association of skill with glibness. Punk's attitude to rhythm was crucial to its sense of difference from other popular genres. It tended to submerge syncopation in its rhythmic patterns – the main reason for the 'undance-ability' of much punk rock. 'Buzzsaw drone' was the typical punk guitar sound, combined with monadic bass-playing, both evident on the Sex Pistol's 'Anarchy in the UK' on *Never Mind the Bollocks* (Warner Brothers, 1977). This combi-nation 'provided a feeling of unbroken rhythmic flow, enhanced by the breakneck eight to the bar rhythm of much punk rock' (Laing, 1988: 86), adding to the urgency which the lyrics and declamatory vocals evoked.

There were marked differences between late 1970s British and American punk, especially in terms of their antecedents and class associations (see Shevory, 1995: 25ff; also Heylin).

1 UK punk emerged in the mid- to late 1970s, with major performers including the Sex Pistols, the Stranglers, the Clash, the Damned, and the Buzzcocks. Marcus (1989) links the Sex Pistols and punk rock to the French **avant garde** (the Situationist internationale) and Dada cultural movements. Other commentators place it against the Thatcher govern-

ment's **new right** economic and social policies (although Thatcher was not elected until 1979), and the alienation and disenchantment of much British youth, especially, but not exclusively, working-class males.

Further reading: Marcus, 1989; Savage, 1991.
Listening:
The Buzzcocks, 'Orgasm Addict' (1977) on *Singles Going Steady*, EMI, 1980.
The Sex Pistols, *Never Mind the Bollocks*, Warner Brothers, 1977.
The Clash, *London Calling*, Epic, 1979.

2 In the mid- to late 1970s the United States boasted an influential punk scene of its own, especially in New York, and arguably one at times with a higher level of musical sophistication than its British counterparts; leading performers included the New York Dolls, Richard Hell and the Voidoids, Television, and Talking Heads (although marketed as **new wave**). American punk had more bohemian, non-working-class associations than its English counterparts. While US punk enjoyed little commercial success in its heyday, it has persisted and mutated in the last twenty years, being influential on various **alternative** performers, particularly **hardcore**, **thrash**, and **grunge**.

Further reading: Fairchild, 1995; Heylin, 1993; McNeil and McCain, 1996.
Listening:
The Velvet Underground, 'White Light, White Heat' (1968) on *Velvet Underground Live*, Polygram, 1974.
The Ramones, *Ramones*, Sire, 1976.
Richard Hell and the Voidoids, 'Blank Generation' on album of same name, 1977.
Television, *Marquee Moon*, Elektra, 1977.

R & B – *see* **rhythm & blues**

race – *see* **ethnicity**

radio; **FM radio**; **radio formats**; **pirate radio** Until the advent of **MTV** in the late 1980s, radio was indisputably the most important broadcast medium for determining the form and content of popular music. The organization of radio broadcasting and its music formatting practices have been crucial in shaping the nature of what constitutes the main 'public face' of much popular music, particularly **rock** and **pop** and their associated **subgenres**. Radio has also played a central role at particular historical moments in popularizing or marginalizing music **genres**. The discussion here provides a brief history of radio in relation to popular music; sketches the current state of 'music radio'; and outlines the regulation and deregulation of radio, with particular reference to pirate radio.

Radio developed in the 1920s and 1930s as a domestic medium, aimed primarily at women in the home, but also playing an important role as general family entertainment, particularly in the evening. Radio in North America was significant for disseminating music in **concert** form, and helped bring regionally based forms such as western swing and **jazz** to a wider audience. Historically the enemy of the record industry during the disputes of the 1930s and 1940s around payment for record airplay, radio subsequently became its most vital promoter. The reshaping of radio in the 1950s was a key influence in the advent of **rock'n'roll**, while radio airplay became central to commercial success, especially through the popular new **chart** shows. 'Hit radio' was 'one of America's great cultural inventions', revitalizing a medium threatened by **television** (Barnes, 1988: 9). The **DJ** (disc jockey) emerged as a **star** figure, led in the United States by figures such as Bob 'Wolfman Jack' Smith and Alan Freed.

FM radio was developed in the early 1930s, using a frequency modulation (hence FM) system of broadcasting. It did not have the range of AM (amplitude modulation), and was primarily used by non-commercial and college radio until the late 1960s, when demand for its clearer sound quality and stereo capabilities saw the FM stations become dominant in the commercial market. They contributed to what became a dominant style of music radio in the 1970s and 1980s (radio friendly; high production values; relatively 'easy listening': see **classic rock**). With the appeal of FM, the 1970s witnessed a consolidation of the historically established role of radio in chart success: 'Independent program directors became the newest power brokers within the industry, replacing the independent record distributors of the early sixties' (Eliot, 1989: 169). Eliot is referring here to the way in which most radio stations now followed formats shaped by consultants, with a decline in the role of programme directors at individual stations, a situation that has persisted into the 1990s. Though video became a major marketing tool in the 1980s, radio continues to play a crucial role in determining and reflecting chart success.

Radio stations are distinguishable by the type of music they play, the style of their DJs, and their mix of news, contests, commercials, and other programme features. We can see radio broadcasts as a flow, with these elements merging. The main types of radio station include college, student, pirate, and youth radio (e.g. the US College stations; New Zealand's campus radio; and Australia's Triple J network); **State** national broadcasters, such as the BBC; community radio; and, the dominant group in terms of market share, the commercial radio stations. There is a longstanding contradiction between the interests of record companies, who are targeting radio listeners who buy records, still largely those in their teens and early twenties, and private radio's concern to reach the older, more affluent audience desired by advertisers. To some extent, this contradiction has been resolved by niche **marketing** of contemporary music radio.

Station and programme directors act as **gatekeepers**, being responsible for ensuring a prescribed and identifiable sound or format, based on what the management of the station believes will generate the largest **audience** – and ratings – and consequent advertising revenue. The station's music director/the programme director (at smaller stations the same person fills both roles) will regularly sift through new releases, selecting three or four to add to the playlist. The criteria underpinning this process will normally be a combination of the reputation of the artist; a record's previous performance, if already released overseas; whether the song fits the station's format; and, at times, the gut intuition of those making the decision. In the case of the first of these factors, reputation and previous track record, publicity material from the label/artist/distributor plays an important role, jogging memories or sparking interest in a previously unknown artist (for example, on UK BBC Radio One's playlist selection, see Grundy, in York, 1991). Chart performance in either the United States or Britain is especially significant where the record is being released in a 'foreign' market. In choosing whether or not to play particular genres of popular music, radio functions as a gatekeeper, significantly influencing the nature of the music itself. This is illustrated in the shifting attitude of radio to **heavy metal** (outlined by Weinstein, 1991a: 149–61).

Historically, **radio formats** were fairly straightforward, and included 'Top 40', 'soul', and 'easy listening'. Recent formats are more complex, and include 'adult-oriented rock' (AOR), classic hits (or 'golden oldies'), contemporary hit radio, and urban contemporary. Barnes (1988) claims that urban contemporary was once a euphemism for black radio, but it now includes artists working within **black music** genres. In the United States, black listeners constitute the main audience for urban contemporary formats, but the music also appeals to white listeners, particularly in the 12–34 age group.

As channel-switching is common in radio, the aim of programmers is to keep the audience from switching stations. Common strategies include playing fewer commercials and running contests which require listeners to be alert for a song or phrase to be broadcast later, but the most effective approach is to ensure that the station does not play a record the listener does not like. While this is obviously strictly impossible, there are ways to maximize the retention of the listening audience. Since established artists have a bigger following than new artists, it makes commercial sense to emphasize their records and avoid playing new artists on high rotation (ie. many times per day) until they have become hits, an obvious catch-22 situation. The most extreme example of this approach is the format **classic rock**, or classic hits, which only plays well-established hits from the past. This format remains very popular, capitalizing on the nostalgia of the **demographic** bulge who grew up during the 1960s, and who now represent a formidable purchasing group in the market place.

The concern to retain a loyal audience assumes fairly focused radio **listening**. Paradoxically, while the radio is frequently switched on, it is rarely 'listened' to, instead largely functioning as 'aural wallpaper', a background to other activities (on this point, and on *who* is listening to the radio, see **consumption**). Yet high-rotation radio airplay remains vital in exposing artists and building a following for their work, while radio exposure is also necessary to underpin activities like **touring**, helping to promote concerts and the accompanying sales of records. The very ubiquity of radio is a factor here; it can be listened to in a variety of situations, and with widely varying levels of engagement, from the walkman to background accompaniment to activities such as study, domestic chores, and reading (for a succinct discussion of the characteristics of radio, see Crisell, 1994).

The **State** regulates radio in two ways. First, in shaping the commercial environment for radio, primarily through licensing systems, but also by establishing codes of practice – a form of **censorship**. This State practice has at times been challenged, most notably by pirate radio (see below). Second, the State has at times attempted to encourage 'minority' cultures, and local musics (with the two frequently connected), through quota and other regulatory legislation. This is evident in the State support of Polynesian radio in New Zealand (see Wilson, 1994); and in attempts to include more French-language music on Canadian radio, a case which illustrates the difficulties of conflating 'the national' in multi-cultural/bilingual settings. A 1989 hearing of the CRTC (the Canadian Radio-Television and Telecommunications Commission) led to a 1990 regulation stipulating 'that at least 65 per cent of the vocal music played weekly by all Franco-phone AM and FM radio stations, irrespective of format or market, must be French-language song'. This was a modifi-cation of the language and country-of-origin requirements which had existed in Canada for some twenty-five years (see Dorland, 1996, especially the contributions by Filion and Straw). The reaction of the various 'key players' to this situation, and the tensions it created for an industry and artists wanting to remain 'culturally politically correct' but also needing to appeal to the larger, international market, illus-trated 'the double-bind in which Quebec is caught: like other small nations [sic], it feels the need to protect its local products from multinational conglomerates but aims none the less at generating its own international hits . . . the debate under study goes to the very heart of this double bind' (Grenier, 1993: 124).

Pirate radio broadcasts are made by unlicensed broadcasters as alternatives to licensed, commercial radio programming. However, the pirate stations usually rely on the same popular music that is programmed on commercial radio, rarely programming music other than the main pop and rock styles.

A major exception was in the 1960s, when the British pirates challenged the BBC's lack of attention to pop/rock music. British pirate radio in its heyday, 1964–8, was an historical moment encapsulating the intersection of rock as cultural politics and personal memory with market economics and government intervention. Twenty-one different pirates operated during this period, representing a wide range of radio stations in terms of scale, motives, and operating practices.

Chapman (1992) argues that the myth of the pirates is that they were about providing pop music to the disenfranchised youthful listeners, representing a somewhat anarchic challenge to radio convention and commerce, but the reality was rather more commercial. However, given that the BBC's popular music policy was woefully inadequate in the early 1960s, the pirates did cater for a largely disenfranchised audience; they also pioneered some innovative programmes and boosted the careers of leading DJs of the time Kenny Everett and John Peel. As their programming indicated, they were never predominantly about popular music, and were heavily oriented toward advertising. All the pirates were commercial operations: 'though work-place and legal judicial circumstances were not typical, in all other respects these were entrepreneurial small businesses aspiring to become entrepreneurial big businesses' (Chapman, 1992: 167). This was particularly evident in the case of Radio London, set up with an estimated investment of £1.5 million, whose 'overriding institutional goals were to maximize profit and bring legal commercial radio to Great Britain' (ibid.: 80). In this respect, the station succeeded, with the BBC's Radio One, established in 1967 as the pirates were being closed down, borrowing heavily from the practices of pirate radio, and hiring pirate DJs. In New Zealand, prominent pirate radio station Radio Hauraki was inspired by the British pirates (see Blackman, 1988). In contrast to the UK pirates, US pirate radio stations operate on shoestring budgets, broadcast irregularly, rarely attempt to turn a profit, do not solicit advertising, and keep a very low profile. The Federal Communications Commission has an attitude of 'selective enforcement', meaning that it acts on complaints and interference, but does not seek out pirate broadcasters. *(Further reading:* Chapman, 1992; Jones, 1992).

The conventional view of radio as existing in a symbiotic relationship with the music industry, functioning primarily as a secondary 'promotional' medium for the industry's products, has been challenged by some observers:

> Consider it this way: perhaps radio was always the primary medium – the commodity experience we (we rock fans, that is) consumed, music simply a means to that consumption . . . it was not the music which gave meaning to music radio, but music radio which gave meaning to the music   (Berland, 1993: 100).

See: **marketing**
Further reading: Barnard, 1989; Crisell, 1994; Cupitt *et al.*, 1996; Morthland, 1992a; Pease and Dennis, 1995; Turner, 1993.

ragtime   A piano style developed around the turn of the century, ragtime was primarily a **black music** genre with prominent European influences. Ragtime is a composed music although it originated in oral, unwritten traditions; its musical features are a left hand based on **chords**, which are broken up differently on each **beat** (commonly in a four-beat phrase); a **melodic** right hand with complex figuration; and uneven accenting between the two hands (syncopation). Its most famous practitioner was Scott Joplin, whose 'Maple Leaf Rag' remains one of the best-known ragtime compositions. Ragtime was an important formative influence in **jazz** and **R & B**.

Further reading: Clarke, 1990; Gammond, 1991.
Listening:
Scott Joplin never recorded – the recordings attributed to him are made from piano rolls he cut; his compositions are to be found in a variety of piano music.

rap; **hip-hop**   Rap has been regarded as 'the most popular and influential form of African-American music of the 1980s and 1990s' (Erlewine *et al.*, 1995: 921) and 'black America's most dynamic contemporary popular cultural, intellectual, and spiritual vessel' (Rose, 1994: 19). The study of rap is regarded as holding the promise of reinvigorating black studies in the United States (Baker, 1993), while rap and hip-hop's concerns with pastiche, collage, and **bricolage** are seen to exemplify **postmodernist** cultural tendencies (e.g. Manuel, 1995). At the same time, rap music has been highly controversial, with its musical and social merits fiercely debated (see **censorship**).

The antecedents of rap lie in the various story-telling forms of popular music: talking **blues**, spoken passages in **gospel**, and **call and response**. Its more direct formative influences were in the late 1960s, with **reggae**'s **DJ** toasters (a talkover style), and stripped down styles of **funk** music, notably James Brown's use of 'stream-of-consciousness' raps over elemental funk back-up.

Initially a part of a **dance** style which began in the late 1970s among black and Hispanic teenagers in New York's outer boroughs, rap became the musical centre of the broader cultural phenomenon of hip-hop: clothing, attitude, talk, walk, and other collaged cultural elements (see below). Rappers made their own mixes, borrowing from a range of musical sources – sampling – and talking over the music – rapping – in a form of improvised street poetry. This absorption and recontextualization of elements of popular culture marked out rap/hip-hop as a form of pop art, or postmodern culture. The style was also commercially significant, as black youth were 'doing their own thing', bypassing the retail outlets: 'By taping bits of funk off-air and recycling it, the break-dancers were setting up a direct line to their culture heroes. They were cutting out the middlemen' (Hebdige, 1990: 140). Many of the early rappers recorded on **independent** labels, initially on twelve-inch **singles**, most prominently Sugar Hill Records in New York. The **genre** was soon taken up by both white artists and the **majors**.

As with other maturing musical styles, a number of identifiable **subgenres** emerged within rap, including:

1 gangsta rap, which is machismo in orientation, and includes themes of gang violence, drugs, and the mistreatment and abuse of women, often with explicitly violent or sexual lyrics (e.g. Snoop Doggy Dog, Ice T). Musically, a heavy bass is prominent;

2 hardcore rap, which focuses on serious political messages aimed at the black community as a whole (e.g. Public Enemy);

3 reggae rap, often termed ragga or Jamaican ragga, which has a distinctive reggae-style beat and rhythm, with the lyrics spoken rather than sung (e.g. Snow, 'Informer'; Shinehead, 'Jamaican in New York');

4 female rap: female vocalists emphasizing gender solidarity and/or power over men; strong beat, heavy bass (e.g. Salt'N'Pepa; Monie Love);

5 East coast, or Daisy Age rap: the latter term was used to describe the music of De La Soul, picking up on their album cover art. It is characterized by a more mellow musical style, drawing on **doo–wop**, 1960s **soul**, and funk. Leading exponents are De La Soul, P.M. Dawn, and A Tribe Called Quest, who all 'broaden the music's emotional and stylistic palette to fashion complicated aural painting' (Weisband, 1995: 413).

Rap has demonstrated continued vitality, while undergoing **commodification** for a broader (and whiter) market, with the blander commercial rap of performers such as MC Hammer, Kris Kross, Vanilla Ice, Puff Daddy, and Warren G. Rap has been subject to both critical denigration and **censorship** (especially gangsta rap), and cultural praise. The social commentary of hardcore rappers such as Public Enemy has seen them considered in Gramscian terms, as a politically significant form of organic intellectual (see Abrams, 1995).

Although misleadingly sometimes used synonomously with rap, **hip–hop** is the broad term that encompasses the social, fashion, music and dance **subculture** of America's urban, black, and latin (mainly, but not exclusively) youth of the 1980s and 1990s. It embraces rap, break-dancing, graffiti art, music clubs with DJs, athletic attire (baseball caps, basketball boots, etc.). Potter claims that hip-hop culture constitutes a 'highly sophisticated postmodernism' (1995: 13), a self-conscious political practice reclaiming, recycling, and reiterating the past for the common people. He argues that the fundamental practice of hip-hop is one of citation (or signifying), and that, as a result, hip-hop necessarily resists the categories of production and consumption. Three versions of the song 'Tramp' are presented to illustrate this point: Lowell Fulsom's 1966 'original' solo version, Otis Redding and Carla Thomas' 1967 duet remake, and Salt'N'Pepa's 1987 hip-hop track of the same name, which samples from and refers to the earlier versions. Potter calls hip-hop a 'cultural recycling center' and a 'counter-formation of capitalism' (1995: 108). Here the central reference point is Michel de Certeau's theory that consumers trace their own paths through the commodity relations with which they are presented. Other observers (e.g. Mitchell, 1996) critique such grand claims being made (often by white intellectuals) for hip-hop or rap, seeing it in more prosaic terms as a form of black street culture.

There is also debate around the identification of rap and hip-hop as specifically **black music**/culture, which is then presented as a unitary cultural movement (e.g. Rose, 1994). This raises questions about the diasporic nature of rap, and the role played by non-black youth in its development. Many of the essays in Ross and Rose (1994) use rap and hip-hop as points of departure to examine cultural practices among **youth cultures**/subcultures more generally.

Further reading: Boyd, 1994; Cross, 1993; Garofalo, 1994; Light, 1991; Lipsitz, 1994; Mitchell, 1996; Potter, 1995; Rose, 1994; Toop, 1991.

Further listening:

Run DMC, *Raising Hell*, London, 1986 (the first rap album to **crossover** to the pop charts, and thereby bring rap into wider public consciousness).

Genius of Rap: The SugarHill Story, Castle, 1987.

Public Enemy, *It Takes a Nation of Millions to Hold Us Back*, Def Jam/Columbia, 1988.

P.M. Dawn, *Of the Heart, the Soul and Of the Cross: the Utopian Experience*, Gee Street/Island, 1991.

The Fugees, *The Score*, Sony/Columbia, 1996 (a huge international success, adding elements of **R & B**, **soul**, and ragga rock to rap).

Rastafari – *see* **reggae**

raves; rave culture   Raves grew out of semi-legal warehouse parties organized by young entrepreneurs in the United Kingdom and United States in the late 1980s (see **dance-music: house**). Raves are **clubs** held outside established dance venues in unconventional places, such as disused warehouses, aircraft hangars, and tents in farmers' fields; these gatherings have attracted up to 15,000 people in Britain (Thornton, 1995). **Rave culture** is the general term applied to the phenomenon of raves, and the social practices which accompany them, including the use of the drug ecstasy, which provoked a (justifiable?) **moral panic** in the United Kingdom, and a number of other countries (e.g. Australia), during the mid- to late 1990s. The main music at raves is **techno** and other variants of **dance-music**.

Further reading: Tagg, 1994; Thornton, 1995.

Listening: The Shamen, 'Ebeneezer Goode', on *Shamen Collection*, One Little Indian/Virgin, 1996 (this UK chart-topping 1992 single was seen by some as endorsing the use of ecstasy).

realism   Realism (i) offers a window on the world, with popular fictions consistent with their own world, which has consistence and plausibility in relation to ours; (ii) mobilizes a particular kind of narrative, constructed through cause and effect, often with a linear structure – a beginning, a middle, and an end; and (iii) conceals the processes of its own production, and the fact that it is a fiction (Longhurst, 1995: 143). The concept of realism has been applied to popular music, primarily in relation to song lyrics and, associated with this, the nature of specific **genres** at particular points in their development.

In relation to song lyrics, realism asserts 'a direct relationship between a lyric and the social or emotional condition it describes and represents' (Frith, 1988a: 112). This is evident in much study of **folk** song and the analysis of **blues** lyrics, such as reading American postwar urban blues lyrics as expressing their black singers' personal adjustment to urban ghettoization: 'a more detailed analysis of blues lyrics might make it possible to describe with greater insight the changes in male roles within the Negro community as defined by Negroes at various levels of socio-economic status and mobility within the lower class' (Keil, 1966: 74).

Longhurst (1995) suggests that realism can also be applied to the development of **reggae**. In the form of **ska** in the 1960s, reggae was strongly realist in its concern with criminality and Jamaica's 'rude boys', with songs debating whether their activities could be considered a form of social and political protest, or simply anti-social, personally motivated criminality. Later reggae music, especially that of Bob Marley and the Wailers, was also strongly realist, addressing class struggle in Jamaica, and black people's international situation in their struggle against the dominance of 'Babylon' (referring to white-dominated Western society). Black underclasses in Jamaica, and elsewhere, could readily identify with the issues in such songs. With the commercialization of reggae in the 1970s, reggae increasingly concealed the manner of its own production, with studio ironing out of the rough edges of the music.

See: **blues**; **reggae**
Further reading: Middleton, 1990.

record covers An important aspect of **marketing**: 'in the record industry, with the proliferation of product, eye-catching covers have become a salient site for elaborating the position being constituted for the artist within various social and cultural institutions' (Ryan, 1992: 203). The practice of printing song lyrics on covers often signals a 'serious' artist, while the iconography of covers frequently connotes characteristics of the recording's **genre**, for example the emphasis on satanic and apocalyptic themes in classic and thrash **heavy metal** album cover imagery. Cover art has become considered as an artistic form (cf. posters), with the publication of collected volumes of the work of artists such as Roger Dean.

See: **semiotics**

record formats Formats are a significant part of popular music, providing empirical data for historical studies of market cycles, shifting consumer tastes, and changing opportunities for musicians. Formats have exercised a significant influence on the marketing of particular **genres** and their associated artists and **audiences**. Changing **technologies** and their associated formats usually appeal to consumers wanting better sound and to those who possess a 'must have' consumerist orientation to such new technologies, thereby creating fresh markets as older consumers upgrade both their hardware and their record collections (see Eisenberg, 1988).

The major record(ing) formats are the shellac 78; the various forms of vinyl (**albums**, **singles**, and **EPs**); the compact disc (**CD**); and the **cassette audio tape**. The importance of several of these warrants their separate consideration. The discussion here considers the initial historical development of these various formats, and the economic and cultural significance of subsequent shifts in their relative importance.

The first major recording/phonograph companies (Columbia, established in 1889; RCA, 1929, incorporating Victor, formed in 1901; and Decca, 1934 in the United States), were engaged from the inception of the industry in a battle over alternative recording and reproducing technologies. At stake was the all-important market share. The ten-inch 78 rpm shellac disc emerged as the standard by the 1930s, but experimentation and research continued. Not only was sound quality a consideration, arguably even more important was the amount of music that could be placed on a record, offering the consumer 'more value for money'. In the early post-war years, Columbia developed a long-playing hi-fidelity record using the newly developed vinyl. In 1948 Columbia released its twelve-inch 33⅓ rpm LP. Refusing to establish a common industry standard, RCA responded by developing a seven-inch vinyl record, with a large hole in the middle, that played at 45 rpm. After several years of competition between the two speeds, the companies pooled their talents and agreed to produce in both formats. By 1952, the LP had become the major format for classical music and the 45 the format for single records for popular radio airplay, jukeboxes, and retail sales (*Further reading:* Millard, 1995; Sanjek, 1988).

Since the 1950s, there have been marked shifts in the popularity of various recording formats. The 1980s saw the decline of the vinyl single, world-wide sales of which dropped by a third from 550 million in 1980 to 375 million in 1988. The global sales of vinyl LPs continued their decline into the 1990s, while CD sales continued to show a significant increase. Globally, unit sales in 1992 were 1.55 billion cassettes, 1.15 billion CDs, 130 million LPs, and 330 million singles. Vinyl made a limited 'comeback' in the mid-1990s in the US market: the number of vinyl albums sold nearly doubled to 2.2 million in 1995, the most recent year for which sales figures are available, with several major artists choosing to release albums on vinyl before the CD (e.g. Pearl Jam, Hootie and the Blowfish).

Plasketes suggests that the rise of the CD 'simultaneously laid the foundation for a new **subculture** of vinyl collectors', and that the market for vinyl, although diminished, remains viable (Plasketes, 1992: 109). But most observers regard the vinyl LP as now clearly outmoded, particularly since 'the future (geographic) growth areas for sound carriers are Asia and Africa, both continents where mass markets have been created by the compact cassette' (Laing, 1990: 235). The CD single has also emerged as a major recording and marketing medium. New technologies such as erasable or recordable compact discs and Mini-Discs hold out the quality of digital sound with the additional cachet of the ability to record, although they are also accompanied by industry concerns over **piracy**.

Opinions differ on the relative musical and cultural value of vinyl and the CD. For those still emotionally tied to vinyl, 'The boom in the used record store business can largely be attributed to the growing number of CD converts selling their entire record collection on their way to buying their first disc player' (Plasketes, 1992: 116). Others prefer the scale of the **record cover** art on vinyl albums. Performers are equally effected by the shifts in formats. Historically, with a few significant exceptions (e.g. Led Zeppelin), performers have generally relied on the single to promote their album release. Commercial success without a single has now become more common. Whatever the aesthetic status of the vinyl single, its material significance lay in its availability to artists with limited resources. The seven-inch 45 and the 12-inch dance single, with their specialist market tied to the club scene, offer such performers only a partial substitute, while many independent record companies cannot afford CDs, further restricting the market options available to their artists.

See: **albums**; **cassette audio tape**; **charts**; **CD**; **singles**

recording – *see* **sound recording**

reggae; **ska**; **Rastafari**   The collective term for a number of successive forms of Jamaican popular music, including ska and rocksteady, picked up in the West since the 1960s, reggae has had an influence on popular music vastly disproportionate to its relatively limited commercial success.

Reggae initially developed in the 1950s when Jamaican musicians combined indigenous folk music with **jazz**, African and Caribbean rhythms, and New Orleans **R & B**. The resultant hybrid was **ska**. In the early 1960s, ska was exported to the United Kingdom, with some **chart** success (eg. the Skatalites, Millie Small). In the mid-1960s, influenced by American **soul** music, ska's 'hyper' rhythms gave way to the slower, loping beats of rocksteady. Around the end of the 1960s, these styles of Jamaican popular music came to be known as reggae, which 'embellished the bedrock rhythms of ska and rocksteady with political and social lyrics, often influenced by Rastafarianism, racial pride, and the turbulent Jamaican political climate. The rhythms ebbed and flowed with the hypnotic, jerky pulse that has become reggae's most identifiable trademark' (Erlewine *et al.*, 1995: 938), along with the bass and choppy rhythm tracks. Key early figures included Toots and the Maytals, The Wailers, Burning Spear, and Jimmy Cliff.

While the influences of ska and reggae were evident in some Western popular music (e.g. the Spencer Davis Group's 'Keep on Running', 1967), the **genre** had only a cult following outside of Jamaica. This changed in the 1970s, with Island Record's popularization of Bob Marley and the Wailers. Marley himself became a cult figure, revered among many young blacks, even more so after his death in 1981 (see White, 1989), and reggae was subsequently influential on many 'white' performers (e.g. The Police, The Clash, UB40). Reggae continued to evolve, with 'toasting' (a **DJ** talkover style) and dub forms in the 1980s, both of which demonstrated the importance of the **record producer** and the Jamaican **sound system** to the genre.

Listening:

Toots and the Maytals, *Funky Kingston*, Island, 1973.

Peter Tosh, *Equal Rights*, Columbia, 1977.

Bob Marley and the Wailers, *Legend: the Best of Bob Marley and the Wailers*, Island, 1984.

Gary Clail, *Keep the Faith*, Sony, 1995.

Glen Brown and King Tubby, *Termination Dub 1973–1979*, Blood and Fire/Chant, 1996.

Lee Perry, *The Producer Series/Words of My Mouth*, Trojan, 1996 (compiles Perry's 1970s work).

There was a ska revival in the United Kingdom in the late 1970s, primarily associated with Coventry and the Two Tone record label. Bands with both black and white members worked with elements of reggae, ska, dub, and rock (e.g. UB40, the Specials, Madness, Selector, Bad Manners). Their record **lyrics** were politically and socially conscious, often containing British working-class themes and criticizing the 'establishment'.

Listening:
The English Beat, *I Just Can't Stop It*, IRS, 1980.
Madness, *Complete Madness*, Stiff, 1982.
The Specials, 'Ghost Town' (1981), on *The Specials: The Singles Collection*, Chrysalis, 1991.

Reggae is strongly associated with **Rastafari**, variously considered as a social movement, a religious cult, and a youth **subculture**, which came out of the ghettos of Kingston, Jamaica, in the 1950s. Rastafarianism preaches the divinity of Haile Selassie of Ethiopia, characterizes white domination as 'Babylon', and advocates a black return to Africa, focused on Ethiopia. Rastafarian males grow their hair in long, plaited dreadlocks, while women cover their heads, use no cosmetics, and wear long, modest dresses. Rastas wear woollen caps coloured green (Ethiopia), red (for blood of their brothers), yellow (the sun), and black (their skin). The use of marijuana ('ganja') is also given a religious significance. Rastafarianism, at least at the level of cultural style, was widely adopted among 'black' groups internationally, for example among the Maori in New Zealand. Reggae plays a major role in communicating the ideals of the movement, through reggae artists acting as role models, and through the themes and lyrics of the music.

Reggae has maintained a commercial and artistic presence through into the 1990s, often forming an important constituent of other popular music genres. It remains a minority taste, although several more contemporary reggae pop hybrids (Aswad, UB40) have achieved chart success, as have some **rap** performers who utilize reggae rhythms, such as Shinehead (*Unity*, Elektra, 1988).

See: **realism**

Further reading: Bishton, 1986; Davis, 1992; Jones, 1988; Ward, 1992b (includes discography); White, 1989.

reissues – *see* **back catalogue**

retail – *see* **marketing**

rhythm & blues (R & B)   In its earliest forms, R & B was one of the most important precursors of **rock'n'roll**, and a crucial bridge between **blues** and **soul**. George accords R & B a socio-economic as well as a musical meaning, linking it to a black community sense of identity 'forged by common political, economic and social conditions' (1989: xii).

The earliest R & B artists emerged from the American big band and swing **jazz** era (in the 1930s and 1940s), playing **dance music** that was louder, used more electric instrumentation, especially the new bass guitar, and accentuated **riffs**, boogies, and vocals. The first popular style of R & B was jump blues, which blended a horn-dominated line-up with swing rhythms from jazz, and general **chord** structures and riffs from blues. Several different styles evolved: vocal 'shouters' (e.g. Big Joe Turner); instrumentalists, especially saxophonists, with strong jazz connections; and smoother, urbane vocal styles. Associated with independent labels (e.g. Speciality), jump blues was popular in cities with growing black communities, especially Los Angeles. Louis Jordan was the most prominent performer, enjoying considerable **crossover** success through the 1940s and early 1950s.

In the early 1950s, 'race' music, as it was termed in the industry, was renamed R & B by *Billboard* magazine. While popular on its own charts, and black radio stations, it received little airplay on white radio stations. Indeed, R & B records were sometimes banned because of their explicit sexual content, such as Hank Ballard's 'Work With Me Annie', Billy Ward's 'Sixty Minute Man', and the Penguin's 'Baby Let Me Bang Your Box'. Jerry Wexler, an **A & R** man at Atlantic, helped shape jump blues into more commercial styles, which pointed the way for rock'n'roll. Around the same time, piano-based New Orleans R & B also crossed over, especially with the success of Fats Domino (e.g. 'Ain't That a Shame', 1955).

R & B was a major part of rock'n'roll. Some would argue that it *was* rock'n'roll, appropriated by white musicians and record companies, for a white audience. R & B elements were merged into the various styles of **rock**, including British R & B of the 1960s (e.g. The Rolling Stones, The Pretty Things, Them) and subsequently into **disco**, **funk**, and **rap**. Indeed, so broad has been the presence of R & B, that the term is sometimes used as a general name for the corpus of **black music**. Contemporary R & B swingbeat groups like Boyz II Men and SWV can be regarded as examples of the genre returning to its black roots.

Further reading: George, 1989; Gillet, 1983.

rhythm; **riff** – *see* **beat**

riot grrrls – *see* **gender**

rock – *see* **rock'n'roll**

Rock Against Racism An organization and movement which conducted a partially successful mass campaign to confront the racism arising in the harsh urban landscapes of inner-city Britain in the 1970s. Rock Against Racism (RAR) used demonstrations, concerts, a magazine, and records to mobilize upwards of half a million people: 'black and white people, outside conventional politics, inspired by a mixture of socialism, punk rock and common humanity, got together and organized to change things' (Widgery, 1986: 8).

In February 1981 *Rock Against Racism's Greatest Hits* (Virgin) was the first album done as a political gesture, providing a precedent for the subsequent efforts of Amnesty International, Band Aid, *et al*. Leading groups and artists also contributed to mass concerts and carnivals, which served to politicize while providing entertainment. Successful anti-National Front rallies were held, and a magazine, *Temporary Hoarding*, was selling 12,000 copies per issue by 1979. While the campaign failed to stop racist attacks, far less racism, it was a factor in the sharp decline of the National Front's share of the vote in the general election of 1979, following the fascist organization's surge of support in the mid-1970s.

RAR strengthened the idea that popular music could be about more than entertainment, and in a sense provided the inspiration for similar campaigns in the 1980s. But Street notes the manner in which the RAR campaign illustrates 'the delicacy of the relationship between a cause and its music', as the reliance on the music as the source of unity and strength threw into sharp relief differences of stylistic affiliations. Political strategies were 'played out and resolved in terms of musical choices', a process which indicated 'the limitations of a politics organized around music' (1986: 78; and see **politics**).

Further reading: Denselow, 1990: ch. 8; Frith and Street, 1992; Widgery, 1986.

Listening:

Tom Robinson Band, *Power in the Darkness*, Capitol, 1978.

rock criticism – *see* **music press**

rockabilly An early fusion of **black** and **country** musics in the American South, predating (just) and overlapping with **rock'n'roll**, with its peak in the mid-1950s. **Blues**-inspired and **bluegrass**-based, rockabilly was described by exponent Carl Perkins as 'blues with a country beat'. Primarily a male form, key figures included Perkins, Gene Vincent, Eddie

Cochrane, and Elvis Presley (the Sun sessions). Guralnick claims the form started and ended with Elvis.

Rockabilly tended to be a rigid and strictly defined form, with imitation at its core (at least in the 1950s):

> Its rhythm was nervously up-tempo, accented on the offbeat, and propelled by a distinctively slapping bass. The sound was always clean, never cluttered, with a kind of thinness and manic energy that was filled by the solid lead of Scotty Moore's guitar or Jerry Lee's piano. The sound was further bolstered by generous use of echo (Guralnick, 1989: 68).

Rockabilly was subsequently carried on by late 1950s and 1960s performers such as Roy Orbison and the Everly Brothers, and into the 1980s by revivalists like the Stray Cats. Rockabilly was an influence on the work of many rock'n'roll performers, including the early Beatles. More recently, bands like The Blasters and Jason and the Scorchers played a style of rock infused with elements of rockabilly, **country and western**, and **punk**.

Further reading: Guralnick, 1992 (includes discography).
Listening:
Elvis Presley, *The Complete Sun Sessions*, RCA, 1987.
The Blasters, 'Marie Marie' (1981); from *The Blasters Collection*, Slash/Warner Brothers, 1990.
Rock This Town: Rockabilly Hits, vols 1 and 2, Rhino, 1991.

rock'n'roll; **teddy boys**; **rockers**; **rock**; **classic rock**   Rock 'n'roll was the **genre** of popular music that emerged when black **rhythm & blues** songs began to get airplay on radio stations aiming at a wider, predominantly white audience, and when white artists began re-recording black R & B songs. R & B, American **country** music, and 1940s and 1950s **boogie-woogie** music are all elements of early rock'n'roll. Some writers (e.g. Gammond, 1991; Garofalo, 1997) conflate it with rock, which became the more general label for the various styles which mutated from rock'n'roll. Two main

youth subcultures were associated with rock'n'roll: teddy boys and rockers.

Alan Freed, a Cleveland **DJ**, is usually given credit for coining the phrase 'rock'n'roll' in the early 1950s. However, as Tosches (1984) documents, the style had been evolving well before this. The term 'rock'n'roll', with its sexual connotations, was popularized in the music of the 1920s. In 1922, **blues** singer Trixie Smith recorded 'My Daddy Rocks Me (With One Steady Roll)' for Black Swan Records, and various lyrical elaborations followed from other artists through the 1930s and 1940s.

In April 1954, Bill Haley and the Comets made the single 'Rock Around the Clock'. The record was a hit in America, then world-wide, eventually selling 15 million copies. It represented a critical symbol in the popularization of the new musical form. Subsequent major figures included Chuck Berry, Little Richard, and, in particular, Elvis Presley.

The new music provoked considerable criticism, with many older musicians contemptuous of rock'n'roll. British jazzman Steve Race, writing in *Melody Maker*, claimed:

> Viewed as a social phenomenon, the current craze for rock'n'roll material is one of the most terrifying things ever to have happened to popular music . . . Musically speaking, of course, the whole thing is laughable . . . It is a monstrous threat, both to the moral acceptance and the artistic emancipation of jazz. Let us oppose it to the end   (cited in Rogers, 1982: 18).

Other criticism focused on the moral threat, rather than the new teenage music's perceived **aesthetic** limitations. To many, rock'n'roll appeared hostile and aggressive, epitomized by Elvis Presley's sensual moves.

Music Central sums up the contemporary status of the genre:

> The prominence of the guitar, a substantial beat, the orientation to young people, and the blatant sexuality of the songs and the performers were, and still are, some of the basic building blocks of rock'n'roll. Since the

261

1950s, the phrase has come to mean many different things and encompass a wide assortment of sub-genres: progressive rock, punk rock, acid rock, heavy metal, country rock, glitter rock, new wave, alternative rock . . . all variations on a 40-year old theme (*Music Central 96*).

Originally a British phenomenon, **teddy boys**, or 'teds', first appeared in the mid-1950s. Mainly from unskilled backgrounds, the teds had been left out of youth's new affluence. Their style included hair worn in elaborate quiffs (the 'duck's arse' style, etc.) dressed with grease, long, pseudo-Edwardian drape jackets (hence the name), thick crepe-soled shoes ('brothel creepers') and thin string ties: 'the "Teddy boy" appropriation of an upper-class style of dress "covers" the gap between largely manual, unskilled near-lumpen real careers and life chances, and the "all-dressed-up-and-nowhere-to-go" experience of Saturday evening' (Hall and Jefferson, 1976: 48). The teds' music preferences were early rock'n'roll and **rockabilly**. New Zealand and Australian imitative versions of the teds in the 1950s were termed 'bodgies'.

The teddy boys' activities centred around rock'n'roll music, coffee bars and cafes with juke boxes, and pubs. They were involved in riots in cinemas and dance halls during the advent of rock'n'roll, and in the 1958 race riots in the United Kingdom: 'the ted was uncompromisingly proletarian and xenophobic' (Hebdige, 1979: 51). There were teddy boy revivals in the 1970s and 1980s, although the 'modern' teds' dress and demeanour carried rather different connotations, being more reactionary and closer to their working-class machismo parent culture.

In Britain in the 1960s, the teds evolved into **rockers** (also known as bikers, or greasers, especially in the United States). The rockers wore black leather jackets, jeans and boots, had greased hair and rode motorbikes. Largely low-paid, unskilled manual workers, they were a male-oriented subculture; female followers rarely rode bikes. Willis (1978) sees a homology between the rocker's masculinity, rejection of middle-class lifestyle, the motorbike, and the preference for rock'n'roll.

The rockers' key value was freedom, and their preferred music was 1950s rock'n'roll: Elvis, Gene Vincent, and Eddie Cochrane. The rockers clashed violently with the **mods** in 1963–4 at southern English holiday resorts, producing a **moral panic**. They have never entirely vanished as an identifiable subculture, although contemporary bikers show a preference for **heavy metal**.

Rock is the broad label for the huge range of styles that have evolved out of rock'n'roll. Rock is often considered to carry more weight than **pop**, with connotations of greater integrity, sincerity, and **authenticity**. **Classic rock** is a term originally used for a **radio** format concentrating on playing 'tried and proven' past **chart** hits which will have high listener recognition and identification (see Barnes, 1988). Also known as 'oldies' or 'gold', classic rock playlists are largely drawn from the Beatles through to the end of the 1970s, and emphasize white rock performers such as Cream, The Doors, Led Zeppelin, Creedence Clearwater Revival, and The Who. The format became prominent in part because of the consumer power of the ageing post-war **baby boomers**, and the appeal of this group to radio advertisers. Classic rock has also become a loosely defined genre and a general marketing category.

See: **hard rock**

Further reading:

(a) on rock'n'roll; rock; classic rock: Brown, 1992; Cohn, 1970; DeCurtis and Henke, 1992a; Gillet, 1983; Tosches, 1984; Ward *et al.*, 1986.

(b) on teddy boys; rockers: Brake, 1985; Cohen, 1980; Gelder and Thornton, 1997; Hebdige, 1979; Melley, 1970; Willis, 1978.

Listening:

Elvis Presley, 'Heartbreak Hotel' (1956) and 'Hound Dog' (1956), on *The Top Ten Hits* (double album compilation), RCA, 1987.

rockumentaries – *see* **film**

roots   Term variously used to refer to (i) an artist's sociological and geographical origins, and the relationship between these and their music; (ii) the audience/environment in which the artist's career is rooted; and (iii) more generally, for artists who are considered the originators of musical styles/**genres** (see, for example, Guralnick's study (1989) of 'major roots musicians' in **rockabilly**, **C & W**, and **blues**). Roots is often a genre-specific term, being most frequently used in relation to styles such as **folk**, the blues, and various **world musics**. It is also often a constituent of populist notions of **authenticity**. Musically, roots is based on the notion that the sounds and the style of the music should continue to resemble its original source. Acceptance of this can lead to a questioning of 'traditional' artists using musical hi-tech equipment.

See: **authenticity**; **folk culture**

salsa   Salsa is Spanish for 'sauce' or 'spice', and has been used in relation to music since the 1920s in a similar fashion to 'funky'. As Negus observes,

> three distinct 'identity claims' have been made on behalf of salsa music as a musical **genre**. First, that it is Cuban in origin and essence. Second, that it is a music that expresses the lives and dreams of working-class Puerto Ricans. Third, that it is a music that expresses a broader pan-Latin consciousness   (1996: 114).

He goes on to show that these claims are difficult to sustain.

For many musicians and commentators, salsa is a euphemism for Cuban music. The word salsa was used for many years by Cuban musicians before the genre became popularized in New York in the late 1960s, and salsa provided a neutral marketing label to bypass the US economic blockade of Cuba following the Castro-led revolution of 1959. Concord Picante, the salsa label of the Concord **jazz** company, helped popularize the genre in the 1980s. Historically significant salsa musicians include Celia Cruz, known as the Queen of Salsa, and mambo bandleader Tito Punte, while Ruben Blades is the most prominent contemporary salsa performer.

The staple musical elements present in salsa – the son and the clave (see Negus, 1996: 115–16) – are derived from essentially Cuban styles. However, this direct link between

265

salsa and Cuba is problematic, given that salsa is produced mainly by Cubans and Puerto Ricans living in New York and Puerto Rico. Further, a number of other features have been detected in the music, including Puerto Rican 'folk-loric' forms such as the bomba, big-band jazz, **soul**, **call and response** patterns from work songs, and even **funk** and **rock** elements (Negus, 1996: 117). Accordingly, it seems more appropriate to consider salsa as a hybrid genre.

The association between salsa and working–class Puerto Ricans has been argued using content analysis of song **lyrics** (eg. Padilla, 1990). This assumes an intrinsic connection between social context, the production and reception of the music, and song lyrics. Claims for salsa's expression of a pan-Latin consciousness are similarly based. Negus shows how the case of Ruben Blades demonstrates the difficulties with any such straightforward correspondences, arguing instead for a more complex process of mediation of the music. Blades, who was born in Panama, educated at Harvard, and lives in New York, writes and performs socially committed songs, which began to reach a wider audience following his signing to Elektra in 1984.

Negus sees here a common problem that theorists of dias-pora have encountered: 'once in circulation, music and other cultural forms cannot remain "bounded" in any one group and interpreted simply as an expression that speaks to or reflects the lives of that exclusive group of people' (1996: 121; on this point, see **black music**).

Further reading: Hardy and Laing, 1990: entries on Ruben Blades, Celia Cruz, Tito Punte; Padilla, 1990; Negus, 1996: 113–22.
Listening:
Celia Cruz, *Celia and Johnny*, Voya, 1975.
Ruben Blades, *Nothing But the Truth*, Elektra, 1988.
Ruben Blades, *Buscando America*, Elektra, 1994.

sampling The practice of using computer technology to take selected extracts from previously recorded works and using them as parts of a new work, usually as a background sound to accompany new vocals. Sampling has been the subject of considerable controversy, with debate around issues of authorship and creativity, the nature of musicianship, **authenticity**, and the legality of the practice.

See: **copyright**; **rap**; **technology**

Further reading: Beadle, 1993 (includes a useful discography); Goodwin, 1990; Jones, 1992.

Listening:

De La Soul, *3 Feet High and Rising*, Tommy Boy, 1989.

KLF (Kopyright Liberation Front) [*sic*] *The History of the Jams aka The Timelords*, TUT, 1989.

Jive Bunny and the Mixmasters, *Jive Bunny: The Album*, Telstar, 1989.

San Francisco sound – *see* **psychedelic rock**

scene – *see* **alternative scenes**; **locality**

Seattle scene; Seattle sound   In 1992 the Seattle music scene came to international prominence, closely linked with the mainstream breakthrough of **alternative** music promoted by American college **radio**. Nirvana's second album and major-label debut *Nevermind* (Geffen, 1991) topped the *Billboard* charts; Pearl Jam and Soundgarden were major drawcards at the second Lollapalooza touring music **festival** in 1992, and both bands also enjoyed huge record sales. The Seattle sound broadly referred to a group of bands initially recording with Seattle's Sub Pop **independent** record label, which were known for their **grunge** sound.

The Seattle scene and the grunge music with which it was associated became the most written-about phenomenon in contemporary popular music since the birth of **punk**. Major labels scoured Seattle for unsigned bands or internationally sought out grunge-oriented performers (e.g. Australia's Silverchair). The film *Singles* (Cameron Crowe, 1992), set amidst the Seattle scene, was widely publicized and commercially successful. The popularization of grunge-related fashion saw spreads in *Elle* and *Vogue* touting highly expensive flannel shirts from the world's most famous designers. The Seattle sound became a marketing ploy for the **music industry**, as well as an ideological touchstone for **Generation X**. ' "Seattle" defines the source of the phenomenon and organizes its often disparate expression. In writing about the Seattle scene, critics are not just chronicling a random success story. They are grappling with the notion of a geographically specific scene itself' (Bertsch, 1993).

A combination of factors explained why this took place in Seattle: the ability of Sub Pop to feed into the **majors**; many good bands of similar style; the strong local alternative scene, linked to the Universities of Washington and Evergreen State (the latter a progressive, no-grades school with an alternative-oriented radio station); and the city's geographical separation from Los Angeles (Kirschner, 1994). Critics emphasized the purity and **authenticity** of the Seattle scene as a point of origin, defining bands like Nirvana in opposition to the mainstream. The foundations for the success of bands such as Nirvana and Soundgarden were laid throughout the 1980s by earlier alternative music scenes. What had changed, suggests Bertsch, was that by the early 1990s it had become easier and quicker for new alternative or **indie** bands to attract the attention of major labels or commercial radio, and to move to major labels and achieve some mainstream success:

> By the summer of 1991, the reasonably rapid rise of Jane's Addiction and popularity of the 'alternative' Lollapalooza rock festival that lead singer Perry Farrell organized clearly heralded a significant change in the 'natural laws' of commercial success. The success of the Seattle scene is thus neither an accident of fate, nor a testament to the superiority of Seattle bands' music. It is, rather, the product of many different scenes and the labor that went into them (Bertsch, 1993).

Seattle is part of a nationwide American indie **subculture**.

See: **alternative scenes**; **locality**
Further reading: Bertsch, 1993; Garofalo, 1997; Kirschner, 1994.
Viewing: Hype! (Doug Pray, 1996); *Singles* (1992).

semiotics – *see* **structuralism**

session musicians – *see* **musicians**

sexuality   Sexuality refers to the expression of sexual identity,
through sexual activity, or the projection of sexual desire and
attraction; this occurs primarily in relation to other people, but
can also be related to material or cultural artifacts. Sexuality and
desire are central human emotions, or drives, which have been
an essential part of the appeal of the **culture/entertainment
industries**, including popular music, and the social processes
whereby performers and their **texts** operate in the public arena.
Popular music is also a significant area of culture in which sexual
politics are struggled over. (For a comparison of how these
concepts and processes operate in film, see Hayward, 1996.)

   Sexuality is central to discussions of how male and, more
frequently, female performers are conceived of – socially
constructed – as sex objects or symbols of desire. Here certain
forms of subjectivity and **identity** are projected as 'normal',
traditionally white, male sexuality. The operation of this
process is a major focus in studies of **music video** and
stars/stardom, and in relation to particular **genres**. It
involves considerations of the nature of spectatorship and the
(gendered) gaze, utilizing conventions primarily developed in
film studies (see for example Kaplan, 1987 on music video).

   Sexual ambiguity is central to many forms of popular music,
which has frequently subverted the dominant sexuality
constructed around male–female binaries. Discussion has
concentrated on exploring the relationship between sexual
orientation, public personas, and a performer's music. Some
performers openly represent or subvert and 'play with' a range
of sexualities. Others constitute themselves, at times very
self-consciously, as objects of heterosexual desire, or as icons

for different ('deviant') sexualities and their constituencies. Early 1950s male stars were 'adored objects', catering to both homosexual desire and female consumption (e.g. Elvis Presley). Later performers include representations of the homoerotic (e.g. Madonna, Morrissey of The Smiths, Suede); androgyny (Bowie during the Ziggy period); the effeminate (the Cure), and asexuality (Boy George); bisexuality (Morrissey, Suede); and gay and lesbian (Freddie Mercury; k.d. lang). The application of such labels, their connotations, and their relationship to 'real' gay communities have been at times strongly contested (see Geyrhalter, 1996).

Some genres and performers are linked to particular sexualities or communities. For example, **disco** generally celebrates the pleasure of the body and physicality, and is linked to the gay community and specific **club scenes**; **heavy metal** has traditionally been associated with overt masculinity (though see Walser, 1993, who contends that the genre has historically been actively *made* as male), as have some forms of rock (**hard rock/cock rock**).

The **lyrics** of many mainstream **pop** songs deal with heterosexual love, desire, longing, and lust; some deal with other sexual orientations and sexual practices, such as the Kinks' 'Lola'. Some songs function at an ironic, 'in joke' level, like The Village People's 'In the Navy' and 'YMCA'. Some openly support or express solidarity with particular sexualities, for instance Tom Robinson's 'Glad to be Gay'. Other musical **texts** criticize non-heterosexuality or openly express homophobic or misogynist views (see **rap**). There is considerable argument over whether these texts are 'read' by their **listeners**, **audiences**, and **fans** in any straightforward manner, or whether the artists' intended or **preferred readings**, embedded in the text, are acknowledged, let alone assimilated into individual and social values and meanings.

See: **gender**; **hard/cock rock**; **lyric analysis**

Further reading: Frith and McRobbie, 1990; Henderson, 1993; Negus, 1996: 123–33; Reynolds and Press, 1995; Savage, 1988; Stringer, 1992.

Listening:

Little Richard, 'Tutti Frutti' (1956), on *The Georgia Peach*, Specialty, 1991.

Lou Reed, 'Walk on the Wild Side' (1973), on *Walk on the Wild Side: the Best of Lou Reed*, RCA, 1977.

The Smiths, 'This Charming Man' (1983), on *The Smiths: Best of 1*, Warner Brothers, 1992.

Frankie Goes to Hollywood, 'Relax' (1984), on *Bang! Greatest Hits*, 2TT/Island, 1994.

Suede, 'Pantomime Horse', 'Animal Nitrate', on *Suede*, Nude/Columbia, 1993.

singer songwriters – *see* **songwriters**

singles; **EPs**   Historically often referred to as '45s' (the rpm), the single is a record(ing) format of considerable historical importance, though its contemporary status and influence is at issue. The single was originally a seven-inch vinyl format, with an 'A-side', the recording considered most likely to receive radio airplay and **chart** 'action', and a 'B-side', usually seen as a recording of less appeal. A few B-sides have achieved chart success along with their 'A' counterparts: 'double-sided hits' (now termed 'double A-sides'), such as several of the Beatles' singles. An EP is an 'extended play' single, a vinyl seven inch, usually with four songs. In the United Kingdom the EP represented an early form of 'greatest hits' package, with attractive **record covers**, and outsold **albums** until the early 1960s.

In the early 1950s, the vinyl single overtook its shellac 78 counterpart as the dominant music industry **marketing** vehicle. Singles became the major selling format, the basis for **radio** and **television** programming, and the most important chart listing, with the last two in an apparently symbiotic relationship. Singles appealed to young people with limited disposable income. For the record companies, singles were cheaper to produce than an album, and acted as market 'testers'. While singles success was important for performers and the record

271

companies in itself, it was also important as a means of drawing attention to the accompanying, or subsequent album, with the release of both being closely related. With a few significant exceptions (e.g. Led Zeppelin), performers generally relied on the single to promote their album release. This approach became the 'traditional' construction of record marketing through the 1960s and 1970s. Album compilations of singles, either by one performer or from a **genre** or style of music became an important market. While some performers with high-charting singles were 'one hit wonders', singles success frequently launched careers, leading to an album deal and moves from **independent** to **major** labels.

In the 1980s new single formats gained an increasingly significant market share. There was a massive increase in sales of **cassette** singles in America, which sold 32.7 million in the first half alone of 1989, already surpassing the 1988 full-year total of 22.5 million. In 1990, Swedish band Roxette's 'Listen to Your Heart' became the first single to hit No. 1 in the United States without being released as a vinyl 45. Twelve-inch singles, including remixes, became an important part of the **dance music** scene, and, accompanying the general rise of the **CD** format, the CD single also began to emerge as a popular marketing form and consumer preference.

At the same time, the single increasingly became a device for marketing an album. Negus (1992: 65) documents the decline of the vinyl single through the 1980s. In the United States, sales of singles from 1979–90 declined by 86 per cent (from 195.5 million to 27.6 million units), and despite the growth of new formats, total sales of singles declined by 41 per cent. In Britain the single's decline was less dramatic, with total sales falling by 21 per cent, from 77.8 million in 1980 to 61.1 million in 1989. This reflected the continued industry practice in the United Kingdom of releasing one or two singles prior to the issue of an album. The relative decline of the single reflected the higher costs of the new formats, and the pressure to produce a video to accompany a single, a practice which was regarded as necessary for supporting radio airplay and chart success (see **music video**).

Performers were affected by the shift to the CD format. Whatever the **aesthetic** status of the **rock/pop** single, its material significance lay in its availability to artists with limited resources as a recording medium. The seven-inch 45 and the twelve-inch dance single, with their specialist market tied to the club scene, offer such performers only a partial substitute. Linked to this is the point that many of the independent record companies cannot afford CDs, restricting the market options available to their artists.

In the 1990s, 'the overall life of the single in the charts, due to radio airplay, draws attention to the album, and this is what counts as the primary measure of the commercial "life" of a recording' (Breen, 1996: 189). The single is now less important, with sales in all formats having declined in the past decade, but remains crucial to commodifying pop music for the **teen** market.

The appeal of particular singles is assessed primarily by the placing achieved in the charts, as well as the record's longevity there (it should be noted that these are not quite the same thing). Making subsequent assessments of the commercial, and thereby presumed cultural, impact of a single on the basis of total sales and the length of time spent in the charts is a common practice (see Whitburn, 1988).

See: **charts**; **recording formats**
Further reading: Frith, 1988b: 11–23; Negus, 1992: 105–6.

ska – *see* **reggae**

skiffle   A musical **genre** which emerged out of **jazz** in Britain in the early 1950s, skiffle was arguably more significant as a catalyst than as a musical style. Skiffle appealed as a 'do-it-yourself' style of music, and thousands of groups sprang up. It had a simple rhythm section (homemade string bass and washboard), augmented by banjo and guitars. The most successful performer was Lonnie Donnegan, who drew on American **blues** and **folk**, especially the work of Woody

Guthrie and Leadbelly (e.g. 'Rock Hardin' Line'). By the early 1960s skiffle had developed into **beat** and instrumental groups (the Shadows) using electric instrumentation. Skiffle was influential as a training ground for beat musicians, such as John Lennon's Quarrymen.

See: **beat**
Further reading: Bradley, 1992; Longhurst, 1995.
Listening:
Lonnie Donnegan, *The EP Collection*, See For Miles, 1992 (remasters of his work up to 1962, including a substantial biography).
Viewing: Dancing in the Street, episode 3, 'So You Wanna Be a Rock'n'Roll Star'.

skinheads; **Oi!**   A youth subculture, first appearing in Britain in the late 1960s, skinheads were a working-class reaction to the **hippies** and their own social marginalization. They made a virtue of working classness: hair cropped to the scalp, working shirts and short jeans supported by braces, and heavy boots (often cherry red Doc Martens; accordingly, skinheads were sometimes referred to as 'bootboys') formed the standard uniform. Often associated with football hooliganism, skinheads became increasingly racist, and were involved in attacks against immigrants, especially Asians. While targets for neo-Nazi recruitment by the National Front, skinheads were largely apolitical. By the late 1960s, they had become highly visible and a clear example of 'folk devils'. English skinheads espoused traditional conservative values: defence of their local territory, hard work, and extreme patriotism; essentially they attempted to magically recover the traditional working-class community (Clarke, 1976). Skinheads became an international phenomenon, present in North America, Europe (especially Germany, where they were linked to Nazi revivalism), and Australia and New Zealand, though these were groups essentially derivative of their British counterparts. Skinheads have remained a visible subculture into the 1990s.

Originally skinheads' musical preferences embraced **black music** genres: **ska**, bluebeat, and **reggae**, in contradiction to their racism; and subsequently 'Oi!'. Oi! first appeared in 1981 as a manifestation of British **punk rock**. It was characterized by a loud, driving guitar sound, basic and abrasive with nihilistic and often racist lyrics – Oi! groups adopted skinhead dress style, and played at National Front meetings. The most prominent performers were the 4 Skins and Rose Tattoo, though they attained only limited commercial success. Sham 69, though not normally considered an Oi! band, also developed a strong skinhead/National Front following. Oi! was often denigrated: 'violent, ugly, unintelligent' music (Taylor, 1985: 69); and 'yob rock' (Larkin, 1995: 153; referring to the 4 Skins).

See: **moral panic**; **youth subcultures**
Further reading: Larkin, 1995.
Listening:
The 4 Skins, *The Good, the Bad, and the 4 Skins*, Secret, 1982.
Sham 69, *The First, the Best, and the Last*, Polydor, 1980.
Viewing: Romper Stomper, G. Wright, 1992 (film on Melbourne's skinheads and racism in Australia).

social history (of popular music) – *see* **history**

social movements – *see* **politics**

song families – *see* **cover versions**

songwriters; **songwriting**; **Brill Building**; **singer songwriters** In comparison with the writing on other roles in the music industry, and the nature of the creative process in popular music, the role of the songwriter has not received much sociological or **musicological** attention. The limited amount of published work has concentrated on song composition, the process of songwriting, and the contributions of leading songwriters, especially those associated with the Brill Building in New York. Some songwriters have been accorded

auteur status, especially when they have later successfully recorded their own material (e.g. Carole King), or are performing as singer songwriters.

There are numerous examples of songwriters exercising considerable influence over artists and styles. In the 1950s Leiber and Stoller got an unprecedented deal with Atlantic to write and produce their own songs; the resulting collaborations with performers such as the Drifters and Ben E. King produced sweet **soul**, a very self-conscious marriage of **R & B** and classical instruments, notably the violin. In the 1960s Holland, Dozier, Holland contributed to the development of the **Motown** sound. In the 1970s Chin and Chapman composed over fifty British Top 10 hits in association with **producers** Mickie Most and Phil Wainman, 'using competent bar bands (Mud, Sweet) on to whom they could graft a style and image' (Hatch and Millward, 1987: 141), to produce highly commercial **power pop**, **glitter rock**, and **dance music**.

In the late 1950s and early 1960s a factory model of songwriting, combined with a strong **aesthetic** sense, was evident in the work of a group of songwriters (and music publishers) in New York's **Brill Building**: 'the best of **Tin Pan Alley**'s melodic and lyrical hallmarks were incorporated into R & B to raise the music to new levels of sophistication' (Erlewine *et al.*, 1995: 883). The group included a number of outstanding songwriting teams: the more pop-oriented Goffin and King; Mann and Weil; and Barry and Greenwich; the R & B–oriented Pomus and Sherman, and Leiber and Stoller. Several also produced, most notably Phil Spector, Bert Berns, and Leiber and Stoller, who wrote and produced most of the Coasters' hits. One factor which distinguished the group was their youth: mainly in their late teens or early twenties, with several married couples working together, the Brill Building songwriters were well able to relate to and interpret **teenage** dreams and concerns, especially the search for **identity** and romance. These provided the themes for many of the songs they wrote, especially those performed by the **teen idols** and **girl groups** of the period. Pomus and Sherman, and Leiber and Stoller, wrote some of Elvis Presley's best material.

Collectively, the Brill Building songwriters were responsible for a large number of **chart** successes, and had an enduring influence. The role of such songwriters, however, was weakened with the **British invasion** and the emergence of a tradition of self-contained groups or performers writing their own songs (most notably the Beatles), which weakened the songwriting market.

The term **singer songwriters** has been given to artists who both write and perform their material, and who are able to perform solo, usually on acoustic guitar or piano. An emphasis on lyrics has resulted in the work of such performers often being referred to as song poets, accorded auteur status, and made the subject of intensive **lyric analysis**. The **folk** music revival in the 1960s saw several singer songwriters come to prominence: Joan Baez, Phil Ochs, and especially Bob Dylan. Singer songwriters were a particularly strong 'movement' in the 1970s, including Neil Young, James Taylor, Joni Mitchell, Jackson Browne, and Joan Armatrading, all still performing and recording at the end of the 1990s. In the 1980s the appellation singer songwriter was applied to, among others, Bruce Springsteen, Prince, and Elvis Costello; and in the 1990s to Tori Amos, Suzanne Vega, Tracy Chapman, Toni Childs, PJ Harvey, and Björk. This recent female predominance led some observers to equate the 'form' with women performers, due to its emphasis on lyrics and performance rather than the indulgences associated with male-dominated styles of **rock** music. The application of the term to solo performers is problematic, in that most of those mentioned usually perform with 'backing' bands, and at times regard themselves as an integral part of these. Nonetheless, the concept of singer songwriter continues to have strong connotations of greater **authenticity** and 'true' **auteurship**.

See: **auteur**
Further reading: Groce, 1991; Shaw, 1992 (includes discography); Sicoli, 1994.
Listening:
Carole King, *Tapestry*, Ode, 1971.

Neil Young, *Harvest Moon*, Warner Brothers, 1992.

Tracy Chapman, *Matters of the Heart*, Elektra, 1992.

Alanis Morissette, *Jagged Little Pill*, WEA, 1996.

Viewing: *Dancing in the Street*, episode 2, 'Be My Baby' (featuring Leiber and Stoller).

soul; northern soul   Originally a secular version of **gospel**, soul was the major black musical form of the 1960s and 1970s. Soul had originally been used by **jazz** musicians and listeners to signify music with a greater sense of **authenticity** and sincerity. As it developed in the 1960s, soul was a merger of gospel-style singing and **funk** rhythms. Funk was originally used in the 1950s to describe a form of modern jazz which concentrated on 'swing' and became used in the 1960s in **R & B** and soul music, especially for the recordings of 'Soul Brother Number One', James Brown.

Guralnick defines soul as 'the far less controlled, gospel-based, emotion-baring kind of music that grew up in the wake of the success of Ray Charles from about 1954 on and came to its full flowering, along with Motown, in the early 1960s' (1991: 2). The **genre** was often ballad in form, with love as a major theme. Soul became closely identified with several **independent** record labels: Atlantic, Stax/Volt, and **Motown**, each with its own 'stable' of performers and an identifiable sound, and associated with particular geographic locations and music **scenes**, like Detroit, Philadelphia, or the Southern US states. Soul was politically significant through the 1960s, parallelling the Civil Rights movement. Soul singers of note to emerge in the 1950s included Sam Cooke and Jackie Wilson; in the 1960s Bobby Bland, Aretha Franklin, Otis Redding, and Percy Sledge, whose 1966 single 'When a Man Loves a Woman' was the first southern soul record to **cross over** and top both the R & B and pop **charts**.

Soul had ceased to be an identifiable genre by the late 1970s, gradually being absorbed into various hybrid forms of **black music** and **dance music** more generally. That its major performers and their records still enjoy a considerable following is indicated by the sales of soul compilation albums, and the international success of the film *The Commitments* (Alan Parker, 1991) and its soundtrack of soul **covers**.

Northern soul is a regional cult in the UK Midlands, based around ballroom/**club culture** and all-night dancing to 1960s Motown and independent label (e.g. Cameo Parkway, Verve) soul records chosen for their 'danceability', for example The Exciters. Northern soul became prominent in the early 1970s, with the Wigan Casino, a First World War dance hall, being declared by *Billboard* to be the world's best discotheque. The subculture has maintained itself, with **fanzines**, continued all-nighters, and record compilations. (See Chambers, 1985: 137ff., 'Northern Soul', Q magazine, no. 125, February 1995: 62–5.)

See: **Motown**

Further reading: Erlewine *et al.*, 1995; Garofalo, 1997; Guralnick, 1991; Hirshey, 1985; Ritz, 1985.

Listening:

James Brown, *Live at the Apollo*, Polydor, 1963.

Aretha Franklin, *30 Greatest Hits*, Atlantic, 1986.

Otis Redding, *The Very Best of Otis Redding*, Rhino, 1993.

sound; **stereophonic sound**; **amplification** In physical, scientific terms, sound is the sensation caused in the ear by the vibration of the surrounding air, or what is or may be heard. Musical sound is produced by continuous and regular vibrations (cf. noise, disorganized sound). In popular music studies, primary interest has been on changes in the nature of sound reproduction and recording, especially the manner in which new **technologies** have influenced the nature and product.

Stereophonic sound was first developed for use in film theatres in the 1930s, with home stereo systems as scaled-down versions. In 1931 the first three-way speaker systems were introduced. The sound was divided into high, middle, and low frequencies, with each band sent to three different transducers in the loudspeaker, each designed to facilitate best that part of the sound spectrum: the large 'woofer' for the bass, a mid-range driver, and the smaller 'tweeter' for the treble. Due to the depression, and the difficulty of reaching agreement on a common stereo standard (compared with the battle over **recording formats**), this system was not turned into a commercial product until the late 1950s.

In the 1950s, tape was the format to first introduce stereo sound into the home. Read and Welch observe that the 'introduction of the stereo tape recorder for the home in 1955 heralded the most dramatic increase ever seen for a single product in home entertainment' (1977: 427). The increased sales of magnetic tape recorders and prerecorded tape forced the record companies to develop a competing stereo product, particularly for the classical music audiophile. By the 1960s, stereo sound was incorporated into the loudspeakers used in home stereos. December 1957 saw the first stereo records introduced to the market. These were not intended for the mass market, and sales were initially not high, but home stereos became popularized during the 1960s, in part based on the technological breakthrough of the transistor, invented in 1948.

The use of electrical signals to increase (amplify) the loudness of sounds, **amplification** was especially important in the history of popular music, enabling larger live **audiences** and contributing to the development of new instruments, especially the electric guitar, and sounds, for example in Chicago or electric **blues**. *Non*-amplification is sometimes associated with an ideology of **authenticity**: for instance, **folk music**'s traditional privileging of acoustic instruments, and the largely negative response from the folk music community to Bob Dylan's 'going electric' in the mid-1960s.

See: **sound recording**; **sound mixers**
Further reading: Gelatt, 1977; Jones, 1992; Millard, 1995: ch. 10; Read and Welch, 1977.

sound recording; **sound mixers** Sound recording is the process of transferring 'live' musical **performance** onto a physical product (the recording). The history of sound recording is one of technical advances leading to changes in the nature of the process, and the tasks and status of the associated labour forms. New recording technologies have opened up new creative possibilities (see **sampling**), and underpinned the emergence of new **genres**, notably **techno** and various other styles of contemporary **dance-music**. In sum, different technologies enable and sustain different **aesthetics**.

In the recording studio, the work of the sound mixer, or sound engineer,

> represents the point where music and modern technology meet. A sound mixer must know the characteristics of hundreds of microphones and a variety of acoustic environments, and how to employ them to best record a musical instrument; the capabilities and applications of a large array of sound-processing devices; the physical capacities of recording media for accepting and reproducing sounds; the operation of various recording machines; and, finally, how to balance or 'mix' at a recording console the electronic impulses coming into a studio 'control room' from a variety of live and prerecorded studio sound sources so as to produce a tape that contains a recognizable and effective musical experience   (Kealy, 1979: 208).

Kealy traces how, initially designated as 'technicians', sound mixers have converted a craft into an art, with consequent higher status and rewards.

Further reading: Cunningham, 1996; Gelder and Thornton, 1997; Jones, 1992; Millard, 1995.

Listening:

Examples from various periods illustrate advances in sound recording, at times accompanied by greatly increased use of studio time; compare the following:

Robert Johnson, 'Love in Vain' (originally recorded 1936–7), on *The Complete Recordings*, Columbia, 1990.

Elvis Presley, 'That's Alright Mama' (1956), on *The Complete Sun Sessions*, RCA, 1987.

Beach Boys, 'Good Vibrations', on *Smiley Smile*, Capitol, 1967.
Pink Floyd, *Dark Side of the Moon*, Capitol, 1973.
Dire Straits, *Love Over Gold*, Warner Brothers, 1982.
The Prodigy, *Music for the Jilted Generation*, Mute, 1994.
Underworld, *Second Toughest in the Infants*, Wax Trax/TVT, 1996.

sound systems   In addition to home stereo systems, there are more mobile forms of sound reproduction, important to particular lifestyles. Sound system is the term given to large, heavily amplified mobile discos and their surrounding **reggae** culture. These initially emerged in Jamaica, from the 1950s onwards, and were subsequently transplanted to Britain with the influx of Caribbean immigrants.

> The basic description of a sound system as a large mobile hi-fi or disco does little justice to the specificities of the form. The sound that they generate has its own characteristics, particularly an emphasis on the reproduction of bass frequencies, its own aesthetics and a unique mode of consumption   (Gilroy, 1997: 342).

The sound system is centred on records rather than live performance. Another mobile form of sound system is the Walkman, which had a major impact when it was introduced during the 1980s (see Negus, 1992).

See: **phonograph**; **sampling**; **technology**
Further reading: Gilroy, 1997; Jones, 1992; Millard, 1995.

sounds – *see* **locality**, and entries on various sounds

soundtracks – *see* **film**

stars; **stardom**   Stars are individuals who, as a consequence of their public performances or appearances in the mass media, become widely recognized and acquire symbolic status. Stars are seen as possessing a unique, distinctive talent in the cultural forms within which they work. Initially associated with the Hollywood film-star system, stardom is now widely evident in sports, television, and popular music. While there is a large body of theoretically oriented work on film stars (see Hayward, 1996 for a helpful overview), the study of stardom in popular music is largely limited to personal biographies of widely varying analytical value.

The important question is not so much 'what is a star?', but how stars function within the **music industry**, within textual narratives, and, in particular, at the level of individual fantasy and desire. What needs to be explained is the nature of emotional investment in pleasurable images. 'Stars are popular because they are regarded with some form of active esteem and invested with cultural value. They resonate within particular lifestyles and cultures' (O'Sullivan *et al.*, 1994: 207), and represent a form of escapism from everyday life and the mundane.

Stardom in popular music, as in other forms of popular culture, is as much about illusion and appeal to the fantasies of the audience as it is about talent and creativity. Stars function as mythic constructs, playing a key role in their **fans'** ability to construct meaning out of everyday life. Such stars must also be seen as economic entities, who are used to mobilize **audiences** and promote the products of the music industry. They represent a unique commodity form which is both a labour process and product. Audience identification with particular stars is a significant marketing device. For example, Madonna must be considered as much an economic entity as a purely cultural phenomenon, as over the course of her career she has generated more than $500 million in world-wide music sales for Time Warner. Madonna represents a bankable image, carefully and continually constructed in an era of media globalization. Several popular music stars have continued to generate enormous income after their death, which freezes their appeal in time while enabling their continued marketing through both the **back catalogue** and previously unreleased material (e.g. Elvis Presley, Jimi Hendrix, Bob Marley, and Kurt Cobain of Nirvana).

Yet the enormous fascination with stars' personal lives suggests a phenomenon which cannot simply be explained in terms of **political economy**. Fans both create and maintain the star through a ritual of adoration, transcending their own lives in the process (see **fans**). Stars appeal because they embody and refine the values invested in specific social types. See, for instance, Kylie Minogue in the 1980s as 'the girl next door' (see Rex, 1992), and Bruce Springsteen, whose image is founded on **authenticity**. Contemporary 'established' stars are frequently at pains to exercise considerable control over their artistic lives, perhaps because this has often been hard won. All have an ability to retain an audience across time, either through reinventing their persona and image, or through exploring new avenues in their music. Many have produced a substantial body of work, often **multimedia** in form, while seeking, to varying degrees, new ways of reinterpreting or reaffirming popular music styles and traditions. In these respects, such stars are frequently considered to be **auteurs**.

The two most extensively considered popular music stars are Elvis Presley and the Beatles (see the huge number of entries both have generated in Leyser's 1994 bibliographic guide; Marcus (1991a) offers a fascinating account of the ongoing cultural preoccupation with 'the King' since his death in 1977). Here, however, I want to use as brief illustrations of the discourse around stardom in popular music two more recent stars: Bruce Springsteen and Madonna.

Initially a cult figure, during the 1980s Bruce Springsteen became the most successful white rock star since Elvis. 'Scrupulous attention to recording and performance, generous live sets, obvious loyalty to and identification with audience gets fanatical loyalty from them: he may be the last true rock star' (Clarke, 1990: 1108). Springsteen's blue-collar bravado tempered with a broadly humanitarian sincerity appeared to strike a universal chord. His success was linked to his vision and ideals, and at times he appears almost obsessively dedicated to his audience and his music: 'You know what rock'n'roll is?' asked Springsteen in 1978, 'It's me and my band going out to the audience tonight and growing older with that audience' (Sinclair, 1992: 333). Springsteen combined an avoidance of the indulgences of the **rock** star lifestyle, with an image of authenticity and the common touch. His songs related to people's lives, their work stresses, financial hassles, and emotional difficulties. Springsteen continued the alienation and critical distance from American society expressed by Bob Dylan, but did so by inverting some of the overt countercultural critiques of the 1960s:

> Operating *within* the assumptions of the dominant, male-defined culture – hard work, patriotism, cars, girls, marriage, and the promise of the American dream – his criticism comes back in a more profound and basic way. He proposes no war, no drugs to alter consciousness – just life in the USA for ordinary people   (Pratt, 1990: 188).

The construction of a popular music star's persona or image may change across time, occasionally in a calculated attempt to redefine a performer's audience and appeal. The continued success of Madonna is an example. By the end of the 1980s Madonna was a superstar, arguably one of the best-known women in the world and certainly one of the most discussed and analysed figures in popular culture. The multimedia contract she signed with Time Warner in 1992, said to be worth $60 million, was indicative of the economic value her cultural impact represented. Madonna is a star whom many critics and fans love to hate, a performer who 'used a licentious image and a little-girl voice to keep at the pinnacle of pop for the better part of the eighties' (Shapiro, 1991: 156). To many, her success rests on artifice and media manipulation, but as Considine points out: 'What her critics forget, however, is that manufactured sensation is usually short-lived, and contrived art is almost always conservative, while Madonna's career has been neither' (1992: 662).

A number of commentators have observed how Madonna has been able to reinvent her persona constantly, and retain a high degree of creative control over her work. Her audience appeal and commercial success lies primarily in **performance**, through both concerts and **music video**, and her ability to keep herself in the public eye, and the creation and maintenance of image is central to her success. Through the later 1980s, Madonna's stardom was underpinned by her charismatic personality and captivating stage presence, with her overt **sexuality** appealing to young males, and her predominantly girl fans identifying with her strong character and emphasis on being her 'own person', in control of her sexuality and her career (see her book *Sex*, New York: Warner Books, 1992). At the same time, 'Madonna's carnivalesque transgressions of gender and sexuality, the source of much pleasure for her fans, are extremely disturbing to her haters, and often this hate is focused on the body and expressed in a discourse about the body' (Schulze *et al.*, 1993: 24). Madonna is constantly reinventing herself, a process which is a necessary part of ensuring her enduring star status (cf. David Bowie). Her public image has shifted from the earlier virgin and vamp to screen siren, from raunchy second-hand clothes-shop dresser to a Marilyn Monroe glamorous persona, exemplified by her starring role in the popular musical *Evita* (Alan Parker, 1996). Her audience has arguably aged along with her in the process.

Springsteen and Madonna are the popular music stars of the past fifteen years who have generated the greatest amount of academic (and popular) analysis and discussion. In sum, the discourse surrounding them shows how stardom has become a construct with a number of dimensions: the economic, the cultural, and the **aesthetic** or creative – the relationship between stardom and **auteurship**.

See: **fans**

Further reading: on stardom generally, and in relation to film stars, see Hayward *et al.*, 1994; on Madonna, see Schwichtenberg, 1993; on Springsteen, see Marsh, 1987; for bibliographic guidance on particular 'rock stars/pop stars', see Leyser, 1994.

State; **State cultural policy**; **regulation/deregulation of broadcasting**; **content quotas** The State can be defined as the Government and its institutional agents, especially the civil service, but also the police and the military. In social and political theory there are two major, competing theories of the nature of the State and its operation: (i) liberal, pluralist views, which see the State as operating neutrally in 'the public interest'; and (ii) Marxist-oriented views, which see the State as upholding the interests of the ruling or dominant groups in society. Within these two extremes, there is a continuum of views (see O'Sullivan *et al.*, 1994 for a succinct overview). The State has often been ignored in analyses of popular music, though there is a tradition of work on cultural policy, at both the central and local State level. Several commentators have suggested that popular music researchers need to pay more attention to the State (see Bennett *et al.*, 1993; Negus, 1996).

State cultural policies have been largely based on the idealist tradition of **culture** as a realm separate from, and often in opposition to, that of material production and economic activity. This means that government intervention in its various forms – subsidy, licensing arrangements, protectionism through quotas, and so on – is justified by the argument which has been clearly elaborated by Garnham:

> 1. that culture possesses inherent values, of life enhancement or whatever, which are fundamentally opposed to and in danger of damage by commercial forces; 2. that the need for these values is universal, uncontaminated by questions of class, gender and ethnic origin; and 3. that the market cannot satisfy this need   (1987: 24).

A key part of this view is the concept of the individual creative artist, with the associated cultural policy problem defined as 'one of finding audiences for their work rather than vice versa' (ibid.). This ideology has been used by elites in government, administration, intellectual institutions, and **broadcasting** to justify and represent sectional interests as general interests, thereby functioning as a form of cultural **hegemony**. Seeing classical music, ballet, and the theatre as **high culture** or 'the arts' legitimizes both their largely middle-class consumption and their receipt of State subsidy. **Popular culture** is then constructed in opposition to this,

287

as commercial, inauthentic, and so unworthy of significant government support. Such a dichotomized high–low culture view is unsustainable, yet it nonetheless remains a widely held and still powerful ideology.

State attitudes and policies toward popular culture are a significant factor in determining the construction of meaning in popular music. At the level of attitudes, State cultural policies are indicative of the various views held about the very concept of **culture** itself, debates over government economic intervention in the market place versus the operation of the 'free market', the operation of **cultural imperialism**, and the role of the State in fostering national cultural **identity**. There have been some notable attempts on the part of the State to use particular forms or **genres** of popular music to foster a particular ideology and engender national solidarity, while at the same time marginalizing or actively persecuting other genres (e.g. Nazi Germany in the 1930s – see Negus, 1996; for other examples, see Garofalo, 1992b). The use of national anthems is a small but significant part of such efforts.

In the case of popular music, government attitudes have generally, but not exclusively, tended to reflect a traditional conservative view of 'culture' (see the high culture tradition), which is used to justify non-intervention in the 'commercial' sphere. Yet this non-intervention exists in tension with frequent governmental concern to regulate a medium which, at times, has been associated with threats to the social order: **moral panics** over the activities of **youth subcultures**, the **sexuality** and sexism of rock, and obscenity. There have been a number of cases where the State has played a significant role in relation to popular music through economically and culturally motivated regulation and intervention. This has usually been to defend national cultural production against the inflow of foreign media products, using trade tariffs, industry incentives, and suchlike, and is focused on popular rather than high culture (see **cultural imperialism**).

State and local governments have increasingly recognized the economic and social potential of popular music. Their intervention 'is becoming increasingly explicit, increasingly programmatic and institutional . . . the role of government has become a crucial factor in the structural organization of rock music at the local, the national and ultimately at the global level' (Bennett *et al.,* 1993: 9). Government music policy has been evident in the former East Germany, Holland, Canada, Australia, New Zealand, and the United States. The issues raised include the defence of national **identity**, the **music industry** as a site for youth employment, and the protection of local markets (see the contributions to Bennett *et al.*, 1993; also Berland, 1991; Breen, 1992, 1996). British State policy on music is still a local phenomenon, with a proliferation of regional and city-based music projects; several writers have raised the cultural implications of these initiatives (especially Cohen, 1991; Street, 1993).

State **regulation/deregulation of broadcasting** occurs with governmental regulation of the airwaves, through (i) limiting the available **radio** frequencies or **television** channels, through licensing policies; (ii) broadcasting codes of practice, which may serve to restrict exposure of 'offensive' material (see **censorship**); and (iii) **content quotas**: governmental legislated provision for minimum fixed proportion of local content on radio (and, sometimes, television) programming. Such quotas are designed to protect local cultural industries from the perceived negative influence of imported, largely US, popular culture. Examples of the application, or the attempted application, of music quotas include New Zealand, Australia, Canada, and France.

See: **broadcasting**; **censorship**; **cultural imperialism**
Further reading: Garnham, 1987; Negus, 1996; Shuker, 1994.

stereophonic sound – *see* **sound**

structuralism; semiotics; post-structuralism

An intellectual enterprise characterized by attention to the systems, relations and forms – the structures – that make meaning possible in any cultural activity or artifact. Structuralism is an analytical or *theoretical* enterprise,

289

dedicated to the systematic elaboration of the rules and constraints that work, like the rules of a language, to make the generation of meanings possible in the first place   (O'Sullivan *et al.*, 1994: 302).

Structuralists' attempts to establish such 'rules of meaning' led to several distinct approaches during the 1970s: semiotics, deconstruction (overwhelmingly a mode of literary analysis, derived from the work of Derrida), and post-structuralism.

'Structuralist' views of popular culture and media forms concentrate on how meaning is generated in media **texts**, examining how the 'structure' of the text (visual, verbal, or auditory) produces particular ideological meanings. Such study is primarily through **semiotics**, the study of signs, which has been applied widely in the study of communications, providing a method for the analysis of both verbal and non-verbal messages. Semiotics distinguishes between signifier, signified, and sign. The signifier can be a word, an image, or a physical object; the signified is the mental concept associated with the signifier; the sign is the association of signifier and signified. Signs may be organized into linked codes, as with dress **fashions**. Social convention may influence the precise nature and strength of the relationship between signifier and signified. Barthes argued that signs can form myths, in that a sign may represent a whole range of cultural values. In addition to associating an image or an object with a concept (denotation), signs also carry connotations, engendering emotions.

In popular music studies, semiology has been used in analyses of **song lyrics**, **music videos**, **record covers**, **youth subcultures**, and photographs (on the last, see Longhurst's instructive decoding of a press photograph of Courtney Love and Sinéad O'Connor at the 1993 MTV Awards, to show how such images/texts contain different levels of meaning; Longhurst, 1995: 163–4). The **musicological** approach can be loosely regarded as a structuralist form of cultural analysis, since it privileges the text by placing the emphasis firmly on its formal properties. Musicologists tackle popular music as music, using conventional tools derived from the study of more traditional or classical forms of music: **harmony, melody, beat, rhythm,** and the lyric. However, this preoccupation with the text in itself has been critiqued for its lack of consideration of music as a social phenomenon. In traditional musicology, the music itself becomes a disembodied presence, lacking any social referents. The concept of musical codes is a structuralist approach to investigating how meaning is conveyed in musical texts, and has also been used to inform discussions of competence, and the differing ability of listeners to decode or interpret musical texts (see Middleton, 1990).

Post-structuralism

> is hard in practice to separate from structuralism. It is more alert to psychoanalytic theories and the role of pleasure in producing and regulating meanings than was the highly rationalist early structuralism. Post-structuralism is also more concerned with the external structures (social process, class, gender, and ethnic divisions, historical changes) that make meaning possible   (O'Sullivan *et al.*, 1994: 304).

This shifted the focus from the text to the reader/viewer/listener. Within popular music studies, post-structuralist ideas have informed discussions on the nature and significance of **class, gender,** and **ethnicity** in relation to changes in the production and consumption of music.

It is worth noting that some discussions of popular music do not use these concepts (of structuralism etc.) explicitly, perhaps reflecting their distaste for the sometimes arcane terminology associated with such analyses (e.g. Negus, 1996; Shuker, 1994). At the same time, however, these authors use many of the ideas associated with the structuralist/post-structuralist discourse.

Further reading: Longhurst, 1995; Middleton, 1990.

style – *see* **fashion; genre; youth subcultures**

subcultures – *see* **youth subcultures**

subjectivity – *see* **identity**

surf music; **surfies**   A short–lived but influential musical phenomenon, surf music was a regional scene associated with a
subculture, which became a marketing label. The majority of
surf music recordings were issued between 1961 and 1965, with
their **chart** success largely confined to Southern California.
The style has continued as something of a cult **genre**.

Surf music was the most guitar-oriented style of early
rock'n'roll, and had enormous influence on subsequent electric guitar playing styles. Dick Dale was the acknowledged
father of surf rock, developing a reverb guitar sound which
evoked the waves and 'runs' of surfing, a teenage subculture
which initially developed in California and Hawaii in the late
1950s. Dale developed a technique based on the tremolo
playing used in Middle Eastern plucked instruments such as
the bouzouka, sustaining notes by plucking strings up and
down. The surf music craze was sparked by Dale and the
Del-Tones' 1961 single 'Let's Go Trippin' (subsequently
covered by the Beach Boys on their album *Surfin' USA*,
Capitol, 1963), with hundreds of surf bands emerging.

Surf was Californian good time music, with references to
sun, sand, and (obliquely) sex, also hot rods and drag racing.
Surf music provided the soundtrack for the beach movies of
the period, and for documentaries celebrating surfing and
the associated lifestyle (e.g. *The Endless Summer*, Dir. Bruce
Brown, 1966; *Crystal Voyager*, George Greenough, 1978).

There was a strong surf instrumental vein, with the Surfaris
('Wipe Out', 1963), the Chantays ('Pipeline', 1963), and the
Ventures all making the national charts. The most commercially successful surf performers were vocal duo Jan and Dean,
and the Beach Boys, who became the leading and most
enduring of the surf bands. Creatively led by Brian Wilson,
the Beach Boys were heavily influenced by the 1950s vocal
group style and **harmonies** of the Four Freshmen and Chuck
Berry's rock'n'roll; their early hit 'Surfin' USA' is based on
Berry's 'Sweet Little Sixteen'. The Beach Boys largely aban-

doned surfing themes and broadened their scope after 1963, with the thematically linked album *Pet Sounds* (Capitol, 1966) and the single 'Good Vibrations' (1966) their crowning achievements.

Initially an upper working-class, male-dominated, American subculture, surfers (the term **surfies**, of Australian origin, has become the more common label) emerged with the popularization of surfing on the US West Coast in the 1950s, partly due to the new lighter and cheaper 'Malibu' boards. The surfboard was the crucial component of the subcultural style, which also included dress (board shorts, or 'baggies', Hawaiian shirts, and wet suits) and surf music. Its core values were leisure, as a form of conspicuous consumption, and individualism, primarily expressed through the skill and enjoyment of surfing. The surfie subculture soon spread to other locations where there was surf; most notably Hawaii, Australia, and New Zealand (see Stratton, 1997).

Surf music experienced a revival in the 1980s, and continues to maintain a cult status associated with specialist labels (eg. Surfdog); though now only rarely played, it has become an element of more contemporary genres, while its guitar sound continues to be influential.

Further reading: Charlton, 1994; Erlewine *et al.*, 1995; Garofalo, 1997; Miller, 1992 (includes discography); White, 1994.

Listening:

The Beach Boys, 'Surfin' USA' (1963), on *The Beach Boys: Twenty Golden Greats*, Capitol/EMI, 1978.

Dick Dale, *King of Surf Guitar: Best of Dick Dale*, Rhino, 1989.

MOM: Music for Our Mother Ocean, Surfdog/Interscope, 1996 (includes Pennywise covering 'Surfin' USA', Pearl Jam covering 'Gremmie Out of Control', an obscure 1964 surf single, and other contemporary alternative bands performing songs with surf themes and guitar sounds: Soundgarden, 'My Wave', Silverchair, 'Surfin' Bird', and the Ramones, 'California Sun').

Viewing: *Dancing in the Street*, episode 2, 'Be My Baby'.

syncreticism – *see* **appropriation**

taste cultures; lifestyles American sociologist Herbert Gans developed the concept of taste cultures in the 1960s, to refer to the differentiation of cultural consumption among social groups, and the manner in which such patterns were shaped. A taste culture is a group of people making similar choices, with these being related to similar backgrounds: class and education are the key determinants of membership in taste cultures. In its contemporary formulations, the term is usually conflated with Bourdieu's concept of **cultural capital**.

Lifestyles are distinctive configurations of cultural **identity** and sets of social practices which are associated with particular consumption groups, taste cultures, and **subcultures**. Although it is used in a number of contradictory ways, 'it provides an important focus for attention in studies of culture and communication in the 1990s' (O'Sullivan *et al.*, 1994: 167). In an anthropological sense, lifestyle refers to particular forms of symbolic consumption. Lifestyle also refers to significant rhetorics and discourses in play in the production or regulation of modern cultural life. There is debate over the degree of individual autonomy/choice involved in the construction of lifestyles, and the extent to which they allow for a genuine plurality of expression, including resistance.

Both concepts, and the associated debates, have informed popular music studies of **audiences** and **consumption**.

Further reading: Featherstone, 1987; Tomlinson, 1991.

techno   Techno emerged as a musical style and **meta genre** in the 1980s, partly associated with new, computer-generated, sound/composition technologies available to musicians. Techno is often conflated with **house** and **ambient** music, or used contiguously with the whole corpus of contemporary **dance-music**. Techno became closely associated with a particular social setting, being the staple music at large-scale parties – **raves** – which, along with the associated use of the drug ecstasy, generated considerable controversy (and **moral panic**) in the early to mid-1990s in the United Kingdom.

The defining musical characteristics of techno are, in most cases, a slavish devotion to the beat, and the use of rhythm as a hypnotic tool (usually 115–60 beats per minute (BPM)), primarily, and often entirely, created by electronic means; a relative lack of vocals; and a significant use of **samples**. There are a number of variants, or **subgenres** within techno, often linked with particular record labels or regional **scenes**. The 'proto-techno' of the original Detroit creators of techno in the United States shows a mixture of influences, especially influential German electronic band Kraftwerk's 'assembly line technopop', and the **funk** of George Clinton and Parliament. From this basis came 'Detroit techno', a stripped-down, aggressive funk sound, played mostly on analogue instruments and characterized by a severe, pounding rhythm, and 'hard-core techno', **speed metal** tunes played on Detroit techno instrumentation. Subsequent variants included the more accessible and commercial 'techno-rave'; 'breakbeat', a style using speeded-up **hip-hop** beat samples; and 'tribal', with rhythm patterns and sounds drawing on Native American and **world music**. Some techno performers have moved progressively with and through a number of these styles; for example, the Shamen's initial recordings combined **psychedelic rock** with hardcore **rap** rhythms, while their later work makes greater use of samples, drum machines, and heavily amplified guitar sounds.

See: **dance-music**
Further reading: Thornton, 1995.

Listening:
The Shamen, *Boss Drum*, Epic, 1992.
Leftfield, *Leftism*, Hard Hands/Columbia, 1995.
Underworld, 'Born Slippy', on *Trainspotting: Original Soundtrack*, EMI, 1996.

technology In sociological usage technology embraces all forms of productive technique, including hand-working, but the more popular use of technology is synonomous with machinery. Both understandings of the term are evident in considerations of the relationship between popular music and technology. While the creation of music and innovations in technology have historically always been related, discussions of this relationship have consciously avoided overbalancing into technological determinism: the notion that the form(s) of technology are the principal factor producing cultural/ social change.

Technology is part of some definitions of popular music, with attempts to maintain a distinction between a 'folk mode' predicated on live **performance**, and a mass culture form associated with recording. The latter is criticized as 'only commercial . . . leaving the profound and innate potential of the medium for cultural and aesthetic expression still un-developed' (Cutler, 1985: 142). However,

> the widespread use of inexpensive multitrack recorders and the spread of homemade cassette networks are giving rise to another form of folk music that fits neither cate-gory. Likewise the use of turntables and microphones in rap music contradicts the easy combination of recording and mass culture (Jones, 1992: 5).

Technology has played a significant role in shaping the evolution of popular music, with each new development allowing the emergence of a 'new' sound. Technological changes in recording equipment pose both constraints and opportunities, with new recording formats offering fresh marketing opportunities, while also affecting the nature of consumption. A major development was the rise of the compact disc (**CD**). Innovations such as **music video** and electronic technologies of composition have generated a certain amount of 'technophobia'. Negus makes an intriguing comparison between contemporary antipathy to such developments and the hostile reception initially accorded the piano (Negus, 1992: 31).

See: **formats**; **sound recording**
Further reading: Jones, 1992; Millard, 1995; Negus, 1992.

teddy boys – *see* **rock'n'roll**

teenagers; **teenyboppers**; **teen idols**   A teenager is a person in their teens (13–19 years of age), and a teenybopper is a teenage girl who follows the latest fashions in clothes, hairstyles, and **pop** music. First used in the late 1950s, teenybopper soon acquired strongly derogatory connotations, being applied to girl **fans** and their preferred artists and musical styles: teen idols and 'teen rock'. Teen idols represented a blander, less rebellious version of **rock'n' roll**, and the music of Paul Anka, Bobby Vee, Bobby Vinton, and Tommy Sands prospered in the charts in the early 1960s. Successful female singers following 'the same pallid formula' (Friedlander, 1996: 72) included Leslie Gore and Connie Francis. The clean-cut teen idols projected a mixture of sexual appeal and innocent youth to a receptive teenage market.

Academic analysis has concentrated on the social construction of teenagers as an identifiable social group, their musical preferences, and their (declining) significance as a market (see **demographics**; **youth culture**). Profiles of popular music **consumption** show a clear pattern of age and gender-based **genre** preferences. Teenagers are traditionally a major **audience** for, and consumers of, popular music, especially pop, **dance music**, **bubblegum**, and **power pop**. Other genres will frequently include variants and performers aimed at the teenage market, such as the 'soft' **rap** of Kriss Kross and Snow; the 'lite' **heavy metal** of Bon Jovi. That girls enjoy commercial pop music more than boys reflects the segmented nature of the market, with certain performers having a clear appeal for younger listeners, particularly girls, and being marketed as such; for example, Kylie Minogue, Duran Duran, Bananarama, and New Kids on the Block in the 1980s, and Take That, Boyzone, and the Spice Girls in the 1990s. A major genre of music magazines are aimed at the teenybopper/younger market (e.g. *Smash Hits*). The majority of their readers are girls, who buy them partly for their pin-up posters, reflecting their frequent obsession with particular stars and what has been termed 'teenybopper bedroom culture'.

See: **pop**

Further reading: Friedlander, 1996; Frith and McRobbie, 1990; McRobbie and Garber, 1976.

Listening:

Connie Francis, *The Very Best of Connie Francis*, Polydor, 1963.

New Kids on the Block, *Hangin' Tough*, Columbia, 1988.

Bobby Vee, *Bobby Vee*, Legendary Masters Series, EMI, 1990.

television   Television has been an important mode of distribution, promotion, and formation for the **music industry**. The discussion here is of free-to-air, broadcast television, and the popular music programmes which form part of its schedules (**MTV** and similar cable channels are dealt with separately). It is worth noting, however, that popular music plot themes, music segments, and signature tunes are also an important part of many programme **genres**, especially those aimed at children (e.g. *Sesame Street*) and adolescents (e.g. *Beverley Hills 90210*; *Ren and Stimpy*).

A contradictory relationship has historically existed between television and popular music. Television is traditionally a medium of family entertainment, collapsing class, **gender**, ethnic, and generational differences in order to construct a homogeneous audience held together by the ideology of the nuclear family. In contrast, many forms of popular music,

especially **rock'n'roll** and its various mutations, have historically presented themselves as being about 'difference',
emphasizing individual tastes and preferences. The rock tradition viewed television as 'always after the event – young
viewers might have learned to move and dress directly from
the TV screen, but the assumption was that it was a window
on the real youth world that was somewhere out there' (Frith,
1988c: 212).

The introduction of public broadcast television in the
United States and the United Kingdom in the 1950s coincided with the emergence of rock'n'roll. Television helped
popularize the new music, and established several of its
performers, most notably Elvis Presley, as youth icons. Indeed,
television was quick to seize the commercial opportunities
offered by the emergent youth culture market of the 1950s.
'Television became devoted, at least in part, to the feature of
televisual musical products for an audience that spent much
of its leisure time and money in the consumption of pop
music goods' (Burnett, 1990: 23). This led to a proliferation
of television popular music shows. The better-known of these
on US television included *American Bandstand*, one of the
longest running shows in television history (1952–), *Your Hit
Parade* (1950–9), and *The Big Record* (1957–8). Britain had
Juke Box Jury and *Top of the Pops*, both starting in the late
1950s, and *The Old Grey Whistle Test*. In 1963 *Ready Steady
Go!* began showcasing new talent, who usually performed
live, compared to *Top of The Pops'* staid studio lip-synchs with
backing from a house orchestra.

The contemporary role of these programmes is illustrated
by *Top of the Pops*, which has in recent years enjoyed a revival
and increased audiences – 8.4 million viewers weekly in 1995.
'In the past twelve months, the programme has been trans-
formed from an insipid showcase for mainstream single releases
and unwatchable dance bands to a varied and bold show
featuring album tracks, more live performances, new acts and
celebrity presenters' (*The Times*, 22 February 1995, p.23: '*Top
of the Pops* back on track').

Television's presentation of rock music prior to the advent

299

of **music video** (MV) was generally uninspiring. Performers either straightforwardly performed, even if at times in an impressively frenetic manner (as with The Who's debut effort on *Ready Steady Go!*) or mimed to their recordings in a pseudo-live setting. There were a few notable experiments through the 1960s and 1970s to incorporate additional visual elements (see Shore, 1985, for a full history of the development of music video in relation to television).

The 1980s success of MTV boosted televised music videos, reshaping the form and the broadcast programmes based on it. In the United States and Canada, nearly every major city now has its own televised music video show, with several nationally syndicated. MV programmes have also become a stock part of television channel viewing schedules in the United Kingdom and Western Europe, and New Zealand and Australia. Yet only in the latter two countries, which have just recently acquired cable television and do not yet have widely available satellite reception, have such programmes retained the dominance they initially achieved during the 1960s, with continued high audience ratings. Popular music programmes are competing against other genres for scheduling space, while the **demographic** significance of the youth audience has declined in the 1990s.

Mainstream television's MV programmes remained significant primarily because of their importance to advertisers, as they draw a young audience whose **consumption** habits are not yet strongly fixed. A number of case studies have illustrated the factors at work in the emergence and nature of popular music programmes on commercial television, particularly the place of such programmes within scheduling practices and the process of selection of the music videos for inclusion on the programme. Of particular interest are the links between such programmes, advertising, and record sales. While it is difficult to prove a direct causal link, as with **radio** airplay and **chart** 'action' there is evidence that exposure on such programmes has an influence on record purchases. The nature of such programmes, and their tendency to play music videos which are shortened versions of the associated song, have exercised considerable influence over the way in which videos are produced and their nature as audio-visual and **star** texts (see Negus, 1992: 97). Also significant, especially in smaller nations such as Australia, New Zealand, and the Netherlands, is the status of locally produced music videos compared with their imported counterparts, which are competing for space on such programmes, a form of **cultural imperialism**.

See: **MTV**; **music video**
Further reading: on Australia, see Stockbridge, 1992; on New
   Zealand, Shuker, 1994; on the United Kingdom, Frith, 1993).

Tex–Mex   A **genre** associated with Chicano, Mexican, and Texan musicians, Tex Mex is very eclectic, blending **rock**, **country**, **R & B**, **blues**, and traditional Spanish and Mexican music. Although the genre had a much longer history, it emerged as a marketing label in the 1980s, primarily with the commercial success of Los Lobos ('one of America's most distinctive and original bands', Erlewine *et al.*, 1995: 484).

Further reading: Lipsitz, 1994.
Listening:
Los Lobos, *How Will the Wolf Survive*, Slash, 1984.

text; **textual analysis**; **preferred readings**; **textual poaching**
The term text has traditionally been used to refer to an author's original words, or a prose work – especially one recommended for student reading. More recently, as a **cultural studies** term, text refers to any media form that is self-contained: television programmes, recordings, films, and books. Popular music texts are quite diverse, and include recordings, record sleeve covers, and **music videos**. The most prominent are sound recordings, in various formats, and their packaging (**record covers**, **box sets**, etc.). In addition there are several other important forms of popular music texts: musical performances, especially **concerts**, **DJ discourse**, music videos, music magazines, posters, T-shirts, tour

brochures, and **fan** club merchandise. These texts are frequently interconnected and mutually reinforcing.

Textual analysis is concerned with identifying and analysing the formal qualities of texts, their underpinning structures and constituent characteristics. As such, it has become closely associated with **semiotic** analysis, often linked to psychoanalytical concepts. In the case of popular music, textual analysis takes several forms. The most important is the examination of the musical components of songs, including their lyrics, in their various recorded formats. This approach is primarily associated with **musicology**: the study of the formal properties of music *qua* music. The application of musicology to popular music **genres** has proved difficult and contentious.

Other forms of popular music texts, such as record covers, concerts, music video, **lyric analysis**, and DJ talk have been examined through various approaches to content and discourse analysis. While texts are usually analysed independently, they can also be considered collectively, as with content analysis of **chart** share in terms of genres, record labels (**majors** compared to **independents**: see **market cycles**), and the proportion of artists who are women. A similar approach has been applied to **radio** and **MTV** airplay.

A point of debate around popular culture is its ideological role in reinforcing and reproducing dominant values through their representation in popular texts. Critics who concentrate on the text itself, often using concepts from semiotic and psychoanalytic analysis, argue that there frequently exists in the text a **preferred reading**, that is, a dominant message set within the cultural code of established conventions and practices of the producers or transmitters of the text. However, while many consumers may, at least implicitly or subconsciously, accept such preferred readings, it must be kept in mind that it is not necessarily true that the audience do so as a whole. In particular, subordinate groups may reinterpret such textual messages, making 'sense' of them in a different way. This opens up the idea of popular resistance to, and subversion of, dominant cultures. This notion has informed analysis of the nature and reception of popular song lyrics, and music videos.

Textual poaching refers to the manner in which fans interact with texts 'to actively assert their mastery over the mass-produced texts which provide the raw materials for their own cultural productions and the basis for their social inter-actions', becoming 'active participants in the construction and circulation of textual meanings' (Jenkins, 1997: 508). This active engagement with texts has been termed 'poaching' by de Certeau, who applied it to reading; others have applied it to various forms of popular culture. Popular music fans and **subcultures** can be considered textual poachers, articulating texts.

See: **audience**, **fans**; **subcultures**
Further reading: Jenkins, 1997.

thrash metal; **speed metal**   An influential **subgenre** of **heavy metal**, sometimes referred to as speed metal, and overlapping with **hardcore** (Erlewine *et al.*, 1995, combines hardcore and thrash as a genre category). Largely a US phenomenon, thrash developed out of hardcore and **punk**, and became a journalistic convenience for guitar-based non-mainstream metal, usually played faster and louder. In common with heavy metal generally, thrash has been accused of being depressing, encouraging teenage suicides, and of being associated with satanism, violent concerts, and a predominantly male audience. Adherents of thrash are attracted by the sheer volume and pace of the music, but also by the subgenre's problem-oriented lyrics, which are at both the global and personal levels, and by thrash bands' lack of a commercialized image.

Weinstein (1991a) and Breen argued that the new era of speed metal represented by Metallica, Anthrax, and others is generating a new form of 'the true rock experience', which runs in direct contradiction to 'the established expectation of pleasure and fun often associated with rock music' (Breen, 1991: 191). This new form is apocalyptic in its visions of negation, and constructed through the live concert as much as its recorded forms.

See: **heavy metal**

timbre Tone quality as it relates to the characteristic differences among singing voices or musical instruments.

See: **voice**

Tin Pan Alley In the late 1800s, **songwriters** and publishers began congregating in a section of New York city, which became known as Tin Pan Alley from the 'tinny' sound of the upright pianos used there. Tin Pan Alley dominated mainstream American popular music from around 1900 through to the late 1940s.

> Tin Pan Alley songs were for white, urban, literate, middle- and upper-class Americans. They remained practically unknown to large segments of American society, including most blacks . . . and the millions of poor, white, rural Americans . . . clustered in the South and scattered across the lower Midwest. These two groups had their own distinctive types of music, oral tradition music (Charles Hamm, cited in Garofalo, 1997: 43).

It was characterized by its association with sheet music, as composing and publishing were the main sources of revenue for those involved. Tin Pan Alley catered to popular tastes, incorporating and homogenizing elements of new musical styles as they emerged, especially **ragtime**, **blues**, and **jazz**. The overwhelming proportion of its songs focused on romantic love, and helped celebrate and legitimize changes in sexual codes of behaviour in America in the 1920s. Tin Pan Alley songs catered to young women, often from middle-class families, who in the 1920s and 1930s were moving to work in the larger American cities: 'female record purchasers and radio listeners could appreciate the exhilaration of finding "someone" in the newly freed social space of the impersonal city' (Horowitz, 1993: 39).

In the early 1950s, the transition from Tin Pan Alley to **rock'n'roll** reflected important demographic, social, and cultural shifts in American society.

Further reading: Garofalo, 1997; Horowitz, 1993.

tours; **touring**   A tour is a scheduled, consecutive series of **concerts** in different centres; tours can be of short duration, with a small number of concerts over a period of several weeks, or can be world affairs, lasting for up to two years.

For the band or performer who has risen beyond the purely local, further commercial success is closely linked to touring, which is especially necessary to promote a new release and build up an audience. Tour schedules are frequently extremely gruelling, resembling 'package' vacation tours, with performers playing different cities each night and much of the intervening time consumed by travel. Tour books, band biographies, and many classic songs document 'life on the road', with its often attendant excesses, and exhilaration at audience enthusiasm coupled with fatigue. Mike Campbell, guitarist with Tom Petty and the Heartbreakers, commented in a 1981 interview:

> I always like it the first couple of weeks, but it can get to you after that. These four walls get real old. If you're not going to chase women or do a bunch of drugs, there's not a lot left on the list. Another thing about touring is coming off the stage, where there is all this energy and adrenalin, and rushing back to the hotel and the silence. Going from one extreme to the other is real disconcerting   (Stambler, 1989: 335).

Tours expose performers and their music to potential fans and purchasers, building an image and a following. Tours were important historically for helping 'break' English bands in the United States at various times, and this remains more generally true for the present national and international touring scenes. The nature of tour concerts is an oddly ambivalent one. On the one hand, for the **fan** it is a rare opportunity to see a favourite performer, especially if they live in locations where the opportunity may come literally once in a lifetime. On the other hand, for the performer each concert blurs into a series of 'one night stands' and the challenge is to maintain a freshness to each performance.

The monotony of touring is captured in *The Big Wheel*, a 'novel' about a band's tour of America, written by Bruce Thomas, the bass player with Elvis Costello and the Attractions:

> We travelled thousands of miles between Holiday Inns that were exactly the same, to see some of the world's most famous sights only from a window across the city. At other times we stayed in places I wish I'd never seen. Or I slept through some of the most spectacular scenery in the world, not because I wasn't interested but because I was bloody knackered. This was the band's third time round the world in three years. Round and round and round the world we had gone until it all blurred together (Thomas, 1991: 20).

There exists a clear hierarchy of tours. For a relatively unknown act, seeking to publicize a new or first release and create an audience, opportunities for live work will be few, and pub and university or polytechnic campus circuits remain essential. The scale of most 'national' tours is very localized, covering only a dozen or so centres. For established visiting bands and local acts, which have broken into the **charts** and the market place, there are larger scale national tours. These still chiefly play selected main centres, where venues and audiences are large enough to (hopefully) make the exercise economically viable. At the top end of the scale are the global tours of the top international acts, which are massive exercises in logistics and marketing – and also hugely profitable. Recent examples include tours by Michael Jackson and Dire Straits, Janet Jackson's 1989–90 'Rhythm Nation' Tour, The Rolling Stones' 'Voodoo Lounge' Tour of 1994–5, and the Kiss reunion tour of 1996–7.

During the record industry's affluent years of the early

1970s, tours by major acts were associated with legendary excess and expense. Eliot cites one publicity manager:

> I was working with Zeppelin, Bad Company, the Rolling Stones. It was the heyday of rock excess, when everybody was rolling in money and there were limousines to take you to the bathroom. The company rule was 'Whatever it takes, you do it to keep everyone happy' (Eliot, 1989: 173).

This was unsustainable when the record industry retrenched in the mid-1970s, and companies began to cut back on tour support and set such expenditure off against bands' future earnings.

Nevertheless, through the 1980s and 1990s, touring and the associated live concerts remained the best way to maintain audience interest in a successful act and a key factor in breaking a new one. 'Virtually every rock group eagerly toured behind the release of a new album, with record companies assuming all expenses, paying the acts nothing more than per diems' (ibid.: 169). These tours are about promotion as much as performance. Artists appear on radio and television shows, make personal appearances at record stores, and generally do anything that will help promote sales. Such tours work to strictly controlled budgets, with the act usually paying for everything out of record sales before the allocation of royalties. If record sales are good, the performer(s) make money. On the other hand, the Grateful Dead, who toured extensively in the 1970s without 'hits', became heavily indebted to their record label, Warner Brothers, and were on the road for five years before generating any income from royalties.

While most tours by popular musicians are commercial affairs, there have been significant tours supporting political causes, such as the Amnesty International tour of North America in 1988, in support of the human rights organization, which is estimated to have added some 20,000 new members to the organization in the United States alone; and the Red Wedge tour in support of the British Labour Party's election campaign in 1987 (see Denselow, 1990; Garofalo, 1992b;

Street, 1986). Another variant is the package tour, where a group of artists are placed on the same bill. This was a popular style of tour during the 1960s, when it was important for internationally popularizing **British beat** performers, and has resurfaced with the successful Lollapalooza tours of 1991 onward, which put together a number of **alternative** acts.

See: **film: rockumentaries**

transculturation – *see* **globalization**

tribute bands – *see* **musicians**

trip-hop – *see* **dance-music**

V

voice 'Popular music is overwhelmingly a "voice music". The pleasure of singing, of hearing singers, is central to it', and 'there is a strong tendency for vocals to act as a unifying focus within the song' (Middleton, 1990: 261, 264). Discussions of the role of the voice within popular music have focused on the relationship between **lyrics**, melodic types, and the singing styles (vocal **timbres**) of various **genres** and performers. A key **semiological** notion is the 'grain' of the voice (very broadly, its 'feeling'), as opposed to the direct meaning of lyrics, and the way in which particular styles of voice convey certain sets of emotions, often irrespective of the words they are singing.

A number of authors have discussed how the voice is used in popular music, particularly with regard to **rock**. Three main aspects are evident. First, attempts to distinguish between 'black' and 'white' voices, which tend to see the 'black' voice as demonstrative and communicating through a variety of vocal techniques, and the 'white' voice as more restrained and restricted. A second distinction is between 'trained' and 'untrained' voices, with the former found in a range of older popular musics rather than more contemporary forms (e.g. minstrel shows). The 'untrained' voice is important in signifying **authenticity** in rock, such as the 'straining' quality of high voices as indicating great effort, naturalness, and a lack of artifice. A third approach has been to associate specific genres with vocal styles, which are linked in turn to **gender**. The main example of this is the discussion of **cock rock** (as male) and '**teenybop**' (as female) by Frith and McRobbie (1990), which has been built upon by others (e.g. Shepherd, 1991). Shepherd notes that the hard, rasping vocal sound typical of 'cock' or **hard rock** is 'produced overwhelmingly in the throat and mouth, with a minimum of recourse to the resonating chambers of the chest and head'; he contrasts this with the 'typical vocal sound of woman-as-nurturer: soft and warm, based on much more relaxed use of the vocal chords and using the resonating chambers of the chest', present in much **pop** music (1991: 167).

Moore argues that such distinctions are problematic because of their essentialist assumptions: 'they emphasise only one aspect of vocal production, and attempt to read meaning into the voice's presence on the basis of that single aspect', ignoring that a multitude of factors characterize a vocal style (1993: 42). He suggests and elaborates four such factors: the register and range which any particular voice achieves; its degree of resonance; the singer's 'heard attitude' to pitch; and the singer's heard attitude to rhythm. Moore usefully illustrates these through a discussion of the vocal styles of Bill Haley, Little Richard, Fats Domino, and Elvis Presley.

As Frith (1989) observes, it is the way in which singers sing, rather than what they sing, that is central to their appeal to listeners. Compare, for instance, the vocal styles of Elvis Presley, Björk, Margot Timmins (the Cowboy Junkies), Johnny Rotten (Sex Pistols), and Mick Jagger.

See: **hard rock**; **heavy metal**; **punk**
Further reading: Middleton, 1990; Moore, 1993; Shepherd, 1991.

women in rock – *see* **gender**

world music; **world beat**   While it can be considered a **meta genre**, world music is really more of a marketing category. World music became prominent in the late 1980s, as a label applied to popular music originating outside the Anglo-American nexus. The term was launched in 1987 as a new category of popular music by eleven independent British, European, and American record labels specializing in music from Third World countries, including Earthworks. In the United States, the term **world beat** was used rather than world music. It is necessary to distinguish between world music situated within the Western music industry, and 'world musics which are defined as objects of ethnomusicological study' (Mitchell, 1996: 118).

World music was encouraged by the interest in, enthusiasm for, and borrowings from non-Western national musical styles by Western artists such as David Byrne, Peter Gabriel, and Paul Simon – though Simon's use of African forms, notably in *Graceland* (Warner Brothers, 1986), has proved contentious (see **appropriation**). Peter Gabriel also set up and runs the influential Real Life world music label. Sweeney (1981) defines the category primarily through a series of exclusions: world music is not part of the Anglo-American **pop** and

311

rock mainstream, nor local re-creations of it; not artificially preserved folklore; and not North American **roots** music like **country** and **blues**. He sees it as popular through its regular use by ordinary people, being performed, and danced and listened to, especially via **radio** or **cassette**. A further characteristic is world music becoming self-defined by virtue of musical **festival** programming (especially the success of WOMAD: World of Music, Arts, and Dance, established by Peter Gabriel in 1982), and media and public interest.

The marketing of world music, and the guides to it, usually construct the category around national **identity**, even though that is clearly tenuous, given the diversity of styles within particular countries. As such, discussions of world music will embrace, among others, Rai music from Algeria, Nigerian juju, Caribbean zouk, and Brazilian bossa nova. Hybrid forms like the Anglo-Indian **bhangra**, and Franco-American cajun and zydeco are also included under this broad rubric.

Perhaps more so than other forms of popular music, world music is open to processes of hybridization and musical acculturation.

Further reading: Barrett, 1996; Broughton *et al.*, 1994; Frith, 1989: introduction; Guilbault, 1993; Mitchell, 1996; Waterman, 1991.

youth – *see* **counter culture**; **demography**; **youth cultures**; **youth movies** (in **film**)

youth cultures; **youth subcultures**   As the contributors to a recently edited reader demonstrate, while there is no consensus about the definition of a subculture, they can broadly be considered to be social groups organized around shared interests and practices (Gelder and Thornton, 1997: part 2). Subcultures often distinguish themselves against others; factions of the larger social group, they usually set themselves in opposition to their parent culture, at least at a cultural level.

In the mid–1970s, rather than being part of a coherent **youth culture**, it seemed to many observers that youth consisted of a mainstream majority, and minority subcultures whose distinctiveness was shaped largely by the social class and ethnic background of their members (cf. the **counter culture** of the 1960s, and the view of youth as a generational unit). Sociological interest concentrated on the various youth subcultures, whose members were seen to rely on leisure and style as a means of winning their own cultural space, and thus represented cultural oppositional politics at the symbolic level.

Music is one of a complex of elements making up subcultural style. Its role in terms of pleasure and **cultural capital**

313

is similar to that played out among more mainstream youth, but in an accentuated form. The relationship between popular music and youth subcultures was comprehensively explored in a number of influential studies during the 1970s and early 1980s. Collectively, these argued what became a frequently asserted thesis: that youth subcultures appropriate and innovate musical forms and styles as a basis for their **identity**, and, in so doing, assert a counter-cultural **politics**. This perspective was primarily associated with writers linked to the United Kingdom's influential Birmingham Centre for Contemporary Cultural Studies (BCCCS), whose views became more widely accepted. (*Further reading:* Gelder and Thornton, 1997: pt 2; Hall and Jefferson, 1976; Hebdige, 1979; Willis, 1978; and see **cultural studies**.)

For the writers associated with the BCCCS, subcultures were regarded as 'meaning systems, modes of expression or life styles developed by groups in subordinate structural positions in response to dominant meaning systems, and which reflect their attempt to solve structural contradictions rising from the wider societal context' (Brake, 1985: 8). Hebdige starts from the premise that style in subculture is 'pregnant with significance', illustrating this through a comprehensive analysis of various spectacular subcultural styles: **beats** and hipsters in the 1950s, **teddy boys** in the 1950s and 1970s, **mods** in the early 1960s, **skinheads** in the late 1960s, **Rastas** in the 1970s, **glam rockers** in the early to mid-1970s, and, most visible of all, **punks** in the mid-1970s. In his analysis, subcultures rely on leisure and style as a means of making their values visible in a society saturated by the codes and symbols of the dominant culture. The significance of subcultures for their participants is that they offer a solution, albeit at a 'magical' level, to structural dislocations through the establishment of an 'achieved identity' – the selection of certain elements of style outside of those associated with the ascribed identity offered by work, home, or school. The expressive elements of this style offer 'a meaningful way of life during leisure', removed from the instrumental world of work:

> Subcultures are therefore expressive forms but what they
> express is, in the last instance, a fundamental tension
> between those in power and those condemned to sub-
> ordinate positions and second class lives. This tension is
> figuratively expressed in the form of subcultural style
> (Hebdige, 1979: 132).

The majority of youth pass through life without any
significant involvement in such subcultures. Associated aspects
of subcultural **fashion** and musical tastes may be adopted, but
for 'respectable' youth these are essentially divorced from subcultural lifestyles and values. Members of youth subcultures,
on the other hand, utilize symbolic elements to construct an
identity outside the restraints of **class** and education, an
identity which places them squarely outside of conservative
mainstream society. Membership of a subculture was seen to
necessarily involve membership of a class culture and could be
either an extension of, or in opposition to, the parent class
culture (eg. the skinheads). Writers such as Hebdige were at
pains not to overemphasize this class dimension, and to accord
due analytical weight to **gender** and ethnic factors.

Youth subcultures in the 1970s and early 1980s were an
international phenomenon, but with marked differences.
Subcultural styles in both Britain and the United States essentially developed out of their immediate social context,
reworking commercial popular culture into a subcultural style
which reflected and made sense of their structural social location. This process was not so clear-cut in more culturally
dependent societies. In Canada, for example, the situation
was confused by the nation's historical links with Britain and
France and the marked contemporary influence of its close
proximity to the United States, a situation contributing to
Canada's problem of finding a sense of national identity.
Canadian youth cultures were consequently largely derivative
and any potential oppositional force in them was highly muted
(Brake, 1985).

For the subcultural analysts of the 1970s, **homology** was
central to the consideration of the place of music in youth

subcultures: a 'fit' between the 'focal concerns, activities, group structure and the collective self-image' of the subculture, and the cultural artifacts and practices adopted by the members of the subculture. The latter were seen as 'objects in which they could see their central values held and reflected' (Hall and Jefferson, 1976: 56).

The BCCCS writers' sociocultural analyses represented an original and imaginative contribution to the sociology of youth cultures, but were critiqued for their overemphasis on the symbolic 'resistance' of subcultures, which was imbued with an unwarranted political significance; the romanticizing of working-class subcultures; the neglect of ordinary or conformist youth; and a masculine emphasis, with little attention paid to the subcultural experiences of girls. And while music was regarded as a central aspect of subcultural style, its homological relation to other dimensions of style was not always easy to pin down. For example, the skinheads' preferred music changed over time, making problematic any argument for its homological role in skinhead culture. As Hebdige (1979) observed, the 'early' skinheads' preference for elements of black style, including **reggae** and **ska** music, is contradictory considering their racial stance. At times, stylistic attributes were too quickly attributed to a specifically subcultural affiliation, rather than recognizing their generalizability.

Writing at the end of the 1980s, Middleton concludes that subcultural analysis had drawn the connection between music and subculture much too tightly, 'flawed above all by the uncompromising drive to homology' (Middleton, 1990: 161). In part, this arises from the problematic subculturalist dichotomizing of mainstream and oppositional musics, locating itself 'within the broader terrain of the ideological politics of style organized around an opposition of center and margin' (Grossberg, 1992: 145).

While this convergence between music and cultural group values is evident in some contemporary youth subcultures, most notably **heavy metal** and **grunge**, subsequent theoretical discussions and case studies suggest that the degree of homology between subcultures and music has been overstated.

Indeed the very value of the concept 'subcultures', and particularly its conflation with oppositional cultural politics, became
seriously questioned. Hebdige, one of the central figures of
1970s subcultural theory, concluded that 'theoretical models
are as tied to their own times as the human bodies that
produce them. The idea of subculture-as-negation grew up
alongside punk, remained inextricably linked to it and died
when it died' (Hebdige, 1988: 8; see also Grossberg, 1992;
Redhead, 1990).

Redhead's detailed reading of post-punk events in the
United Kingdom suggested that the very notion of subculture,
and the emphasis on it as part of a tradition of 'rock authenticity' and opposition at the level of cultural politics, were in
need of revision: 'Such notions are not capable of capturing
the changes in youth culture and rock culture from at least
the late 1970s onwards. They are, moreover, unsatisfactory as
accounts of pop history and youth culture in general'
(Redhead, 1990: 41–2). For many youthful consumers during
the 1980s and 1990s, the old ideological divides applied to
popular music had little relevance, with their tastes determined
by a more complex pattern of considerations than any 'politically correct' dichotomizing of **genres**. This is most evident
in the constituencies for **alternative** and **dance–music**.
Recent research in popular music has retained elements of
the subculturalist approach, but moved towards a more sophisticated understanding of the activities of music audiences,
drawing heavily on the concept of scenes (see Straw, 1992).

See: entries on specific subcultures; **alternative scenes**; **bricolage**;
   locality
Further reading: Gelder and Thornton, 1997.

youth movies – *see* **film**

FURTHER RESOURCES AND BIBLIOGRAPHY

In addition to the books and articles listed here, I have made extensive use of music magazines and the Internet. These provide current and often extensive information on particular music scenes, genres, and performers, and the activities of record companies.

1 Music magazines

Billboard
Guitar Player
ICE: The CD News Authority
Melody Maker
MOJO
Music Week
NME
Pavement
Q,
Rip It Up
Rolling Stone (US and Australian editions; especially the annual Yearbook)
VOX

In addition to their print versions, several of these have Web sites. *Addicted to Noise* is on-line only; see below.

2 Selected Internet World Wide Web (WWW) sites

Note that these are subject to change (and in accessing you use only the section within <>). An enormous number of other sites can be accessed through these.

Addicted to Noise, excellent current reviews and columns: <http://www.addict.com>

Perfect Beat: The Pacific Journal of Research Into Contemporary Music and Popular Culture: <http://www.elm.mq.edu.au/pbeat/pbeat.htm>

Rolling Stone, Australia: <http://www.rstone.com.au/>

The RoJaRo Index, a bibliographic guide to the music press: <http://www.notam.uio.no/rojaro/>

Internet Underground Music Archive, an excellent starting point: <http://www.iuma.com/index.html>

Music Resources on the Internet: <http://www.music.indiana.edu/misc/music-resources.html>

NME's Web site: <http://nme.com/>

Q magazine is also on-line: <http://www.erack.com/QWeb/>

Internet Music Resource Guide: <http://www.teleport.com/~celinec/music.html>

3 Bibliography

Abbs, P. (1975) *Reclamations: Essays on Culture, Mass-Culture and the Curriculum*, London: Heinemann.

Abrams, N. (1995) 'Antonio's B-Boys: Rap, Rappers, and Gramsci's Intellectuals', *Popular Music and Society*, 19, 4: 1–20.

Adorno, T., with the assistance of G. Simpson (1941) 'On Popular Music', reprinted in: Frith, S. and Goodwin, A. (eds) *On Record: Rock, Pop, and the Written Word*, New York: Pantheon Books.

—— (1976) 'Perennial Fashions: Jazz', in *Prisms*, London: Neville Spearman; trans. S. and S. Weber (first published 1955).

—— (1991) *The Culture Industry: Selected Essays on Mass Culture*, ed. J. Bernstein, London: Routledge.

Agger, B. (1992) *Cultural Studies as Critical Theory*, London: Falmer Press.

Aizlewood, J. (ed.) (1994) *Love is the Drug*, London: Penguin.

Anderson, B. (1983) *Imagined Communities*, London: Verso.

Ang, I. (1991) *Desperately Seeking the Audience*, London and New York: Routledge.

Arnett, J. (1996) *Metalheads: Heavy Metal Music and Adolescent Alienation*, Boulder, CO: Westview Press.

Arnold, M. (1869) *Culture and Anarchy*, reprinted 1993, Cambridge: Cambridge University Press.

Ash, J. and Wilson, E. (1992) *Chic Thrills: A Fashion Reader*, London: HarperCollins.

Aufderheide, P. (1986) 'Music Videos: The Look of the Sound', in Gitlin, T. (ed.) *Watching Television*, New York: Pantheon Books.

Baker, H., Jr (1993) *Black Studies, Rap and the Academy*, Chicago: University of Chicago Press.

Bangs, L. (1990) *Psychotic Reactions and Carburetor Dung*, ed. G. Marcus, London: Minerva.

—— (1992a) 'The British Invasion, in DeCurtis, A. and Henke, J. (eds) *The Rolling Stone Illustrated History of Rock and Roll*, 3rd edn, New York: Random House, pp. 199–208.

—— (1992b) 'Bubblegum', in DeCurtis, A. and Henke, J. (eds) *The Rolling Stone Illustrated History of Rock and Roll*, 3rd edn, New York: Random House, pp. 452–4.

—— (1992c) 'Heavy Metal', in DeCurtis, A. and Henke, J. (eds) *The Rolling Stone Illustrated History of Rock and Roll*, 3rd edn, New York: Random House, pp. 459–64.

—— (1992d) 'Protopunk: the Garage Bands', in DeCurtis, A. and Henke, J. (eds) *The Rolling Stone Illustrated History of Rock and Roll*, 3rd edn, New York: Random House, pp. 357–61.

Banks, J. (1996) *Monopoly Television: MTV's Quest to Control the Music*, Boulder, CO: Westview Press.

Barlow, W. (1989) *Looking Up At Down: The Emergence of Blues Culture*, Philadelphia: Temple University Press.

Barnard, S. (1989) *On the Radio: Music Radio in Britain*, Milton Keynes: Open University Press.

Barnes, K. (1988) 'Top 40 Radio: A Fragment of the Imagination', in Frith, S. (ed.) *Facing the Music*, New York: Pantheon Books.

Barnes, R. (1979) *Mods*, London: Eel Pie Publishing.

Barnet, R. J. and Cavanagh, J. (1994) *Global Dreams: Imperial Corporations and the New World Order*, New York: Simon & Schuster.

Barrett, J. (1996) 'World Music, Nation and Postcolonialism', *Cultural Studies*, 10, 2 (May): 237–47.

Barrow, T. and Newby, J. (1996) *Inside the Music Business*, London and New York: Routledge.

Baxter-Moore, N. (1996) 'Reelin' and Rockin': Genre-bending and Boundary-crossing in the "East Coast Sound" ', unpublished paper, Dept of Politics, Brock University, Ontario.

Bayton, M. (1990) 'How Women Become Musicians', in Frith, S. and Goodwin, A. (eds) *On Record: Rock, Pop, and the Written Word*, New York: Pantheon Books.

Beadle, J. (1993) *Will Pop Eat Itself?: Pop Music in the Soundbite Era*, London: Faber & Faber.

Becker, H. (1997) 'The Culture of a Deviant Group: The "Jazz" Musician', in Gelder, K. and Thornton, S. (eds) *The Subcultures Reader*, London and New York: Routledge (first published 1963).

Bennett, A. (1997) ' "Going Down to the Pub!": The Pub Rock Scene as a Resource for the Consumption of Popular Music', *Popular Music*, 16, 1: 97–108.

Bennett, H. S. (1990) 'The Realities of Practice', in Frith, S. and Goodwin, A (eds) *On Record: Rock, Pop, and the Written Word*, New York: Pantheon Books.

Bennett, T., Frith, S., Grossberg, L., Shepherd, J., and Turner, G. (1993) *Rock and Popular Music: Politics, Policies, Institutions*, London: Routledge.

Berland, J. (1991) 'Free Trade and Canadian Music: Level Playing Field or Scorched Earth?', *Cultural Studies*, 5, 3: 317–25.

—— (1993) 'Radio Space and Industrial Time: The Case of Radio Formats', in Bennett, T. *et al.* (1993) *Rock and Popular Music: Politics, Policies, Institutions*, London: Routledge.

Bertsch, C. (1993) 'Making Sense of Seattle', *Bad Subjects*, 5 (March/April).

Bishton, D. (1986) *Black Heart Man*, London: Chatto & Windus.

Bjornberg, A. and Stockfelt, O. (1996) '*Kristen Klatvask fra Vejle*: Danish Pub Music, Mythscapes and "Local Camp" ', *Popular Music*, 15, 2: 131–48.

Blackman, A. (1988) *The Shoestring Pirates*, Auckland: Hauraki Enterprises.

Blake, A. (1992) *The Music Business*, London: Batsford.

Bloom, B. (1987) *The Closing of the American Mind*, New York: Simon & Schuster.

Bloomfield, T. (1993) 'Resisting Songs: Negative Dialectics in Pop', *Popular Music*, 12, 1: 13–31.

Bordo, S. (1993) ' "Material Girl": The Effacements of Postmodern Culture', in Schwichtenberg, C. (ed.) *The Madonna Connection: Representational Politics, Subcultural Identities, and Cultural Theory*, St Leonards, NSW: Allen & Unwin, pp. 265–90.

Bourdieu, P. (1984) *Distinction: A Social Critique of the Judgement of Taste*, London: Routledge & Kegan Paul.

Boyd, T. (1994) 'Check Yo Self, Before You Wreck Yo Self: Variations on a Political Theme in Rap Music and Popular Culture', *Public Culture*, 7: 289–312.

Boyd-Barrett, O. and Newbold, C. (1995) *Approaches to Media: A Reader*, London: Arnold; New York: St. Martin's Press.

Brackett, D. (1995) 'The Politics and Musical Practice of Crossover', in Straw, W. *et al.* (eds) *Popular Music – Style and Identity*, Montreal: Centre for Research on Canadian Cultural Industries and Institutions.

Bradley, D. (1992) *Understanding Rock'n'Roll: Popular Music in Britian 1955–1964*, Buckingham: Open University Press.

Brady, L. (1994) *Rock Stars/Pop Stars: A Comprehensive Bibliography, 1955–1994*, Westport, CT: Greenwood Press.

Brake, M. (1985) *Comparative Youth Culture*, London: Routledge & Kegan Paul.

Brand, G. and Scannell, P. (1991) 'Talk, Identity and Performance: The Tony Blackburn Show', in Scannell, P. (ed.) *Broadcast Talk*, London: Sage, pp. 201–26.

Brantlinger, P. (1990) *Crusoe's Footprints: Cultural Studies in Britain and America*, London and New York: Routledge.

Breen, M. (1991) 'A Stairway to Heaven Or a Highway to Hell?: Heavy Metal Rock Music in the 1990s', *Cultural Studies*, 5, 2 (May): 191–203.

—— (1992) 'Global Entertainment Corporations and a Nation's Music: The Inquiry Into the Prices of Sound Recordings', *Media Information Australia*, 64 (May), pp. 31–41.

—— (1993) 'Making it Visible: The 1990 Public Inquiry into Australian Music Copyrights', in Frith, S. (ed.) *Music and Copyright*, Edinburgh: Edinburgh University Press, ch. 6.

—— (1995) 'The End of the World as We Know It: Popular Music's Cultural Mobility', *Cultural Studies*, 9, 3 (October): 486–504.

—— (1996) 'The Popular Music Industry in Australia: A Study of Policy Reform and Retreat 1982–1996', PhD thesis, Victoria University of Technology, Melbourne.

Brennan, S. (1996) 'Student Radio – An Alternative Culture', *SITES*, 33: 87–101.

Broughton, S., Ellingham, M., Muddyman, D., and Trillo, R. (eds) (1994) *World Music: The Rough Guide*, London: The Rough Guides.

Brown, C. T. (1992) *The Art of Rock and Roll*, 3rd edn, Englewood Cliffs, NJ: Prentice-Hall.

Burnett, R. (1990) 'From a Whisper to a Scream. Music Video and

Cultural Form', in Roe, K. and Carlsson, V. (eds) *Popular Music Research*, NORDICOM, University of Goteborg.

—— (1996) *The Global Jukebox: The International Music Industry*, London and New York: Routledge.

Carney, G. (1990) 'Geography of Music: Inventory and Prospect', *Journal of Cultural Geography*, 10, 2: 35–48.

Carr, I., Fairweather, D., and Priestley, B. (1988) *Jazz: The Essential Companion*, London: Paladin.

Cawelti, J. (1971) 'Notes Toward an Aesthetic of Popular Culture', *Journal of Popular Culture*, 5, 2 (Fall): 255–68.

Chambers, I. (1985) *Urban Rhythms: Pop Music and Popular Culture*, London: Macmillan.

—— (1986) *Popular Culture: The Metropolitan Experience*, London: Methuen.

Chapman, R. (1992) *Selling the Sixties: The Pirates and Pop Music Radio*, London and New York: Routledge.

Chapple, S. and Garofalo, R. (1977) *Rock'n'Roll Is Here To Pay: The History and Politics of the Music Industry*, Chicago: Nelson-Hall.

Charlton, K. (1994) *Rock Music Styles: A History*, 2nd edn, Madison, WI: Brown & Benchmark.

Chester, A. (1970) 'Second Thoughts on a Rock Aesthetic: The Band', *New Left Review*, No. 62, London; reprinted in Frith, S. and Goodwin, A. (1990) *On Record: Rock, Pop, and The Written Word*.

Christenson, M. (1995) 'Cycles of Symbolic Production? A New Model to Explain Concentration, Diversity and Innovation in the Music Industry', *Popular Music*, 14, 1: 55–93.

Christgau, R. (1982) *Christgau's Guide: Rock Albums of the '70s*, London: Vermillion.

—— (1990) *Christgau's Record Guide: The '80s*, London: Vermillion.

Clarke, D. (ed.) (1990) *The Penguin Encyclopedia of Popular Music*, London and New York: Penguin.

Clarke, D. (1995) *The Rise and Fall of Popular Music*, London: Viking/ The Penguin Group.

Clarke, J. (1976) 'The Skinheads and the Magical Recovery of Community', in Hall, S. and Jefferson, T. (eds) *Resistance Through Rituals: Youth Subcultures in Post-War Britain*, London: Hutchinson/ BCCCS.

Clayson, A. (1995) *Beat Merchants*, London: Blandford.

Cline, C. (1992) 'Essays from Bitch: The Women's Rock Newsletter with Bite', in Lewis, L. A. (ed.) *The Adoring Audience: Fan Culture and the Popular Media*, London: Routledge.

Cloonan, M. (1995) 'Popular Music and Censorship in Britain: An Overview', *Popular Music and Society*, 19, 3 (Fall): 75–104.

—— (1996) *Banned! Censorship of Popular Music in Britain: 1967–92*, Aldershot: Arena.

Cohen, Sarah (1991) *Rock Culture in Liverpool: Popular Music in the Making*, Oxford: Clarendon Press.

—— (1993) 'Ethnography and Popular Music Studies', *Popular Music*, 12, 2: 123–38.

—— (1994a) 'Identity, Place and the "Liverpool Sound"', in Stokes, M. (ed.) *Ethnicity, Identity and Music*, Oxford: Berg.

—— (1994b) 'Moral Panic, the Media and British Rave Culture', in Ross, A. and Rose, T. (eds) *Microphone Fiends*, London and New York: Routledge.

—— (1995) 'Localizing Sound', in Straw, W. *et al.* (eds) *Popular Music – Style and Identity*, Montreal: Centre for Research on Canadian Cultural Industries and Institutions.

Cohen, Stanley (1980) *Folk Devils and Moral Panics*, Oxford: Robertson.

Cohn, N. (1970) *WopBopaLooBopLupBamBoom: Pop From the Beginning*, St. Albans: Paladin/Granada.

—— (1992) 'Phil Spector', in DeCurtis, A. and Henke, J. (eds) *The Rolling Stone Illustrated History of Rock and Roll*, 3rd edn, New York: Random House, pp. 177–88.

Collins, J. (1993) 'The Problem of Copyright: The Case of Ghana', in Frith, S. (ed.) *Music and Copyright*, Edinburgh: Edinburgh University Press, ch. 8.

Collis, J. (ed.) (1980) *The Rock Primer*, Harmondsworth: Penguin.

Considine, J. D. (1992) 'Madonna', in DeCurtis, A. and Henke, J. (eds) *The Rolling Stone Illustrated History of Rock and Roll*, 3rd edn, New York: Random House, pp. 656–62.

Cooper, B. L. (1981) 'A Popular Music Perspective: Challenging Sexism in the Social Studies Classroom', *The Social Studies*, 71: 1–8.

—— (1992) 'A Review Essay and Bibliography of Studies on Rock'n'roll Movies, 1955–1963', *Popular Music and Society*, 16, 1: 85–92.

—— (1993) 'Awarding an "A" Grade to Heavy Metal: A Review Essay' [of Walser, and Weinstein], *Popular Music and Society*, 17, 3: 99–101.

Crisell, A. (1994) *Understanding Radio*, 3rd edn, London and New York: Routledge.

Cross, B. (1993) *It's Not About a Salary: Rap, Race and Resistance in Los Angeles*, New York: Verso.

Cunningham, M. (1996) *Good Vibrations: A History of Record Production*, Chessington: Castle Communications.

Cupitt, M., Ramsay, G., and Shelton, L. (1996) *Music, New Music and All That: Teenage Radio in the 90s*, Sydney: Australian Broadcasting Authority.

Curran, J., Morley, D., and Walkerdine, V. (eds) (1996) *Cultural Studies and Communications*, London and New York: Edward Arnold.

Curtis, J. (1987) *Rock Eras: Interpretations of Music and Society 1954–1984*, Bowling Green, OH: Bowling Green State University Press.

Cusic, D. (1990) *The Sound of Light: A History of Gospel Music*, Bowling Green, OH: Bowling Green State University Press.

—— (1996) *Music in the Market*, Bowling Green, OH: Bowling Green State University Press.

Cutler, C. (1985) *File under Popular*, London: November Books.

Dancing in the Street, BBC 10-part series on the history of rock.

Dannen, F. (1991) *Hit Men: Power Brokers and Fast Money Inside the Music Business*, New York: Vintage Books.

Davis, S. (1992) *Reggae Bloodlines: In Search of the Music and Culture of Jamaica*, New York: Da Capo Press.

DeCurtis, A. (ed.) (1991) 'Rock and Roll Culture', *South Atlantic Quarterly*, 90, 4.

—— (1992) 'Bruce Springsteen', in DeCurtis, A. and Henke, J. (eds) *The Rolling Stone Illustrated History of Rock and Roll*, 3rd edn, New York: Random House, pp. 619–25.

DeCurtis, A. and Henke, J. (eds) (1992a) *The Rolling Stone Illustrated History of Rock and Roll: The Definitive History of the Most Important Artists and Their Music*, 3rd edn, New York: Random House.

DeCurtis, A. and Henke, J. (eds) (1992b) *The Rolling Stone Album Guide: Completely New Reviews*, New York: Random House.

Denisoff, R. S. (1986) *Tarnished Gold: The Record Industry Revisited*, New Brunswick, NJ: Transaction.

Denselow, R. (1990) *When The Music's Over: The Story of Political Pop*, London: Faber & Faber.

DeRogatis, J. (1996) *Kaleidoscope Eyes: Psychedelic Rock from the '60s to the '90s*, NJ: Citadel Press/Carol Publishing.

Dixon, W., with D. Snowden (1989) *I Am the Blues: The Willie Dixon Story*, London: Quartet Books.

Dorland, M. (ed.) (1996) *The Cultural Industries in Canada: Problems, Policies and Prospects*, Toronto: James Lorimer & Company.

Downing, D. (1976) *Future Rock*, St. Albans: Panther.

Draper, R. (1990) *Rolling Stone Magazine: The Uncensored History*, New York: Doubleday.

Du Gay, P. and Negus, K. (1994) 'The Changing Sites of Sound: Music

Retailing and the Composition of Consumers', *Media, Culture and Society*, 16, 3: 395–413.

Dunbar-Hall, P. and Hodge, G. (1993) *A Guide to Rock'n'Pop*, 2nd edn, Marrickville, NSW: Science Press.

Dychtwald, K. (1989) *Age Wave*, Los Angeles: Tarcher.

Dyer, R. (1990) 'In Defence of Disco', in Frith, S. and Goodwin, A. (eds) *On Record: Rock, Pop, and the Written Word*, New York: Pantheon Books.

Eddy, C. (1992) 'The Metal Explosion', in DeCurtis, A. and Henke, J. (eds) *The Rolling Stone Illustrated History of Rock and Roll*, 3rd edn, New York: Random House, pp. 465–73.

Eisenberg, E. (1988) *The Recording Angel: Music, Records and Culture From Aristotle to Zappa*, London: Pan Books.

Eliot, M. (1989) *Rockonomics: The Money Behind the Music*, New York and Toronto: Franklin Watts.

Endres, T. G. (1993) 'A Dramatic Analysis of Family Themes in the Top 100 Country Songs of 1992', *Popular Music and Society*, 17, 4: 29–46.

Ennis, P. H. (1992) *The Seventh Stream: The Emergence of Rock'n'Roll in American Popular Music*, Hanover and London: Wesleyan University Press.

Erlewine, M., Bogdanov, V., and Woodstra, C. (eds) (1995) *All Music Guide to Rock* [AMG], San Francisco: Miller Freeman.

Evans, L. (1994) *Women, Sex and Rock'n'Roll: In Their Own Words*, London: Pandora/HarperCollins.

Ewen, S. (1988) *All Consuming Images: The Politics of Style in Contemporary Culture*, New York: Basic Books.

Eyerman, R. and Jamison, A. (1995) 'Social Movements and Cultural Transformation: Popular Music in the 1960s', *Media, Culture and Society*, 17: 449–68.

Fairchild, C. (1995) ' "Alternative" Music and the Politics of Cultural Autonomy: The Case of Fugazi and the D.C. Scene', *Popular Music and Society*, 19, 1: 17–36.

Featherstone, M. (1987) 'Lifestyle and Consumer Culture', *Theory, Culture and Society*, 4: 55–70.

Felder, R. (1993) *Manic, Pop, Thrill*, Hopewell, NJ: Eco Press.

Fenster, M. (1995) 'Two Stories: Where Exactly is the Local?', in Straw, W. *et al.* (eds) *Popular Music – Style and Identity*, Montreal: Centre for Research on Canadian Cultural Industries and Institutions.

Fink, M. (1989) *Inside the Music Business: Music in Contemporary Life*, New York: Schirmer/Macmillan.

Finnegan, R. (1989) *The Hidden Musicians: Music-Making in an English Town*, Cambridge: Cambridge University Press.

Fiske, J. (1989) *Understanding Popular Culture*, Boston: Unwin Hyman.

Fong-Torres, B. (1991) *Hickory Wind: The Life and Times of Gram Parsons*, New York: Pocket Books.

Fordham, J. (1991) *Jazz on CD: The Essential Guide*, London: Kyle Cathie.

Fornas, J., Lindberg, U., and Sernhelde, O. (1995) *In Garageland: Rock, Youth and Modernity*, London: Routledge.

Fox, A. (1988) *Rock and Pop: Phillips Collectors Guides*, London: Boxtree.

Friedlander, P. (1996) *Rock and Roll: A Social History*, Boulder, CO: Westview Press.

Friedman, T. (1993) 'Milli Vanilli and the Scapegoating of the Inauthentic', *Bad Subjects*, 9.

Frith, S. (1978) *The Sociology of Rock*, London: Constable.

—— (1983) *Sound Effects: Youth, Leisure and the Politics of Rock'n'Roll*, London: Constable.

—— (1987) 'Towards an Aesthetic of Popular Music', in Leppert, R. and McClary, S. (eds) *Music and Society*, Cambridge: Cambridge University Press, pp. 133–49.

—— (ed.) (1988a) *Facing the Music*, New York: Pantheon Books.

—— (1988b) *Music for Pleasure: Essays in the Sociology of Pop*, Cambridge: Polity Press.

—— (1988c) 'Video Pop: Picking up the Pieces', in Frith, S. (ed.) *Facing the Music*, New York: Pantheon Books, pp. 88–130.

—— (ed.) (1989) *World Music, Politics and Social Change*, Manchester: Manchester University Press.

—— (ed.) (1993) *Music and Copyright*, Edinburgh: Edinburgh University Press.

—— (1996) *Performing Rites: On the Value of Popular Music*, Cambridge, MA: Harvard University Press.

Frith, S. and Goodwin, A. (eds) (1990) *On Record: Rock, Pop, and the Written Word*, New York: Pantheon Books; London: Routledge.

Frith, S. and Horne, H. (1987) *Art Into Pop*, London: Methuen.

Frith, S. and McRobbie, A. (1990) 'Rock and Sexuality', in Frith, S. and Goodwin, A. (eds) *On Record: Rock, Pop, and the Written Word*, New York: Pantheon Books, pp. 371–89 (first published 1978).

Frith, S. and Street, J. (1992) 'Rock against Racism and Red Wedge', in Garofalo, R. (ed.) *Rockin' the Boat: Mass Music and Mass Movements*, Boston: South End Press.

Gaar, G. (1992) *She's a Rebel: The History of Women in Rock and Roll*, Seattle: Seal Press.

Gaines, D. (1991) *Teenage Wasteland: Suburbia's Dead End Kids*, New York: HarperCollins.

Gaines, J. (1993) 'Bette Midler and the Piracy of Identity', in Frith, S. (ed.) *Music and Copyright*, Edinburgh: Edinburgh University Press, ch. 5.

Gambaccini, P., Rice, T., and Rice, J. (1987) *The Guinness Book of British Hit Singles: Every Hit Single Since 1952*, 6th edn, Enfield: Guinness Superlatives; 10th edn, 1995.

Gamman, L. and Marshment, M. (1988) *The Female Gaze: Women as Viewers of Popular Culture*, London: The Women's Press.

Gammond, P. (ed.) (1991) *The Oxford Companion to Popular Music*, Oxford: Oxford University Press.

Garnham, N. (1987) 'Concepts of Culture: Public Policy and the Cultural Industries', *Cultural Studies*, 1, 1 (January): 23–37.

—— (1990) *Capitalism and Communication: Global Culture and the Economics of Communication*, London: Sage.

Garofalo, R. (1992a) 'Understanding Mega-Events', in Garofalo, R. (ed.) *Rockin' the Boat: Mass Music and Mass Movements*, Boston: South End Press.

—— (ed.) (1992b) *Rockin' the Boat: Mass Music and Mass Movements*, Boston: South End Press.

—— (1994) 'Culture versus Commerce: The Marketing of Black Popular Music', *Public Culture*, 7: 275–87.

—— (1997) *Rockin' Out: Popular Music in the USA*, Needham Heights, MA: Allyn & Bacon.

Garon, P. (1975) *Blues and the Poetic Spirit*, London: Eddison.

Gass, G. (1991) 'Why Don't We Do It in the Classroom?', in DeCurtis, A. (ed.) 'Rock and Roll Culture', *South Atlantic Quarterly*, 90, 4.

Gatten, J. (1995) *Rock Music Scholarship: An Interdisciplinary Bibliography*, Westport, CT: Greenwood Press.

Gelatt, R. (1977) *The Fabulous Phonograph, 1877–1977*, New York: Macmillan.

Gelder, K. and Thornton, S. (eds) (1997) *The Subcultures Reader*, London and New York: Routledge.

Gendron, B. (1986) 'Theodor Adorno Meets the Cadillacs', in Modleski, T. (ed.) *Studies in Entertainment*, Bloomington: Indiana University Press, pp. 18–36.

George, N. (1985) *Where Did Our Love Go?*, New York: St Martin's Press.

—— (1989) *The Death of Rhythm & Blues*, New York: Pantheon Books.

Geyrhalter, T. (1996) 'Effeminacy, Camp and Sexual Subversion in Rock: The Cure and Suede', *Popular Music*, 15, 2: 217–24.

Gill, R. (1996) 'Ideology, Gender and Popular Radio: A Discourse Analytic Approach', in Baehr, H. and Gray, A. (eds) *Turning It On: A Reader in Women and Media*, London: Arnold.

Gillet, C. (1983) *The Sound of the City: The Rise of Rock and Roll*, revised edn, London: Souvenir Press.

Gilmore, M. (1990) 'The Season of the Witch Hunt', in Cresswell, T. (ed.) *Rolling Stone: 1990 Yearbook*, Surrey Hills, NSW: Rolling Stone Australia.

Gilroy, P. (1993) *The Black Atlantic: Modernity and Double Consciousness*, Cambridge, MA: Harvard University Press.

—— (1997) 'Diaspora, Utopia, and the Critique of Capitalism', in Gelder, K. and Thornton, S. (eds) *The Subcultures Reader*, London and New York: Routledge.

Goertzel, B. (1991) 'Review Essay. The Rock Guitar Solo: From Expression to Simulation', *Popular Music and Society*, 15, 1: 91–101.

Golding, P. and Murdoch, G. (1991) 'Culture, Communications and Political Economy', in Curran, J. and Gurevitch, M. (eds) *Mass Media and Communications*, London: Edward Arnold, pp. 15–32.

Goode, E. and Ben-Yehuda, N. (1994) *Moral Panics: The Social Construction of Deviance*, Oxford and Cambridge, MA: Blackwell.

Goodwin, A. (1987) 'Music Video in the (Post) Modern World', *Screen*, 28, 3: 36–55.

—— (1990) 'Sample and Hold: Pop Music in the Digital Age of Reproduction', in Frith, S. and Goodwin, A. (eds) *On Record: Rock, Pop, and the Written Word*, New York: Pantheon Books, pp. 258–74.

—— (1991) 'Popular Music and Postmodern Theory', *Cultural Studies*, 5, 2 (May): 174–90.

—— (1993) *Dancing in the Distraction Factory: Music Television and Popular Culture*, Oxford, Minn.: University of Minnesota Press.

Gracyk, T. (1996) *Rhythm and Noise: An Aesthetics of Rock*, Durham and London: Duke University Press.

Grant, B. (1986) 'The Classic Hollywood Musical and the "Problem" of Rock'n'Roll', *Journal of Popular Film and Television*, 13, 4 (winter): 195–205.

Grenier, L. (1993) 'Policing French-Language Music on Canadian Radio', in Bennett, T. *et al. Rock and Popular Music*, pp. 119–41.

Gribin, A.J. and Schiff, M. (1992) *Doo-Wop: The Forgotten Third of Rock 'N' Roll*, Iola, WI: Krause Publications (includes a huge 'sono-graphy').

Groce, S.B. (1991) 'On the Outside Looking In: Professional Socialization and the Process of Becoming a Songwriter', *Popular Music and Society*, 15, 1.

Grossberg, L. (1986) 'Teaching the Popular', in Nelson, C. (ed.) *Theory in the Classroom*, Urbana, IL: University of Illinois Press.

—— (1992) *We Gotta Get Out of This Place: Popular Conservatism and Postmodern Culture*, New York: Routledge.

Grossberg, L., Nelson, C., and Treichler, P. (eds) (1992) *Cultural Studies*, London and New York: Routledge.

Guilbault, J. (1993) *Zouk: World Music in the West Indies*, Chicago: University of Chicago Press.

Guralnick, P. (1989) *Feel Like Going Home*, London: Omnibus Press.

—— (1991) *Sweet Soul Music: Rhythm and Blues and the Southern Dream of Freedom*, London: Penguin.

—— (1992) 'Rockabilly', in DeCurtis, A. and Henke, J. (eds) *The Rolling Stone Illustrated History of Rock and Roll*, 3rd edn, New York: Random House, pp. 67–72.

Gurevitch, M., Bennett, T., Curran, J., and Woollacott, J. (eds) (1982) *Culture, Society and the Media*, London: Methuen.

Gurley, T. and Pfefferle, W. (1996) *Plug In: The Guide to Music on the Net*, Englewood Cliffs, NJ: Prentice-Hall.

Haggerty, G. (1995) *A Guide to Popular Music Reference Books: An Annotated Bibliography*, Westport, CT: Greenwood Press.

Hakanen, E. and Wells, A. (1993) 'Music Preference and Taste Cultures Among Adolescents', *Popular Music and Society*, 17, 1: 55–69.

Halfacree, K. and Kitchin, R. (1996) ' "Madchester Rave On": Placing the Fragments of Popular Music', *Area*, 28, 1: 47–55.

Hall, D. (1994) 'New Age Music: A Voice of Liminality in Postmodern Popular Culture', *Popular Music and Society*, 18, 2: 13–21.

Hall, S. (1993) 'Minimal Selves', in Gray, A. and McGuigan, J. (eds) *Studying Culture*, London: Edward Arnold, pp. 134–8.

Hall, S. and Jefferson, T. (eds) (1976) *Resistance Through Rituals: Youth Subcultures in Post-War Britain*, London: Hutchinson/BCCCS.

Hall, S. and Whannel, P. (1964) *The Popular Arts*, London: Hutchison.

Hall, S., Critcher, C., Jefferson, T., Clarke, J. and Roberts, R. (1978) *Policing the Crisis*, London: Macmillan.

Hansen, Barry (1992a) 'Doo-Wop', in DeCurtis, A. and Henke, J. (eds) *The Rolling Stone Illustrated History of Rock and Roll*, 3rd edn, New York: Random House, pp. 92–101.

—— (1992b) 'Rhythm and Blues', in DeCurtis, A. and Henke, J. (eds) *The Rolling Stone Illustrated History of Rock and Roll*, 3rd edn, New York: Random House, pp. 17–20.

Hardy, P. and Laing, D. (eds) (1990) *The Faber Companion to Twentieth Century Popular Music*, London: Faber & Faber.

Harker, D. (1980) *One For The Money: Politics and Popular Song*, London: Hutchinson.

Harley, R. (1993) 'Beat in the System', in Bennett, T., Frith, S., Grossberg, L., Shepherd, J., and Turner, G. (eds) *Rock and Popular Music: Politics, Policies, Institutions*, London: Routledge.

Harron, M. (1988) 'Pop as a Commodity', in Frith, S. (ed.) *Facing the Music*, New York: Pantheon Books, pp. 173–220.

Hatch, D. and Millward, S. (1987) *From Blues to Rock: An Analytical History of Rock Music*, Manchester: Manchester University Press.

—— (1995) 'Enterprise on the New Frontier: Music, Industry and the Internet', *Convergence*, 1, 2.

Hayward, P., Mitchell, T., and Shuker, R. (eds) (1994) *North Meets South: Popular Music in Aotearoa/New Zealand*, Sydney: Perfect Beat Publications.

Hayward, P. and Orrock, G. (1995) 'Window of Opportunity: CD-ROMs, The International Music Industry and Early Australian Initiatives', *CONVERGENCE*, 1, 1: 61–79.

Hayward, S. (1996) *Key Concepts in Cinema Studies*, London and New York: Routledge.

Hebdige, D. (1979) *Subculture: The Meaning of Style*, London: Methuen.

—— (1988) *Hiding in the Light: On Images and Things*, London: Comedia/Routledge.

—— (1990) *Cut 'N' Mix: Culture, Identity, and Caribbean Music*, London: Comedia/Routledge.

Henderson, L. (1993) 'Justify Our Love: Madonna and the Politics of Queer Sex', in Schwichtenberg, C. (ed.) *The Madonna Connection: Representational Politics, Subcultural Identities, and Cultural Theory*, St. Leonards, NSW: Allen & Unwin, pp. 107–28.

Herman, G. and Hoare, I. (1979) 'The Struggle for Song: A Reply to Leon Rosselson', in Gardner, C. (ed.) *Media, Politics and Culture*, London: Macmillan.

Herzhaft, G. (1992) *Encyclopedia of the Blues*, Fayetteville: University of Arkansas Press.

Hesmondhalgh, D. (1996a) 'Is This What You Call Change? Post-Fordism, Flexibility and the Music Industries', *Media, Culture and Society*, 18.

—— (1996b) 'Rethinking Popular Music after Rock and Soul', in Curran, J., Morley, D., and Walkerdine, V. (eds) *Cultural Studies and Communications*, London and New York: Arnold.

Heylin, C. (ed.) (1992) *The Penguin Book of Rock and Roll Writing*, London: Penguin.

—— (1993) *From the Velvets to the Voidoids: A Pre-Punk History for a Post-Punk World*, London: Penguin.

—— (1995) *Bootleg: The Secret History of the Other Recording History,* New York: St. Martin's Press.

Hill, D. (1986) *Designer Boys and Material Girls: Manufacturing the 80's Pop Dream,* London: Blandford Press.

Hill, T. (1991) 'The Enemy Within: Censorship in Rock Music in the 1950s', in DeCurtis, A. (ed.) 'Rock and Roll Culture', *South Atlantic Quarterly,* 90, 4.

Hirshey, G. (1985) *Nowhere to Run: The Story of Soul Music,* New York: Penguin.

Hoggart, R. (1957) *The Uses of Literacy,* Harmondsworth: Penguin.

Horowitz, D. (1993) 'The Perils of Commodity Fetishism: Tin Pan Alley's Portrait of the Romantic Marketplace, 1920–1942', *Popular Music and Society,* 17, 1: 37–53.

Houghton, M. (1980) 'British Beat', in Collins, J. (ed.) *The Rock Primer,* Harmondsworth: Penguin, pp. 149–78.

Hudson, R. (1995) 'Making Music Work? Alternative Regeneration Strategies in a Deindustrialised Locality: The Case of Derwentside', *Transactions, Institute of British Geographers* (New Series), 20, 4: 460–73.

IFPI (1990) *World Record Sales 1969–1990: A Statistical History of the Recording Industry,* ed. and compiled M. Hung and E. G. Morencos, London: International Federation of the Phonographic Industry.

Jameson, F. (1984) 'Postmodernism, or the Cultural Logic of Late Capitalism', *New Left Review,* 146 (July/August): 53–93.

Jenkins, H. (1997) 'Television Fans, Poachers, Nomads', in Gelder, K. and Thornton, S. (eds) *The Subcultures Reader,* London and New York: Routledge.

Jipson, A. (1994) 'Why Athens?', *Popular Music and Society,* 18, 3: 19–31.

Jones, Simon (1988) *Black Culture, White Youth: The Reggae Tradition from JA to UK,* London: Macmillan.

Jones, Simon and Schumacher, T. (1992) 'Muzak: On Functional Music and Power', *Critical Studies in Mass Communications,* 9: 156–69.

Jones, Steve (1992) *Rock Formation: Music, Technology, and Mass Communication,* Newbury Park, CA: Sage.

—— (1993) 'Music and Copyright in the USA', in Frith, S. (ed.) *Music and Copyright,* Edinburgh: Edinburgh University Press, ch. 4.

—— (1995a) 'Recasting Popular Music Studies' Conceptions of the Authentic and the Local in Light of Bell's Theorem', in Straw, W. *et al.* (eds) *Popular Music – Style and Identity,* Montreal: Centre for Research on Canadian Cultural Industries and Institutions.

—— (1995b) 'Covering Cobain: Narrative Patterns in Journalism and Rock Criticism', *Popular Music and Society,* 19, 2: 103–18.

Kaplan, E. A. (1987) *Rocking Around the Clock: Music Television, Postmodernism, and Consumer Culture*, New York: Methuen.

Kaufman, G. (1997) 'Steering Sub Pop Into the Future', *Addicted to Noise*, 3.02 (February).

Kealy, E. (1979) 'From Craft to Art: The Case of Sound Mixers and Popular Music', in Frith, S. and Goodwin, A. (eds). *On Record*: pp. 207–20.

Keil, C. (1966) *Urban Blues*, Chicago: University of Chicago Press.

Keil, C. and Feld, S. (1994) *Music Grooves*, Chicago and London: University of Chicago Press.

Kennedy, D. (1990) 'Frankenchrist versus the State: The New Right, Rock Music and the Case of Jello Biafra', *Journal of Popular Culture*, 24, 1: 131–48.

Kirschner, T. (1994) 'The Lalapalooziation of American Youth', *Popular Music and Society*, 18, 1: 69–89.

Kocandrle, M. (1988) *The History of Rock and Roll: A Selective Discography*, Boston: G.K. Hall.

Kong, L. (1995) 'Popular Music in Singapore: Exploring Local Culture, Global Resources, and Regional Identities', *Environment and Planning D: Society and Space*, 14, 3 (June): 273–92.

Kotarba, J. A. (1994) 'The Postmodernization of Rock and Roll Music: The Case of Metallica', in Epstein, J. S. (ed.) *Adolescents and Their Music: If It's Too Loud, You're Too Old*, New York and London: Garland Publishing.

Kruse, H. (1993) 'Subcultural Identity in Alternative Music Culture', *Popular Music*, 12, 1: 33–41.

Laing, D. (1986) 'The music industry and the "cultural imperialism" thesis', *Media, Culture and Society*, 8: 331–41.

—— (1988) 'The Grain of Punk: An Analysis of the Lyrics', in McRobbie, A. (ed.) *Zoot Suits and Second Hand Dresses: An Anthology of Fashion and Music*, Boston: Unwin & Hyman, pp. 74–101.

—— (1990) 'Record sales in the 1980s', *Popular Music*, 9, 2.

Larkin, C. (ed.) (1995) *The Guinness Who's Who of Indie New Wave*, 2nd edn, London: Guinness.

—— (ed.) (1993) *The Guinness Encyclopedia of Popular Music*, concise edn, London: Guinness.

Lealand, G. (1988) *A Foreign Egg in our Nest? American Popular Culture in New Zealand*, Wellington: Victoria University Press.

Lee, S. (1995) 'An Examination of Industrial Practice: The Case of Wax Trax! Records', in Straw, W. *et al.* (eds) *Popular Music – Style and Identity*, Montreal: Centre for Research on Canadian Cultural Industries and Institutions.

333

Bibliography

Lewis, G. H. (ed.) (1993) *All That Glitters: Country Music in America*, Bowling Green, OH: Bowling Green State University Press.

Lewis, L. A. (1990a) 'Consumer Girl Culture: How Music Video Appeals to Girls', in Brown, M. E. (ed.) *Television and Women's Culture*, London: Sage.

—— (1990b) *Gender Politics and MTV: Voicing the Difference*, Philadelphia: Temple University Press.

—— (ed.) (1992) *The Adoring Audience: Fan Culture and the Popular Media*, London: Routledge.

Leyser, B. (1994) *Rock Stars/Pop Stars: A Comprehensive Bibliography 1955–1994*, Westport, CT: Greenwood Press.

Light, A. (1991) 'About a Salary or a Reality? Rap's Recurrent Conflict', in DeCurtis, A. (ed.) 'Rock and Roll Culture', *South Atlantic Quarterly*, 90, 4.

Lipsitz, G. (1994) *Dangerous Crossroads: Popular Music, Postmodernism and the Poetics of Place*, London and New York: Verso.

Longhurst, B. (1995) *Popular Music and Society*, Cambridge: Polity Press.

Lopes, Paul (1992) 'Aspects of Production and Consumption in the Music Industry, 1967–1990', *American Sociological Review*, 57, 1: 46–71.

Lull, J. (ed.) (1992) *Popular Music and Communication*, 2nd edn, Newbury Park, CA: Sage.

McAleer, Dave (1994) *BEATBOOM! Pop Goes the Sixties*, London: Hamlyn.

McClary, S. (1991) *Feminine Endings: Music, Gender, and Sexuality*, Oxford, Minn.: University of Minnesota Press.

McClary, S. and Walser, R. (1990) 'Start Making Sense! Musicology Wrestles with Rock', in Frith, S. and Goodwin, A. (eds) *On Record: Rock, Pop, and the Written Word*, New York: Pantheon Books, pp. 277–92.

McDonnell, Judith (1992) 'Rap Music: Its Role as an Agent of Change', *Popular Music and Society*, 16, 3 (Fall): 89–108.

McEwen, J. (1992) 'Funk', in DeCurtis, A. and Henke, J. (eds) *The Rolling Stone Illustrated History of Rock and Roll*, 3rd edn, New York: Random House (includes discography).

McLeay, C. (1994) 'The "Dunedin Sound" - New Zealand Rock and Cultural Geography', *Perfect Beat*, 2, 1 (July): 38–50.

McNeil, L. and McCain, G. (1996) *Please Kill Me: The Uncensored Oral History of Punk*, New York: Grave Press.

McRobbie, A. (ed.) (1988) *Zoot Suits and Second Hand Dresses: An Anthology of Fashion and Music*, Boston: Unwin & Hyman.

334

—— (1991) *Feminism and Youth Culture: From 'Jackie' to 'Just Seventeen'*, Basingstoke: Macmillan.

McRobbie, A. and Garber, J. (1976) 'Girls and Subcultures: An Exploration', in Hall, S. and Jefferson, T. (eds) *Resistance Through Rituals: Youth Subcultures in Post-War Britain*, London: Hutchinson/ BCCCS.

Malone, B. C. (1985) *Country Music USA*, Austin: University of Texas Press.

Manuel, P. (1995) 'Music as Symbol, Music as Simulacrum: Postmodern, Premodern, and Modern Aesthetics in Subcultural Popular Musics', *Popular Music*, 14, 2: 227.

Marcus, G. (1989) *Lipstick Traces: A Secret History of the Twentieth Century*, Cambridge, MA: Harvard University Press.

—— (1991a) *Dead Elvis: A Chronicle of a Cultural Obsession*, New York: Penguin.

—— (1991b) *Mystery Train*, 4th edn, New York: Penguin (first published 1977).

—— (1992) 'Anarchy in the UK', in DeCurtis, A. and Henke, J. (eds) *The Rolling Stone Illustrated History of Rock and Roll*, 3rd edn, New York: Random House, p. 594–608.

Marsh, D. (1983) *Before I Get Old: The Story of The Who*, New York: St. Martin's Press.

—— (1987) *Glory Days: A Biography of Bruce Springsteen*, New York: Pantheon Books.

—— (1989) *The Heart of Rock and Soul: The 1001 Greatest Singles Ever Made*, New York: Plume/Penguin.

—— (1992) 'The Who', in DeCurtis, A. and Henke, J. (eds) *The Rolling Stone Illustrated History of Rock and Roll*, 3rd edn, New York: Random House, pp. 395–406.

Martin, C. (1993) 'Traditional Criticism of Popular Music and the Making of a Lip-synching scandal', *Popular Music and Society*, 17, 4: 63–81.

Mellers, W. (1974) *Twilight of the Gods: The Beatles in Retrospect*, London: Faber & Faber.

—— (1986) *Angels of the Night: Popular Female Singers of Our Time*, Oxford: Blackwell.

Melley, G. (1970) *Revolt Into Style*, London: Penguin.

Mercer, K. (1988) 'Monster Metaphors: Notes on Michael Jackson's Thriller', in McRobbie, A. (ed.) *Zoot Suits and Second Hand Dresses: An Anthology of Fashion and Music*, Boston: Unwin & Hyman.

Meyer, D. C. (1995) 'The Real Cooking is Done in the Studio: Toward a Context for Rock Criticism', *Popular Music and Society*, 19, 1 (spring): 1–15.

Middleton, R. (1990) *Studying Popular Music*, Milton Keynes: Open University Press.

Millard, A. J. (1995) *America on Record: A History of Recorded Sound*, Cambridge: Cambridge University Press.

Miller, J. (1992) 'The Beach Boys', in DeCurtis, A. and Henke, J. (eds) *The Rolling Stone Illustrated History of Rock and Roll*, 3rd edn, New York: Random House, pp. 192–8.

Milner, A. (1991) *Contemporary Cultural Theory: An Introduction*, Sydney: Allen & Unwin.

Mitchell, T. (1996) *Popular Music and Local Identity*, London and New York: Leicester University Press.

—— (1997) 'New Zealand on the Internet: A Study of the NZPOP Mailing List', *Perfect Beat*, 3, 2: 77–95.

Mitsui, T. (1993) 'Copyright in Japan: A Forced Grafting and the Consequences', in Frith, S. (ed.) *Music and Copyright*, Edinburgh: Edinburgh University Press, ch. 7.

Montgomery, M. (1986) 'DJ Talk', *Media, Culture and Society*, 8, 4 (October): 421–41.

Moore, A. F. (1993) *Rock: The Primary Text – Developing a Musicology of Rock*, Buckingham, PA: Open University Press.

Morley, D. (1992) *Television, Audiences, and Cultural Studies*, London: Routledge.

Morthland, J. (1992a) 'The Payola Scandal' in DeCurtis, A. and Henke, J. (eds) *The Rolling Stone Illustrated History of Rock and Roll*, 3rd edn, New York: Random House, pp. 121–3.

—— (1992b) 'The Rise of Top 40 AM' in DeCurtis, A. and Henke, J. (eds) *The Rolling Stone Illustrated History of Rock and Roll*, 3rd edn, New York: Random House, pp. 102–6.

—— (1992c) 'Rock Festivals' in DeCurtis, A. and Henke, J. (eds) *The Rolling Stone Illustrated History of Rock and Roll*, 3rd edn, New York: Random House, pp. 174–9.

Mungham, G. (1976) 'Youth in Pursuit of Itself', in Mungham, G. and Pearson, G. (eds) *Working Class Youth Culture*, London: Routledge & Kegan Paul.

Murdoch, G. and Phelps, G. (1973) *Mass Media and the Secondary School*, London: Schools Council/Macmillan.

Murray, C. S. (1989) *Crosstown Traffic: Jimi Hendrix and Post-War Pop*, London: Faber & Faber.

—— (1991) *Shots From the Hip*, London: Penguin.

Music Central 96, CD-ROM, Microsoft.

Myers, H. (ed.) (1992) *Ethnomusicology: An Introduction*, London: Macmillan.

Negus, K. (1992) *Producing Pop: Culture and Conflict in the Popular Music Industry*, London: Edward Arnold.

—— (1996) *Popular Music in Theory*, Cambridge: Polity Press.

Nelson, P. (1992) 'Folk Rock', in DeCurtis, A. and Henke, J. (eds) *The Rolling Stone Illustrated History of Rock and Roll*, 3rd edn, New York: Random House, pp. 313–18.

Neuenfeldt, K. (ed.) (1997) *The Didjeridu: From Arnham Land to Internet*, London and Sydney: John Libby/Perfect Beat Publications.

Nicholson, G. (1991) *Big Noises: Rock Guitar in the 1990s*, London: Quartet.

Norman, P. (1981) *SHOUT!: The Beatles in Their Generation*, New York: Simon & Schuster.

Nuttal, J. (1968) *Bomb Culture*, London: MacGibbon & Kee.

O'Brien, K. (1995) *Hymn to Her: Women Musicians Talk*, London: Virago Press.

O'Brien, L. (1995) *She Bop: The Definitive History of Women in Rock, Pop and Soul*, London: Penguin.

O'Sullivan, T., Hartley, J., Saunders, D., Montgomery, M., and Fiske, J. (1994) *Key Concepts in Communications*, London: Routledge.

Oliver, P. (ed.) (1990) *Black Music in Britain*, Buckingham: Open University Press.

Owens, T. (1995) *Bebop: The Music and its Players*, New York, Oxford: Oxford University Press.

Paddison, M. (1993) *Adorno's Aesthetics of Music*, Cambridge: Cambridge University Press.

Padilla, F. (1990) 'Salsa: Puerto Rican and Latin American Music', *Journal of Popular Culture*, 24: 87–104.

Palmer, Robert (1995) *Rock & Roll: An Unruly History*, New York: Harmony Books. This is a companion to the PBS/BBC 10–part television series, *Dancing in the Street*.

Palmer, T. (1970) *Born Under a Bad Sign*, London: William Kimber.

Parker, M. (1991) 'Reading the Charts – Making Sense of the Hit Parade', *Popular Music*, 10, 2: 205–17.

Pearsall, R. (1975) *Edwardian Popular Music*, Newton Abbot: David & Charles.

—— (1976) *Popular Music of the Twenties*, Newton Abbot: David & Charles.

Pease, E. and Dennis, E. (eds) (1995) *Radio – The Forgotten Medium*, New Brunswick and London: Transaction Publishers.

Perry, S. (1988) 'The Politics of Crossover', in Frith, S. (ed.) *Facing the Music*, New York: Pantheon Books, pp. 51–87.

—— (1992) 'The Sound of San Francisco', in DeCurtis, A. and Henke, J. (eds) *The Rolling Stone Illustrated History of Rock and Roll*, 3rd edn, New York: Random House, pp. 362–9.

Peterson, R. A. (1990) 'Why 1955? Explaining the Advent of Rock Music', *Popular Music*, 9, 1: 97–116.

Peterson, R. A. and Berger, D. G. (1975) 'Cycles in Symbolic Production: The Case of Popular Music', *American Sociological Review*, 40; republished in Frith, S. and Goodwin, A. (eds) *On Record: Rock, Pop, and the Written Word*, New York: Pantheon Books, pp. 140–59.

Pichaske, D. (1989) *A Generation in Motion: Popular Music and Culture in the Sixties*, Granite Falls, Minn.: Ellis Press (first published in 1979).

Pickering, M. (1986) 'The Dogma of Authenticity in the Experience of Popular Music', in McGregor, G. and White, R. S. (eds) *The Art of Listening*, London: Croom Helm, pp. 201–20.

Pickering, M. and Green, T. (eds) (1987) *Everyday Culture: Popular Songs and the Vernacular Milieu*, Milton Keynes: Open University Press.

Plasketes, G. (1992) 'Romancing the Record: The Vinyl De-Evolution and Subcultural Evolution', *Journal of Popular Culture*, 26, 1: 109–22.

Potter, J. and Wetherell, M. (1987) *Discourse and Social Psychology: Beyond Attitudes and Behaviour*, London: Sage.

Potter, R. (1995) *Spectacular Vernaculars: Hip-Hop and the Politics of Postmodernism*, Albany, NY: SUNY Press.

Pratt, R. (1990) *Rhythm and Resistance: Explorations in the Political Use of Popular Music*, New York: Praeger.

Puterbaugh, P. (1992) 'The Grateful Dead', in DeCurtis, A. and Henke, J. (eds) *The Rolling Stone Illustrated History of Rock and Roll*, 3rd edn, New York: Random House, pp. 370–7.

Read, O. and Welch, W. L. (1977) *From Tin Foil to Stereo: The Evolution of the Phonograph*, Indianapolis: Howard Sams.

Redhead, S. (1990) *The End-Of-The-Century Party: Youth and Pop Towards 2000*, Manchester: Manchester University Press.

Reich, C. (1972) *The Greening of America*, New York: Penguin.

Reid, J. (1993) 'The Use of Christian Rock Music by Youth Group Members', *Popular Music and Society*, 17, 2: 33–45.

Reisman, D. (1950) 'Listening to Popular Music', *American Quarterly*, 2; republished in Frith, S. and Goodwin, A. (eds) *On Record: Rock, Pop, and the Written Word*, New York: Pantheon Books.

Rex, I. (1992) 'Kylie: The making of a Star', in Hayward, P. (ed.) *From Pop to Punk to Postmodernism: Popular Music and Australian Culture from the 1960s to the 1990s*, Sydney: Allen & Unwin, pp. 149–59.

Reynolds, S. and Press, J. (1995) *The Sex Revolts, Gender, Rebellion and Rock'n'Roll*, London: Serpent's Tail.

Richards, C. (1995) 'Popular Music and Media Education', *Discourse: Studies in the Cultural Politics of Education*, 16, 3: 317–30.

Rimmer, D. (1985) *Like Punk Never Happened: Culture Club and the New Pop*, London: Faber & Faber.

Riordan, J. (1991) *Making it in the New Music Business*, Cincinnati: Writer's Digest Books.

Ritz, D. (1985) *Divided Soul: The Life of Marvin Gaye*, London: Collins/ Grafton.

Roach, C. (1997) 'Cultural Imperialism and Resistance in Media Theory and Literary Theory', *Media, Culture and Society*, 19: 47–66.

Robinson, D., Buck, E., Cuthbert, M. *et al.* (1991) *Music at the Margins: Popular Music and Global Diversity*, Newbury Park, CA: Sage.

Rockwell, J. (1992) 'The Emergence of Art Rock', in DeCurtis, A. and Henke, J. (eds) *The Rolling Stone Illustrated History of Rock and Roll*, 3rd edn, New York: Random House (includes discography) pp. 492–9..

Roe, K. (1983) *Mass Media and Adolescent Schooling*, Stockholm: Almqvist and Wiksell.

—— (1990) 'Adolescent's Music Use: A Structural-Cultural Approach', in Roe, K. and Carlsson, U. (eds) *Popular Music Research*, pp. 41–52.

Roe, K. and Carlsson, U. (eds) (1990) *Popular Music Research*, NORDI-COM, University of Goteborg.

Rogan, J. (1988) *Starmakers and Svengalis*, London and Sydney: MacDonald & Co.

Rogan, J. (1992) *Morrissey and Marr: The Severed Alliance*, London: Omnibus Press.

Rogers, D. (1982) *Rock'n'Roll*, London: Routledge & Kegan Paul.

The Rolling Stone Interviews: 1967–1980 (1981) New York: St. Martin's Press/Rolling Stone Press.

The Rolling Stone Record Guide (1984) ed. Marsh, D., with Swenson, J., New York: Random House/Rolling Stone Press.

Romanowski, W. (1993) 'Move Over Madonna: The Crossover Career of Gospel Artist Amy Grant', *Popular Music and Society*, 17, 2: 47–68.

Romanowski, W. D. and Denisoff, R. S. (1987) 'Money for Nothin' and the Charts for Free: Rock and the Movies', *Journal of Popular Culture*, 21, 3 (winter): 63–78.

Romney, J. and Wootton, A. (1995) *Celluloid Jukebox: Popular Music and the Movies Since the 50s*, London: BFI.

339

Rose, Tricia (1994) *Black Noise*, Hanover: Wesleyan University Press.

Ross, A. and Rose, T. (eds) (1994) *Microphone Fiends*, London and New York: Routledge.

Rosselson, L. (1979) 'Pop Music: Mobiliser or Opiate?', in Gardner, C. (ed.) *Media, Politics and Culture*, London: Macmillan.

Rothenbuhler, E. (1985) 'Commercial Radio as Communication', *Journal of Communication*, 46, 1: 125–44.

Rothenbuhler, E. and Dimmick, J. (1982) 'Popular Music: Concentration and Diversity in the Industry, 1974–1980', *Journal of Communications*, 32 (winter): 143–9.

Rubey, D. (1991) 'Voguing at the Carnival: Desire and Pleasure on MTV', in DeCurtis, A. (ed.) 'Rock and Roll Culture', *South Atlantic Quarterly*, 90, 4.

Russell (1993) 'The "Social History" of Popular Music: A Label Without a Cause?', *Popular Music*, 12, 2: 139–46.

Rutten, P. (1991) 'Local Popular Music on the National and International Markets', *Cultural Studies*, 5, 3 (October): 294–305.

Ryan, B. (1992) *Making Capital from Culture: The Corporate Form of Capitalist Production*, Berlin and New York: Walter de Gruyter.

Sadler, D. (1994) 'Playing to the Music: Consumer Electronics, the Music Business and the Video Game', unpublished paper.

Samuels, S. (1983) *Midnight Movies*, New York: Collier/Macmillan.

Sanjek, R. (1988) *American Popular Music and Its Business: The First Four Hundred Years. Volume III: From 1900 to 1984*, New York: Oxford University Press.

Santelli, R. (1993) *The Big Book of the Blues: A Biographical Encyclopedia*, New York: Penguin.

Sardiello, R. (1994) 'Secular Rituals in Popular Culture: A Case for Grateful Dead Concerts and Dead Head Identity', in Epstein, J. S. (ed.) *Adolescents and Their Music: If It's Too Loud, You're Too Old*, New York and London: Garland Publishing.

Savage, J. (1988) 'The Enemy Within: Sex, Rock and Identity', in Frith, S. (ed.) *Facing the Music*, New York: Pantheon Books.

—— (1991) *England's Dreaming: Sex Pistols and Punk Rock*, London: Faber & Faber.

Schaefer, J. (1987) *New Sounds: A Listener's Guide to New Music*, Cambridge, MA: Harper & Row.

Schulze, L., White, A., and Brown, J. (1993) 'A Sacred Monster in Her Prime: Audience Construction of Madonna as Low-Other', in Schwichtenberg, C. (ed.) *The Madonna Connection: Representational Politics, Subcultural Identities, and Cultural Theory*, St. Leonards, NSW:

Allen & Unwin, pp. 15–38.

Schwichtenberg, C. (ed.) (1993) *The Madonna Connection: Representational Politics, Subcultural Identities, and Cultural Theory*, St. Leonards, NSW: Allen & Unwin.

Scoppa, B. (1992) 'The Byrds', in DeCurtis, A. and Henke, J. (eds) *The Rolling Stone Illustrated History of Rock and Roll*, 3rd edn, New York: Random House, pp. 309–12.

Selvin, J. (1994) *Summer of Love*, New York: Plume/Penguin.

Shapiro, B. (1991) *Rock and Roll Review: A Guide to Good Rock on CD*, Kansas City: Andrews and McMeel.

Shaw, A. (1986) *Black Popular Music in America*, New York: Macmillan.

Shaw, G. (1992) 'Brill Building Pop', in DeCurtis, A. and Henke, J. (eds) *The Rolling Stone Illustrated History of Rock and Roll*, 3rd edn, New York: Random House, pp. 143–52.

Shepherd, J. (1986) 'Music Consumption and Cultural Self-Identities', *Media, Culture and Society*, 8, 3: 305–30.

—— (1991) *Music as Social Text*, Cambridge: Polity Press.

Shepherd, J. *et al.* (1977) *Whose Music?*, London: Latimer.

Shevory, T. (1995) 'Bleached Resistance: The Politics of Grunge', *Popular Music and Society*, 19, 2: 23–48.

Shore, M. (1985) *The Rolling Stone Book of Rock Video*, London: Sidgwick & Jackson.

Shuker, R. (1994) *Understanding Popular Music*, London and New York: Routledge.

Shumway, D. R. (1989) 'Reading Rock'n'Roll in the Classroom: A Critical Pedagogy', in Giroux, H. and McLaren, P. (eds) *Critical Pedagogy, the State, and Cultural Struggle*, New York: State University of New York Press.

Sicoli, M. L. (1994) 'The Role of the Woman Songwriter in Country Music', *Popular Music and Society*, 18, 2: 35–41.

Sinclair, D. (1992) *Rock on CD: The Essential Guide*, London: Kyle Cathie.

Small, C. (1987) 'Performance as Ritual', in White, A. (ed.) *Lost in Music: Culture, Style and the Musical Event*, London: Routledge.

—— (1994) *Music of the Common Tongue*, London: Calder (first published 1987).

Smith, Graham (1997) Reviews of recent folk music books, *Popular Music*, 16, 1: 127–30.

Smith, Giles (1995) *Lost in Music*, London: Picador.

Smucker, T. (1992) 'Disco', in DeCurtis, A. and Henke, J. (eds) *The Rolling Stone Illustrated History of Rock and Roll*, 3rd edn, New York: Random House, pp. 561–72.

Spencer, J. (ed.) (1991) *The Emergence of Black and the Emergence of Rap*, a special issue of *Black Sacred Music: A Journal of Theomusicology*, 5, 1 (spring).

Stambler, I. (1989) *The Encyclopedia of Pop, Rock and Soul*, revised edn, London: Macmillan.

Stanford, C. (1996) *Kurt Cobain,* New York: Random House.

Steward, S. and Garratt, S. (1984) *Signed, Sealed, and Delivered: True Life Stories of Women in Pop*, Boston: South End Press.

Stockbridge, S. (1990) 'Rock Video: Pleasure and Resistance', in Brown, M. E. (ed.) *Television and Women's Culture*, London: Sage.

——(1992) 'Rock Music on Australian Television', in Hayward, P. (ed.) *From Pop to Punk to Postmodernism: Popular Music and Australian Culture from the 1960s to the 1990s*, Sydney: Allen & Unwin, pp. 68–88.

Storey, J. (1993) *An Introductory Guide to Cultural Theory and Popular Culture*, New York and London: Harvester Wheatsheaf.

Stratton, J. (1982) 'Between Two Worlds: Art and Commercialism in the Record Industry', *Sociological Review*, 30, 1: 267–85.

—— (1983) 'What is Popular Music?', *Sociological Review*, 31, 2: 293–309.

—— (1997) 'On the Importance of Subcultural Origins', in Gelder, K. and Thornton, S. (eds) *The Subcultures Reader*, London and New York: Routledge.

Straw, W. (1990) 'Characterizing Rock Music Culture: The Case of Heavy Metal', in Frith, S. and Goodwin, A. (eds) *On Record: Rock, Pop, and the Written Word*, New York: Pantheon Books, pp. 97–110.

—— (1992) 'Systems of Articulation, Logics of Change: Communities and Scenes in Popular Music', in Nelson, C., Grossberg, L., and Treichler, P. (eds) *Cultural Studies*, London and New York: Routledge.

Straw, W. *et al.* (eds) (1995) *Popular Music – Style and Identity*, Montreal: Centre for Research on Canadian Cultural Industries and Institutions.

Street, J. (1986) *Rebel Rock: The Politics of Popular Music*, Oxford: Blackwell.

—— (1993) 'Local Differences?: Popular Music and the Local State', *Popular Music*, 12, 1: 42–56.

—— (1995) '(Dis)located?: Rhetoric, Politics, Meaning and the Locality', in Straw, W. *et al.* (eds) *Popular Music – Style and Identity*, Montreal: Centre for Research on Canadian Cultural Industries and Institutions.

Stringer, J. (1992) 'The Smiths: Repressed (But Remarkably Dressed)', *Popular Music*, 11, 1: 16–26.

Sturmer, C. (1993) 'MTV's Europe: An Imaginary Continent?', in Dowmunt, T. (ed.) *Channels of Resistance: Global Television and Local Empowerment*, London: BFI/Channel Four Television.

Sweeney, P. (1981) *The Virgin Directory of World Music*, London: Virgin Books.

Swingewood, A. (1977) *The Myth of Mass Culture*, London: Macmillan.

Szatmary, D. P. (1991) *Rockin' in Time: A Social History of Rock and Roll*, 2nd edn, Engelwood Cliffs, NJ: Prentice-Hall.

Tagg, P. (1982) 'Analysing Popular Music', *Popular Music*, 2: 37–67.

—— (1989) '"Black Music", "Afro-American Music" and "European Music" ', *Popular Music*, 8, 3: 285–98.

—— (1990) 'Music in Mass Media Studies: Reading Sounds for Example', in Roe, K. and Carlsson, U. (eds) *Popular Music Research*, NORDICOM, University of Goteborg, pp. 103–14.

—— (1994) 'From Refrain to Rave', *Popular Music*, 14, 3: 209–22.

Tanner, J. (1981) 'Pop Music and Peer Groups', *Canadian Review of Sociology and Social Anthropology*, 18, 1: 1–13.

Taylor, P. (1985) *Popular Music Since 1955: A Critical Guide to the Literature*, London: G. K. Hall.

Théberge, P. (1991) 'Musicians' Magazines in the 1980s: The Creation of a Community and a Consumer Market', *Cultural Studies*, 270ff.

—— (1993) 'Technology, Economy and Copyright Reform in Canada', in Frith, S. (ed.) *Music and Copyright*, Edinburgh: Edinburgh University Press, ch. 3.

Thomas, B. (1991) *The Big Wheel*, London: Penguin.

Thomas, H. (1995) *Dance, Modernity and Culture*, London and New York: Routledge.

Thompson, D. (1994) *Space Daze: The History and Mystery of Ambient Space Rock*, Los Angeles: Cleopatra.

Thornton, S. (1994) 'Moral Panic, the Media and British Rave Culture', in Ross, A. and Rose, T. (eds) *Microphone Fiends*, London and New York: Routledge.

—— (1995) *Club Cultures: Music, Media and Subcultural Capital*, London: Polity Press.

Tomlinson, J. (1991) *Cultural Imperialism*, London: Pinter.

Tong, R. (1989) *Feminist Thought: A Comprehensive Introduction*, London: Routledge.

Toop, David (1991) *Rap Attack 2*, London: Serpent's Tail.

Tosches, N. (1984) *Unsung Heroes of Rock'n'Roll*, New York: Scribners.

Trondman, M. (1990) 'Rock Taste – On Rock as Symbolic Capital. A Study of Young People's Tastes and Music Making', in Roe, K. and

Carlsson, U. (eds) *Popular Music Research*, NORDICOM, University of Goteborg, pp. 71–86.

Tucker, K. (1992) 'Alternative Scenes: America; Britain', in DeCurtis, A. and Henke, J. (eds) *The Rolling Stone Illustrated History of Rock and Roll*, 3rd edn, New York: Random House (includes useful discographies).

Tunstall, J. (1977) *The Media Are American*, London: Constable.

Turner, G. (1992) 'Australian Popular Music and its Contexts', in Hayward, B. (ed.) *From Pop to Punk to Postmodernism: Popular Music and Australian Culture from the 1960s to the 1990s*, Sydney: Allen & Unwin.

—— (1993) 'Who Killed the Radio Star?: The Death of Teen Radio in Australia', in Bennett, T., Frith, S., Grossberg, L., Shepherd, J., and Turner, G. (eds) *Rock and Popular Music: Politics, Policies, Institutions*, London: Routledge, pp. 142–55.

—— (1994) *British Cultural Studies: An Introduction*, revised edn, Boston: Unwin Hyman.

Vassal, J. (1976) *Electric Children: Roots and Branches of Modern Folkrock*, New York: Taplinger.

Valentine, G. (1995) 'Creating Transgressive Space: The Music of kd lang', *Transactions: Institute of British Geographers* (new series), 20, 4: 434–46.

Vermorel, F. and Vermorel, J. (1985) *Starlust: The Secret Fantasies of Fans*, London: W. H. Allen.

Vincent, R. (1996) *Funk: The Music, the People, and the Rhythm of the One*, New York: St. Martin's/Griffin.

The Virgin Encyclopedia of Rock (1993), M. Heatley, (ed.) London: Virgin Press.

Vogel, H. L. (1994) *Entertainment Industry Economics: A Guide to Financial Analysis*, 3rd edn, New York: Cambridge University Press.

Vulliamy, G. and Lee, E. (1982) *Popular Music: A Teacher's Guide*, London: RKP.

Walker, J. (1987) *Cross-Overs: Art Into Pop/Pop Into Art*, London and New York: Comedia.

Wallis, R. and Malm, K. (1984) *Big Sounds from Small Countries*, London: Constable.

—— (eds) (1992) *Media Policy and Music Activity*, London: Routledge.

Walser, R. (1993) *Running With the Devil: Power, Gender and Madness in Heavy Metal Music*, Middletown, CT: Wesleyan University Press.

Ward, E. (1992a) 'The Blues Revival', in DeCurtis, A. and Henke, J. (eds) *The Rolling Stone Illustrated History of Rock and Roll*, 3rd edn,

New York: Random House, pp. 343–7.

— (1992b) 'Reggae', in DeCurtis, A. and Henke, J. (eds) *The Rolling Stone Illustrated History of Rock and Roll*, 3rd edn, New York: Random House, pp. 586–93.

Ward, E., Stokes, G., and Tucker, K. (1986) *Rock of Ages: The Rolling Stone History of Rock and Roll*, New York: Rolling Stone Press/Summit Books.

Waterman, C. A. (1991) *Juju: A Social History and Ethnography of an African Popular Music*, Chicago: Chicago University Press.

Weinstein, D. (1991a) *Heavy Metal: A Cultural Sociology*, New York: Lexington.

— (1991b) 'The Sociology of Rock: An Undisciplined Discipline', *Theory, Culture and Society*, 8: 97–109.

Weisband, E., with Marks, C. (eds) (1995) *SPIN Alternative Record Guide*, New York: Vintage/Random House.

Welsh, R. (1990) 'Rock'n'Roll and Social Change', *History Today* (February), pp. 32–9.

Whitburn, J. (1988) *Billboard Top 1000 Singles 1955–1987*, Milwaukee, MI: Hal Leonard Books.

White, A. (ed.) (1987) *Lost in Music: Culture Style and the Musical Event*, London: Routledge & Kegan Paul.

White, T. (1989) *Catch a Fire: The Life of Bob Marley*, revised edn, New York: Holt, Rinehart and Winston.

— (1994) *The Nearest Faraway Place: Brian Wilson, The Beach Boys, and the Southern California Experience*, New York: Henry Holt & Co.

Whiteley, S. (1992) *The Space Between the Notes: Rock and the Counter-Culture*, London: Routledge.

Widgery, D. (1986) *Beating Time: Riot'n'Race'n'Rock'n'Roll*, London: Chatto & Windus.

Williams, R. (1983) *Keywords*, London: Fontana.

Willis, P. (1978) *Profane Culture*, London: Routledge.

Willis, P. et al. (1990) *Common Culture: Symbolic Work at Play in the Everyday Cultures of the Young*, Milton Keynes: Open University Press.

Wilson, H. (ed.) (1994) *The Radio Book 1994*, Christchurch: Christchurch Polytechnic.

York, N. (ed.) (1991) *The Rock File: Making it in the Music Business*, Oxford: Oxford University Press.

Zappa, F., with Occhiogrosso, P. (1990) *The Real Frank Zappa Book*, London: Pan Books.

NAME INDEX

A Tribe Called Quest 248
Abba 98, 207
Abbs, P. 164
Abdul, Paula 94, 201, 202
AC/DC 162
Adam and the Ants 152
Adorno, T. 15, 82, 89, 136, 137, 176, 177, 230
Aerosmith 132, 159, 161
Amazing Rhythm Aces 74
Amos, Tori 19, 277
Anderson, Laurie 21, 22
Ang, I. 16
Anka, Paul 297
Anthrax 162, 303
Apache Indian 26
Aphex Twin11
Archies 37
Armatrading, Joan 297
Armstrong, Louis 174
Arnold, M. 164
Ash 36
Aswad 256

B-52s 8, 9, 214
Bach 13
Bad Brains 159
Bad Company 158, 159
Bad Manners 256
Badfinger 231

Baez, Joan 134, 135, 277
Ballard, Hank 258
Bananarama 94, 151, 298
Band, the 131
Bangs, L. 35, 37, 161, 197
Banks, J. 202, 222
Barnes, Jimmy 159
Barnes, K. 101, 241, 243
Barnett, R. (and Cavanagh, J.) 58
Barra McNeils 43
Barry (and Greenwich) 276
Barthes, R. 107
Basie, Count 174
Bauhaus 154, 155
Baxter-Moore, N. 43
Beach Boys 282, 292–3
Beatles 6, 12, 17, 18, 18, 20, 25, 35, 36, 53, 96, 128, 150, 190, 204, 231, 234, 235, 260, 263, 271, 277, 284
Beck, Jeff 175, 207
Becker, Howard 182–3
Bee Gees 98
Bennett, T. 289
Berland, J. 246
Berliner 219
Berns, Bert 276
Berry, Chuck 131, 166, 261, 292

Bertsch, C. 268
Big Star 231
Bikini Kill 145
Bjork 277, 310
Bjorn Again 98, 207
Black Flag 132, 159, 160
Black Sabbath 162
Blades, Reuben 265, 266
Bland, Bobby 278
Blasters 74, 260
Bloom, B. 164–5
Blues Magoos 141
Blur 36, 53
Bon Jovi 151, 159, 162, 298
Bourdieu, P. 52, 77, 79, 84, 294
Boston 9, 13
Bowie, David 18, 152, 270, 286
Boy George 213, 270
Boys II Men 103, 258
Boyzone 298
Brackett, D. 27, 76–7
Brake, M. 152, 314
Breen, M. 69, 147, 162, 273, 303
Brinsley Schwarz 9, 236
Brooks, Garth 73, 74
Broughton, S. xiii
Brown, Arthur 235
Brown, C. 138–9
Brown, Glen 255
Brown, James 18, 77, 138, 139, 247, 278, 279
Browne, Jackson 277
Brubeck, Dave 173
Burnett, R. 59, 220, 222, 227, 299
Burning Spear 255
Bush 157
Buzzcocks 238, 239
Byrds 23, 24, 35, 74, 135, 136, 170, 231
Byrne, David 311
Byrne, Johnny 124

Cale, John 21
Campbell, Mike 305
Campion, Sarah 124
Can 13
Captain Beefheart 18
Carey, Mariah 203
Carpenter, Mary Chapin 73
Carpenters 6
Carr, Leroy 28
Carroll, Jim 124
Cars 214
Carter Family 73
Cash, Johnny 73
Cash, Rosanna 74
Cawelti, J.17
Chambers, I. 86, 90, 146
Chandra, Sheila 26
Chapman, R. 245
Chapman, Tracy 277, 278
Chapple, William 226
Charles, Ray 154
Charlton, K. 155
Cheap Trick 231
Chemical Brothers 92
Chieftains 43
Chicago 9
Childs, Toni 277
Chills 103, 104, 231
Chimes 75
Chinn and Chapman 226, 276
Chocolate Watch Band 141, 148
Christenson, M. 60
Christgau, R. 20, 197
Circle Jerks 132, 159
Clail, Gary 255
Clannad 43
Clapton, Eric 24, 31, 203
Clark, Dick 216
Clark, J. 33
Clarke, D. 98, 148
Clarke, Stanley 175
Clash 238, 239, 255
Clean 104
Cliff, Jimmy 255
Clinton, George 138, 295

Cloonan, M. 44, 45
Clovers 102
Coasters 102, 276
Cobain, Kurt 110, 157, 283
Cochrane, Eddie 259, 263
Cohen, Sarah 113–4, 144, 177–8, 179, 206
Cohen, Stanley 192
Cohn, N. 124, 197
Cold Chisel 159
Coleman, Jazz 14
Collins, J. 70
Connelly, Ray 124
Considine, D. 285
Cooke, Sam 154, 278
Cooper, Alice 132
Cooper, B. 180
Corea, Chick 175
Corrs 43
Coryell, Larry 175
Costello, Elvis (and the Attractions) 9, 19, 214, 277, 306
Count Five 140
Country Joe and the Fish 135
Cow, Henry 138
Cranberries 41, 44
Cray, Robert 31
Cream 30, 31, 235, 263
Creedence Clearwater Revival 263
Crosby, Stills, and Nash 1
Crowe, Cameron 8
Crudup, Arthur 75
Cruz, Celia 265, 266
Crystals 150, 151
Cult 159
Cure 155, 156, 270
Curry, Tim 204
Curtis, J. 166
Cutler, C. 296
Cyrus, Billy Ray 73

Dale, Dick 292, 293
Daltrey, Roger 158

Damned 238
Dave Clark Five 25, 35
Davies, Ray 6
Davis, Miles 174
De La Soul 70, 248
Dead Kennedies 159, 160, 171
Death 162
DeCurtis, A. 14; and Henke, J. 138, 148
Deep Purple 158, 159, 161
Def Leppard 161
Del Lords 171
Demme, Jonathon 131
Depeche Mode 170
Devo 8, 214
Dinosaur Jr 9
Dion and the Belmonts 102
Dire Straits 282, 306
Disposable Heroes of Hiphoprisy 8
Dixon, Willie 30, 75
Dominoe, Fats 32, 258, 310
Donegan, Lonnie 273, 274
Donovan 135
Doors 263
Dorsey, Thomas 154
Downing, D. 233
Dr. Feelgood 236
Drifters, the 276
Ducks Deluxe 236
DuGay, P. 188
Duran Duran 201, 298
Dylan, Bob 18, 32, 51, 74, 134, 135, 181, 277, 280, 285

Eagles 6, 74, 96
Earth, Wind and Fire 138
Echobelly 36
Eddie and the Hotrods 236
Edison, Thomas 219
Eisenberg, E. 190
Electric Prunes 140, 141
Eliot, M. 55, 241, 307
Eliot, T.S. 164
Ellington, Duke 173

Emerson, Lake, and Palmer 13, 14
Engels, Freidrich 188
English Beat 256
Eno, Brian 11, 13, 18, 22
Entwistle, John 190
Enya 43, 44
Erasure 98
Erlewhine, M. (*et al.*) 151, 159, 231, 247, 255, 276, 301
Everley Brothers 260
Everett, Kenny 245
Exciters 279

Fabian, Jenny 124
Fairport Convention 135
Farrell, Perry 268
Fenster, M. 10
Finnegan, R. 206
Fishbone 8
Fiske, J. 117
Flack, Roberta vii
Flying Burrito Brothers 74, 135
Foreigner 159
Four Freshmen 292
Four Seasons 103
4 Skins 275
Four Tops 194
Francis, Connie 297, 298
Frankie Goes to Hollywood 271
Franklin, Aretha 18, 154, 278, 279
Freed, Alan 101, 216–17, 241, 261
Friedlander, P. 297
Frith, S. 3, 4, 17–18, 56, 68, 97, 119, 145–6, 179–80, 181, 208, 230, 251, 299; and Street 225; and McRobbie 310
Fugees xii, 250
Fulsom, Lowell 249
Funkadelic 138, 139

Gabriel, Peter vii, 311, 312
Gaines, J. 69

Gammond, P. 27, 89, 148, 212, 225
Gans, H. 294
Garnham, N. 82, 287
Garofalo, R. 62, 153–4, 217
Gass, G. 107
Gaye, Marvin 77, 194
Gendron, B. 137–8
Genesis 13
George, N. 26, 77, 194, 257
Germs 132
Gerry and the Pacemakers 25, 35, 53, 128
Gill, R. 100
Gillespie, Dizzy 174
Gilmore, M. 45
Gilroy, P. 27, 282
Glitter, Gary 151, 152
Goetzel, B. 13
Goffin, Gerry 150, 276
Goldie 92, 93
Goldstein, Richard 181
Goodman, Benny 173
Goodwin, A. 96, 230
Gordy, Berry 111, 193, 194
Gore, Leslie 297
Graham, Davy 134
Gramsci, Antonio 85, 163
Grant, Amy 51
Grant, B. 129–30.
Grateful Dead 32, 94, 135, 234, 235, 307
Green Day 156
Greer, J. 7
Grenier, L. 244
Gribin, A. (and Schiff, M.) 103
Grossberg, L. 4, 33–4, 95, 96
Guns N' Roses 159
Guralnick, P. 260, 264, 278
Guthrie, Woody 135, 137, 274
Guy, Buddy 31

Haines, Nathan 93
Haley, Bill (and the Comets) 166, 261, 310

Hall, D. 212
Hall, S. 85; and Jefferson, T. 33, 167–8, 262, 316
Ham, Charles 304
Happy Mondays 54, 184
Hardy, P. (and Laing, D.) 146, 148–9, 174, 212
Harker, D. 181
Harris, Emmylou 74
Harrison, George 24, 122
Hatch, D. (and Millward, S.) 27, 207, 276
Hawkwind 233, 234
Hayward, S. 17, 126–7
Heart 41
Hebdige, D. 33, 168, 236, 247, 262, 314–15, 316, 317
Hell, Richard (and the Voidoids) 239
Hendrix, Jimi; (Jimi Hendrix Experience) 18, 20, 21, 235, 283
Herschel, Sir John 164
Hill, D. 225–6, 230
Hill, T. 217
Hole 9,145
Holiday, Billie 174
Holland, Dozier, Holland 276
Hollies 25
Holly, Buddy 8, 166, 204
Hooker, John Lee 30, 31, 178
Hootie and the Blowfish 253
Hornby, Nick 124
Horowitz, D. 304–5
Horslips 43
Hot Chocolate 98
Hurt, Mississippi John 29
Hüsker Dü 9, 160

Ice-T 46–7, 248
Iggy and the Stooges 237
Ink Spots 102
Inspiral Carpets 184

Jackson, Janet 306
Jackson, Mahalia 154
Jackson, Michael 18, 77, 83, 139, 172, 202, 306
Jagger, Mick 310
Jam 36
James 54, 184, 185
James, Skip 28, 29
James, Tommy and the Shondells 37, 75, 231
JAMS, The 70
James, Richard 11
Jameson, F. 229
Jan and Dean 292
Jane's Addiction 268
Jansch, Bert 134
Jarvin, Linda 124
Jason and the Scorchers 74, 260
Jefferson Airplane 135, 234, 235
Jefferson, Blind Lemon 28, 29
Jefferson, T. see Hall, S. and Jenkins, H. 303
Jesus and Mary Chain 155, 156
Jett, Joan (and the Blackhearts) 75
Johnson, Robert 24, 28, 29, 31, 281
Jones, Simon (and Schumacher, T.) 211
Jones, Steve 69, 195, 296
Joplin, Janis 18
Joplin, Scott 246
Jordan, Louis (and the Tympany Five) 30, 257
Journey 159
Joy Division 154, 155, 184
Judas Priest 110

Kansas 13, 234
Kaplan, A. 202
Kaufman, G. 10
Kaye, Lenny 140
KC and the Sunshine Band 98
Kealy, E. 281
Keil, C. 251

Kerouac, Jack 71, 124
King, B.B. 30, 31
King, Ben E. 276
King, Carole 150, 276
King Crimson 233
Kingsmen 140
Kinks 6, 36
Kirschner,T. 7
Kiss 132, 151, 152, 162, 306
Knack 231
Koerner, Alexis (Blues
    Incorporated) 30
Kool and the Gang 138
Kong, L. 149
Kraftwerk 13, 93, 295
Kris Kross 248, 298
Kronos Quartet 21
Kula Shaker 36

L7 145
Labelle 98
Laing, D. 169, 237–8; *see also*
    Hardy and
Landau, J. 17. 20
lang, k.d. 270
Larkin, C. 170–1, 275
Leadbelly 274
Leaves, The 140
Leavis, F.R. 164
Led Zeppelin 30, 159, 254, 263,
    276
Lee, S. 170
Leftfield 296
Lemonheads 9
Lemonpipers 37
Lennon, John 190, 274
Lester, Richard 128
Levi-Strauss, C. 33
Lewis, Jerry Lee 32
Lewis, L. 116, 118
Lieber and Stoller 232, 276
Lindisfarne 135
Lipsitz, G. 34
Little Richard 166, 261, 271,
    310

Living Colour 138
Longhurst, B. 251
Lopes, P. 59
Los Lobos 301
Love, Courtney 290
Love, Darlene 150
Love Tractor 9
Loverboy 159
Loving Spoonful 135, 136
Lowe, Nick 231
Lull, J. 56

McClary, S (and Walser, R)
    208, 209
McEwen, J. 193
McInnes, Colin 124
McIntyre, Reba 73
MacIssac, Ashley 43
McKennitt, Coreena 43
McLachlin, Sarah 44
McLaughlin, John 175
McRobbie, A. 33, 90, 310
Madonna 19, 121, 201, 270,
    283, 285–6
Marcus, G. 22, 197, 238, 284
M/A/A/R/S 70
Malone, Bill 73
Manhatten Transfer 103
Mann and Weil 276
Marley, Bob (and the Wailers)
    112, 251, 255, 283
Marsalis, W. 174
Marsh, D. 20, 197
Martin, George 232
Marx, Karl 188
Massive Attack 93
Mayall, John (Bluesbreakers)
    30
MC5 170
MC Hammer 248
Mercury, Freddie 270
Metallica 132, 162, 163, 303
Meyer, D. 4
Meyers, H. 114, 115
Michael, George vii

Middleton, R. 58, 86, 227, 309, 316
Midnight Oil 224
Millard, S., *see* Hatch and
Ministry 163
Milli Vanilli 21, 94
Minogue, Kylie 94
Mitchell, Joni 277
Mitchell, T. 311
Mitsui, T. 69
Moby Grape 235
Monk, Thelonious 174
Monkees 37
Monroe, Bill 28, 75
Moore, A. 4, 13, 232, 233, 310
Moore, Scotty 260
Morley, D. 16
Morissette, Alanis 24, 278
Moroder, Georgio 98
Morrissey 270
Most, Mickie 276
Mothers of Invention: *see* Zappa
Motors 236
Move 231
Mud 276
Murdoch, G. (and Phelps, G.) 52
Murray, C. 197
My Bloody Valentine 22

Negus, K. 2, 15, 57, 84, 89, 178, 189, 222, 227, 265, 266, 272, 297
Nelson, Willie 73
New Kids on the Block 298
New Order 184
New York Dolls 151, 152, 237, 239
Newman, Randy 181
Nice 13
Nirvana 7, 157, 267, 268
NWA 47–8

Oasis 12, 13, 36, 53, 153, 236
O'Brien, L. 144, 150

O'Brien, Richard 204, 205
Ocean Colour Scene 96
Ochs, Phil 134, 277
O'Connor, Sinéad 290
O'Hara, Mary 22
Ohio Express 37
Ohio Players 138
Oldfield, Mike 213
Orb, The 11
Orbison, Roy 260
Orieles, the 102
Osbourne, Ozzy 110, 132
O'Sullivan, T. (*et al.*) 57–8, 77, 79–80, 142, 152, 189, 192, 229, 283, 289–90, 291, 294
Oswald, John 69
Ozark Mountain Daredevils 74

Paddison, M. 138
Page, Jimmy 207
Parker, Alan 130
Parker, Charlie 174
Parker, Graham and the Rumour 9, 214
Parker, M. 49
Parliament 138, 139, 295
Parnes, Larry 183
Parsons, Gram 6, 74
Parton, Dolly 73
Patterson, Alex 11
Pearl Jam 9, 156, 157, 253, 267, 293
Pearsall, R. xii
Peel, John 245
Penguins 258
Pennywise 293
Pentangle 135
Pere Ubu 9
Perkins, Carl 295
Perry, Lee 255
Perry, S. 77
Pestilence 162
Peterson, R. (and Berger, D.) 59, 185–6

Petty, Tom (and the
    Heartbreakers) 214
Philips, Sam 170
Pickering, M. (and Green, T.) xii
Pink Floyd 13, 14, 96, 233, 282
Pixies 9
PJ Harvey 277
Plant, Robert 158
Plaskettes, G. 253, 254
Plato 164
P.M. Dawn 248, 250
Poco 74
Pogues 43, 44
Poison 162
Police 255
Pomus and Sherman 276
Poneman, Jonathan 10
Portishead 93
Potter, R. 249
Pratt, R. 285
Presley, Elvis 28, 75, 127, 128,
    130, 136, 154, 166, 190, 260,
    261, 263, 270, 276, 281, 283,
    284, 299, 310
Pretty Things 5, 30, 258
Prince; (The Artist Formerly
    Known As Prince) 9, 18, 32,
    41, 131, 133, 138, 139, 146,
    277
Procul Harum 13, 14
Prodigy 92, 282
Public Enemy 248, 250
Puff Daddy 248
Pulp 36
Punte, Tito 265
Pylon 9

Queen 151
Queensryche 41
Quicksilver Messenger Service
    235

Race, Steve 261
Radiohead 14
Rage Against the Machine 8

Rainey, Ma 29
Ramones 239, 293
Rankin Family 43
Raspberries 231
Ravins 102
Rawlins Cross 43
Read, O. (and Welsh, W.) 280
Red Hot Chilli Peppers 162, 163
Redding, Otis 249, 278, 279
Redhead, S. 317
Reed, Lou 271
Reisman, D. 78–9
REM vii, 7, 8, 9, 135, 136, 224
Renbourne, John 134
Replacements 9, 160, 231
Revere, Paul (and the Raiders)
    231
Richard, Cliff 128
Richman, Jonathan (and the
    Modern Lovers) 214
Rimmer, D. 117, 197
Robinson, D. 81
Robinson, Tom 270
Rockwell, J. 12, 13
Roe, K. 108–9
Roe, Tommy 37
Rogers, Jimmie146
Rolling Stones 18, 29, 30, 35,
    41, 96, 122, 190, 235, 258,
    306
Ronnettes 150, 151
Rose, Axl 158
Rose, T. 247, 249
Rose Tattoo 275
Ross, A (and Rose, T.) 249
Rosselson, L. 221
Rothenbuhler, E. 142; (and
    Dimmick, J.) 59
Rotten, Johnny 310
Rubey, D. 202
Russell, D. 166–7
Roxette 272
Roxy Music 13, 151
Run DMC 249
Ryan, B. 251–2

Salt'N'Peppa 248, 249
Sands, Tommy 297
Savage, J. 119, 120, 197
Searchers 25, 53
Schultze, L. 286
Scruton, Roger 164
Seeger, Pete 134
Selassie, Haile 256
Selector 256
Sex Pistols 238, 239
Shadows 274
Sham 69 275
Shamen 250, 295, 296
Sha-Na-Na 103
Shapiro, B. 205
Shepherd, J. 310
Shinehead 248, 257
Shuker, R. 52, 62–3, 155
Shumway, D. 107
Silhouettes, The 103
Silverchair 157, 267, 297
Simon, Paul 12,13, 311
Sinatra, Frank 217
Sinclair, D. 213, 284–5
Siousie and the Banshees 154,
    155, 156
Sisters of Mercy 155, 156
Size, Roni 93
Skatalites 255
Skunk Anansie 145
Slade 151, 231
Sledge, Percy 278
Sly and Robbie (Dunbar) 207
Small, C. 61
Small, Millie 255
Small Faces 5, 158, 191
Smashing Pumpkins 24
Smith, Bessie 29
Smith, Robert 155
Smith, Trixie 261
Smiths 36, 185, 271
Smucker, T. 98
Snoop Doggy Dog 248
Snow 248
Sonic Youth 22, 145

Soul Asylum 9
Soundgarden 267, 268, 293
Southern Death Cult 155
Specials 256
Spector, Phil 150, 226, 232, 276
Spencer Davis Group 255
Spice Girls vii, 94, 151, 298
Springsteen, Bruce 18, 32, 146,
    178, 277, 284–5
Standells 140
Steel, Tommy 128
Steeleye Span 1, 135, 136
Steely Dan 218
Sting 19
Stock, Aiken, Waterman 94,
    187, 226
Stone Roses 54, 184, 185, 231
Stranglers 238
Stratton, J. 195
Street, J. 106, 178, 179, 225, 259
Streisand, Barbara 126
Strong, Andrew 133
Styx 13
Subdudes 42
Suede 8, 36, 270, 271
Suicidal Tendencies 162
Summer, Donna 98, 99
Supergrass 36
Supremes 150, 151
Surfaris 292
Sweeney, P. 311–12
Sweet 151, 152, 231, 276
Sweet Honey on the Rocks 1

T. Rex 12, 36, 152
Tagg, P. 4, 228
Take That 298
Talking Heads 131, 202, 214,
    239
Tangerine Dream 233
Tanner, J. 52, 108
Taylor, James 277
Taylor, P. 196, 275
Television 239
Temple, Julian 124

Temptations, the 194
Théberge, P. 69, 70
Them 140, 258
Thomas, Bruce 124, 306
Thomas, Carla 249
Thompson Twins, The 201
Thornton, S. 54, 111
Throwing Muses 9
Tikaram, Tanita 135
Timmins, Margot 310
TLC 151
Tom Robinson Band 259
Tomlinson, J. 81
Toots and the Maytals 255
Tosches, N. 261
Tosh, Peter 255
Toy Love 102
Tricky 93
Troggs 140, 141, 237
Trondman, M. 79
Tubby, King 255
Tucker, K. 8
Turner, Big Joe 257
2 Live Crew 46

UB40 255, 256
Underworld 282, 296
U2 51, 75

Van Halen 159, 162, 163
Van Morrison 6, 43, 51
Vanilla Ice 248
Vaughan, Sarah 174
Vaughan, Stevie Ray 31
Vee, Bobby 226, 297, 298
Vega, Suzanne 277
Velvet Underground 22, 154,
    170, 237
Verlaines 103
Verucha Salt 145
Village People 270
Vincent, Gene 259, 263
Vinton, Bobby 297
Vogel, H. 83

Vulliamy, G. (and Lee, E.) 105–6

Wainman, Phil 276
Wakeman, Rick 14
Walser, R. 161, 270; *see also*
    McClary and
Ward, Billy 258
Warhol, Andy 22
Warner, Alan 124
Warren G. 248
Waters, Muddy 30
Weinstein, D. 61, 62, 91, 109,
    120, 147, 161, 303
Weisband, E. (*et al.*) 144
Weller, Paul 96
Welsh, Irvine 124
Welsh, R. 95
Wexler, Jerry 258
White, Bukka 28
Whitely, S. 234
Who 5, 6, 20, 24, 36, 53, 132,
    158, 159, 191, 204, 231, 262,
    300
Wicke, P. 106
Widgery, D. 258
Williams, Hank 73
Williams, Raymond 164
Wilson, Jackie 278
Wire 159, 160
Willis, P. 39, 65, 168, 262–3
Wolfman Jack 241
Wonder, Stevie 194

X 8, 9
XTC 214

Yardbirds, The 30
Yes 13, 14
Yoakum, Dwight 73
Young, Neil 6, 277, 278

Zappa, Frank (and the Mothers
    of Invention) 6, 18, 22, 138
Z Z Top 31

SUBJECT INDEX

a capella 1, 102
A & R (artist & repertoire) xii,
    1–2, 84, 195
Acid House 54, 93
acid jazz 173, 175
acid rock 72, 234
aesthetics (and musical value) x,
    xi, 2–4, 17, 18, 35, 75, 137,
    148, 165, 186, 199, 228, 260,
    261, 281; commodity
    aesthetics 187; and muzak 211
affect 4, 117, 210
aficionados 4–5, 117
Afro-American: see black music
age 52, 66, 78; see also
    demography
albums 5–6, 39, 271; album
    charts 49; see also record
    formats
alternative music 6–9, 22, 64,
    78, 170, 223, 267, 308, 317;
    and dance 90; and radio 142
alternative music scenes 9–11,
    103, 113, 120, 144, 184,
    267–8
ambient 11, 43, 212; Ambient
    House 11, 295
amplification: 11, 280
appropriation 11–13, 33, 112,
    198, 311

art rock 13–14, 22, 146, 151,
    174
articulation 14–15, 21, 63
audiences x, 15–16, 21, 56, 81,
    88; 173, 193; and genre 148;
    and Internet 171, 172; and
    stars 283, 284; see also
    consumer sovereignty, fans
auteur; auteurship xiii, 16–20,
    181; and producers 232; and
    songwriters 276–7
authenticity xiii, 3, 6, 20–1, 43,
    80, 138, 162, 164, 229, 268;
    and black music 26, 77; and
    Celtic music 43; and club
    scene 54; and folk 134; and
    indie music 171; and live
    performance 53, 218; and
    lyrics 188; and rock 96, 146;
    and roots 264; and sampling
    267; Springsteen and 284; and
    voice 309; and white blues 31
avant garde; experimental 21–2,
    138, 154, 238

bauhaus 22
baby boomers 23, 72, 95, 263
back catalogue 97, 125, 194,
    207, 283; see also reissues;
    boxed sets

beat 24–5, 57; backbeat 24
Beatlemania 35, 116
beats; beatniks 70–1, 124, 174, 314
bebop 27, 71, 174, 191
behaviourism : *see* effects
bhangra 3, 12, 25–6, 312
black music 3, 26–31, 76, 77, 111, 138, 154, 193, 249, 258, 274, 278
blue notes 27
bluegrass 12, 27–8, 73, 75
blues ix, 1, 12, 28–31, 134, 173, 257, 261, 273, 304, 312; and black music 26, 27; consumption of 52, 64; lyrics of 123, 181, 231, 251; *see also* Chicago/electric blues; classic blues; country blues; jump blues; British R&B
boogie-woogie 12, 31–2, 260
bootlegs 4, 32, 94, 220
bottleneck (slide) guitar 29
boxed sets 24, 29
breakdancing 90
bricolage 11–12, 33–4
Brill Building (songwriters) 275, 276–7
British beat 25, 26, 150, 177, 274, 308
British invasion 25, 34–5, 277; and doo wop 103; and film 128; and garage rock 140
British R&B 30–1, 258
Britpop 12, 36, 184, 231, 235
broadcasting: *see* radio; State; MTV; television
bubblegum 21, 37, 231, 297

call and response 38, 154, 266
cassette audio tape (and players) 5, 38–9, 312; cassette culture 39; *see also* hometaping
cassette singles 272; *see also record formats*

CD 5, 23, 29, 40, 272, 297; *see also record formats*
CD-ROMs; ROMagazines vii, 40–2
Celtic music 43–4
censorship 44–8 ; 244, 257
charts 63, 75, 83, 91, 271, 273, 306; attempts to influence 50 (*see also* payolla); British invasion of American 25, 34, 35; and crossover 27, 73, 76–7; and genres 48; and market cycles 59, 185–6; role of 49–50
Chicago/electric blues 30, 150, 179, 280
Chicago House 92–3
chords 50
Christian metal 162; Christian rock 51
class 16, 51–3, 78, 315
classic blues 29
classic metal 161–2
classic rock 243, 263
classical music viii, ix, 3, 52, 61, 87, 227; and art rock 13, 14
clubs; club culture viii, xiii, 20, 187; and DJs 101–2; and fanzines 120; club scenes 53–5
cock rock 158, 310
college (student) radio 7, 10, 47, 241–2
commodification 55, 72, 187, 223; of audiences 123; of folk 135; of grunge 157; of rap 248
communication 15, 56–7
concentration (of media/music industry) 57–60, 185, 188, 221
concept albums 5–6
concerts viii, 5, 60–2, 122, 187; concert going 64, 65, 118; and film 131; and Grateful Dead 94

conglomerates 68, 82, 83
consumer sovereignty 39, 55–6, 62–3
consumption x, 59, 63–6, 77, 83, 165, 220, 300; cultural significance of 77, 169, 222; and ethnicity 112; and identity 169; and Internet 171–2; and listening 176; modes of xiii, 63, 64–6; and music press 199; and muzak 210; patterns of 63–4; by youth 83
copyright viii, x, xii, 23, 39, 66–70, 171, 211
counter culture/underground 7, 20, 70–2, 94, 151, 313; and film 128–9; and progressive rock 232; and psychedelic rock 234
country blues 28–9, 38
country music; country & western 8, 12, 64, 73–4, 76, 123, 181, 260, 261, 312; and dance 90
country rock 135
cover bands 206–7
cover versions 74–5, 206–7
crossover 76–7, 112; and art rock 14; and Celtic music 43; and country 73, 76; and R&B 27, 76, 257; and soul 193, 278
cultural capital xiii, 4, 16, 21, 64, 77–8, 169, 294, 313
cultural imperialism 79–82, 149, 152, 178
culture industries ix; 82, 220, 269; and commodification 55, 136; and music industry viii, 82–3, 136, 195
cultural intermediaries xii, 84–5; DJs as 101; producers as 232
cultural policy: see State cultural policy

cultural studies xi; and active audience 63, 81, 94, 177; and BCCCS 33, 85–6, 106, 113; development of 85, 106, 114, 222; and music journalism 197
culture 86–8, 221, 287; see also mass culture/society; popular culture
curriculum (and popular music studies) 105–6

dance; dancing 57, 65, 164; and film 90, 129; as social practice 57, 89, 90–1, 111, 118
dance music 26, 77; 91, 140, 175, 278
dance-music ix, xii, 9, 26, 36, 98, 222, 235, 295, 317; and fiction 124; subgenres of 91–3
dance pop 3, 7, 26, 94–5, 187
deadheads 32, 94
death metal 162
Deep House 93
demography; 95–7, 127, 243; see also age, youth
diaspora 27
disco 20, 97–9, 138; and dance 89, 90; and sexuality 270
discourse analysis 99–100
DJ 17, 54, 66, 241, 261; as auteurs 17, 54; and house music 92–3; and payolla 216–17; and pirate radio 245; as stars 241; DJ talk 99–100; DJ toasters 247
doo-wop 1, 102–3, 138, 248
drum'n'bass 93, 174
dub 232, 255
Dunedin sound 9, 103–4, 231

education 87, 105–9
effects 109–110, 156
enculturation 110–11, 134
entertainment industries 82, 83

EPs 271
ethnicity 52, 66, 76, 78,
111–12, 134, 163
ethnography; xii, 113–14
ethnomusicology xi, 3,
114–15
experimental music 21–2

fans; fandom xiii, 4, 121, 151,
155, 187, 306; and aficanodos
4, 117; denigration of 116;
and fiction 124; and film 125;
and genre 145; and identity
16, 117, 122; and music press
199; and stars 284; and tours
306
fanzines 4, 106, 195; and
alternative scenes 10, 11, 106;
and garage rock 141; and
heavy metal 120; and
Northern Soul 279; and Riot
Grrrls 195; and punk 119
fashion 33, 86, 121, 187, 290,
315
feminism xi, 3, 121–2, 144
festivals 29, 122–3, 312; and
film 131; and folk music 134;
Montery Pop 234–5;
Woodstock 218
fiction 123–4
film 7, 123-33; beach movies
292; see also Hollywood
musicals, popular/rock
musicals; rockumentaries;
soundtracks
folk culture 70, 133
folk music 1, 72, 73, 123,
133–5, 280; and authenticity
280; and class 52; and
ethnomusicology 114; and
festivals 122,134; and politics
223; and singer songwriters
134, 277
folk rock 135-6, 174
Fordism; post-Fordism 136, 211

formats xii, xiii, 39, 187; see also
radio; recording formats
Frankfurt School 3, 55, 87,
136–7, 164, 222
functional music: see muzak
funk 7, 8, 138–9, 175, 266,
278, 295; funk metal 162
fusion 177

garage bands; garage rock 35,
140–1; and punk 237
gatekeepers 59–60, 85, 141–2;
DJs as 101–2; MTV as 202;
music critics as 199; radio
programmers as 242
gender 16, 52, 72, 78, 142–5,
163, 298, 315; and vocal style
190
Generation X 71, 97, 268
genre; meta genres; sub genres
viii, x, xii–xiii, 1,4, 6, 11, 56,
84, 145, 195, 204, 210;
commodification of 55; and
consumption preferences 64;
and crossover 76; and cultural
capital 78, 118; definitions of
145–6, 147; fans and 145,
148; hierarchies of 148; and
histories 166; marketing of
186, 187; and moral panic
193; 118, 121, 123; and
national identity 169; and
performance styles 62; and
radio 142; see also individual
genre entries
geography 149–50, 178, 184
girl groups vii, 35, 150–1, 276
glam (glitter) rock 36, 146,
162, 231, 314
globalization ix; and cultural
imperialism 82, 149, 152; and
local 10, 153, 183; and majors
152–3; and rights 68
gospel ix, 1, 12, 27, 102, 138,
150, 153–4

goth/gothic rock; goths 7, 154–6, 193; and 'rock suicide' 110
gramophone: *see* phonograph
grunge 7, 159, 316; and alternative/indie music 7, 156, 267; and Britpop 36; commodification of 157; and dance 90; and film 132; as style 97, 156–7

hard rock 7, 158–9, 161; vocal style in 310
hardcore 132, 144, 145, 159–60, 303
hardtrance 11
harmony 1, 57, 160
heavy rock 108, 158
heavy metal xii, 7, 52; 160, 214, 316; class and 52; criticism of 161; and concerts 61; and dance 90–1; and fanzines 120; and hard rock 158, 161; and radio 142, 242; and 'rock suicide' 110; school commitment and 108–9; and sexuality 270; and subcultures 161; subgenres of 161–2
hegemony 19, 85, 105, 163–4, 192; and State cultural policy 287–8
high culture 17, 85, 87, 164–5, 192, 287
hip-hop vii, 8, 138, 175, 248–9, 295; and doo-wop 103; and trip-hop 103
hippies 72, 168, 234, 274
history 21; boxed sets and 24, 107, 122, 165–7; and emergence of rock'n'roll 95–6; and gender 122, 143; and genre(s) 107, 141, 145, 166; and performers 166; rockumentaries as 131–2; social history 166–7
Hollywood musicals 124–7

home taping 65, 220
homology 167–8, 315–16
hook(s) 37, 57, 168, 226
house 26, 92–3; and *see* Acid House, Ambient House
hybridization 312

identity xii, xiii, 178, 312; and individual/self 26, 57, 71, 129, 169, 276, 314; and fifties rock'n'roll 96; and fandom 117, 122; and local ix, 149, 169; and politics 223, 225; and sexuality 269; subcultures and 78, 169, 314–15
industrial 7; industrial metal 162
independents/indies (record labels): and alternative music 7, 170–1, 267; and alternative scenes 10, 103, 268; and authenticity 20, 171; and girl groups 150; and grunge 156; and hardcore 160; and majors ix, xii, 7, 136, 153, 170, 182, 268; and market cycles 59, 185; and MTV 202; and rap 247; and soul 278
indie music 7, 36, 64, 77, 78, 170, 184; *see also* alternative music
Internet vii, xiii, 11, 120, 141, 171–2

jazz viii, 72, 137, 138, 173–5, 193, 304; and beats 71; and class 52; and clubs 53; contributions to, and influence on other genres 13, 29, 53, 64, 71, 72, 173, 174, 175, 265, 278; and film 124, 126; subgenres of 173–5
jazz rock/fusion 146, 174–5
jitterbugging 89
jump blues 30, 154, 257
jungle 92

labelling theory 192
lifestyles 294
listening 3, 57, 176–7; and radio
  243
lite metal 151, 162, 298
live (music) 53, 63–4, 65, 218,
  307; and punk rock 237;
  regulation of live venues 44;
  see also performance
Liverpool sound/Merseybeat xi,
  25, 34, 53, 144, 177–8
locality x, xii, 10, 53, 81,
  178–9; local scenes 9, 178;
  local sounds ix, 104, 169, 179
lyrics; lyric analysis 13, 57, 277;
  in art rock 13; in blues 251;
  censorship/criticism of 45,
  153, 181; in Christian Rock
  51; and copyright 70; in punk
  rock 237–8; in reggae 251,
  255; in salsa 266; and
  sexuality 270

majors 7, 10, 58–60, 69, 84;
  and authenticity 20; and back
  catalogue 23; and copyright
  80, 81; and Internet 172;
  market concentration of
  58–60; and market cycles 185;
  market dominance of 83,
  152–3, 182–3; and MTV 202
making music 206
managers 183–4
Manchester sound 54, 184–5
market cycles xii, 59, 185–6
marketing 10, 83, 84, 186–8,
  216, 271; of black music 112;
  and genres 146, 186–7; and
  Internet 171–2; and music
  press 198; record covers and
  252; of stars 186, 187
Marxism xi, 3, 55, 188–9, 221
mass culture/society 3, 15, 87,
  181
mediation 63, 189

mega events 62
melody 57, 70, 190
memorabilia 190–1
Merseybeat: *see* Liverpool sound
mods 191–2, 314
moral panic 110, 288; and
  genres 193; and mods and
  rockers 192, 263; and raves
  193, 250; and 'rock suicide'
  110, 155
Motown 150, 191, 193–4, 276,
  278
MTV 142, 162, 187, 200–3,
  213, 300
multi media 40–1
music industry 20, 81, 87, 136;
  Anglo-American dominance
  of 163; and CD ROM 41;
  and commodification 55;
  consolidation of 58, 185; and
  copyright 66, 69; as cultural
  industry 83, 195; economic
  importance of viii; and genre
  145; and Internet vii, 171;
  and marketing 187–8; and
  MTV 201; and music press
  199–200; operation of xii, 83,
  84, 194, 195, 222; and payola
  217; and piracy 220; and stars
  283; women in 121, 143
music journalism 196–200
music press viii, 5, 11, 54, 65,
  106, 187, 195–200
music publishers 66
music video 57, 63, 65, 82,
  84, 163, 269, 286, 297;
  and auteurship 17; and
  commodification 55;
  and dance pop 94; as
  hybrid cultural form 200;
  and television 300–1;
  textual analysis of 203–4;
  women in 121, 143; *see
  also* MTV
musicals viii, 204–5

musicians xiii, 20, 113, 145; definitions of 205–6; hierarchies of 206–7

musicology x, xi, xiii, 17, 228; and aesthetics 3, 165; aspects of 209, 302; debate on value of 208–9; extension of x, 209–10; and education 106, 108; and gender 143; and structuralism 290–1; *see also* ethnomusicology

muzak vii, 210–1; new age as 212

new age 11, 43, 212–13
new country 73, 76
new right 238
new pop 55, 213
new romantics 36, 121, 152, 213
new wave 8, 9, 213–14, 231, 239; and film 131, 213
northern soul 90, 91, 279
'nostalgia rock' 96

Oi! 225, 275

Parents' Music Resource Center 45–6, 109
participant observation 113
payola 50, 101, 216–17
pedagogy (and popular music studies) 106–7, 165
performance; live performance 10, 20, 32, 53, 217–18, 296; performance income 67
phonograph 219
piracy 32, 39, 67, 220, 254
pirate radio 101, 244–6
political economy 189, 220–2, 284
politics x, 6, 56, 71, 222–5, 314
pop music ix, x, xii, 12, 20, 45, 273, 310; as dichotomous with rock 20, 225–6; audience for 64, 297; definitions of ix, 225–6; and girl groups 150; and lyrics 123–4, 270; *see also* individual genres

popular culture 17, 21, 80, 85, 87, 192, 288
popular music: definitions of viii, 226–8
popular/rock musicals 127–31
Post-Fordism: *see* Fordism
postmodernism 3, 33, 229–30; New Age as 212; rap as 247, 249; rock as 230
post-structuralism 291
power pop 35, 231, 297
preferred readings 110, 270, 302
producers 5, 17, 84, 94, 98, 150, 193, 205, 231–2, 276; and pop 226
progressive country 73
progressive rock 13, 22, 72, 141, 151, 174, 232–4; consumption of 52, 64; and counter culture 72, 232
psychedelic/acid rock 7, 72, 135, 141, 155, 235–5, 295
pub rock 9, 113, 235–6, 237
punk (as youth subculture) xii, 168, 236–7, 314; and bricolage 33
punk rock 39, 53, 55, 151, 154; antecedents in garage rock 140–1, 237, and pub rock 235, and avant garde 22; Celtic punk 43; continued influence of 7,8, 156, 159, 260, 303; class and 52; dance in 90; fanzines 119–20; on film 132; live performance of 237; New Wave and 213, 214; and Oi! 275; and politics 223, 235; as reaction to progressive rock 233; and Riot Grrrls 144

quotas 289

R&B: *see* rhythm & blues
race 111; race music 257; racism
217, 224, 225; *see also* Rock
Against Racism
radio viii, xiii, 57, 63, 162, 312;
and censorship 44; and charts
48; consumption of 63, 66,
243; FM radio 241; as
gatekeeper 141–2, 242;
historical development of
240–1; radio formats 73, 83,
241, 242–3; regulation of 244;
see also college radio; pirate
radio
ragtime 27, 67, 173, 246, 304
rap ix, xii, 3, 12, 21, 39, 138,
246–50, 257, 295, 298; as
black music 26, 249;
consumption of 64, 112;
controversy over 46–8, 193,
247, 248; commodification of
248; and sampling 21;
subgenres of 247–8
rastafari 256
rave culture; raves 193, 250,
295
realism 250–1
record companies: *see*
independents, majors, music
industry
record collecting/buying 5, 65,
117
record covers 5, 147, 188,
251–2, 254
record formats 252–4
recording: *see* sound recording
reggae ix, xii, 8, 55, 233,
316; consumption of 52,
64, 112; development of
254–5, 256–7; as folk
culture 133; realism and
251; *see also* ska; two tone;
rastafari

reissues 23, 32; *see also* back
catalogue
retail 44, 49, 188, 212
rhythm & blues (R&B) 25, 27,
29, 34, 35, 49, 64, 76, 112,
153, 158, 175, 191; and black
music 27, 258; controversy
and 258; development of 12,
29, 257–8; influence/
significance of 257, 258
rhythm 24, 70; funk and 138–9
riff 24–5, 31
Riot Grrrls 144–5
ritual 61, 62
rock ix, xii, 12, 84, 137; as art
5, 6, 17; and authenticity 21,
146, 218; and concerts 61,
62; consumption of 63;
contribution to other genres
12, 30, 36, 43, 260; and
cultural capital 79; and
demographics 95–6; and
festivals 122–3; as ideology
(rockist) 144, 166; and lyrics
181; and musicology 208–9;
and PMRC 45; and suicide
109; and voice 309; *see also*
individual genres
Rock against Racism 236,
258–9
rock opera 191, 205
rockabilly 28, 29, 32, 73, 75,
133, 154, 259–60
rockers 168, 192, 262–3
rock'n'roll xii, 12, 24, 25,
29, 32, 34, 45, 55, 75, 76,
137, 263; criticism of 45,
193, 261; and dance 89,
90; and demographics 95;
and film 125; and payola
216–17; *see also* teddy boys;
rockers
rocksteady 254, 255
rockumentaries 131–2
roots (music) 133, 263–4, 312

salsa 169, 265–6
samples; sampling ix, xii, 11, 21, 26, 69, 70, 212, 266–7, 295
San Francisco sound 94, 150, 185
scene x, xii; scenes 43, 113, 134, 141, 150, 169, 178, 184; and gender 144; *see* also alternative scenes, locality
school commitment (and music preferences) 64, 108–9
Seattle scene, sound 11, 150, 267–9
semiotics xii, 34, 290, 309; semiotic democracy 63
session musicians 37, 193–4, 207
sexuality 122, 152, 209, 269–71, 288; and cock rock 158; and Madonna 286; and R&B 258; and rock'n'roll 261; and song lyrics 143, 163, 270
singer songwriters 35, 52, 123, 134, 143, 181, 277; as auteurs 19; and genres 270; as performers 269–70
singles 271–3; singles charts 49
ska 12, 133, 191, 251, 254–5, 256, 316
skiffle 25, 34, 273–4
skinheads 12, 191, 225, 274–5, 316
social history 166–7
social movements 223
song families 75
song narratives 123–4, 150; *see also* lyrics.
songwriters 30, 66, 137, 194; as auteurs 17, 19, 276; and girl groups 150, 276; influence of 276; *see also* Brill Building; singer songwriters
soul x, 26, 103, 138, 150, 153, 154, 181, 194, 278–9; sweet soul 276; *see also* Northern Soul

sound 219, 279–80
sound mixers 84, 205, 281; DJs as 101–2
sound recording ix, xii, 66, 280–2
sound systems viii, 282
soundtracks viii, 57,75, 83, 90, 132–3
speed metal: *see* thrash
stadium rock 159
stars; stardom xiii, 18, 121, 125, 186–7, 196, 203, 280–6, 301; and fans 117–18; and film 101; DJs as 54; and musicals 204; and postmodernism 230
State cultural policy 165, 244, 286–9
structuralism 85, 289–90
style: and glam 151–2; and goths 155; and punk 236; and skinheads 167–8; *see also* fashion; genre; subcultures
subcultures xiii, 5, 20, 70, 108, 113, 118, 124, 143, 193, 292; and film 129, 130; *see also* youth subcultures
subjectivity: *see* identity
surf music; surfies 292–3

taste 39, 77–8, 117; taste cultures xiii, 4, 52, 54, 294
techno 11, 54, 92–3, 138, 295–6
technology ix, 1, 10, 23, 38, 66, 83, 92, 219, 232, 296–7; and genre 147
teddy boys/teds 193, 262, 314
teenagers 116, 297
teenybopper 65, 94, 116, 121, 297, 298, 310; teen idols 226, 276, 297
television viii, 40, 187, 203, 298–301

Tex-Mex 73, 301
text x, 16, 39, 77, 88, 183,
  301–3; music videos as
  202, 203–4; textual
  analysis xii, 145, 221,
  270, 290; textual poaching
  303; *see also* discourse
  analysis
thrash/speed metal viii, 7, 8,
  162, 295, 303–4
timbre 12, 112, 155, 233, 304;
  see also voice, vocal style
Tin Pan Alley 137, 216, 276,
  304–5
tours, touring viii, 7, 61, 96,
  124, 305–8
transculturation: *see* globalization
tribute bands 207
two-tone 192

underground: *see* counter
  culture

vocal styles 12, 22, 28, 38, 150,
  154, 237; *see also* timbre
voice 1, 309–10
vinyl 253, 271, 272

Walkmans viii, 176
women in rock 1, 84; *see also*
  Riot Grrrls
world music; world beat ix, xiii,
  8, 12, 111, 295, 311–12

youth 16, 61, 83; and
  consumption 63, 97; *see also*
  demography, youth
  subcultures.
youth cultures; youth subcultures
  16, 33, 71, 78, 86, 121, 161,
  163, 185, 313–17; and
  homology 167–8, 236; and
  moral panic 193; *see also*
  individual subculutures
youth movies 127–30